Ethnicity, Race,
and American Foreign Policy

ETHNICITY, RACE, AND AMERICAN FOREIGN POLICY

A History

Alexander DeConde

Northeastern University Press
Boston

Northeastern University Press

Library of Congress Cataloging-in-Publication Data

DeConde, Alexander
  Ethnicity, race, and American foreign policy: a history /
Alexander DeConde.
    p. cm.
  Includes bibliographical references and index.
ISBN 1-55553-133-4—ISBN 1-55553-215-2 (pbk.)
  1. Minorities—United States—Political activity—History.
2. United States—Foreign relations. I. Title.
E184.A1D29 1992
327.73—dc20   92-15698

Designed by Susan Shelkrot

Composed in Garamond #3 by Coghill Composition Co., Richmond, Virginia. Printed and bound by The Maple Press, York, Pennsylvania. The paper is Sebago Antique, an acid-free sheet.

MANUFACTURED IN THE UNITED STATES OF AMERICA
98 97 96 95 94   5 4 3 2

CONTENTS

ACKNOWLEDGMENTS

In the years of working on this study I benefited from grants from the Research Council of the University of California, Santa Barbara, and the Institute on Global Conflict and Cooperation situated at the University of California, San Diego, but which serves the entire university system and beyond. Under the auspices of the Rockefeller Foundation I enjoyed a second residency at the Villa Serbelloni, Bellagio, Italy, where I put together an early draft.

Friends and colleagues from my university and elsewhere kindly read drafts or offered advice on my ideas, research, and manner of presentation. Notable among them were my wife Glace, my son A. Christopher De-Conde, Otis L. Graham, Jr., Wilbur R. Jacobs, Robert Kelley, Albert S. Lindemann, Kenneth L. McCann, who labored at times as my research assistant, Cedric J. Robinson, Geoffrey S. Smith of Queens University, Ontario, and the courteous staff of the inter-library loan department at the University of California, Santa Barbara. I am also indebted to anonymous readers who detected serious flaws and thereby helped me to improve the manuscript. To all who assisted, I extend my gratitude.

PREFACE

In recent years the attentive public, policymakers, and others have evinced a considerable interest in the influence of ethnicity and race on the shaping of American foreign policy. Yet much of the literature on the problem is fragmented or impressionistic. No one has yet investigated the subject at length or in sufficient depth to produce a connected history. The few books and the scattered specialized articles touching on it focus usually on episodes in the most recent past or on the activities of European ethnic groups.

This history goes beyond the European connection, reaches farther into the past, and includes a larger spectrum of ethnic and racial groups than have others. To date it is the first synthesis to relate how and why ethnoracial groups have attempted, from the beginning of the nation to approximately the present, to give direction to aspects of foreign policy. It assesses the perceived as well as the actual power of such interest groups and, where possible, the public reaction to their activities. It also examines customary theory on ethnic influence in foreign policy.

Persuasive evidence indicates that ethnoracial affiliation has in general been more important in promoting activity to influence foreign policy than has either class or religion. So, unless class or religion has been or is an essential part of a group's ethnicity, I do not attempt to analyze the separate impacts of groups that are mainly religious or that can be defined essentially in terms of class. We should remember, though, that ethnicity, class, and religion are often intertwined and that for some groups religious affiliation forms an essential part of their identity. The activity of such groups is included in this study.

Experts disagree on the precise definitions of ethnicity and race. I adhere to the usual flexible practice as shown in any good dictionary, which gives those words several meanings. Race, for example, may be used in either a biological or a cultural sense. I employ the terms ethnoracial, ethnocultural, ethnic groups, and obvious synonyms to refer roughly to entities held together by common origin, language, culture, race, color, and/or religion. These groups also possess another common characteristic crucial to this study: a history that can be examined.

I realize that the terms ethnicity and race differ etymologically and in strict usage are distinct. Yet even in scholarly practice the words frequently overlap, while in popular idiom they are often used as though interchangeable. In keeping with common procedure I generally treat them as part of a collective phenomenon. When they seem to function clearly as separate influences, I so indicate. Context, also, should make my usage clear.

Some students of American foreign relations draw a firm line between domestic and international politics. I do not. Oftentimes the differences between them have been fundamental, but their separation has rarely been rigid. As do other contemporary historians, and political scientists too, I proceed from the premise that American relations with the outside world have seldom been divorced from their sociocultural milieu, and are less so now than ever. In consequence, the ethnic groups that are absorbed in national politics can hardly avoid involvement with issues affecting foreign relations.

As the record indicates, ethnic, racial, and religious loyalties are part of a broad pattern in the making of foreign policy. While these allegiances have repeatedly affected relations with other countries and peoples, there is no claim here that they have been exclusive determinants of policy. This perspective is embodied in my central theme, that while ethnoracial considerations have always had an influence on foreign policy, only in specific circumstances can they be considered decisive. From the founding of the nation to the present time, ethnic groups of various origins have applied pressure on government in matters relating to kinfolk abroad, but with mixed results.

Scholars who study ethnic and racial relations in the United States invariably concentrate on minorities, thereby excluding Anglo-Americans. Traditionally, ethnoracial groups have been minorities in comparison to the Anglo-Americans who until recently were the majority. Unlike conventional writers, I treat Americans of English or British stock as belonging to a discernible ethnic group with a traceable history. Their unique power, whether potential or real, in formulating foreign policy forms my second major theme. Other historians have recognized this influence, but they have not, to my knowledge, explored it explicitly in terms of ethnicity and its long-range impact on policy.

Again, as with other terms of loose connotation, my use of Anglo-American merits explanation. Even though over a period of several centuries its meaning has changed, I try to employ it in the political and social context proper for its time. In the colonial period the phrase referred specifically at first to people of English descent and then to those of British origin. Today, especially in its abbreviated form "Anglo," it often is used pejoratively throughout the Western hemisphere to deride all white Americans. Many

apply the word, as they do the acronym WASP (White, Anglo-Saxon, Protestant), to English-speakers, or Euro-Americans, who may or may not have
English blood. When I make generalized use of Anglo, I attempt to do so
without its current negative connotation. I employ the term because of its
extensive usage, because it is widely understood, and because it helps lessen
the monotony of constantly referring to Anglo-Americans.

However we may allude to them, the Americans of British stock have to
be prominent in this study, because from the nation's founding to the present they have been centrally involved in the shaping of foreign policy. Because of their constant presence they are subjected to a more extended and
perhaps harsher or gentler scrutiny than others. There is no intent to hold
them or those in any other ethnic group to impossibly high moral standards
of behavior. In particular I seek to eschew the WASP-bashing currently
evident in some popular literature dealing with sensitive minority issues.
But I do not hesitate to advance my own interpretations.

Much of the data that has been amassed on ethnicity and race casts fresh
light on important aspects of group behavior. Yet scholars and others often
present their judgments on the ethnic politics of foreign policy as a means
of attacking or defending theoretical positions. I attempt to analyze their
arguments without necessarily becoming entangled in the debate. Within
the scope of my primary theme, I stress continuity, and in some instances I
also suggest comparisons with similar problems in other societies.

As with most broad histories, this one is grounded on the extensive sec-
ondary literature that touches on the subject rather than on manuscript
sources. Some data comes from printed documents, memoirs, newspapers,
tracts, or archival materials that I examined in previous researches.

Alexander DeConde
Santa Barbara, California

Ethnicity, Race,
and American Foreign Policy

1

INTERPRETATIONS

American foreign policy at times has been an elitist operation, and it needs the counterbalance that ethnic groups can often give.

Lee H. Hamilton, Congressman, Indiana, Oct. 15, 1979

In 1960, in the new introduction to a well-received book that had been first published ten years earlier, political scientist Gabriel Almond pronounced the triumph of assimilation theory as it pertained to foreign relations. He maintained that "ethnic groups which have historically provided the bases for 'special interest' foreign policies, seriously affecting our decisions insofar as they involved the countries of origin of significant immigrant groups in the U.S. (i.e., the Irish, the Germans, the eastern and southern Europeans, and the Jews)," no longer did so. Declining immigration and these groups' assimilation had markedly "reduced the salience of ethnic origins in the American population," and hence of ethnicity on the formulation of policy. [1]

Fifteen years later, in an equally influential book, sociologists Nathan Glazer and Daniel P. Moynihan argued that "the immigration process is the single most important determinant of American foreign policy." They claimed that the flow of immigrants regulated the ethnic composition of the electorate, permitting the incoming groups to acquire power in international matters because "foreign policy responds to that ethnic composition." They acknowledged that policymakers also reacted to other pressures, "but probably *first of all* to the primal facts of ethnicity." [2]

Glazer and Moynihan may have exaggerated the potency of ethnicity, but developments since Almond's time have made the thrust of his argument more equivocal. His perspective reflected the consensus hypothesis, popular among the historians of the fifties, which homogenized the American past by stressing harmony, playing down conflict, and undervaluing the significance of ethnicity and race. Like many thinkers of his time, whether within or outside the foreign-policy establishment, Almond had absorbed the assimilation hypothesis that underestimated the resilience of the ethnoracial ingredient as a significant influence on the shaping of policy. He spoke, for instance, of "homogeneous standards and values among all groups." Other analysts, especially those concerned with the dynamics of dissent and conflict, now regard the influence of ethnicity in domestic and foreign politics as stronger than ever and a worldwide phenomenon.

This depth of interest in the power of ethnicity in America's domestic and foreign political life is of recent origin. Traditionally, most scholars virtually ignored the ethnoracial influences on foreign policy because they concentrated on other components, components that often reflected their predilections. Many of them were economic determinists who showered attention on the ideology of class, invariably attributing causal power of global significance to economic class. They regarded, and still regard, economics as the engine of history.

Regardless of this or other intellectual partiality, numerous historians also believed that ethnic politics had only a marginal effect on relations with other nations because they perceived minorities as usually being concerned exclusively with special-interest policies. Researchers assumed that the study of contacts between individuals in positions of power, even between leaders of special-interest groups, resulted in a better understanding of foreign affairs than did the investigation of ethnoracial pressure groups. Overall, those who wrote the conventional studies of diplomacy emphasized the importance of following the exchange of notes and of assessing the attitudes of the decision-making elite.

Contemporary investigators of policy-making do that too, but in addition many of them attach value to ethnoracial considerations. They contend that an understanding of how ethnicity and domestic politics interact with foreign policy is critical because of American society's diversity. They also suggest that minority groups are as highly motivated to lobby for specific foreign policies that affect old homelands as they have ever been.

This is a sound perspective, but its deeper significance can be discerned most clearly if we examine the problem of ethnoracial influence historically as a whole. This approach poses difficulties because of the traditional attitudes of scholars. They differ as to the origin of consciously practiced ethnic politics designed to influence American foreign relations. Most of them assume that such activity began late in the nineteenth century with the "new immigrants" and their offspring. These newcomers, the people of color, and the other minorities, made up the *hyphenates* who are usually associated with the special-interest lobbying in international matters. This interpretation also maintains that Americans of British stock did not engage in such politics because they held to no allegiance other than to the United States.

Contrary to this customary wisdom, the holistic idea holds that the people of English ancestry, from the colonial period onward, were as conscious of an ethnic bond with their old homeland as were those in any other group. After the nation came into existence, these Anglo-Americans, behaving in much the same way as the constituency in any special-interest group, engaged in proto-ethnic politics to influence foreign policy. Thus, even though in these formative years ethnic determinism was not identified clearly as such, it existed in spirit if not in name. Since the domestic pressures on foreign policy in this period did not always involve obvious conflict between competing ethnic groups, they are easy to overlook and difficult to assess. It is for these and other reasons that historians generally disregard the ethnoracial element in the making of foreign policy in the early years of the republic and hold other ascriptive determinants of policy in higher regard.

One of the determinants assumed to be potent has been an elitism often identified with the Department of State. This school of thought insists that an elite based on class, ancestry, or other connections, and seemingly immune to minority and other pressures, has always made basic foreign policy. Prominent professional bureaucrats and diplomats, as well as academics, are convinced that it should continue to do so. They condemn what they perceive as the subordination of policy-making to domestic exigencies and deplore especially any dependence it may have on minority politics. They believe that foreign policy should not have to rely on popular support through the ballot box or on the vagaries of public opinion expressed through different means.

Career diplomatist and historian George F. Kennan summarized this elitist perspective. "Our actions in the field of foreign affairs," he wrote, "are the convulsive reactions of politicians to an internal political life dominated by vocal minorities."[3] With faith in its own expertise, the bureaucratic elite to which he belonged insisted that it could do a better job in defining the national interest and setting the goals of diplomacy than could "opportunistic" politicians.

This elite's ability to sway the president often did permit it to operate above the ordinary demands of public opinion. At times it also functioned beyond democratic accountability as required by congress, by the electorate, and sometimes by ethnoracial politics.

Scholars of the elitist persuasion "believe that American foreign policy can be understood only by studying the ideas, the attitudes, and the experiences of the 'people at the top.'"[4] European academics have long favored an analogous approach. In Britain in recent years a modified version of this analytical model has focused on "groups of definable individuals" who form "a foreign-policymaking elite" whose actions can be tracked.[5]

There are those who accept much in the elitist approach but who concentrate on economics as the primary determinant in diplomacy. They contend that capitalism guides the thrust of American foreign policy. Others maintain that ideological and other pressures do more to shape policy than do economic or other forces. Overtly, those who are committed to any of these theories just about disregard the ethnic and racial factors in policy-making.

Among the critics of the theory of ethnic-group pressure as a determinant are those who point out as a defect that it implies a correlation between the numbers in a politically mobilized group and its impact on policy. They say that the ethnic concept fails to account for the imbalance of competing group interests. It discounts the political effectiveness, organizing skills, education, and wealth of particular groups which may permit them to influence policy out of proportion to their size. The Jewish community, for example, has been far more effective in influencing aspects of foreign policy than has the black community five times its size.

Cynics also attack the assumption in ethnoracial theory that there is a direct connection between policy and constituency pressure. In their perspective this premise gives insufficient weight to the predilections of individual policymakers. It discounts evidence that officeholders, groups of people, and public opinion can be manipulated to thwart popular sentiment. It mistakenly treats ethnic constituencies as if they were monolithic in their support of foreign-policy objectives that engage their interest. Sometimes such bodies are unified in their goals, and at other times they are not.

Regardless of these shortcomings, the hypothesis that stresses influence through ethnoracial solidarity attracts adherents because for the most part it works, especially if a group is well organized and has specific goals. This theory is popular also because it fits widely accepted democratic ideology that the policies of the American government reflect the will of the people. Of course, that connection can be tenuous. The politicians who make policy may be more directly responsive to other special interests that raise the large sums of money necessary for staying in power than they are sensitive to a mass public or to a substantial ethnic constituency.

Despite this dependence of officeholders on fund-raisers, the principle of power flowing from the electorate has compelled officials to try, however crudely, to gauge the inclinations of the attentive citizenry. In this vein, theorists in political science explain that "public opinion may influence the behavior of statesmen in their international relations even when it does not exist, or when it is dormant. The knowledge—or the belief, even if mistaken—that the public might react in a given way may have a compelling effect upon the behavior of participants in multilateral diplomacy."[6]

In the past half century, beginning sometime after systematic voter-canvassing techniques came into practice, policymakers tried to go beyond such intuitive responses. They often attempted to fathom public opinion and the attitudes of interest groups through the use of polls. This kind of political sensitivity may have enhanced democratic accountability among officeholders. At the same time, with an expanding electorate and the officeholders' need for campaign support, it increased the susceptibility of the president and members of congress to well-organized and generously financed lobbies.

In recent decades this kind of dependency has mushroomed because of the huge sums required to gain and hold office. Furthermore, in opposition to the elitist paradigm, officeholders have come more and more to view questions of foreign policy as extensions of domestic politics. Hence, when they respond to the international concerns of their well-heeled or efficiently organized, ethnically sensitive constituents who deliver votes, the politicians have been able to justify their actions in terms of democratic ideology.

Political analysts other than those committed to elitist dogma have disputed such reasoning. They argue that constituent-group pressure does not substantively affect national elections and that foreign-policy issues in particular have seldom "gripped the attention of sizable pressure groups."[7] They point out, quite properly, that presidential campaigns have rarely hinged on single issues, especially not on those relating to foreign policy. In this anti-accountability hypothesis it follows that policymakers could virtually ignore the ethnic politics connected to narrow international issues. In many instances officeholders have disregarded such minority pressures without fear of retribution at the polls, but with less frequency in recent years than in the more distant past.

A variation of this hypothesis maintains that ethnic politics often produce results because most Americans are too busy, too apathetic, or too ill-informed to follow the intricacies of foreign policy in circumstances that intensely interest minority voters. In the late 1940s a blue-collar worker, with some exaggeration but also with a ring of truth, explained this lack of popular involvement to a pollster. "Foreign affairs!" the worker said. "That's for people who don't have to work for a living."[8]

Public indifference of this nature at times has had the effect of inflating the power of those voters who do cast ballots specifically to advance the interest of their own ethnic group. Ironically, broad public lack of interest also could contribute to the elitist control of foreign policy that minorities often deplore. In rhetoric, even a populist president such as Harry S Truman took advantage of public passiveness to dominate external affairs as he saw fit. "I make foreign policy," he once stated bluntly.[9] In actuality, he relied heavily on both political and professional advisers; he courted the ethnic vote; and on occasion he even bowed to it.

Truman's actions rather than his words fit a significant corollary of democratic theory that runs counter to the anti-accountability hypothesis. The corollary holds that the decisions of the president and through him the work of his subordinates, especially on the big questions of policy, ultimately require the approval or disapproval of the electorate, regardless of the pockets of indifference within it. The voters exercise their power when they choose or reject the presidents and the members of congress who wrestle daily with international issues.

Knowledge of this eventual accountability, the corollary goes, constrains policymakers to respond in some way to the foreign-policy concerns of even minority constituents. As the United States became more ethnically and racially diverse, officeholders had more need to take special interests into account when dealing with foreign relations. So they became more responsive to minority pressures.

Of course, there are other multiethnic populations in the world where minorities have demanded comparable attention. Great Britain, France, and Germany are among those other nations that have experienced ethnic pressures on specific foreign-policy issues. Other New World countries such as Argentina, Brazil, and Canada at given times have also welcomed a greater number of immigrants in proportion to their original populations than has the United States. Generally, though, these nations have drawn most of their immigrants from a few desired sources. As has the United States, these and other countries have long favored assimilationist doctrine, or policies that would lead to the absorption by the dominant ethnic community of the invited minorities and to their ultimate disappearance.

What has set the United States apart has not been just the number of its immigrants, who since the founding have contributed to about fifty percent of its growth. The United States is unique in the heterogeneity of its people. Among the major nations it is the only one that has either consistently encouraged, or at least permitted, large numbers of permanent immigrants of numerous origins to come to its bosom. It also has always been home for native peoples of color who were dispossessed and for blacks of African origin who were brought to its shores in chains. Largely for these reasons students of popular diplomacy conclude that the influence of ethnic politics on foreign policy "is a uniquely American phenomenon," or another of the nation's ascribed exceptional qualities.[10]

The believers in the old melting-pot idea of the amalgamation of many groups into one with a single national loyalty have long accepted the cultural pluralism that goes along with the unique ethnoracial mix. These disciples of blending also have been prominent among those who questioned the viability of ethnic groups as an influence on foreign policy. Furthermore, these devotees of the melting-pot idea were often wedded to the conviction that ethnic commitment was "a fading phenomenon" in American life as a whole rather than just in special-interest politics. As have been most students of immigration and ethnicity, they were Eurocentric assimilationists who assumed that in a few generations the minorities would shed old ethnic loyalties to accept the Anglo-American model of culture.

In a famous essay in 1893, less than a decade before the melting-pot analogy became popular, historian Frederick Jackson Turner gave the idea of ethnic amalgamation what was then a new twist. As did others of his time, he saw mixing as "the formation of a composite nationality for the American people." But he focused on the frontier, rather than on the more usual forms of acculturation, as the "crucible" that fused Europeans of varied origins into Americans.[11] Regardless of his theory, Turner, like most others who took an elitist approach to the making of American foreign policy, was an Anglo-conformity assimilationist.

Like the assimilationists, the pluralists who began making themselves heard in the early years of the twentieth century, when the new immigrants had crowded into American cities, were Eurocentric. These pluralists were not, however, Anglo-conformists. Like the first apostle of "cultural pluralism," the Jewish-American philosopher Horace M. Kallen, many of them came out of white minority backgrounds. As a rule they viewed assimilation doctrine as "a racism of culture" or as a "forced Americanization" carried out with "ethnic insensitivity and discrimination."[12] Some of them compared this Americanization to coercive acculturation akin to the Russifying and Germanizing that they had detested in the old countries.

A number of these pluralists spoke of a "democracy of nationalities" and of cooperation among European ethnic groups in the United States. They believed that neither democratic politics nor the conduct of foreign policy required homogeneity. This pluralism, which had never attracted a large following, moved underground during the hyphenate hysteria of the First World War. It revived in the twenties primarily among academics, artists, and intellectuals. Their ideas have been characterized as unpopular in "an era in which ethnic concerns faded from consciousness as public issues," but they have gained popularity in the wake of the Second World War, with the widespread acceptance of cultural pluralism.[13]

In general, these new pluralists had no fear of dual loyalties. They portrayed ethnic differences, but not always racial consciousness, as beneficial aspects of American life. Many of them, to a greater extent than had their predecessors, identified democracy with pluralism and elitism with assimilationism. They implied an inherent conflict between the two theories. These pluralists also treated ethnic commitment as an enduring ingredient in the body politic, suggesting that to a degree at least its presence made foreign policy responsive to democratic forces. They maintained that since the American people were divided into many groups, minorities should legitimately compete for power in the conduct of foreign relations. In this perspective, in external affairs as in other areas of political concern, no one group deserved the right to define the national interest.

Even in this expansive vision of American society, the ethnic communities distinguished by race or color — Native Americans, African-Americans, Asian-Americans, Mexican-Americans, and others — were left out. They could fit neither the assimilationist nor the pluralist model of belonging. With increasing frequency, therefore, these outsiders challenged the legitimacy of a society that barred them from full participation in its rituals.

For years the interests of the "colored" minorities had had less effect on foreign relations than those of the smaller white minority groups that the establishment had long excluded. The policymakers rarely acknowledged the wishes of the racial minorities on international matters. This weakness of the non-whites fitted the theory that those interest groups with the most direct access to the decision makers had the greatest impact on policy-making. Only in the 1950s with the rise of the civil rights movement did the "colored" minorities become part of a broader pluralism that permitted them a voice in foreign-policy issues of special interest to them. As these racial pluralists became involved, they more and more questioned the Euro-American dominance of the policy-making institutions.

To explain these considerable recent changes within the mass of American society and their effect on relations with other countries, scholars have advanced hypotheses beyond those we have briefly examined. We shall explore some of those speculations in their chronological context. As for the contradictions in both the popular and scholarly interpretations, they illustrate why the ethnoracial influence in American foreign policy has been difficult to gauge with precision or to assess without biased emotion.

The very nature of ethnic politics compounds the problem. It blurs the distinctions that analysts usually employ to mark off domestic from foreign-policy issues, because ethnic politics are rooted in two places—in the United States and abroad. Even though we may not be able to measure precisely the potency of the ethnoracial element in the formulating of foreign policy, we can examine its role as a determinant or a modifier of policy in given situations and even approximate its power. In broad configuration we can also trace its influence historically.

No one can more sincerely
rejoice than I do, on the
reduction of Canada; and this
is not merely as I am a
colonist, but as I am a
Briton.

Benjamin Franklin, January
1760

2

"UNMISTAKABLY ENGLISH"

From childhood, Americans learn virtually by rote that beginning with Jamestown, founded in April 1607, white colonizers along North America's Atlantic seaboard "produced a culture unmistakably English."[1] Further investigation would reveal that from the start the whites and the indigenous Indians sometimes mingled, often lived side by side, and continuously fought each other. This transplanted English society also quickly attracted limited numbers of other peoples of European origin who contributed to the ethnic and racial heterogeneity that would become one of its distinctive qualities.

Beginning in 1619, when the captain of a Dutch warship sold twenty Africans to the colonists, another racial group involuntarily joined this new society. African slavery started slowly, but by the end of the century it had spread, especially through the southern colonies, where the black presence became striking.

Among the continental Europeans who added to North America's ethnoracial mix, the Dutch were the first to plant their own colony in the region. In 1624 they established New Netherland, comprising roughly the region of present-day New York and New Jersey. In the 1660s a few Huguenots settled in New York. Twenty years later as a group fleeing persecution in the France of Louis XIV, they sought refuge in several of the English colonies. In 1683 Germans began coming, settling mainly in Pennsylvania because the Quaker proprietor, William Penn, recruited them. Protestants from the north of Ireland, many of whom were called Scotch-Irish, also started arriving in significant numbers.

These outsiders quickly aroused animosity among the original colonists, who referred to themselves as "the English" so as to be distinguished from all others. For example, at first, as in New England, the British settlers, whether of English, Scottish, or Welsh origin, accepted the Huguenots with friendliness as suffering fellow Protestants. Later, even though the Huguenots were few and nonthreatening, the British colonists reacted violently against them. In South Carolina even a law of 1697 designed to promote assimilation "could not eliminate continuing English prejudice against the Huguenots in the colony."[2] From the British perspective, the French ethnicity of the newcomers overshadowed the importance of shared religion.

To the north, in Massachusetts Bay, the Puritan leadership attempted with specific measures to discourage non-English peoples, and even those of English blood who were not Congregationalists, from settling there. Nonetheless, in the seventeenth century Britain's North American colonies became home to Dutch, German, French, Irish, Swedes, Spanish, Indians, and blacks from Africa, as well as the British. The minority, non-English white population increased steadily, especially in the following century.

By this time, because of their ethnic and racial composition, the societies in virtually all of the mainland provinces could be regarded as pluralistic, and the whole as an "ethnic complexity."[3] Yet the Anglo-Americans who dominated those settlements did not conceive of them as plural. In their eyes the Atlantic communities were basically English. Through the assimilation of other whites on terms prescribed by themselves, the Anglo-Americans were determined to maintain the colonies' English character and their own privileged position within them. As in their homeland, many of these relocated English men and women were convinced that they were God's newly chosen people and that they must preserve that exalted status.

In the following century Anglo-Americans of a more secular bent shared the ethnoracial views of Benjamin Franklin, who preferred "purely white People" to "swarthy" Europeans and the "Blacks and Tawneys" of Africa and Asia, whom he wanted to exclude from the colonies. He regarded his own English people as among the whitest and certainly as the finest on earth, whether or not they were divinely selected. "I could wish their Numbers were increased," he wrote in 1751. "But," he added, "perhaps I am partial to the Complexion of my Country, for such Kind of Partiality is natural to Mankind."[4]

To the discomfort of Franklin and other Anglo-Americans, between 1749 and 1755 about 37,000 Germans arrived in Philadelphia. They went their own way, spoke their own language, and sought to perpetuate their own customs. This separateness and their increasingly visible presence more and more stirred Anglo-American enmity. Franklin expressed a common reaction to them. "Why should Pennsylvania, founded by the English, become a Colony of *Aliens*, who will shortly be so numerous as to Germanize us instead of our Anglifying them[?]" he wrote. They "will never adopt our Language or Customs, any more than they can acquire our Complexion." Several years later he denounced the Germans as knaves, wretches, and rascals "burthensome to the old Settlers."[5] He favored measures to keep the Germans out of Pennsylvania.

This early nativist resentment directed against foreign white ethnic groups such as the German, Dutch, and Irish occasionally touched on larger issues of policy. In North America the bloodshed between the colonists, as between English and Spanish, and English and French, often originated in dynastic, economic, or other rivalries. Seldom, though, was it free of ethnic antagonisms, which affected the people in the colonies and, at times, the foreign policies of the European powers involved. The French and Indian War—known in Europe as the Seven Years' War—which broke out first in the colonies in 1754 aroused such feelings of ethnoracial chauvinism.

During this conflict Franklin and the other British leaders who suspected the German settlers of disloyalty to the crown watched them closely. These Germans now made up the largest non-British white ethnic group in the colonies, but still they were most concentrated in Pennsylvania, where the Anglo-American elite continued to resent them and to condemn their alleged clannishness. It demanded of them an allegiance which required acceptance of English values in politics as well as in religion and language.

Christian Sauer, a leader of the Pennsylvania Germans, denounced this pressure for assimilation as well as the other discriminatory actions against his people. He wrote in 1758 "that the English Nation consists of proud and conceited people who denigrate all others, who oppress all those nations of whom they can be master."[6] Regardless of the ethnic frictions, the Germans ultimately supported the British against the French and in the process acquired a degree of political influence.

Contemporaries, as well as later historians such as Francis Parkman, depicted the French and Indian War itself in ethnoracial terms as a struggle between the Anglo-Saxons and Latins. Ethnically conscious colonial leaders such as Franklin made this view quite clear. As a British victory seemed assured, he urged the retention of Canada so that "all the country from the St. Lawrence to the Mississippi will in another century be filled with British people."[7]

In these years more and more of the white arrivals who took up residence in the colonies were Irish. After the Germans, they became the largest portion of the minority European population. Even though the great majority of these newcomers, some 250,000 of them, were Scotch-Irish Protestants from Ulster and less than a fifth were Catholics from southern Ireland, the English settlers disliked them all and discriminated against them all.

The governing elite demonstrated a similar prejudice against other minorities because by this time the outsider population had grown to such an extent that many within the British populace regarded ethnic diversity as a menacing feature of colonial life. Increasingly conspicuous among these varied peoples were the enslaved blacks. According to widely accepted estimates their numbers had grown rapidly until, toward the latter part of the eighteenth century, they amounted to about twenty percent of the population.

Regardless of this diversity and the group animosities it engendered, everywhere in the colonies the English remained the majority people who dominated culture, social life, and politics. They still looked upon *their* colonies as English preserves to be maintained as such. They tolerated the European settlers of different ethnicity but only out of the necessity to retain them as a source of labor and to avoid constant conflict. These Anglo-Americans also accepted the presence of some Indians because they came with the land, but in most instances the English settlers continued to fight the native Americans with deadly effect. Like the other Europeans, the Anglo-Americans detested the blacks they imported to serve them, exploited them, and treated them virtually as subhumans.

Those who considered themselves English also resented almost any social or political assertiveness by the minority whites. With few exceptions, the Anglo-Americans continued to insist that the other ethnoracial groups must acknowledge their superiority. Understandably, as with conquerors and majority peoples everywhere, those on the top were intent upon perpetuating their own way of life against all comers.

This pride in Englishness peaked during, and remained unwavering immediately after, the Seven Years' War. Colonial intellectuals, such as the poet Francis Hopkinson, stressed that "We in America are in all respects Englishmen" who are tied to the mother country with the "strongest bonds of love." The colonials assumed that the "English people, . . . despite even the separation of some by three thousand miles of ocean, were essentially a unitary homogeneous order with a fundamental common interest."[8]

The delight in English preeminence worldwide faltered a bit as colony and mother country quarreled, but it did not diminish. What was lost in this escalating confrontation was the British sense of political union with the majority white colonists. The ethnoracial identification with most of them was hardly touched.

On both sides of the Atlantic pamphleteers and others repeated often that the colonies stood as children to their mother. These writers argued that the Anglo-American family should remain intact. The authorities in London also desired to maintain that familial cohesion, but they injured it by trying to bring the colonists, as though they were stubborn children, to obedience through discipline. Other leaders who also wished to avoid a break played down the idea of punishment. They stressed instead the ethnic bond as a unifier. As William Pitt the Elder announced in the House of Commons in March 1776, "The Americans are the sons, not the bastards of England."[9]

As the quarrel escalated into revolution, many of the rebelling colonists still expressed pride in "having descended from the illustrious stock of Britain."[10] But this macro-ethnic bond did not bring reconciliation. Furthermore, because in a sense the Britons in the transatlantic family fought among themselves in a kind of civil war, ethnic antagonism did not fit into the American Revolution's pattern of causation. Micro-ethnic emotions, nonetheless, did influence the attitudes of the colonists of Scotch, Scotch-Irish, Irish, and Welsh origin toward the coming of, and the waging of, the war. Generally these ethnic groups were more hostile toward the mother country than were the colonists of English descent.

At times the patriot leaders showed sensitivity to ethnic nuances of this nature. Even though most of these men were staunchly Protestant, they urged the Catholics in Ireland to rise in rebellion so as to weaken the British war capabilities in America. In the case of the French in Canada the earlier hostility between them and the Anglo-Americans affected the course of the revolutionary struggle.

In the Quebec Act of May 1774, passed by Parliament after years of deliberation with the purpose of "securing Quebec's position and loyalty under the British crown," the London government had guaranteed the French-Canadians a number of ethnic, religious, legal, and other liberties. These concessions to old Catholic enemies, as well as the expansionist features of the law, had infuriated the Anglo-American colonists to the south, who had designated it one of London's several intolerable measures against them. On October 21, for instance, the First Continental Congress attacked the legislation, maintaining that its framers had included the idea of a French community with the intent of detaching the "dominion of Canada . . . from our interests by civil as well as religious prejudices."[11]

Ironically, four days later the delegates played down their anti-French prejudices. In a surface display of camaraderie, they invited the *Canadiens* to join them in the struggle against the British by sending delegates in May of the following year to the Second Continental Congress in Philadelphia. The French-Canadians did not respond as desired to this appeal, nor later to a second plea for cooperation. In the fall and winter, nonetheless, patriot expeditions headed by Richard Montgomery and by Benedict Arnold attacked Quebec to gain its support through force. The invaders failed to win over the French there, as did the efforts of a congressional commission of two Catholics and two Protestants.

Even though the *Canadiens* did not identify with the people on either side, the Anglo-Americans could not gain their allegiance; neither party could overcome the mutual ethnic distrust of long standing. In a sense the old communal animosities, along with the *Canadiens'* general satisfaction with the British acceptance of their collective identity, prevented Quebec from entering the American union. In the Declaration of Independence the Anglo-Americans reverted openly to their ethnic bias by denouncing the Quebec Act.

Obviously, as the Canadian fiasco revealed, the old animosities between the Anglo-Americans and the French could not easily vanish. They still ran deep in 1778, when France and the new American nation became allies. Among the British empire Loyalists many could not comprehend, therefore, why the United States had "allied itself to her natural, professed, and most dangerous enemy." Even committed rebels could not truly shed their dislike of the French and readily subordinate their predominantly English consciousness to the larger revolutionary cause.

French leaders understood this ethnic attachment. As one of them remarked of their new allies, "They are English as regards Frenchmen, but Americans towards the English."[12] As long as two years after the signing of the alliance, patriot Simeon Baldwin could speak at Yale University on "Whether the Alliance with France will be beneficial to the Inhabitants of America." He concluded that it would not.[13]

Even as the French helped make America's proclaimed independence a reality, the former British colonists still could not bring themselves to trust fully as allies those whom they had long been accustomed to hating. The Anglo-Americans manifested an even stronger aversion to the Spaniards who, while not formal allies, at least fought concurrently against the common British foe. As for the minority colonists such as the Germans and the Irish, they had no real trouble aligning themselves with the patriot cause. Although their animosity toward the Anglo-American elite persisted, before the end of the Revolutionary War they had largely accepted the reality of that elite's predominance in what became the basis for American nationality.

When the revolutionary hostilities ceased, the Anglo-American suspicion of French and Spanish motivation carried over into the peace-making in Paris in 1783. The British negotiators sought to take advantage of this mistrust and of their own blood tie to the American leadership to drive a wedge between the Americans and their French ally. This tactic succeeded to an extent, because the American commissioners suspected the French of treachery. In consequence, and in violation of a commitment not to nego-tiate a separate peace, the Americans in Paris bargained on their own with the British. Thus suspicion between the allies, based in part on ethnic dif-ferences, affected the terms of the treaty that confirmed independence.

The blood connection of most Americans with the old homeland also had an impact on the nation's foreign relations under the Articles of Confeder-ation and under the constitution that came into existence in 1789. More than ninety-five percent of the men who established these governments were of British Protestant stock. Despite the recent hostilities, when most of these founding fathers thought about foreign relations they could not shake off an emotional attachment to their land of origin. They identified what they perceived as the evolving American nationality with Britishness.

Yet, following the revolution even more than during the colonial period, America's populace was multiethnic and multiracial, a characteristic that set the new nation apart from the generally more homogeneous countries of Europe which dominated world affairs. No ethnic group in the United States could claim a clear majority, but among whites almost sixty percent were of English origin. These Anglo-Americans set the standard for a national loyalty that governed political behavior pertaining to foreign relations.

Regardless of the differences within this group over politics, economics, and other domestic issues, it exercised an extensive control over the state and hence over its foreign policy. Its leaders could not conceive of a North America, regardless of its diversity, as a place where all the inhabitants would merge into one people, as did the farmer and essayist Michel-Guil-laume-Jean de Crèvecoeur, who had emigrated from France to America in 1759. He wrote of the new American society as a caldron wherein "individ-uals of all nations are melted into a new race of men," or in other words, a new ethnic community. Nor did the Anglo-Americans regard themselves as fitting his often-cited observation that "the American, this new man," was "either an European, or the descendant of an European."[14] As in the past, most white Americans thought of themselves "as modified Englishmen rather than as a product of a European amalgam."[15]

Indeed, these Anglo-Americans quickly expressed concern over the possibility of dual loyalty among the white minority groups, especially among the recent immigrants from continental Europe. At the constitutional convention in Philadelphia in 1787, for instance, New York's socially and politically conservative Gouverneur Morris, among others, had feared that such newcomers would infiltrate congress before becoming properly assimilated. He urged that they be kept out of the senate with a long residency requirement of fourteen years.

They must be monitored, Morris assumed, because, in the words of a recent analyst, they "would retain their attachment to the interests of the countries from which they emigrated, and engage in what much later would be called ethnic lobbying."[16] Morris himself warned, "Admit a Frenchman into your Senate, and he will study to increase the commerce of France: an Englishman, he will feel an equal bias in favor of that of England."[17]

Morris and other founding fathers did not, of course, associate such allegedly questionable allegiance with ethnic politics as the term is currently used. Other than the Anglo-American population, American society had not yet produced significant ethnically organized groups that could influence the politics of foreign policy.

Still, the fathers deplored almost any kind of political opposition as a threat to national unity. From an elitist range of vision, they stressed a harmony among whites that did not in fact exist. As in the colonial period, the Anglo-Americans sought to assimilate most Europeans in keeping with British standards. They consciously ignored diversity, excluding racially identifiable outsiders, such as Indians and blacks, from their conception of community.

The words of John Jay, taken from the *Federalist* papers, are often quoted to lend authority to this narrow definition of the communal bent of America's population. "Providence has been pleased to give this one connected country to one united people," he asserted, "a people descended from the same ancestors, speaking the same language, professing the same religion, attached to the same principles of government, very similar in their manners and customs."[18] Even though this description lacked a realistic foundation in the new nation as a whole, it probably seemed accurate enough to the Anglo-American elite that Jay, who was himself of mixed European ancestry, addressed.

Two years later, when the geographer Jedidiah Morse also discussed the perceived characteristics of the newly independent American people, he followed the same theme, labeling them "Anglo-Americans" and stressing their descent "from the English." As applied to whites, his assumptions were sound. About seventy-five percent of them could trace their origins to

England, Scotland, and Ulster. Unlike many of his contemporaries, Morse believed that the mixing of these people of British stock with the Dutch, Irish, Germans, and others, did not diminish the overall feeling of "racial" unity with England.[19] He, too, ignored Indians and blacks.

This point of view carried over into the state legislation that granted national citizenship and into the constitution of 1787, which gave congress the power to enact laws regulating naturalization. On March 26, 1790, after lengthy debate, congress approved the first federal naturalization law. That statute, which left the details of implementation to the states, set a uniform standard for preserving European predominance by restricting eligibility for citizenship to those who were free white persons. It thus denied to the first-generation non-whites who might enter the country any opportunity to participate in the politics which shape foreign policy. The racial attitude implicit in the legislation would affect important aspects of foreign relations for generations to come.

A similar ethnoracial consciousness affected the political structure of the national government. President George Washington and others in the administration usually denounced organized resistance to their policies as "faction." Among these leaders, Secretary of the Treasury Alexander Hamilton, an ardent Anglophile, was especially concerned over real or possible opposition to close relations with Britain. He headed what London called the "British interest" in the United States. In particular, he distrusted Secretary of State Thomas Jefferson's handling of foreign affairs because in some matters Jefferson evinced a distaste for Britain, appeared too enamored of the French, and thus headed a faction.

To advance toward his goal of intimacy with the old mother country, Hamilton worked closely with Major George Beckwith, a secret British agent operating out of Canada whom some "considered in no other light than as a petty Spy." Hamilton told Beckwith that "I have always preferred a connexion with you, to that of any other country, *we think in English*, and have a similarity of prejudices and of predilections."[20] Hamilton also informed the British government that if it wished it could circumvent Jefferson and could always reach the president through him. Thus in 1790–92 significant diplomacy with Britain bypassed the State Department because the treasury secretary and his friends, for ethnic and other reasons, chose to dominate this aspect of external relations.

In part as a consequence of this pro-British foreign policy, pursued by the Hamiltonians regardless of an alliance with France that remained in force, around 1793, when England and France went to war, two national political parties arose. Essentially, men of Anglo-American stock dominated both parties, but those most concerned with the ethnic connection with Britain had greater power in the Federalist party than in the opposing Democratic-Republican party. The Republicans favored friendship with France for political and ideological reasons, however, and not because of any ethnic affiliation or any explicit desire to harm England.

While important in itself, party affiliation did not change most people's emotional identification with old homelands. In November 1794, for instance, John Jay, now a staunch Federalist sent as a special envoy to London to avert a possible war, negotiated a commercial treaty with Britain which many of the Irish in the United States and most Republicans deplored. Pressure-group politics and foreign lobbying came into play through partisan clubs known as democratic societies, dominated often by Irish and German anti-Federalist ethnic groups. The clubs were also openly patronized by Joseph Fauchet, the French minister to the United States, who along with the minority and Republican politicians encouraged their attacks on the Jay treaty.

Within the government the only officer who openly opposed the agreement was Secretary of State Edmund Randolph. The Hamiltonian Federalists accused him of conspiring with Fauchet to sabotage the treaty and thereby advance French causes within the country. When the extreme Federalists forced his resignation, Randolph blamed a "British faction" for his fate. Despite the furor, in the following June Washington ratified Jay's treaty, and Americans began a rapprochement with the mother country. Its major motif was "a wide and unique community of interests," based in large measure on ethnic affinity, that had been interrupted by the revolution.[21]

In the following year Charles-Maurice de Talleyrand-Périgord, a French aristocrat residing in the United States as a private citizen, found evidence of this attachment striking. "*America is . . . completely English*," he noted, "*that is England still has the advantage over France in drawing from the United States all benefit that one nation can draw from the existence of another.*"[22]

The French sought to overcome their disadvantageous position in this triangular relationship by seeking extended privileges within the scope of their alliance, by meddling in American politics, and by bribing members of congress. The bribes and other pressures gained the French some backing from individual legislators and from a few other officials, which permitted them to affect some small issues of foreign policy. In the main, though, the French efforts failed.

The French tampering did bring into the open, however, what would become a basic principle in ethnic politics: without strong domestic support in the structure of a legitimate opposition in the American party system, foreign agents could not significantly sway foreign policy. As a rule, such outsider activity cannot match the influence of strategically placed indigenous interest groups, such as those composed of Federalist Anglophiles. Inside groups, moreover, could at times make or break specific policies.

In keeping with this evolving principle, Federalists inveighed against foreign interference in the nation's internal politics, condemning those who cooperated with the French as disloyal. In his Farewell Address in September 1796, Washington gave notable expression to this reaction against the "insidious wiles of foreign influence" by decrying the lobbying of foreigners "as one of the most baneful foes of Republican Government." He attacked those who would place the interests of another country in the center of domestic politics. That practice endangered the state because it "would sever" leaders "from their Brethren and connect them with Aliens."

Washington also advised against "a passionate attachment of one Nation for another," warning that "sympathy for the favourite nation" leads to "quarrels and wars." Regardless of their land of birth, or attachment to it, all Americans should give their primary allegiance to the new nation. Yet, Washington and his advisers allowed the affection for ancestral England to influence their shaping of foreign policy, particularly in a confrontation with France.[23]

John Adams, the next president, distrusted aspects of Britain's policy but along with his advisers greatly admired her and felt deeply the attachment to her as his mother country. This bond, as reflected in Federalist foreign policy, exacerbated the already raw relations with France. When, for example, Theodore Sedgwick, a Federalist leader in the senate, heard that the French, in what became known as the XYZ affair, had humiliated the American envoys sent to Paris to negotiate a settlement of differences, he exulted. "It will," he said, "afford a glorious opportunity to destroy faction."[24] This Federalist attitude, the aggravations by the French, the ethnic connection with Britain, and other causes in 1798 plunged the country into the Quasi-War with France.

Immediately Sedgwick and like-minded Federalists wished to take advantage of the conflict to wipe out immigrant support for the Republican party, which they regarded as tainted with disloyalty because of its record of friendliness toward France. They also desired an alliance with England. The often Anglophile extremists among them agitated to enlarge the Quasi-War. To achieve these goals they sought popular support through the exploitation of a white nativism linked to a still potent Francophobia.

During the course of these French hostilities, which were confined to small naval engagements, political activists in Ireland fled the failed but bloody revolution of the United Irishmen. Through this society of Protestant radicals headed by the rebel lawyer Theobald Wolfe Tone, they had hoped to set up an Irish republic. Many of the losers took refuge in the United States, to become naturalized citizens in numbers exceeding those of all other nationalities. Supported by kin who had arrived earlier, these newcomers continued their agitation for an independent Ireland. To facilitate the achievement of that objective, most of them joined the ranks of the Jeffersonian Republicans. Both the Catholic and Protestant Irish disliked the pro-British stance of the Federalist party as well as its aristocratic pretensions.

In the seaboard cities where the Irish-Americans constituted a strategically placed minority, they took to the streets to denounce government policy. They also organized the American Society of United Irishmen to further their anti-English revolutionary cause, achieving sufficient success to alarm the British minister, who formally protested their activities to the American government.

This kind of repercussion from ethnically oriented politics, and the tactics of the Irish-Americans in particular, angered the Federalists. They moved to muzzle these foreign-born critics of their foreign policy and also to curb their ability to engage in ethnic politics. In June and July 1798 the Federalists in congress secured the passage of legislation affecting naturalization, the status of aliens in the country, and civil liberties. All of the measures, usually designated the Alien and Sedition laws, were designed to exclude the minority immigrants from political life and hence from influencing foreign policy. As Harrison Gray Otis of Massachusetts expressed the Federalist outlook, the Anglo-Americans "did not wish to invite hordes of wild Irishmen, nor the turbulent and disorderly of all parts of the world to come here with a view to disturb our own tranquility."[25]

Other Federalists, such as Rufus King, the United States' minister in London, wanted to prevent the Irish from disfiguring "our true national character," meaning a presumed Anglo-Saxon distinctiveness.[26] These leaders, who had difficulty in accepting the idea of a legalized opposition, believed that the ethnic politics of minority groups possessed no legitimacy. These nativists assumed, too, that in acting to prevent aliens from gaining access to political power, they were serving the national interest as well as that of their own core group. In their eyes the two interests were one and the same.

Regardless of the restrictive Federalist laws, between 1789 and 1800 Irish-Americans constituted 55 percent of all aliens naturalized. By this time, also, Catholics may have accounted for 20 percent of the Irish population.[27] In critical spots these Irish-American voters may have exerted substantial influence on policy. In elections in New York and Pennsylvania in 1799, they claimed to have provided the margin of victory for the Democratic-Republicans.

Irish-Americans believed also that they had contributed significantly to Jefferson's victory in the presidential election of 1800. Congress thereafter repealed the discriminatory Alien acts. Jefferson himself took note of those who presumedly had organized the "Irish vote" by rewarding them with government jobs. As the conventional wisdom has it, the Irish community thus became confirmed in its allegiance to the Democratic-Republicans.

Despite this concern with Irish-American support and his wariness toward England that so alarmed Federalists, Jefferson as president usually approached other ethnoracial issues touching on consequential aspects of foreign policy from the British viewpoint that he had known since childhood. For example, as did other Anglo-Americans, he believed that in the future, through "rapid multiplication," Anglicized Americans, unblemished by racial mixture, "speaking the same language, governed in similar forms, and by similar laws," would "cover the whole northern, if not the southern continent."[28] Such faith in the capability of the whites, and in their supposed superiority over others, governed aspects of his administration's relations with black revolutionaries on Saint Domingue, the West Indies colony belonging to France.

From the white American point of view the problem had begun in August 1791 when slaves on the island rose against their French masters. President Washington, Jefferson, and other Americans feared that the uprising would spread to the United States and ignite a race war "which will probably never end but in the extermination of one or the other race."[29] So the American government sent arms and ammunition to the white planters to help them suppress the insurrection, but to no avail. Under the leadership mainly of Toussaint Louverture, a talented former slave originally from Guinea, the blacks and mulattoes in June 1793 toppled the planter regime. Fifteen thousand of the French survivors fled to the United States, particularly to the south, where they received succor and sympathy.

Beginning in 1797, as part of the Quasi-War with France, the Adams administration cooperated with the blacks on Saint Domingue and encouraged them to assert their independence from France. Yet the president took a strong stand against acknowledging their regime as self-governing. For racial reasons, he explained, closer relations would constitute a danger to the United States, meaning mainly to its slaveholding states.

Jefferson had no love for Toussaint; as president he too encouraged trade with Saint Domingue, but hardly anything more. He did not wish to impair restored friendly relations with France, which still claimed dominion over the colony. For reasons similar to those of Adams, he also opposed a truly independent status for the slave regime. As did many of his contemporaries, Jefferson felt that Toussaint's example of black dominance menaced white security in every slaveholding region in the United States.

This fear accounted in part for Jefferson's support of Napoleon Bonaparte's attempt to reconquer the island. That effort, as is well known, ran into difficulties which contributed to American success in obtaining Louisiana in May 1803. In November the blacks compelled a large French army to sign an armistice and then to capitulate to the British. Blacks and mulattoes also forced all the whites who still remained on their part of the island to flee.

As to Louisiana, the Jeffersonians pushed aside Spanish protests that the purchase of that territory was illegal. They justified the acquisition and the imposition of American dominion over the Indians and Spaniards in Louisiana with a number of reasons, but especially with an ingrained assumption of Anglo-Saxon superiority. They viewed this heritage as endowing them with a moral right to rule over these allegedly inferior peoples and to populate the continent with their own kind. Jeffersonians employed a similar rationale in seeking to wrench the Floridas from Spain.

Meanwhile, on January 1, 1804, the former slaves of Saint Domingue proclaimed independence, named their state Haiti, and then massacred the whites who remained on their soil. In the United States the slave-owning planters, who lived in fear of similar uprisings by their own blacks, reacted with horror. These Southerners, who in effect dominated the national government, maintained the practice of shunning the Haitians. Thus, the United States refused formally to recognize this first free black nation in the modern world. As all of those involved in the decision knew, race more than anything else governed this nonrecognition policy.

All the while, for ethnic and other reasons, Americans took a keen interest in the struggle between Great Britain and Napoleonic France, which had resumed in May 1803. Initially most of them favored Britain. As the uncompromising Federalist Timothy Pickering explained with an often-repeated sentiment, they loved her because she was "the country of our forefathers."[30] Ultimately, Americans became indirectly involved in the Anglo-French conflict through the War of 1812. Ethnic determinism had no direct part in that conflict's origins or in its conclusion. Yet from the American perspective micro-ethnic considerations touched some aspects of it significantly.

Among minority groups, the Irish-Americans greeted the war enthusiastically. In the course of the hostilities, when American forces invaded Canada, the government in Washington expected cooperation, if not aid, from the French populace. Largely for ethno-religious reasons, no help materialized. As in the past, the French-Canadians distrusted the prejudices of the Americans more than they did those of the British. At the same time the American strike at the Floridas, which was in part strategic and which brought all of West Florida into the Union, had in it the ethno-religious emotion of Spanish-hating.

In the view of many historians, Anglophobia also had a compelling role in the war hysteria. Yet where it existed it often had shallow roots. Some Americans spoke sadly of war with "the land of our fathers" and many were determined to prevent the hostilities from seriously weakening the ethnic bond with Britain.

New Yorker De Witt Clinton, for instance, lauded the English language for keeping Americans together and extinguishing "stubborn prejudices and violent animosities" which could divide them. Others shared the sentiment of New Englander Edward Everett as expressed in December 1814. "I may presume," he said, "that there is not one who hears me, that does not regard it as a matter of congratulation and joy, that our fathers were Englishmen." He stressed the widespread feeling among Anglo-Americans that England was a nation "of common blood." In this outlook, shared frequently by historians, the war was an "anomaly" in the close relationship between kindred peoples.[31]

Just as the American establishment recognized the intimacy of the ethnic connection with Britain, so it did an assumed blood relationship between many of the slaves in the United States and the people of West Africa. Jefferson, James Madison, James Monroe, and others saw in this perceived African kinship a possible escape from the dilemma of a black-white relationship in the United States that filled them with foreboding.

Some of these leaders were slaveholders, and others disliked racial slavery, but all of them believed in the innate inferiority of the Africans, whom they regarded as incapable of assimilation in their white-dominated society. Jefferson feared that, because of these ineradicable distinctions between the whites and the blacks and the animus they engendered, if the slaves were emancipated and remained in the country a race war would follow. The solution to this quandary that he and thinkers of similar persuasion found most acceptable was the gradual emancipation of slaves followed by their shipment out of the country, mainly to West Africa.

On January 1, 1817, the mostly Southern whites who held to similar ideas tried to put them into effect by founding the American Society for the Colonization of Free People of Color of the United States, or as it became known generally, the American Colonization Society. It sought to interest emancipated blacks in returning to African homelands, which in reality they never knew, and undertook to provide them with transport there. The organizers hoped to rid the country of blacks and thereby maintain the white establishment's assimilationist ideal without obvious hypocrisy.

Knowledgeable blacks quickly discerned the true intent of the scheme. A month after the society had been organized, three thousand of them crammed into Philadelphia's Bethel Church to protest, pointing out that the planned colonization would "stigmatize the free Negro population, and it countenanced the perpetuation of human bondage and encouraged it by seeking to remove free blacks."[32]

The colonization effort proceeded anyway with a settlement in 1822 on Africa's west coast which the society had acquired through barter and called Liberia. The plan did not work as desired because "Africans simply refused to go to Liberia or support colonization," thereby making it clear to all who were willing to accept reality that the numerous people of African origin would remain a permanent feature of American society.[33] The always obvious presence of these blacks, however powerless their status might be, along with the existence of Liberia, maintained the racial link with West Africa which in the future would at least sway an aspect of the nation's foreign relations.

While this African connection was languishing, the bond with the peoples of Europe, despite revolution, wars, and four decades of slowing immigration, grew stronger. The voluntary immigrants, mostly from the British Isles and elsewhere in northeastern Europe, kept alive the nation's white ethnic and cultural diversity. As in the past, however, the non-Anglo immigrants seldom influenced the foreign policies which the old elite continued to formulate and dominate.

With considerable fervor the Anglo-American establishment proceeded with its desire to Americanize all other white ethnic groups in keeping with its own now well-established model. Even though this Americanizing became a source of friction between the minorities and the elite, it succeeded well enough to satisfy much of the white populace, which could still think of itself as fundamentally, if not unmistakably, English. As usual, such assimilation did not apply to the non-whites.

In the case of the Indians, Euro-American racial enmity promoted more of the wars that exterminated many of their tribes and dispossessed others. A few governmental and intellectual leaders, such as Jefferson, at times spoke of the Indians as mingling with the whites "to become one people." Others, such as President James Monroe, explained on the other hand that "it is impossible to incorporate them [the Indians], . . . in any form whatever in our system."[34]

As from the beginning of European settlement, the whites as a whole viewed the indigenous peoples with their usual scorn as "unassimilable," as "savage bloodhounds," as "bloodthirsty barbarians," and as subhuman obstacles to the advancement of "civilization." The Indians had to be removed to make room for the Caucasians. Congress and all the presidents of the early nineteenth century favored this policy as a matter of principle, but Andrew Jackson stands out because, through the use of military force, he made it rigorous. In the racial combat of the Jacksonian era against the Indians, the whites perceived themselves as preserving their "uniquely American identity" that sprang from English soil. They also pursued this ethnoracial objective in their foreign policy.

3
RACISM AND EXPANSION

Another [shallow phrase] is
"Anglo Saxon race." This
patronymic is meant for
those who know as much
about who the Angles and
who the Saxons were as they
do of those Jewish affiliations
which run back to the
twelve sons of Jacob. Oh,
miserable humbug of
History!

National Intelligencer,
Jan. 15, 1848

In 1820, after the start of a new surge in immigration, for the first time the census listed the newcomers by their country of origin. Its data showed that most of them still came from the British Isles but also that fresh groups of northwestern Europeans had begun thronging to America's port cities, where many remained. Along with the old-stock white Americans, some of them pushed westward in search of economic betterment through farming. Others provided much of the labor for the building of roads, canals, and factories. All of them affected the fabric of America's life and culture.

Even though a significant number of these recent arrivals became involved in politics, they rarely influenced the thrust of foreign policy. Regardless, they still retained a lively interest in the affairs of their homelands. Those who formed "by far the largest group" among these newcomers were the Irish, the majority of whom were now Catholic.[1] They were the most persistent among the minorities in trying to affect an important aspect of the nation's foreign relations.

Wherever these ethnically sensitive new or old Irish-Americans congregated, they expressed solidarity with the revolutionary causes on the island they had left. While the activists who remained at home struggled for religious and ethnic emancipation, the American Irish supported them directly or through associations known as the Friends of Ireland. These friends sent a stream of money along with addresses of encouragement to the Catholic Association in Dublin, headed by Daniel O'Connell, a reforming nationalist who made it the foremost civil rights organization in Ireland. Functioning as a mobilized ethnic group determined to affect the course of relations with Great Britain, the friends also pressured the government in

Washington to aid their kin in their old homeland. These politically active Irish-Americans did win support from some elected officials but without noteworthy effect on the British connection.

At this time ethnoracial concerns in a small way also affected relations with a number of recently independent nations in Latin America, most of whom had done away with slavery. South America's liberator, Simón Bolívar, planned to bring together in Panama representatives from the American republics to discuss Western hemisphere issues. In November 1825 the organizers of the conference invited the United States to participate with the hope of persuading its policymakers to transform the Monroe Doctrine into a multilateral hemispheric agreement, or even an alliance. President John Quincy Adams decided to send delegates, but racial considerations immediately caused him difficulty.

The agenda provided for a discussion on abolishing the African slave trade and on the question of the participating powers' possibly recognizing Haiti as free and independent. These topics, as well as the expected presence of black and mulatto delegates from other countries, aroused opposition in the senate, particularly among its race-conscious Southerners.

John M. Berrien of Georgia, for example, objected to an American presence at the conference because formerly mutinous slaves would represent some of the newly independent nations. He foresaw as a danger that these delegates, when dealing with the representatives from the United States, would be treated as the equals of whites. Other opponents spoke contemptuously of the allegedly mongrel Creole leaders, reflecting the Anglo-American perspective that "the three primary racial stocks in Latin America—Iberians, native Americans, and Africans, and the 'mixed races'" were all low in the human scale.[2] As a consequence of these fears, even though the senate finally approved the sending of two delegates, the idea of participation had meager real support.

When the Panama congress did meet for three weeks in June and July 1826, it accomplished little. The representatives from the United States never took part. Even so, the Latin American leaders who had gone ahead with the congress learned of the abuse that had been heaped on them and their kind in Washington. Thus, soon after most of the Hispanic peoples to the south had achieved independence, the negative ethnoracial sentiment common among Americans affected the Hispanics' attitude toward and relations with the United States.

Meanwhile, to the north, the descendants of earlier British settlers regarded the continuing arrival of European immigrants as an obstacle to the kind of national unity they prized. In this migratory wave only the British suffered no hostility, because they were seen as posing no assimilative problem. They blended so easily that the dominant Anglo-Americans considered them "invisible immigrants," or hardly aliens at all in the usual sense. Yet these newcomers, too, clung to old ethnic loyalties. They were "patriotic John Bulls" who, like other immigrants, reacted strongly to foreign-policy issues that affected their old homeland.[3] Overall in these decades the number of British arrivals who moved into America's cities and farms shrank in proportion to the other incoming ethnic groups. The Anglo-American control of foreign affairs, however, suffered no decline.

Regardless, the "Protestant nationalists" of Anglo descent perceived in the widening involvement in politics of the multiplying minority immigrants a threat to their position of power. Convinced that their "patterns of life could be imposed on others," the white nativists mobilized to do so and to vent their anti-foreign feelings.[4] Beginning in 1835 the political organizations they controlled, usually on a local basis, sought to limit the influence of immigrants, especially of the Catholics, in American society. In the following decade the agitation of these xenophobes became almost a fixed feature of political life.

Externally, the nativists rationalized their bigotry, for instance against Indians and Hispanics, with notions of exceptionalism and mission. These Anglo-Americans had long viewed the peoples who inhabited Mexico in particular as beneath them, maintaining that they, like others from Latin America, belonged to a substandard mixed race. As Mexico's first minister to Washington observed, "The arrogance of those republicans does not allow them to see us as equals but as inferiors. With time they will become our sworn enemies."[5]

This ethnoracial antagonism stands out as a cause for the revolt of the Anglo colonists in Mexico's province of Texas. When the skirmishing began in 1835, the rebels' foremost leader, Stephen F. Austin, expressed a view of the struggle common among his people. It was being waged, he wrote, by a "mongrel Spanish-Indian and negro race, against civilization and the Anglo-American race."[6]

Knowledgeable Mexicans, especially those who were aware of the northerners' attitudes, took it for granted that the Anglo-Americans had fomented the uprising for racial reasons. Within the United States also, people generally regarded the difficulties as racial, seeing the struggle as a clash between the white Texans of their own kind and the half-breeds of Indian and Spanish stock. All over the country, but especially in the South, newspapers and popular sentiment expressed approval of the rebel cause.

After Texas had won its de facto independence in May 1836, those Americans who favored its annexation talked constantly of the ethnoracial affinity between themselves and the white Texans. As the Anglo-Americans did for themselves, they claimed for the Texans an innate superiority over Mexicans. Alexander Stephens, a Georgia politician, expressed a common attitude. "They are of the Americo-Anglo-Saxon race," he said. "They are from us, and of us; bone of our bone, and flesh of our flesh."[7] Another Southerner declared that Texas' fate would "effect, for weal or for wo[e], through ages yet to come, millions of the Anglo-Saxon race."[8] Mexican leaders who were aware of this attitude reacted in analogous ethnoracial terms, telling their people, for example, to struggle to retain Texas because theirs was a "war of race, of religion, of language, and of customs."[9]

The American opponents of annexation also frequently acted out of ethnoracial motivation, but from a standpoint that differed from that of the expansionists. For instance, the abolitionists, many of whom were believers in white supremacy, viewed the Texas annexation effort as part of a conspiracy by a slave-owning oligarchy that presumedly dominated the foreign-policy establishment. William Jay, a leading publicist of this theory, expressed abolitionist disgust in a few words, complaining that "even American diplomacy must be made subservient to the interests of the slaveholders."[10]

As the agitation over the events in Texas continued, ethnoracial emotions affected the attitudes toward, and relations with, China and Britain. In the Opium War of 1839–41, fought in a period regarded as intensely Anglophobic, the Anglo-American elite gave little consideration to the right or wrong of the adversaries' positions. Along with the Protestant missionaries, who were Britain's chief apologists, it denounced the Chinese and sided strongly with the British. Former president John Quincy Adams, for one, stretched the facts to maintain that Britain had "the righteous cause." American journalists such as James Gordon Bennett of the New York *Herald* saw the struggle as racial, as "between the Caucasian and Tungusian races." These writers, of course, "supported their fellow Anglo-Saxons."[11] Even the leaders of opinion who had been Anglophobic on some other issues hailed the victory as belonging to the United States as well as to England.

In the meantime a financial panic and then a depression struck the country. In addition to inflating the popular fears of job competition from the minority newcomers, the depression intensified white nativist emotions against them, especially against the Irish. As the Irish-Americans became more Catholic, more numerous, more well-to-do, and more active politically, officeholders curried their favor. To British visitors it seemed that "the Irish were wooed by all parties."[12] In 1843 a more distant observer, in

Dublin, protested the politicking of this nature by Robert Tyler, the president's son. "He knows that our countrymen have much political power in America," the critic said. "He is anxious to gain their suffrages for his party; these are cheaply purchased by a few hollow-hearted and fiery speeches in favour of Irish independence."[13]

True enough, the Irish-Americans, through organizations such as the Friends of Ireland founded several years earlier, stepped up their aid to the nationalist anti-British groups in their motherland. To the old-stock nativists this ethnic solidarity took on the aspect of an "uprising against the assumed superiority of the 'original Americans'."[14]

These nativists found the political activity of the organized white minority ethnic groups, or merely their presence, so distasteful that they resorted to violence. For example, between May 6 and 8, 1844, gangs in Philadelphia systematically gutted the homes of Irish-Americans. Mobs looted and burned two Catholic churches and a seminary. In July nativist riots left thirteen people dead and fifty wounded. The motivation behind this bloodletting was more anti-Irish than anti-Catholic, but the religious and ethnic elements were so mixed that they could not be separated.

As one consequence of this Protestant ethnic fury, anti-foreignism as well as expansionism became a foremost issue in the presidential campaigning of 1844. After the election, expansionism remained in the forefront of foreign policy, leading the two major parties to put aside, while not abandoning, white nativism as a compelling concern. By mid-1845, therefore, this anti-immigrant agitation as a political movement had lost much of its initial force.

At the same time, expansionist fervor led to a confrontation with Britain over the vaguely defined Oregon country. Although many Americans were deeply aroused by the issue, however, few of them phrased their sentiments in hateful racial or ethnic slurs against the British. In the recent past there had been diplomatic clashes with Britain over a number of issues and even loose talk of war. For instance, in 1837 a rebellion in Canada had attracted support from Americans who had intervened on their own, thus roiling relations with London. When the uprising quickly collapsed, so did the harsh rhetoric.

Two years later the American and British governments quarreled over the boundary between Maine and New Brunswick. Then they bickered over the arrest in New York of Alexander McLeod, a Canadian deputy sheriff, for murder and arson connected with the 1837 rebellion. They also squabbled over the mutiny of slaves on an American ship, the *Creole*, mainly because the defiant blacks found refuge in British Nassau. In the United States the

Anglo-American elite blamed the Irish and other Anglophobes for much of the furor as well as for the popular heat that these episodes generated.

Anglophiles dismissed the talk of war "between the two nations of the earth the most closely knit together by the bands of a common origin" as absurd.[15] In August 1842 the bitterness of these confrontations, along with the festering differences on the Canadian frontier, were swept away in an effort of diplomacy suffused with a sense of Anglo-Saxon brotherhood that produced the Webster-Ashburton treaty. The senate approved this arrangement, which fixed a compromise boundary in the northeast, with the largest majority it had ever given a treaty. Historians generally hail this settlement as having prevented war, as marking a new rapprochement between Britain and the United States, and as exemplifying how two kindred civilized peoples could resolve disputes.

Yet the differences over the Oregon country remained unresolved. The Americans demanded all of it as far north as Russian America at latitude "fifty-four forty." Some of them took seriously the possibility of war over the boundary line. Among Irish-Americans hopes again ran high that such a conflict would bring in its wake freedom to their old homeland. Their expectations were illusory. Practical diplomacy and the strong feelings of kinship between the American and English elites, based on "the ties of common blood, language, & laws," prevailed.[16] These considerations helped resolve the Oregon dispute peacefully in June 1846 through a compromise, favorable to the United States, which set the boundary at the 49th parallel.

As historian Reginald Horsman explained, "the sense of Anglo-Saxon racial community, combined with respect for British power and ability, helped mute the most strident demands for war." As with the Maine dispute, most American politicians were loath to battle their "Anglo-Saxon brethren."[17]

Other writers have also suggested that war at this time with Britain, "another Anglo-Saxon nation, would have been unthinkable." With some frequency historians have analyzed the outcome of the Oregon dispute in terms tinged with ethnic bias. One who followed in this tradition said that in Oregon "American pioneers were confronted by sterner stuff than Spaniards or Mexicans," and hence would not again fight the kindred British.[18]

When it came to the shedding of Mexican blood to acquire Texas and California, however, the pioneers of expansionist stripe exhibited no hesitancy. "We can now thrash Mexico into decency at our leisure," one of their spokesmen said.[19] This attitude and the Americans' generally low regard for their brown southern neighbors had contributed to the rising animosities which in May 1846, after the United States had annexed Texas, brought on war with Mexico.

Novelist William Gilmore Simms expressed a sentiment common among the Anglo-Americans. He praised war and urged his countrymen "to obey our destiny and blood," insisting that "our destiny is conquest." A year later he wrote that "Never Don or Savage yet with the Saxon could endure!" As with the Texas uprising, Mexicans, too, often viewed this conflict in racial terms. For instance, early in 1847 Mexico's Antonio López de Santa Anna clung to his position of leadership by telling his people that the Americans were making war upon "their race and their religion." Some Mexicans depicted Americans as detestable beings who "scarcely have the look of men."[20]

In the United States newspaper editors, politicians, and others invariably focused on race when referring to the Mexicans. As during the Texas revolution, most commentators stressed the alleged inferiority of the Mexicans or dismissed them contemptuously as a given to miscegenation. Shared by the leaders of the country, this popular sentiment implied that because of their racial characteristics the Mexicans deserved the violent treatment they were receiving.

Sarcastically, the abolitionist poet James Russell Lowell expressed the conviction of many Americans

> Thet Mexicans worn't human beans,—an ourang outang nation,
> A sort o'folks a chap could kill an' never dream on 't arter,
> No more'n a feller'd dream o'pigs thet he hed hed to slater. . . .
> An' kickin colored folks about, you know,'s a kind of national.[21]

The Whigs and the others who, for a cluster of reasons, opposed the war also nurtured a racial distaste for the Mexicans, whom they characterized as a "wretched people." The *Richmond Whig* perceived the conflict in terms "of the Caucasian and Anglo-Saxon, pure white blood, against a mixed and mongrel race, composed of Indians, negroes, and Spaniards, all three degenerated by the admixture of blood and colors."[22]

The overwhelming American victory in the Mexican War appeared to confirm these notions of Anglo-Saxon superiority implicit in the gospel of Manifest Destiny. It also induced the formulators of foreign policy to attempt to infuse this doctrine and the racism in it with a moral quality. As had conquerors since antiquity, they talked enigmatically about a divinely imposed duty to regenerate their backward southern neighbors. Ironically, those who took for granted that Mexicans were so retarded as to require uplifting through force did so mainly because white Americans had defined the Mexicans as such.

The rhetoric of a special destiny had an appeal well beyond American borders, but especially in Britain. Despite striking foreign-policy differences with the United States at this time, England's leaders expressed a "racial" sympathy for the American conquest. Even Lord Palmerston, Britain's foreign minister, spoke most warmly of the American victories as illustrating the transcendent worth of the Anglo-Saxon. Many in the United States who shared this belief were also convinced that the nation's "future glory" would be achieved through "a bond of cordial, and, . . . imperishable love" with England.[23]

This idea of a racially determined preeminence figured prominently in the debates on terminating the Mexican War and in the making of a peace settlement. Numerous believers in destined expansion desired to seize all of Mexico. Others objected to the acquiring of another mass of dark-skinned peoples. The objectors prophesied that if the allegedly degraded Mexicans were incorporated into the nation, they would in time build up enough gall to seek to share in the privileges of citizenship. Then they would corrupt Anglo-American institutions.

Lewis Cass, a politician of presidential ambition who shared the prevailing views against any mixture of white Americans with supposed racial inferiors, earlier had expressed what became the core argument of those who opposed the all-Mexico movement. "We do not want the people of Mexico, either as citizens or subjects," he said. "All we want is a portion of territory which they nominally hold, uninhabited, or, where inhabited at all, sparsely so, and with a population which would soon recede, or identify itself with ours."[24]

Even more adamant in their aversion to full annexation than the northerners such as Cass were the spokesmen for America's South. John C. Calhoun, the South Carolina apostle of racism, who had opposed the war, stated, for example, "I know . . . that we have never dreamt of incorporating into our Union any but the Caucasian race—the free white race. . . . I protest against such a union as that" with Mexico. "Ours, sir, is the Government of a white race" with which the Mexicans are not fit to be connected.[25]

While the Americans and Mexicans were hurling insults at each other and shedding blood, a famine stemming from a blight on potatoes, a staple food for many Europeans, and from the insensitivity of British authorities to the plight of the people, struck in Ireland. Beginning in February 1847, the resulting misery on their island drove thousands of impoverished Irish to America's shore. Within four years more than a million immigrants, who were now overwhelmingly Catholic and imbued "with hatred in their hearts for the British," streamed into the country.[26] They transformed the character of the Irish-American community and rapidly altered the base of minority ethnic politics.

In August 1848, in the course of this mass migration, a group of militants in Ireland that had broken away from the idealistic but impractical leadership of the nationalist Young Ireland movement rebelled against English rule. Even though this uprising quickly collapsed, it inspired the creation of Irish Republican clubs in New York and other American cities. These societies backed the Young Irelanders and other nationalists, especially in their anti-British endeavors, and provided money for them to purchase guns.

Leaders of the failed revolt such as John Mitchel, a talented Presbyterian revolutionary from Ulster, also fled to the United States, where ethnic kin gave them warm receptions. The plight of these refugees and their success in organizing groups to support Irish independence intensified the already strong Irish-American hatred of England. Now, with increased numbers and more sophistication than in the past, the Irish-Americans used the power of their votes with sufficient effect to aggravate, more effectively than in earlier efforts, American relations with the British government. They hoped that ultimately their enhanced political potency would promote Irish independence.

Sure enough, politicians promptly recognized the new growth in Irish power. In the campaign of 1848, and in those that followed, the competition among candidates for Irish-American votes became a prominent feature of the electioneering. Officeholders also listened more carefully to the overseas concerns of the local Irish. In January 1852, for instance, a delegation of two hundred Irish-Americans gained access to the White House to plead with President Millard Fillmore to intercede with the British for the release of revolutionary Young Irelanders banished to Australia. He expressed sympathy but said he could not interfere in Britain's internal affairs.

In areas such as New York City, where by 1855 Irish-Americans constituted more than a third of the electorate, politicians found the need to defer to their wishes more and more compelling. At the same time the increased presence of "poor, vicious, and degraded Irishmen" brought to a boil the old nativist hatred of outsiders that had been simmering just below the surface of American life for about a decade.

In addition to the Irish, a substantial number of German newcomers felt the force of this revived nativist ire. Between 1846 and 1855, upward of a million Germans entered the United States, more than a few of them having fled revolution as well as the potato disease. Many, but not all, were well received. The substantial number of Catholics among them in particular aroused resentment. Those Germans who had been revolutionaries, known usually as "forty-eighters," gained prominence through involvement in politics. The forty-eighters' activism stirred the ethnic consciousness of established German-Americans. It attracted into political action even some of those who had been divided or were apathetic about their roots. This reaching out for political power hardened whatever antagonism the old-stock nativists felt toward the German-Americans.

When politicians did cater to the German-American voters as they did to the Irish-Americans, the nativist fear increased. Nonetheless, the foreign-born became naturalized and tried to make their votes count. In 1852 the German-American vote was thought to have helped elect Franklin Pierce to the presidency. Four years later German-American voters again presumedly took a crucial part in presidential politics.

Despite their naturalization, most German-Americans defended their right to maintain ethnic differentiation against assimilationist pressure. Many argued for pluralism, for a durable ethnicity, and for the conservation of their own culture. This assertiveness was one of the qualities that compounded the Anglo-American irritation toward this ethnic community. Unlike the Irish-Americans, however, the German-Americans at this time did not as a cohesive group attempt to influence foreign policy that could have had an impact on kin in Europe.

With their numbers and new activism, the German-Americans certainly had the potential to affect at least limited aspects of foreign policy. They did not engage in ethnic lobbying largely because, lacking a connection to a united homeland, they were fragmented by old-world religious and regional loyalties. Yet, like other elements of the immigrant population in many cities and despite the Anglo-American distaste for many of them, the German-Americans had become too numerous and too involved in national politics for the traditional parties to antagonize them openly.

Outwardly, the nativists denounced all the minority newcomers because they differed from them in customs, dress, and sometimes in language and religion. Fundamentally, though, with immigration surging toward annual levels higher than any yet reached, the Anglo-Americans feared the incoming foreigners with a renewed ferocity because they now appeared more capable than ever before of challenging the established power structure. With the avowed purpose of preserving the predominance of the English "racial" strain, these nativists expanded their small, often secret, anti-foreign and anti-Catholic societies.

In 1849 nativists had established the Order of the Star-Spangled Banner, which quickly gained a large following. When questioned about their association, members feigned ignorance, responding, "I know nothing." So in 1853 the New York newspaper editor Horace Greeley dubbed them the "Know Nothings." The name stuck. As hostility to immigrants, especially Catholics, swept across the northern states because of the newcomers' naturalization and sharply increased politicking, the Know Nothing nativism captured public imagination and flourished.

As with their predecessors, many of these xenophobes were convinced that the best way to restore American society to an Anglo-Protestant purity it had never known was to purge it of foreign and Catholic influences. Ironically, the Americans who a few years earlier had sent shiploads of food and thousands of dollars to the Irish during their famine again attacked the Irish-Americans as though they were scum. In 1854 this attitude led the nativists to organize their own American Party. In the following year the Know Nothing Order spread to 31 states. In the election of 1856 it garnered 21 percent of the popular vote. By that time also, 7 governors, 8 senators, and 104 national representatives had gained election after campaigning on anti-Catholic, anti-foreign platforms.

Nativists, and other Americans as well, had assumed that the Know Nothings' popularity, based on appeals to bigotry, would bring them the presidency. That did not happen for a number of reasons, but especially because many voters became disgusted with their tolerance for lawless violence and because when Southern members of the American Party changed its antislavery stance, Northerners bolted. Moreover, as civil conflict approached, the nativist conception of what a white American should be was overwhelmed by the pressing concerns over racial slavery. When the party dissolved, its Northerners became absorbed into the Republican party. Through it, as recent scholarship indicates, the Know Nothing "ethnocultural and religious animosities did not cease influencing the electorate."[27] In doing so, those sentiments also continued to affect the shaping of foreign policy.

The Know Nothing hatred that most newcomers experienced apparently toughened their ethnic cohesiveness. When such solidarity also produced disciplined voting, the power of minority groups increased. A few historians have asserted that in 1860 the votes of German-Americans contributed significantly to the election of Abraham Lincoln. Others have persuasively disputed this claim. Regardless, the Republican party courted German-American voters while also engaging in a mostly anti-Catholic "blatant solicitation of nativist support."[28] To advance his candidacy among ethnic voters, Lincoln even purchased a German-language newspaper, struggled to learn German, and when elected rewarded German-Americans with jobs in government. He and other politicians of both major parties assumed that ethnic votes could be, and perhaps were, vital in the election.

Thus, the German-Americans and the Irish-Americans were again reminded that ethnic solidarity possessed actual or potential political power. To a greater extent than ever, such cohesion formed the basis for the ethnic politics that gave clout in foreign policy to the white minorities that were involved with developments in old homelands.

Another episode, not connected directly with America's ethnic politics at this time, illustrates nonetheless how feelings about race could affect dealings with foreigners, could touch on the closeness of the bond with the British, and could reveal the fragility of American Anglophobia. In the *Arrow* War that began in 1856 when Chinese authorities seized the lorcha *Arrow*, which ran opium while flying the Union Jack, American officials supported the British. American marines also joined British forces in assaulting Canton. Even though the British and the French were the aggressors, opinion in the United States as expressed in the press was overwhelmingly anti-Chinese and pro-British. One newspaper editorialized that "the enfeebled Mohammedan and Mongol races are destined" to fall before the Anglo-Saxons just as the Mexicans and Indians "melt away before the advance of American settlers."[29] Other journalists, and naval officers too, even urged Americans to enter the war alongside their "Anglo-Saxon cousins."

In June 1859, after Britain and her allies had defeated the Chinese, the victors sent representatives to Tientsin to deliver the ratified peace treaties. En route they found that the Chinese had blockaded the river leading to the city. Impatient British marines along with French troops attempted to clear the barriers, but artillery fire from the Chinese forts on two shores inflicted heavy losses on men and ships. Commodore Josiah Tattnall of the United States Navy then rushed to the aid of the English, reputedly explaining that "blood is thicker than water," or that he would "be damned if he'd stand by and see white men butchered before his eyes."[30]

Back in the United States Irish-American lobbyists still sought to overcome such sentiment, or any kind of solidarity with the British, by exploiting their expanded political strength. They hoped it would permit them to challenge the Anglo-American power structure so effectively as to influence the area of diplomacy of most concern to them. The effort began in April 1859, when activists living in New York City organized a wing of the Irish

Revolutionary Brotherhood, a society based in Ireland. This American branch took the name Fenian Brotherhood. The Fenians planned to cooperate with revolutionaries abroad and also to foment a war between the United States and Britain as a means of securing independence for Ireland. They grew in number but bided their time until they felt sufficiently powerful to hurl their challenge.

Caution should have been the watchword of these Irish-Americans, because the Anglo-American grip on foreign policy had not weakened. Moreover, that elite still detested the Irish for their Catholicism and their anti-British agitation. So, along with their enhanced political leverage, the Irish-Americans experienced a deeper and more widespread hatred than they had known previously. As the Civil War approached, both this antagonism and the strident Fenian activity abated.

Those historians who view that war mainly from the perspective of the white antagonists maintain that neither in its causes nor in its results does it fit an ethnoracial pattern. They shunt aside race, ignore blacks as an integral part of the American population, slight the widespread Southern fears of a race war, and analyze the struggle primarily in terms of the kindred white belligerents. As did the participants themselves and observers of similar outlook, these historians usually characterize the conflict as one of brother against brother. As the *Times* of London explained this perspective, the struggle was "a war between men sprung from a race and speaking a language from which we are also sprung and which we also speak."[31] Yet in the North masses of non-British immigrants, such as the Irish and the Germans, fought for the Union cause, frequently in ethnic regiments. A third of the Union army was foreign-born.

From the beginning of the struggle, also, meaningful aspects of foreign policy pivoted on the issue of race. For decades Southerners had blocked the formal recognition of Haiti, arguing, for instance, that to grant it would be "a reward for the murder of masters and mistresses by black slaves."[32] On the other hand, anti-slavery abolitionists such as Lydia Maria Child and William Jay had long denounced the government for refusing to recognize Haiti. They pointed to the inconsistency of Washington's having accorded recognition to Texas shortly after it had proclaimed independence while still denying it to Haiti. They and others persevered in stressing the obvious political incongruities, but as had others in the past, they slighted the fundamental reason for the double standard—the racial biases of those in power.

Most of the policymakers had been white Southerners or officials beholden to them. When with secession these primary opponents of Haitian recognition lost their posts of power within the federal government, they could no longer exercise a veto over the formulation of national policy. In December 1861, therefore, President Abraham Lincoln called for the recognition of "Hayti and Liberia." Even though Liberia had become an independent state in 1847, it too had failed to receive American recognition because of race. So, along with regularizing relations with Haiti, Lincoln's government extended recognition to Liberia. The United States was the last of the Western nations to open normal diplomatic relations with that African country.

All the while, the concept of shattered white brotherhood and the issue of race weakened an important aspect of Union diplomacy. From the start of the war, Lincoln's government would not acknowledge openly that it was fighting racial slavery. A number of European leaders who were attracted to the Union cause therefore held back the support they might otherwise have given it. The many in Britain who, for instance, felt moral outrage against slavery apparently for this reason acquiesced in their government's pro-Confederate policy.

Only with Lincoln's issuing of the Emancipation Proclamation in January 1863 did numerous British anti-slavery groups pledge "sympathy for the cause of the North." Henry Adams, the son of the American minister in London, hailed it as doing more for the Union "than all our former victories and all our diplomacy."[33] After the proclamation's implementation, the image of the Union among the British, Netherlanders, Italians, Spaniards, and other Europeans improved, and racial slavery ceased to be an important foreign-policy concern.

When the war ended and slavery was abolished, the racial worries over the place of blacks in American society remained prominent, but the nativist passions toward the white minorities had subsided. Minority ethnic politics even gained a degree of tolerance. After 1867 this politicking benefited from the Fourteenth Amendment, which affirmed "the primacy of national over state citizenship" and assured Americans fundamental rights regardless of their place of birth within the Union.[34]

During this time of social and constitutional upheaval, the Irish-Americans were among the first to benefit from the changes. Right after the war, they had employed their strategically located political strength with fresh effectiveness in lobbying for help to their old homeland. Their rising power also coincided with a deterioration in relations with Britain that had occurred during the conflict. At the same time, the Fenian Brotherhood's membership had expanded considerably, making it possible soon thereafter for the movement again to acquire a high visibility. In addition, Fenianism became a significant, though not a driving, force in foreign policy because many Irish-Americans believed that "it was necessary for everyone of Irish blood to do all in his power" to help liberate the Irish at home.[35] By the spring of 1865, the Fenians had become ready to move against England.

The British viewed the revived Fenian agitation as part of "a vast conspiracy" against them and were alarmed by it. They urged the American government to curb the brotherhood. When the administration of Andrew Johnson did nothing, Sir Frederick Bruce, the British minister in Washington, reported that its inactivity was governed by the weight of Irish-American ballots. He explained that the "Irish party, owing to their compact organization, exercise, unfortunately for us, a powerful influence in American politics."[36] Yet Fenian militancy did not become truly threatening until the following year.

The Fenians collected large sums of money, held conventions, and organized a shadow government for the Irish republic that they hoped to establish. They raised a uniformed army recruited in part from among veterans of Irish origin who had served in the Union forces during the war. These recruits drilled and paraded openly in American cities. Charles Francis Adams, the American minister in London, denounced the Fenians as "agitators laboring not for the interests of the United States, but to make them subservient to their designs against a foreign country."[37]

In the spring of 1866, armed Fenians launched several small raids into Canada, which the British protested. The first large incursion came in June when eight hundred Fenians occupied the outpost of Fort Erie. They defeated a force of inexperienced Canadian volunteers, but when organized military reinforcements arrived, the Fenians retreated. The Canadians suffered twelve dead and the Fenians eight, as well as some wounded. President Johnson did not issue a proclamation forbidding such violations of the neutrality laws until five days after the raid.

The Fenians viewed their strikes against Canada as acts of war on behalf of an oppressed people. Numerous other Americans seemed to accept this reasoning. Others considered the Fenian assaults legitimate reprisal for Confederate raids on Union towns launched from Canadian soil during the Civil War. At the same time, the Democrats courted the Irish-American vote. They were reluctant, therefore, to support strong measures against the Fenians. There were Democrats who even attributed the defeats they suffered in the elections in October to the defections of the Irish-Americans from their usual support of the party.

In Britain the authorities feared that the attention American politicians paid to the Irish vote might persuade one of the major parties to embrace the Fenian cause, an action that could inflict heavy damage on relations between the two countries. When the Fenians in England rose in 1867, they did so in part with such an objective in mind. They hoped to raise the flag of Irish freedom long enough to galvanize the Irish-Americans into supportive action. The uprising promptly failed. The American Irish could do nothing about it, and neither of the American political parties committed itself to the Irish cause. Yet the revolutionary zeal among young Irish-Americans did not diminish. Moreover, Johnson and his political allies remained anxious to hold the Irish-Americans to their usual Democratic allegiance, while the Radical Republicans sought to win them to their side.

In the presidential campaign of 1868, it seemed unlikely that the Fenians could deliver the Irish-American vote en masse. They simply lacked the necessary cohesion to do so. Unaware of this weakness, the British leadership believed that "under the circumstances of the Presidential elections" neither party would do anything to injure the sensibilities of Irish-Americans if at all possible. It was assumed that the American government would intervene against the Fenians only if they brought its connection with Britain to an unbearable crisis.[38]

When Ulysses S. Grant won the election and became president, he too tolerated the Fenians out of a concern for Irish-American political power. During his tenure, in May 1870 from St. Albans, Vermont, the Fenians staged their last major raid on Canada. A volley of rifle fire from a small force of defenders drove off two hundred invaders. After that assault, coincident with a decided improvement in Anglo-American relations, Fenian power fizzled. The brotherhood itself survived until 1886, when another revolutionary society, the Clan-na-Gael (United Brotherhood) took up Ireland's cause in America. The Fenians had acquired their impressive, though brief, influence because many of those in positions of power within the American government had assumed that their activities represented the sentiments of a considerable body of Irish-American voters.

Despite their political clout and six years of taking advantage of America's strained official relations with London, the Fenians never even came close to bringing about the war with Britain that they desired. They failed for a number of reasons, but primarily because they never could compete on equal terms with the power of the Anglo-American elite. As from the start, the British-Americans, or others favorable to them, controlled the apparatus of government.

With their numerous powerful allies in Washington, the British, despite their worries, never really had cause for deep despair. The elites in both

Britain and the United States prized their blood relationship as well as the comity between themselves and their countries to such an extent that they would not permit the Fenians, or Irish-Americans in general, to place that friendship in any serious danger.

The Fenians did have at least one noteworthy effect on relations with Britain, however. Their activities helped persuade the prime minister, William Gladstone, and others that the Irish question had "an American dimension" or a transatlantic blood relationship of its own which could not be readily dismissed. For that and other reasons, British officialdom turned with more constructive attention than in the past to Irish grievances.

It is to the interest of
civilization that the English
speaking race should be
dominant in South Africa,
exactly as it is . . . that the
United States . . . should be
dominant in the Western
Hemisphere.

*Theodore Roosevelt, March 20,
1896*

4

ETHNIC TRANSFORMATION

In 1864, with the Civil War still raging, the State Department urged government recruitment of European immigrants. Congress responded by legalizing the importation of contract laborers. It wished to encourage the "immigration of skilled industrial workers, chiefly from Great Britain." Under the new contract system, non-British workers also arrived. Although few of them were unskilled, their mere presence alarmed organized labor leaders and others. These nativists demanded some form of restriction. So in August 1882, in the first federal law controlling aspects of immigration, congress excluded criminals, paupers, and other undesirables. Less than three years later, with the Foran Act, which was directed against southeastern Europeans, it declared contract labor illegal.

These laws, with their "favored treatment" of British immigrants and bias against others, marked a continuation in anti-foreign prejudice rather than, as is often suggested in the traditional literature, a resurgence of a dormant emotion.[1] A similar continuity in ethnic attitudes was reflected in aspects of foreign policy.

Regardless of the restrictive intent embedded in law, masses of immigrants who had the potential of altering the nation's ethnic base, of transforming society, and of contributing ultimately to a reorienting of foreign policy, streamed into the country. In the seventies one out of four European immigrants had come from the British Isles. In the eighties this ratio fell to one in eight.

From the mid-eighties onward, even though representative groups of varied continental Europeans had been coming for years, the recent arrivals were called new because their kind had not been seen before in the United

States in large numbers. Most of these immigrants came from southeastern Europe, but others arrived from Asia until barred by exclusionary laws. The whites were not really fresh types, nor in physical characteristics were they much different from the old immigrants, but their ethnicity, traits, religions, and loyalties contrasted markedly with those of the already established Euro-Americans.

These new groups arrived at a time when the socio-racial ideas adapted from the writings of naturalist Charles Darwin and popularized by others, such as the British philosopher Herbert Spencer and the American sociologist William Graham Sumner, were gaining converts by the thousands. These and other intellectuals of like mind conveyed the message that select Caucasians—or essentially those who were of their own kind—were inherently superior to other peoples. The writings of such thinkers fed a constantly present racialism evident in European and other societies as well as in the United States.

Regardless of their scholarly veneer, the socialized Darwinian theories did not differ much from earlier ethnoracial doctrine. This continuity with past attitudes accounted in part for the widespread acceptance of these scientifically packaged ideas, which in turn facilitated their use by the Anglo-American establishment in formulating policy to exclude the newcomers from the inner circles of government. For this reason, among others, the changes in the population blend did not immediately affect the traditional thrust of foreign policy.

In a number of instances, nonetheless, old and allegedly new ethnic concerns in external relations overlapped. The Irish-Americans, for instance, felt the ancestral attachment as strongly as ever. As in the past, they contributed money to support nationalist revolutionaries in the old homeland while pressuring the government in Washington to intervene in the British-Irish struggles. The *Irish-American Almanac* put the ethnic emotion of the American-born Irish into verse, saying that

> Columbia the free is the land of my birth
> And my paths have all been on American earth
> But my blood is as Irish as any can be,
> And my heart is with Erin afar o'er the sea.[2]

With similar feeling for their ancestral land, the German-Americans, as they had in previous years, used muscle in politics, but now under considerably changed circumstances. At this time Germany's drive for unification contributed to an intensified and broad, rather than provincial, ethnic consciousness among most Americans of German stock. In the interest of their now rising former homeland, many of them strove for greater involvement in issues relating specifically to foreign relations.

During the Franco-Prussian War, German-American groups held mammoth rallies in major cities which raised money to help wounded brethren overseas, to celebrate Prussian victories, and to gain the sympathy of other Americans. In these activities the German-Americans succeeded to a considerable extent by appealing to old Anglo-American ethnic prejudices, as in portraying the war as a struggle between the Germanic and Latin "races." They also argued that it served the interest of the United States to back Prussia, pointing out that many in Germany had supported the Union cause during the Civil War, while the French under Napoleon III had invaded Mexico.

In keeping with this expanded concern in ethnic politics, the leaders of German-American communities established a national society to foster better relations between the Germany newly united in 1871 and the United States. For a while it seemed that the German-Americans had overcome the religious and regional fragmentation inherited from their homeland. "Today no longer does the immigrant come as Prussian, Hanoverian, Bavarian, Swabian, or Saxon," community leaders asserted. "No! he comes as German."[3] Even though German-American nationalists did not become strident until two decades later, they envisioned their national organization as a potential lobby for expanding the power of their ethnic community in the international affairs of special interest to it.

Ethnoracial concerns of a different kind affected a few other aspects of foreign relations. For instance, racism as well as greed and naiveté ran through the effort of President Ulysses S. Grant to acquire Santo Domingo. In a long paper in 1869 he tried to justify annexation with racial reasoning, arguing that it would help resolve communal tensions at home. The island, he wrote, was capable of "supporting the entire colored population of the United States, should it choose to emigrate."[4]

Many in the senate attacked the scheme for diametrically opposing reasons. They did not want to bring more people of color into the Union. The leading opponent, Charles Sumner of Massachusetts, chairman of the Foreign Relations Committee, insisted that the United States as "an Anglo-Saxon Republic" should not take in "colored communities" where the "black race was predominant." For racial and other reasons, Secretary of State Hamilton Fish also took a stand against annexation. So in June 1870 the senate killed the president's annexation treaty. His plan, whether or not sincere, for a "congenial home" for the "emancipated race in the South" thus collapsed.[5]

Grant also dabbled with the idea of intervening in Cuba's Ten Years' War, which had begun two years earlier. He wished to recognize the rebel regime as independent of Spain, hoping also that later he could annex the island. A number of reasons led Fish and others in the government to oppose this plan, too, but they again made a point of the racial grounds. They did not want Cuba's mixed population of blacks and others to come into the Union.

Race stands out as well among the concerns that concurrently affected relations with the kingdom of Hawaii. In 1873, a year in which a severe financial panic struck the nation, American officials sought an arrangement whereby the kingdom would turn Pearl Harbor over to them in exchange for allowing Hawaiian sugar free access to the United States market. Enraged native Hawaiians saw the proposal as a device to control their homeland and erode their status within it. In September, therefore, the monarch's native guard mutinied against its white officers. Such opposition forced the Hawaiian government to reject the plan. The native population then launched a movement of "Hawaii for Hawaiians" with anti-American overtones which remained present in the islands for the next two decades.

Another foreign-policy issue of these years that was charged with ethnic, but not racial, emotion sprang from the renewal of an old American desire to acquire Canada. Anglo-Americans favored annexation for economic reasons and because they perceived it as a first step toward the reuniting of the entire "Anglo-Saxon race." For decades such sentiment had been unable to attract sufficient support in either the United States or Canada to overcome the resistance of the French-Canadians, who feared that in any union American assimilationist pressure would destroy their ethnic identity. Within Canada's governmental structure the distinctiveness of the French community still had constitutional protection.

For a while in 1885, after the authorities in Canada had executed Louis Riel, a failed French-Canadian rebel, a desire for change seemed popular. Annexationism gained followers even in French Quebec, but in the next few years that sentiment collapsed. Moreover, despite the desire of the Anglo-American elite in the United States for northward expansion, it would not resort to force against its own kind in Britain and Canada to bring it about.

All the while, politicians in both parties continued to vie for the Irish-American vote. Its importance in crucial New York City mushroomed when the Irish there captured control of Tammany Hall. With the intent of pulling them out of the Democratic party, the Republicans courted them, now even with concessions on some foreign-policy issues. As usual, the Democrats appeased the Irish-Americans on many, but not all, of the matters dear to them so that these ethnic voters would not leave their traditional fold.

From 1875 onward, the foreign-policy concerns of Irish-Americans centered on Charles Stewart Parnell, a Protestant nationalist landlord who led the Irish Land League, an organization founded in Dublin in 1879 to promote the ownership of property in the place of tenancy. He and other Irish leaders also used the league to rally their people to the cause of independence, or to home rule, in a campaign that captured headlines in Ireland, England, and America. In 1880 Parnell toured the United States in behalf of the league, traveling 11,000 miles, raising thousands of dollars, and addressing a joint session of congress. There he claimed "that the public opinion and sentiment of a free country like America is entitled to find expression wherever it is seen that the laws of freedom are not observed."[6]

Parnell and home rule excited Irish-Americans much more than had any other cause since Fenianism. In the early eighties they held mass meetings from the Atlantic to the Pacific to express solidarity with him. Despite their disappointing experience with Fenianism, they still believed that through ethnic politics they could give direction to aspects of foreign policy of passionate interest to them. Hence they continually pressed the government in Washington to back the home-rule movement.

In the presidential campaign of 1884, Irish-American voters were courted by both parties. Many deserted the Democratic party to support James G. Blaine, the Republican candidate, who had an Irish mother and as secretary of state had been friendly to Irish hopes. Yet when Samuel D. Burchard, a Protestant clergyman, in Blaine's presence condemned the opposition as the party of "Rum, Romanism, and Rebellion," Blaine did not rebuke him. Many angered Irish-Americans turned to Grover Cleveland, the Democratic candidate, who won. Blaine believed that Burchard's slur caused him to lose New York, where Irish votes were crucial, and hence the election.

In June 1886, when Cleveland as president delivered a strong speech in favor of Irish autonomy, Irish-American politicking again appeared to produce results. In August 1888 its clout in the senate at least contributed to the defeat of the Bayard-Chamberlain treaty, which provided for the settlement of an old fisheries dispute with Britain. Two days after that rejection, when Cleveland sent an ostensibly anti-British message to congress over the issue, Irish-Americans deluged him with telegrams of praise. In that same year, in an effort to attract their votes, the platforms of both national parties expressed sympathy for Irish home rule.

Late in October, on the eve of the election, another aspect of ethnic politics, the affinity of Anglo-Americans for their old homeland and their influence on government, became headline news. Sir Lionel Sackville-West, the British minister in Washington, indiscreetly revealed that he preferred the Democratic candidate Cleveland because he had usually been "favorable and friendly towards England."[7] This disclosure led to the minister's swift dismissal and expulsion. Democrats feared that his now publicized preference might turn the Irish-Americans away from Cleveland. Later some of these voters claimed that they had decided the outcome. Historians, too, usually maintain that the episode may have cost Cleveland the election. Yet, while it ruffled relations with Britain, it did not dilute the growing power of Anglo-Saxonism.

Henry James, the novelist, expressed succinctly the Anglo-Saxonist sense of community prevalent at the time. "I can't look at the English-American world . . . save as a big Anglo-Saxon total," he said, "destined to such an amount of melting together that an insistence upon their differences becomes more and more idle and pedantic."[8]

Attitudes such as this, as well as the Sackville-West fiasco, stirred the ethnic consciousness of the declining number of British immigrants, many of whom had recently established a British-American Association to give their own ethnic politics specific direction as a counter to Irish-American influence on policy-making. The organization rapidly gained a healthy membership, attracted Anglophile allies with similar biases, and made its weight felt in support of the usual Anglo-American stance on external issues. In cooperation with anti-Catholic nativist groups, it also exerted noteworthy political power in domestic affairs.

Similarly, anxiety over foreign policy sparked a renewed political activity of retribution among the German-Americans. They were upset by Cleveland's policy in Samoa, where at this time American and German interests clashed. Supposedly, because he took a tough stand against strong-arm German tactics there, German-American voters turned against him to help elect Benjamin Harrison. Like the activist Irish-Americans, the many German-Americans who were convinced that their votes had decided the election of 1888 had an exaggerated estimate of their potency in this instance and in other matters affecting foreign relations.

As for the Irish-American voters, since politicians tried not to antagonize them, their ethnic politics, as in the Sackville-West affair, could hardly avoid creating diplomatic problems with Britain. Their moral and financial support for home rule, for instance, gave the movement a vitality and stamina in Ireland that aroused British anger. Irish-American political power, however, could not formulate foreign policy, could not overcome English contempt for the Irish, could not deeply damage overall Anglo-American relations, and could not win autonomy for kin in the old homeland. It suffered from the fall from power and the death of Parnell in 1891, which ended the home-rule agitation. Along with a renewed Anglo-Saxon racism, the decline of home rule as an issue also diminished, but did not eliminate, whatever impact Irish-American ethnic politics had on foreign policy.

Ethnoracial politics of another kind now directly affected relations with China. Chinese laborers, who had first arrived in California immediately after the Mexican War, quickly experienced discrimination and some violence in the goldfields there because they differed conspicuously "from the Anglo-American root stock."[9] Since the Chinese were few, however, their presence did not at first arouse a more widespread white nativist ire. Indeed, in July 1868 Secretary of State William H. Seward signed with Anson Burlingame, representing China, a treaty that permitted the Chinese to immigrate into the United States without restriction. It also promised them protection against maltreatment under the terms of a most-favored-nation clause.

Two years later, as the number of Chinese immigrants increased, the senate refused to grant them the right of naturalization. All the while, the nativists and other Caucasians in California and elsewhere in the west inspired riots against them. Denis Kearney, himself an Irish immigrant, stirred emotions with the slogan "The Chinese must go!" In Los Angeles in 1871, mobs animated with similar biases shot or hanged some twenty Chinese. In the east as well as on the West Coast, whites wanted to shut out the Chinese, arguing that because of their color they could never be assimilated. This racist thinking, which "enveloped all segments of the new American society," assumed that the pot that supposedly blended Euro-Americans into one people would not melt the Asians. They were, in the words of a senator who complained to President Rutherford B. Hayes, "a cold pebble in the public stomach which cannot be digested."[10] Thus, before the end of the decade, the fear of a flood of Chinese could be discerned through much of the nation.

Even though the railroad magnates persuaded federal judges to overturn successive anti-Chinese measures in California and elsewhere, both major parties adopted a program to terminate Chinese immigration. In the senate James G. Blaine declared in hyperbolic rhetoric that "either the Anglo-Saxon race will possess the Pacific slope, or the Mongolians will possess it." He and others repeated the conventional dogma that Asians could never "make a homogeneous element" within the white population. "They are of a different race," another senator echoed, "and are incapable of being brought into assimilation."[11]

When the census of 1880 revealed that 75,000 Chinese lived in California, making up almost ten percent of the population, the exclusionists gained more support. In acknowledgment of their pressure, congress in May 1882 for the first time proscribed an ethnoracial group, primarily because the Chinese did not fit the white assimilationist thesis. The statute congress enacted "suspended," but did not actually bar, Chinese immigration for ten years. Congress amplified and renewed the law in 1884, 1888, and 1892, giving to exclusion a sense of permanency. The racial prejudice in this legislation left a nasty mark on diplomacy. To appease the exclusionists, the federal government, which had taken control of the whole immigration-and-naturalization process in 1891, consciously violated Chinese rights under the Burlingame treaty.

One author has declared that these "attitudes towards the Chinese in the United States, and particularly in California, . . . had a direct effect on public opinion and on lawmakers in Australia and British Columbia."[12] Before the close of the nineteenth century, Canada, Australia, and other English-speaking countries raised barriers similar to those in the United States against Chinese immigrants.

As could have been expected, the Chinese government and many of its people found these officially sanctioned discriminations humiliating. When stories of more abuse—such as a massacre of twenty-eight Chinese in Rock Springs, Wyoming, in September 1885 and bloody anti-Chinese riots in Denver, Seattle, many California towns, and elsewhere—reached China, they contributed to the anti-American missionary riots in Chungking and in two towns in Kwangsi province. As President Grover Cleveland told the nation, "Race prejudice is the chief factor in originating these disturbances, and it exists in a large part of our domain, jeopardizing our domestic peace and the good relationship we strive to maintain with China."[13]

In the United States the Chinese immigrants had no vote, no hope, and no desire for the kind of assimilation prescribed by white nativists. The Chinese also could do practically nothing to prevent their maltreatment. They were as helpless as had been the foreigners in their own land who for centuries had been discriminated against as inferior barbarians. Ironically, along with other Western powers, the United States countered China's ethnoracial prejudice against Caucasians by employing force. Against China's tradition and will, these Western nations compelled her to treat whites as equals and to admit them to her territory. United States gunboats patrolled Chinese coasts and rivers to protect the lives and property of unwanted missionaries and other Americans.

The Chinese government, which had no warships it could send to intimidate the United States, could only lodge official protests against Washington's statutory restrictions and the violence against its people. It did so repeatedly, insisting that exclusion "is an unnecessary discrimination against the Chinese race."[14] The objections had no effect on the politicians who enacted the exclusionary laws and formulated foreign policy. The negative effect of this white prejudice on relations with China persisted well into the future. It belied the myth, arising in Washington, of a special friendship between the two countries.

Southeastern Europeans, too, had difficulty in meeting assimilationist standards, although much less than did the Chinese. As outsiders, these European immigrants also suffered ethnoracial humiliations they could not easily overcome. Unlike the Chinese, however, they had slowly acquired some influence in matters of foreign policy. Among these newcomers the first to attempt, in conjunction with earlier arrivals, to sway the American government to act on behalf of their kin abroad were the Jews.

Both Sephardic and Ashkenazi Jews from southern, western, and central Europe had long been represented in North America. The Sephardim had been trickling into the country since 1654. Although they often had been denied the right to vote or hold elective office, they became active in community affairs in the 1790s after achieving "political equality in the five states in which they were most numerous."[15] In 1840, several years after the Ashkenazim had begun arriving from Germany, American Jews became involved in the politics of foreign policy.

With the support of Christian missionaries, this ethnoreligious group of some 15,000 members persuaded but did not pressure President Martin Van Buren to protest the persecution of Jews in Damascus who had been charged with ritual murder. "For the first time in American Jewish life Jews . . . organized themselves politically to help a Diaspora Jewry in distress."[16] In November 1859, after their community had grown with the arrival of thousands of Ashkenazim, American Jews organized themselves nationally by establishing the Board of Delegates of American Israelites, which "by its very existence as a united group impressed the State Department."[17] From then on, through consistent, organized lobbying, Jewish organizations petitioned Washington to act, for example, on behalf of persecuted ethnoreligious brethren in Morocco, Serbia, Romania, and Russia. The State Department protested, but with mixed results.

Jewish ethnic politicking became more effective following the assassination of Tsar Alexander II in March 1881, which produced anti-Semitic laws and a wave of riots against Jews in European Russia. Within the next few years, thousands of these hounded people fled to the United States, where they found themselves separated by language and culture from the already established Jewish community dominated by the earlier immigrants from Germany and the Habsburg empire. Regardless of their differences, however, the two groups cooperated on an international issue because of a common worry for persecuted kin abroad. Most of the concerned Jews were new immigrants, but the leaders came principally from the earlier migration. Through their joint organizations, they persuaded the White House to remonstrate against the Russian pogroms and the maltreatment of Jews in the Ottoman empire and in Austria-Hungary.

In 1892 Representative Irvine Dungan of Ohio introduced a resolution in congress that called for the severing of diplomatic relations with Russia. It failed to pass, but that year the national platforms of the Republican and Democratic parties contained planks which expressed compassion for abused Jews. Among the purportedly new ethnic groups, the Jews thus quickly stood out in their ability to bring organized political influence to bear on foreign policy. Their effectiveness rose from a widespread sympathy they elicited among other Americans because of the brutalities they had suffered, and from organized political activity by earlier immigrants. Other factors in the Jews' successful lobbying were an intelligentsia with access to policymakers and to the public and the support of wealthy Jewish leaders who had already established themselves in American society.

Another group prominent among the European newcomers were the Italians, who had settled in various sections of the country but were crowded mainly into the cities of the northeast. About 30,000 of them, mostly from Sicily and southern Italy, had chosen to live in New Orleans. There on March 4, 1891, owing in large part to ethnic animosities, a mob of white nativists lynched eleven Italians and Italian-Americans who had just been acquitted of a murder charge. As revealed in the press and elsewhere, most nativist Americans endorsed the bloodletting. Theodore Roosevelt called it "a rather good thing" and boasted about it before "various dago diplomats." The slaughter enraged Italians and Italian-Americans everywhere. Under pressure from them, the Italian government protested, demanded punishment of the murderers, and asked compensation for the victims' families.

When Secretary of State Blaine reacted haughtily, Italy severed full diplomatic relations. Many Americans believed rumors that the modern Italian fleet might attack coastal cities. The more emotional nationalists welcomed the idea of war. From Georgia the White House received an offer, among others, to raise a company of soldiers "to invade Rome, disperse the Mafia, and plant the stars and stripes on the dome of St. Peter's."[18]

When President Benjamin Harrison followed a calmer course by essentially apologizing to Italy and indemnifying the families of the victims, the crisis passed. Italian-Americans were outraged by the terms of the settlement because it did not address the issues of apprehending the killers and dampening anti-Italian prejudice. Like the Chinese, these Italians in the United States suffered prejudice and lacked political power, but unlike the Asians they already had sufficient numbers at least to be heard. Although scorned, they had on their own made a small difference in foreign affairs. Some of them had organized, pursued redress for discrimination with the backing of their old homeland's government, helped produce an international crisis, and because of it obtained a modicum of justice.

This episode, along with the expanding of ethnic politics, took place in the ambience of an institutionalized racism that had risen and fallen but had never died. The Ku Klux Klan, with a membership carried over mainly from the post–Civil War era, the American Protective Association, founded in 1887, and other white nativist movements exploited the ethnoracial hatreds inherent in a widely accepted old-stock xenophobia. These organizations attacked blacks, Jews, Catholics, and minority newcomers in general. They also wanted to throttle most minority immigration.

During the 1890s the white supremacists tried to rid the country of blacks by reviving the idea of returning them to Africa, this time to the Congo. With this goal in mind, these nativists urged the government to formulate a policy that would open Africa for this purpose.

As in the pre–Civil War years, this attitude toward blacks and immigrants mixed with an exuberant Anglo-Saxonism. Much of the citzenry believed, as did the Congregational clergyman Josiah Strong, that "surely, to be a Christian and an Anglo-Saxon and an American in this generation is to stand at the very mountaintop of privilege."[19] In 1894, within this climate of Anglo self-esteem, a group of nativist intellectuals in New England, who were disturbed in particular by the influx from southeastern Europe but also by the presence of colored minorities, formed the Immigration Restriction League. Historian John Fiske served as its first president. Its members were convinced that true Americanism could come only from those of Anglo-Saxon, Protestant origin.

Two other prominent historians, George Bancroft and John Lothrop Motley, linked this restrictionist outlook to foreign relations. They often stressed that quality of racial stock, or ethnic origin, was of crucial importance in the nation's choice of policymakers. They believed without doubt that those who were best endowed, either through divine or scientific selection, to formulate a foreign policy in keeping with the nation's greatness were people of their own kind.

This generally well-educated elite stood firm in its commitment to Anglo-Saxon racism, even though no "Anglo-Saxon race" ever existed and no one could logically define the term Anglo-Saxon. To many outsiders humorist Finley Peter Dunne's biting characterization appeared to come close to the mark. "An Anglo-Saxon," he explained, ". . . is a German that's forgot who was his parents. They're a lot iv thim in this counthry."[20]

Intellectuals and political leaders such as Henry Cabot Lodge, naval officer Alfred Thayer Mahan, and Albert J. Beveridge publicized many of the claims to extreme preeminence associated with Anglo-Saxonism. These believers were not alone. Educated thinkers in other societies shared similar racialist ideas. Common in such reasoning in the United States since its earliest days was the often-repeated notion that God had prepared the Anglo-Saxons, the "elect race," to rule over others inferior to themselves.

Despite these effusions that stressed race in the sense of ethnicity, scholars and others contended that the Anglo-American community was not an ethnic group like those composed of the new immigrants with their close ties to distant homelands. In keeping with this outlook, those who continued to leave Britain for the United States, as in the past, were rarely treated as foreigners.

Social analysts also maintained that in the United States the British sense of group identity seldom endured beyond the second generation. Considerable evidence suggests, to the contrary, that the British ethnic bond retained its vitality for many generations. Anglo-Americans had a pride in their origins and old-world connection that was as strong as, and perhaps more compelling than, in any other ethnic group. The Anglo-Americans still insisted, with a record of success attributable to their ethnic consciousness as well as to other reasons, that others must assimilate to their ways.

At this time the governing elite's already heady Anglo-Saxonism, in part as a reaction to the transformation of the nation's ethnic base by the most recent arrivals, acquired a new prominence. For example, for more than a decade Lodge, who has been portrayed as both an Anglophobe and an Anglicized American, had sought enactment of a literacy law as a means of blocking additional new immigration. He backed restriction out of the conviction that the immigrants from the "lower races" did not assimilate well and threatened "the Anglo-Saxon race of the United States."[21] He and other Anglo-American politicians and intellectuals wanted to eliminate this imagined danger while it was still in its assumed infancy. From a broad perspective, this attitude contained little that was unusual. Governing elites that perceived themselves as vulnerable often responded with such hostility to newcomers.

The unique quality in this Anglo-American ethnic consciousness was the depth of its transatlantic character. It found expression in various forms, as for example in the patriotism preached by nationalist societies such as the Daughters of the American Revolution. As in earlier decades, the protagonists of this nationalism stressed their true or assumed origins as sons and daughters of Great Britain. They insisted that the Anglo-Saxons had created the United States and that only they could sustain its true character.

Even though the racism in this Anglo-Saxonism contained nothing basically new, historians often depict it as different from that of the previous decades, primarily because of its connection to Darwinian thought. Now science appeared to confirm the idea that the backward "races" would collapse before the push of more highly civilized peoples, as the Anglo-Saxonists had always assumed. This conception of conflict between unlike peoples stood at the center of the Anglo-American bond, or what many termed the "blood relationship." That connection, especially between the elites, continued to draw the United States and Britain together even as the fundamental Anglo character of the American population was diminishing and fewer Americans could identify with a British heritage. Almost daily the mosaic quality of America's ethnoracial groups was becoming more intricate.

Still, those of Anglo stock clutched the idea that they were the truest of Americans while dismissing those deriving from other stock as something less. The Anglo-Americans often disparaged most others of foreign origin as "hyphenates," a term of opprobrium that came into use at this time. It was not applied to those of British ancestry. Anglophiles of whatever origin, and other ethnically conscious Americans such as Theodore Roosevelt, whose roots were Dutch and Scotch, quickly seized upon the hyphenate slur and gave it wide exposure. In a speech in 1895, for instance, Roosevelt inveighed against "the hyphenated American—the German-American, the Irish-American," and others, urging his listeners to "be Americans pure and simple."[22]

Many Anglo-Americans perceived themselves precisely in this manner. "Most families of pure English descent," one of them explained to a British newspaperman in 1896, "have been in this country so long that they have become Americans and nothing else." When, therefore, Irish-Americans, "who provided the most strident anti-Anglo-Saxonist propaganda," and other minorities criticized Britain's policies, her leaders dismissed their complaints as the prattling of biased hyphenates. Some Anglo-Americans even viewed the attitude of the outsiders as a kind of reverse racism, an anti–Anglo-Saxonism designed to keep alive "well over a hundred years of American Anglophobia."[23]

Diplomatic scholars often attribute a crisis in relations with Britain at this time to such a conception of Anglophobia. The confrontation began in 1894 over a boundary dispute between Venezuela and British Guiana. In theory Cleveland's government intervened to uphold the Monroe Doctrine. When the British rejected his overtures to help resolve the differences, Cleveland and his secretary of state, Richard Olney, took a belligerent attitude.

In a message to congress on December 17, 1895, the president suggested the use of force if necessary to run the boundary, apparently against the British. This announcement met with greater popularity than had much of his other diplomacy, supposedly because it pleased the Anglophobes. Yet neither Cleveland nor Olney was an Anglophobe, and they had no intention of turning the controversy into a war. Regardless, their stance dismayed the Anglophiles, who perceived it as a reckless bid for Irish-American votes. It also alarmed the policymakers in London.

For years Britain's leaders had stressed the ethnic bond with "our American cousins." They spoke repeatedly of "the trans-Atlantic branch of our race," as if the two peoples were one. "The notion of identity of race was central in British thinking about America," a British analyst explains. "The United States was regarded as an Anglo-Saxon country, and little attention was paid to the other diverse strains which went to make up its population." Indeed, it "was treated as a branch of the British Empire" which because of an unfortunate quarrel had broken away.[24]

Since those in power in Britain, like American leaders, still greatly prized the attachment, both groups were determined that the current misunderstanding should not be allowed to produce more regret in the family relationship. In Britain men of prominence such as Arthur J. Balfour declared "that the idea of war with the United States of America carries with it something of the unnatural horror of civil war."[25] Similarly, in January 1896 Joseph Chamberlain, the colonial secretary, asserted that war between the two nations "would be an absurdity as well as a crime." They were closer "than any other nations on the face of the earth."

In the United States Anglo-American intellectuals expressed analogous sentiments. In that same month *The Evangelist*, a Presbyterian journal, announced that "Next to our own country, we love England, the land of our fathers, and the bitterest calamity that could happen to both nations would be fratricidal and suicidal war." Several thousand Britons signed an "Anglo-

American Memorial" which said that "all English-speaking peoples united by race, language, and religion, should regard war as the one absolutely intolerable mode of settling the domestic differences of the Anglo-American family."

Despite his strong words against Britain, Olney was fundamentally an Anglophile who took great pride in his English ancestry. Several months later, when the crisis had passed, he wrote that "there is no general and rooted hatred by Americans of the English people. On the contrary, if there is anything the Americans are proud of, it is their right to describe themselves as of the English race." Leaders in both countries spoke of "race sentiment" as bringing about the peaceful settlement.[26]

In the view of most historians, after the passing of this crisis British-American relations underwent "a deep and enduring transformation." They usually describe it as a "great" rapprochement to distinguish it from the other rapprochements that the relationship, as is usual in family quarrels, seemed occasionally to require. This idea of an abrupt change has the quality of hyperbole. For a striking rapprochement to take place, there has to be deep estrangement. Relations between the two countries, on the contrary, had a remarkable record of continuity in friendship based in good measure on ethnicity. Yet, for strategic, political, and international reasons as well, the official relationship did become conspicuously closer.

Even many Americans who could claim no British ancestry approved of the rapprochement, partially because traditionally they had felt a veneration for Britain and her culture. At the same time, Anglophobia remained strong among ethnic groups such as the Irish-American. In general, though, now as before, Anglophobia did not sink deep roots. It found virtually no acceptance among the policy-making elites. Despite some bitter quarrels and harsh rhetoric, since 1815 Britons and Americans had rarely been truly hostile toward each other. Even their diplomatic differences often contained more smoke than fire. The disagreements invariably ended amicably.

As in any family, even the deepest of amity suffers temporary setbacks. In January 1897, for instance, as one result of the rapprochement, Britain and the United States concluded a treaty that provided for the compulsory arbitration of virtually all issues between them. Behind this agreement, negotiated by Olney, stood the idea of precluding the possibility of war between two kindred peoples. In May, with a mere three votes short of a two-thirds majority, the senate defeated the treaty. Even some senators committed to British-American friendship were unwilling to give up a vital power in foreign affairs.

Anglo-Saxonists, however, attributed the result to the usual Anglophobia. Irish-Americans appeared to give substance to this supposition. They claimed responsibility for the senate's action because they viewed the pact as the possible beginning of an alliance. Another arbitration treaty in 1905 suffered a like fate for similar reasons. Despite these setbacks for the Anglo-American establishment, in other areas of foreign policy in these years it practically ignored the Irish-Americans.

At the same time, the stronger official relationship between their countries led British statesmen and the more ardent Anglophiles in America to bid openly for "a re-united Anglo-Saxondom," "common citizenship," or a "race alliance." Chamberlain, for instance, hoped that in war or peace "the Stars and Stripes and the Union Jack would wave together over an Anglo-Saxon alliance."[27] The British imperialist Cecil Rhodes "placed the dream of Anglo-American union above any other ideal."[28] Men such as these maintained that in terms of perceived ethnicity as well as of common geo-political interests the two countries were natural allies. Yet, in part because of concern over minority ethnic reactions in the United States, the idea of an "Anglo-Saxon alliance" never rose much beyond rhetoric.

The white racial idea behind the rhetoric did not, however, die. It found a sufficiently prominent place in the planks of the major political parties to affect issues of foreign policy. The Republican platform of 1896, for one, sought to commit the government to preventing the "mixed races from Mexico and Central America" from entering the Union. It wanted to restrict admission to "the English-speaking peoples of North America." Yet the party's politicians also wished to "control" peoples of color within the reach of American power, as in the Hawaiian Islands.[29]

In the 1890s the close relationship of these islands with the United States contributed to a drastic demographic change. Hawaii's whites of American origin, who dominated the government and had tied its economy to that of the United States, had imported Asians to work their sugar and pineapple plantations. Along with the whites, these laborers came to outnumber the indigenous Hawaiians, who thus became a minority in their own islands. The future of the Hawaiians appeared grim because, as the population became more and more multiracial, the "Hawaii for Hawaiians" movement lost vigor.

Liliuokalani, an aging anti-foreign queen who inherited her throne in 1891, tried to revive the movement, took steps to curb the power of the whites in her government, and sought to improve the status of her own people. Her actions so alarmed the minority American residents in Honolulu that in January 1893 they overthrew her. They established a provisional government and immediately petitioned for annexation to the United States. The native Hawaiians were powerless to prevent the coup.

When President Cleveland investigated the revolution, he learned that the queen's "colored" subjects were overwhelmingly opposed to annexation. Anti-white, anti-American native organizations fought the proposal, but the revolutionaries dismissed this agitation with the argument "that the native Hawaiians were incapable of knowing what was good for them and that their wishes in the matter should therefore not be given weight."[30]

The president, who thought differently, concluded that the queen had been dethroned unjustly. He realized, though, that to restore her to power in the face of a determined white opposition he would have resort to force. He understood also that congress would not authorize violence against the expatriate American revolutionaries on the islands for the benefit of the Polynesians. So Cleveland put aside both the idea of annexation and of restoration, and waited.

Other Americans kept annexationist sentiment very much alive, always with a focus on race. Theodore Roosevelt, for one, thought that the government should take Hawaii "in the interests of the white race." In congress and elsewhere, still others expressed opposition to the acquiring of Polynesians, Chinese, Japanese, half-breed Portuguese, and other "dusky" people. They insisted that Hawaii would merely "add another race problem" to the Union.[31]

Fear of Japan weakened their argument. She aroused worry because of the large number of Japanese in the Hawaiian Islands who regarded themselves as citizens and representatives of the Japanese empire. When Tokyo protested the treaty of annexation, ethnic concern stood out. Japan's spokesmen maintained that the action imperiled the status quo in the Pacific, ignored her rights in the islands, and jeopardized the welfare of her people there because Americans discriminated against them.

As the Japanese had perceived, the whites desired acquisition particularly for, but not exclusively for, racial reasons. The *Hawaiian Star,* a radical annexationist newspaper, capsulized this attitude. "The annexation of Hawaii is for the benefit of the Hawaiian, the Latin, and the Anglo-Saxon races of these Islands," it explained. "It is not and it does not pretend to be for the benefit of the Asiatics. It is meant as a bar to the Asiatics."[32] The United States consummated the acquisition on July 7, 1898, on the crest of a wave of patriotic emotion that in April had plunged the nation into the war with Spain.

In Honolulu, where the Hawaiian flag came down and the Stars and Stripes went up, most native Hawaiians boycotted the ceremony. The few who were present wept. An American anti-imperialist writer commented bitterly, "what matter the victims whose consent was lacking? Are they not poor, feeble, dark-skinned child-like persons, unworthy of lordly Anglo-Saxon recognition?"[33]

As for the causes of the Spanish-American War, one of the more thorough analyses of that conflict concludes that "irrational impulses rather than calculated strategic, economic, ideological, or religious considerations" moved Americans to demand war.[34] Among these impulses, another study suggests, ethnic antipathy should rank high. The stereotype image of Spaniards as dark, tyrannical, and barbarous inferiors who possessed an "inner core of cruelty," it contends, provided "both incentive and justification for America's immediate intervention in Cuba."[35] Even though President William McKinley opposed the shedding of blood, he believed that he could not resist this war fever rooted in both ethnic jingoism and nebulous humanitarian feelings for the plight of the Cuban rebels. Many students of the conflict have concluded that he capitulated to the jingoes.

The elitists who both desired and managed the brief war virtually ignored the feelings of the new immigrants and of other minorities—but of course used them on the battlefields. The ethnoreligious ingredients took the form of old anti-Hispanic, anti-Catholic hostility, of claims "that the Anglo-Saxon was superior to the Latin," of ethnoracial exceptionalism, and of an "intense national hate" for those of the "Latin race."[36] The contempt directed against the Spaniards, Cubans, and Filipinos as encompassed in the notions of the New Manifest Destiny were as ugly as those in the war with Mexico and similar to other ethnoracial effusions in the American past.

In this atmosphere Anglo-Saxon racism reached a highpoint. Olney extolled it as "a patriotism of race as well as of country," maintaining that "the Anglo-American is as little likely to be indifferent to the one as to the other." In their "family quarrels," he added, the English and Americans take liberties with each other that "only the fondest and dearest of relatives indulge in."[37]

In keeping with this sentiment, in July 1898 Anglo-Saxonists in London and New York founded the Anglo-American League, chaired by the British publicist James Bryce and the American editor Whitelaw Reid. In the United States men of wealth, such as the industrialist Andrew Carnegie, served on its executive committee. It sought to further "racial" cooperation between Britain and the United States. In America the league functioned to buttress the already impressive power of the Anglo-American ethnic community. In the following year these lobbyists launched two journals, the *Anglo-Saxon Review* and the *Anglo-American Magazine* published in London and New York, to strengthen further the cultural and other bonds between the two countries.

Yet the rhetoric of Anglo-Saxonism, with its message "that the Anglo-Saxons were the born rulers of men, the 'uncrowned kings of the world,'" had little appeal for the masses in most of the other ethnic groups.[38] Many of them, not just the Anglophobes, found the term as well as the claims offensive. In some western states people even held meetings to protest the power of Anglo-Saxonism. But they could neither counterbalance the influence of that cult nor refute the reality of British and American industrial and other leadership in the world, a status which the Anglo-Saxonists seldom failed to laud.

As in the past, Britain's elite continued to nurture Anglo-Saxonism. Many ordinary Britons, too, favored the United States in its war against Spain because of the "ties of blood" that bound the "sons of the self-same race." In both countries those who wielded power portrayed the conflict as virtually a "war of races." Darwinian law, they said, doomed Spain to defeat before the might of the more fit Anglo-Saxons. As expressed by Washburn Hopkins, a professor at Yale University, "Spain bends to America" because she must "by the higher law of racial superiority." Spaniards, on the other hand, ridiculed the American inconsistency of "rushing off to liberate negroes in Cuba while lynching negroes at home."[39]

Many Americans, however, were unaware of Cuba's racial mosaic. When American soldiers and their officers first met some of their Cuban allies, they were surprised to find that many were black and "only partially civilized." The Anglo liberators characterized these people, as they had other non-whites, as "born of a mongrel spawn of Europe, crossed upon the fetiches of darkest Africa and aboriginal America." Obviously, in this perspective, the Cubans were incompetent to govern themselves. "The 'Cuba Libre' of the blacks," an American observer warned, "would be a veritable hell upon earth, a blot upon Christian civilization."[40]

After defeating Spain and occupying Cuba, the Americans allowed their racial perceptions to govern the debates over whether or not the island should be independent. Even the most well-informed and supposedly enlightened leaders acted on racist assumptions, assumptions that permeated the culture of most nations in the Western world. The imperialists insisted that, like the majority of non-Anglo peoples, the Cubans were incapable of self-government. To gain territory, however, these expansionists were willing to put aside the problem of the Teller Amendment, which prohibited the acquisition of Cuba, and also to suppress their distaste for the mingling of Anglos with more black and brown people. Even though infused with the same biases as the imperialists, the anti-imperialists refused to overlook color even in the interest of national expansion. They opposed any annexation that would result in statehood.

In the controversy over Cuba's future, both political parties wanted her devoid of her blacks and mulattoes. In turn, for racial reasons also, the Cubans had no love for the Americans. As much as, if not more than, anything else, racial antipathy soured relations with the Cubans, whom the Americans had just fought to liberate. So deep were these feelings that "the prospect of war between the Americans and Cubans loomed as a real possibility in the minds of many American officials."[41]

That same prejudice guided the American presence in the Philippines. There, in the cause of white supremacy, the United States turned from a policy of cooperating with Tagalog insurgents against the Spanish colonial regime to one of teaming with the defeated Spaniards against the Filipinos. This attitude permeated the discussions over the future of the Philippines. In a kind of standard argument applied to peoples of color, both the imperialists and anti-imperialists pronounced the Filipinos incapable of governing themselves. The imperialists such as Alfred Thayer Mahan urged acquisition as a duty that white American "race patriots" must assume.[42] They explained that tutelage under these self-designated superiors could uplift and regenerate the Filipinos.

The anti-imperialists, on the other hand, had little faith in such regeneration. As with Cuba and Hawaii, they feared that annexation would lead to the incorporation of brown people into the Union, thereby endangering the purity of the old Anglo-American stock. Senator John W. Daniels of Viriginia said, for instance, of the Filipinos that "their race forbid it; their climate forbid it; their condition in all respects forbid it." Some contemporaries believed that not a single senator favored taking in Filipinos as potential citizens. Other anti-imperialists stated simply that they did not want to "bring into the American system a lot of Malays, Chinese Mestizos" and others of "inferior race."[43]

In general, the anti-imperialists opposed annexation not out of sympathy for the Filipinos' desire for freedom or even out of a humanitarian sensitivity for the abuses they suffered. As with the Cubans and Hawaiians, the anti-imperialists did not want Filipinos because they feared any possible dilution of the white American "race." Like the imperialists, who despised the Filipino because he was "entirely devoid of the sturdy manhood of the Anglo-Saxon," the anti-imperialists embraced the racism that ran through much of American society.[44] Both sides sought to influence foreign policy for racial reasons, but the imperialist side did so more successfully.

On December 21, 1898, while the imperialists and anti-imperialists were debating and before the senate had approved annexation, President McKinley "usurped" its "power by proclaiming American sovereignty over the Philippines." He ordered General Elwell S. Otis, the American commander there, to announce Spain's cession and to extend military government throughout the archipelago. To soothe the feelings of the Filipinos who had expected independence, the president announced that America's mission was "benevolent assimilation" with just rule. Ironically, Otis, who was entrusted to carry out this policy, believed that the Filipinos were incapable of benefiting from such enlightened dominion because they wanted only "to loot and kill every white man" in the islands.[45]

A month earlier, in keeping with British sentiment that "would welcome the Americans in the Philippines as kinfolks and allies united with us in the Far East," the poet Rudyard Kipling had written "The White Man's Burden," subtitled "The United States and the Philippine Islands."[46] It urged Americans to get on with the conquest of the archipelago. Kipling rushed his verses off to Theodore Roosevelt and had them published first by the New York *Sun* on February 5, 1899, the day before the senate by a close vote approved the peace treaty with Spain that provided for the annexation of the islands according to American constitutional procedure.

Filipinos, particularly the Tagalogs, fiercely resisted the American colonialist program, making it clear to all that the president, his advisers, and the imperialists in general had underestimated their desire for self-determination. The American army therefore carried out its misnamed mission of benevolence with bullet and bayonet, with concentration camps, and with policies of "kill and burn," torture, and take no prisoners. As one soldier explained, "It kept leaking down from sources above that the Filipinos were 'niggers,' no better than Indians, and were to be treated as such."[47]

Despite the opposite intentions of many Americans to help or uplift the victims, critics could characterize the war against the Filipinos as a slaughter based on race. American military and political leaders often rationalized the brutalities of their soldiers with the usual contempt for peoples of color. They categorized the Filipinos, who also resorted to cruelties, as backward and innately subordinate to whites, insulting them also with racial slurs such as "nigger," "savage," and "goo-goo."

Within the United States only one prominent ethnoracial group, the African-American, identified with the embattled Filipinos. It did so out of an "affinity of complexion." Bishop Alexander Walters of the National Afro-American Council expressed most sensitively the black community's opposition to the obvious thrust of American foreign policy. He maintained that "had the Filipinos been white and fought as bravely as they have, the war would have been ended and their independence granted a long time ago."[48]

Such dissent had no effect on American policy; the negative racial assumptions behind the war remained virtually intact. Three years of warfare brought death to at least 18,000 Filipino "insurgents" in combat and to more than 100,000 civilians, mainly from the hunger and disease that accompanied the violence. American combat deaths numbered slightly more than 4,000.[49]

The American racial biases, which blinded the public as well as reputedly knowledgeable intellectuals to the atrocities in the conquest, were also reflected in the recommendations of the First Philippine Commission in 1900, headed by educator Jacob Gould Schurman. He hoped that "the Federal Constitution could be amended so as to provide for the perpetual exclusion of Asiatic countries from partnership in our great American Republic."[50] Widespread convictions held that the peoples of the newly acquired territories such as Hawaii and the Philippines should not be entrusted with governing themselves in their own islands unless the controlling faction was white and preferably Anglo-American.

Solidarity with the British in the Boer War had a greater impact on American foreign policy than it did on the concurrent conflict in the Philippines. Efforts to involve Americans in the clash between Briton and Boer had begun earlier, as far back as 1877 when Britain annexed the Transvaal, a Boer republic. Denouncing the act as aggression, the Afrikaners had looked to the United States for help. Their leader, Paul Krüger, appealed personally to the American government to protest the annexation. He received no response. Few Americans, other than attentive blacks, were interested in Africa at this time. As for the Anglo-American elite, it simply did not wish to become involved.

Other clashes between Britons and Boers followed, but they did not lead to open warfare until October 1899, at the height of the new British-American rapprochement. The attitude of Secretary of State John Hay, a passionate Anglophile, did much to shape governmental policy toward the conflict. A month earlier he had written that "as long as I stay here no action shall be taken contrary to my conviction that the one indispensable feature of our foreign policy should be a friendly understanding with England."[51]

Unlike Hay and others in the government, much of the American public, particularly the Dutch-, German-, and Irish-Americans, felt that the Boers had been wronged and hence sympathized with them. Notable among those who took exception to this sentiment were the American blacks who followed the events in South Africa. At first they viewed the struggle as between whites with little in it to concern them. As they learned more of the ingrained racialism in Afrikaner society, they "became increasingly hostile to the Boers."[52] Yet they also questioned British racism. Congress reflected the general public's attitude. Accordingly, the mixed American reaction to the struggle put the rapprochement with the British to its first significant test.

Britain's conduct of the war, particularly under General H. Herbert Kitchener, aroused worldwide protest. His campaign, like that of the Spaniards in Cuba, included concentration camps, destruction of food and water supplies, and harsh treatment of civilians. Continental Europeans welcomed the Boer successes, as did many non-Anglos in the United States. Their anti-British attitude took various forms, most of them intellectual, unofficial, and ineffectual.

Feeling the pull of Anglo-Saxon "racial" affinity, President McKinley and Secretary of State Hay quickly took a pro-British position. Throughout the war, in consequence, the American government followed a policy of allowing all kinds of aid to Britain. Angered Boers could do nothing to block it, in good part because the administration stifled congressional opposition. It also blunted the attacks of Irish-American publicists and politicians who denounced its policy. Secretary Hay had constantly to deny rumors of a secret alliance with Britain.

Establishment leaders such as Alfred Thayer Mahan feared that unsavory elements among the citizenry would take advantage of the sympathy for the Boers to disrupt the understanding with Britain. Other elitists pointedly differentiated between Boer and British "racial" characteristics, designating the Boers as the inferiors. One writer labeled the conflict "a race war." In nearly every instance, prominent Englishmen who brought their country's case before the American public through the media "appealed for support on grounds of the supposed racial affinity of Britons and Americans and the superiority of Anglo-Saxon culture."[53]

In contrast, as early as January 1900, William Jennings Bryan, the Democratic leader, appealed to pro-Boer sentiment for votes by attacking McKinley's pro-British policy. In July the Democratic platform extended sympathy to the Boers, hailed their courage, and denounced "the ill-concealed Republican alliance with England." Yet this stance had little effect on the election, partially because a British victory seemed inevitable. Pro-Boer appeals also failed because the public was not deeply aroused and because, except for the Irish-Americans, the Boers had no significant constituency of their own in the United States that would lobby for them.

McKinley, Hay, and the others like them in the Anglo-American elite made it clear that their support of Britain was based "primarily on racial considerations," a commitment that took precedence over morality, ideology, and other issues. As Mark Twain wrote, "Even wrong—and she is wrong—England must be upheld." Henry Cabot Lodge explained "that however much we sympathize with the Boers, the downfall of the British Empire is something which no rational American could regard as anything but a misfortune for the United States."[54] These sentiments, along with America's virtual alliance with Britain, discouraged possible intervention by European powers and thus helped to assure the annihilation of the Boer republics.

This ethnic primacy in American foreign policy had counterparts in European imperialist conceptions, some of them similar in their ethnocentrism to Anglo-Saxonism. The condescending idea that somehow a variety of divine beings had endowed whites with civilizing missions had ancient origins. It never died, but in the late nineteenth century pseudoscientific laws that were embraced as though divine brought to it new sponsors.

Regardless of its roots, this concept of "racial" mission had popular followings in countries such as France, Germany, and Russia, as well as in Britain and the United States. While not exclusive to white societies, that theory and the idea of exceptionalism were generally associated with white racism because the Europeans often used them to rationalize their dominion over peoples of color. The American governance of islands that had been acquired or that were dominated by the United States at the end of the century fit this pattern. The islands were populated by a hodgepodge of ethnic groups and formed the nucleus of what has been termed "America's Negro empire."[55]

In nearly every instance, the whites did not want to bring these dominated blacks and mixed bloods into the Union on the basis of equality with "Anglo-Saxon" Americans. As a congressman from Kentucky put it, we should not "open wide the door by which these negroes and Asiatics can pour like the locusts of Egypt into this country."[56] Accordingly, in April 1900 congress passed the Foraker Act for the governing of Puerto Rico as an unorganized territory.

That law and the supreme court decisions that followed in the insular cases were all based on racial reasoning. They said, in effect, that the constitution had ethnoracial limitations which supported the theory that the Filipinos and Puerto Ricans who had been annexed through force were, because of their color, not fit to become American citizens. Foreigners, as in Latin America and Asia, noted this institutionalized racism. It affected their attitudes toward the United States in both official and less formal relations.

At home at this time, Americans with colored skins had little influence over the conduct of any kind of government policy, let alone in international relations. Thus, regardless of their desire for change, they could not soften the nation's ethnoracial harshness in its relations with other peoples. The newcomers from southeastern Europe had a larger, but still small, impact on international policy. They, too, could hardly dent the dominance of the Anglo-Americans in giving meaningful form to foreign policy. Yet in small ways in these last years of the nineteenth century, more minority groups than in the past had begun to demonstrate their concern over policy that affected their old homelands. On rare occasions they had even been influential.

5
Hyphenate Hysteria

There is a possible danger that the race feeling in America may manifest itself in such forms as will inflame the pride and passion of the Japanese to an uncontrollable degree. There is a possible danger that the popular passion in either or in both countries might be aroused to such a pitch that no Government could restrain it.

Outlook, Dec. 14, 1907

Despite the resentment of the old-stock Americans against them, in the new century many among the nation's white minorities who had attained the vote struggled to enter government so as to participate directly in the making of policy. When leaders in these ethnic groups attained office as well as political power that was consequential enough to be felt on a national scale, they used it primarily to influence policy on issues affecting former homelands. At first this increase in hyphenate clout intruded only in minor ways on the nativist establishment's management of foreign policy. Even so, the traditional power brokers generally deplored this outsider effort to alter the policy-making system.

Prominent Anglo-Americans often condemned the new ethnic politicians and their constituents as untrustworthy because they supposedly held to dual loyalties that worked against the national interest as perceived in establishment terms. As a nativist historian later put it, the minority peoples were "mongrels with a divided allegiance . . . hyphenates, whose hyphen, like the kiss of Judas, is a link for treachery."[1] Like a drug-resistant virus, this kind of ethnoracial bias would remain potent in much of American historiography for decades into the new century.

This xenophobic outlook was not unique to the Anglo-Americans. Most ethnic groups that hold power distrust all except those who are like themselves. Yet, despite their denunciation of dual allegiance, the Anglo-Americans, like the hyphenates, had always coupled loyalty to the United States with an affection for their own mother country. They even defined American national character in terms of their own ethnic heritage, thereby making it an extension of Anglo-Saxonism.

This link between Americanism and Anglo-Saxonism facilitated the negotiations in 1900 between John Hay and Britain's ambassador in Washington, Sir Julian Pauncefote, for a treaty allowing the United States to construct but not fortify a transoceanic canal across Central America. In this instance the Anglo ethnic bond did not prove strong enough to overcome the opposition to the agreement within the senate.

The Irish-Americans, who lobbied against the treaty because it appeared favorable to Britain, assumed that they had caused its defeat. The Anglo-American elite decried the result because it roiled the harmony of relations with Britain. In the elitist perspective, a minority had meddled in foreign affairs where it should not. Even though Irish-American opposition remained active, in the next year the senate approved a similar but modified canal treaty.

By this time American Jews, whose numbers had swelled with thousands of recent arrivals from Russia, Romania, and Poland, had become almost as active in ethnic politics as had the American Irish, and with increasing competence. More and more Jewish leaders gained access to politicians who listened to them and were willing to act on behalf of their organizations dedicated to helping distressed ethnoreligious kin throughout the world. The effectiveness of such politics came to affect United States relations with Russia.

The motivation for the ethnic mobilization at this time arose out of the worsening condition of the Jews in Russia and Romania. In Russian lands they suffered persecution in some three hundred instances starting in 1900. The most notorious of the pogroms struck Kishinev, the capital of Bessarabia, in April 1903, and was followed by others across the country. Horrified by this bloodshed, American Jews sponsored anti-Russian demonstrations throughout the country. They deluged the White House with letters and petitions urging pressure on Tsar Nicholas II to stop the brutalities.

Secretary of State Hay heeded the protests. In a gesture widely publicized for its political impact, he made American displeasure known to St. Petersburg. "The victims were Jews," he said of the Russian violence, "and the assault was the result of race and religious prejudice."[2] Nicholas retreated from, but did not abandon, his anti-Jewish position. Nonetheless, President Theodore Roosevelt, who was not himself free of the anti-Semitic sentiments of his time, won Jewish approbation for at least attempting to do something for persecuted brethren just before elections in 1904, when he sought the presidency in his own right.

Still, the pogroms continued. Prominent American Jewish lobbyists such as the banker Jacob H. Schiff even urged military intervention in Russia to stop the bloodshed, a course of action that Roosevelt rejected. When mobs in Odessa and elsewhere in November 1905 massacred thousands of Jewish men, women, and children, more than 50,000 American Jews marched in protest through the streets of New York City.

Schiff also acted on his own by organizing a number of Jewish and other banking firms in the United States to block the extension of credit to Russia, which was then financially hard-pressed in its war with Japan. He wanted "to make the Russian government feel that it cannot continue forever with immunity its shameful policy towards its Jewish subjects."[3] The bankers did lend money to Japan, an action that has been assumed to have affected American policy toward the belligerents, although to an extent unmeasurable.

After this venture into international affairs, these ethnoreligious leaders increased their political effectiveness. In November 1906 they launched the American Jewish Committee, a lobby that swayed policy relating to a commercial treaty of 1832 with Russia which permitted her to bar American Jews from entering the country. The imperial government enforced the provision. The Jewish organizations in the United States protested vehemently, sought government intervention, and pointedly reminded key politicians of the Jewish-American swing vote in New York. Whether for humanitarian or political reasons, the Republican and Democratic parties reacted by promising in their 1908 platforms to revise the treaty.

No matter, the Russian government persisted in refusing to honor passports issued to American Jews, arguing that it could not allow them privileges, such as freedom of travel, that it denied to its own Jews. The American Jewish Committee and other groups, which desired precisely such a change for kin in Russia, showered congress with demands for abrogation of the 1832 treaty. They stepped up their advocacy by encouraging anti-treaty rallies in a number of cities. On December 17, 1912, because of the pressure from the "powerful lobby amassed by American Jews and their sympathizers," whose political support he valued, President William H. Taft terminated the treaty.

A Jewish-American congressman hailed the abrogation as "a great victory for human rights."[4] Yet it provided no immediate help to the persecuted Jews and added more bitterness to relations with Russia. The Russians retaliated by raising their tariffs on American goods, by organizing boycotts of some products, and by imposing more restrictions on the Jews within their reach. George F. Kennan, the specialist in Russian affairs, later deplored the effect of such ethnic politics practiced by "maladjusted groups: in our country—Jews, Negroes, immigrants—all those who feel handicapped in the framework of a national society." He maintained that in these years Jews along with liberals "pretty well dominated the formation of American opinion with respect to Russian matters."[5] This was an overstatement, but it indicated that by this time at least one of the nation's new minority groups had acquired a significant, even though not yet powerful, influence in foreign relations.

Concurrently, exclusionist immigration laws continued to exacerbate relations with China. In 1900 and after, through its open-door policy, the American government sought to enlarge the markets in China for its businessmen. Racial issues intruded. Increasingly in exchange for trade the Chinese demanded an end to the official bigotry that barred the immigration of their people to the United States. Evidence of the depth of feeling among the Chinese within the country over the racist treatment they experienced cropped up regularly. "Why can't you be fair?" Wu T'ing-fang, China's minister in Washington, asked newspaper reporters in November 1901 in referring to their disparagement of Chinese immigrants. "Would you talk like that if mine was not a weak nation? Would you say it if the Chinese had votes?"[6]

Neither the protests nor the inconsistency of Americans' insulting the Chinese while seeking them as customers affected the popular and governmental discrimination. Indeed, the white nativists in the Bureau of Immigration embarked on a campaign to tighten the exclusionist policy. In addition to keeping out new immigrants, the federal government as represented by the bureau now attempted to drive the entire Chinese community from the American mainland. Sino-American leaders appealed to the Chinese government and to merchants in China for help, suggesting a termination of the immigration treaty when it came up for review in two years and a boycott of American goods. "If exclusion treaty is renewed for another ten years," spokesmen in San Francisco cabled to the foreign office, "Chinese in the United States will become extinct."[7]

This stepped-up exclusionist program, the repeated violence against Chinese residents in the United States, and the atrocities against homeland Chinese by American troops during the Boxer Rebellion, fed a xenophobia that had always been present among the Chinese. In some parts of China it also produced a specifically anti-American hatred. The educated Chinese who visited the United States and suffered abuse through detainment in filthy quarters summarized this bitterness. "The Americans," they reported, "are a race of pigs."[8]

Such sentiment had no discernible effect on congress. In April 1902, without China's being consulted, it renewed the exclusion laws. Under pressure from its own officials, from intellectuals, and from others, the Chinese government in January 1904 gave notice that in the following December it would abrogate the exclusion treaty that it had accepted a decade earlier. Again ignoring the Chinese anger, congress in that year enacted other laws that made exclusion a national policy of indefinite duration. As John Hay wrote, now "even Confucius could not become an American—though he should seek it with prayers and tears."[9] Yet diplomatists continued to negotiate over the fate of the treaty.

All the while, as the Chinese in the United States had urged, aroused students, merchants, and others overseas organized a boycott of American goods, the first such anti-foreign campaign in China's history. "The Chinese people are in earnest," their ambassador in Washington warned in explaining the aroused emotions in his homeland. "Your exclusion act is humiliating. They would prefer to pay a huge indemnity or surrender a slice of territory rather than be insulted and menaced as they are by the attitude of the United States."[10]

Organized groups in twenty-five Chinese cities endorsed the boycott. Students and others plastered walls with anti-American slogans. They proceeded on the premise, as stated by a prominent merchant, that "when our government proves itself unable to act, then the people must rise up to do so." Accompanied by discriminatory measures against American residents, their schools, and their firms, the boycott went into effect in June in the ports of southern China. The acrimonious feeling behind the agitation came out in the words of an editor. "In order to exclude the Chinese, the United States adopted force, disregarded justice, ignored humanity and violated international treaties," he wrote. "This was a great insult imposed upon all of us four hundred million Chinese."[11]

Over a period of almost eight months, the boycott spread through much of China while also attracting support from Chinese overseas. It especially injured American cotton manufacturers. The anti-American movement, which encompassed more than the boycott, was more widespread and of greater duration. Although this commotion did not end exclusion or other discrimination against the Chinese in the United States, it did reveal the intensity of feelings of the American Chinese as well as of those in China over issues of foreign relations touching on race. It also prompted concessions from President Roosevelt, a believer in the exclusion of "inferior" Chinese but one who also did not want "another race problem" on his hands. In addition, the agitation in China and in the Chinese communities abroad against discrimination halted the momentum of the American government's effort to expel its resident Chinese.

Even though few in number and virtually impotent politically, the pro-boycott Chinese in America had formed an essential ingredient in this troubled Sino-American relationship. They were able to contribute to the pressure on the American government because the ethnic bond had given them temporary leverage with powerful leaders in China. Their trans-Pacific politics demonstrated that on occasion a small, highly motivated ethnic group with concentrated pressure can have greater impact on a foreign-policy issue than its numbers might suggest. Of course, fundamental in the Chinese relationship was the racism in American policy. It took precedence over the economics of the open door; it remained entrenched; and it still rankled.

At the same time, the trans-Pacific lobbying for the boycott had produced among the Chinese in the United States an "increased awareness and concern with their motherland's fate" similar to the feelings of people in other ethnic groups. This aroused "political consciousness" expressed itself clearly in support of China's revolution of 1911. China's nationalist leader, Sun Yat-sen, even called the overseas Chinese "the mother of the revolution." In America's Chinese communities such politicization appeared to have become "permanently rooted."[12]

All the while, the racism that the Chinese in the United States had experienced and were still encountering had an impact on Japanese immigrants, even though they tried to avoid the behavior "that brought upon the Chinese as a whole the contempt of Westerners" and with it exclusion.[13] Notable numbers of Japanese had started migrating to the West Coast around 1885. Even though they never amounted to more than one tenth of one per cent of the nation's population, from the beginning they came to know white resentment and discrimination. As with prejudice against the Chinese, anti-Japanese sentiment gained such strength that, starting in Seattle and San Francisco in 1900, demands arose for the exclusion of the Japanese. Euro-American nativists argued, as they had against earlier pigmented outsiders, that the Japanese were unassimilable because of their color and physical features.

Despite this prejudice, in 1904 when Japan and Russia tangled in a war that many in Asia, and in the West too, viewed as racial, American sentiment initially favored the Japanese. This attitude was based partially on a distrust of the Russians. Seeing in President Roosevelt a friend who had long admired them as a superior Asian people because they had readily adapted to Western ways, the Japanese in May 1905 asked him to act as mediator. After the Russians had agreed, Roosevelt sponsored the diplomacy that stilled the hostilities.

In the course of the peace-making that began in Portsmouth, New Hampshire, in August, Japanese ethnoracial elation crumpled. When the peace terms of September 3 were made public, many in Japan came to believe incorrectly that the Americans had sided with the Russians, thereby denying their country the full benefit of the victory gained in battle. Americans, on the other hand, viewed the Japanese as ungrateful and arrogant. The Japanese-American diplomatic connection, as well as the already strained racial relations between the two countries, began to turn sour. In the United States the swelling dislike of the Japanese combined with the notion of a "yellow peril," which worried even Roosevelt as he reflected on the consequences of Japan's rise to power. At the heart of this yellow-peril idea lay the emotion of racial antagonism toward Asians and a fear of Japan's rising power.

As for the outlook of Asians in general and other peoples of color, including American blacks, they rejoiced in Japan's victory over a powerful nation that they regarded as essentially European. Even the Chinese, who had no love for the Japanese, greeted the outcome with satisfaction. To them as to others, "it was the awakening hope of the Oriental peoples, it was the first blow given to the other race, to that accursed race of the West." Europeans shuddered, interpreting this "victory of a non-white people over a white people," as an analyst concluded, as "the most important historical event" in their lifetime.[14]

In California in March 1905, well before the Russo-Japanese hostilities had ceased, basic racial antipathy unencumbered by geo-political concerns had led the legislature by unanimous vote to memorialize congress to terminate Japanese immigration. In May white nativists in San Francisco formed the Asiatic Exclusion League, which demanded that the laws barring the Chinese be extended to Japanese and Koreans. The league's activity, backed by a membership of over 100,000, along with the racist ambience in the city, in October 1906 generated the conditions for segregating Japanese and Korean schoolchildren.

This expression of white bias, following closely the exclusionist demands and the differences over the outcome at Portsmouth, jolted the Japanese. Even though they too viewed the world from a harsh racist perspective and discriminated against outsiders, they now felt that among foreigners the Americans wished in particular to humiliate them. Yet other white governments in South Africa, Australia, New Zealand, and Canada also enacted laws that excluded people on the basis of race.

To the Japanese at this point, comparative racism seemed irrelevant. They were concerned with the bigotry against their own kind in the United States. On this score, a Japanese newspaper correspondent reminded his people in California that they had behind them a mighty nation. "Struggle, endeavor, and overwhelm the white race," he advised. "The struggle between the races is not only a problem involving interests but is a problem of life and death."[15]

Japan's diplomats held to similar views but expressed them in less extreme terms. In formally protesting the San Francisco discrimination, Japan's ambassador in Washington pointed out that in the United States his people had civil rights guaranteed by a treaty that the government was obligated to enforce. Even though Roosevelt shared the popular biases that had contributed to the dilemma, he had to acknowledge the correctness of the Japanese position. He also realized that the immigration issue had escalated into a foreign-policy crisis which might lead even to war. "The infernal fools in California, and especially in San Francisco," he told his son, "insult the Japanese recklessly, and in the event of war it will be the Nation as a whole which will pay the consequences."[16]

After considerable effort, the president in the following year persuaded the San Francisco school board to rescind its segregation order and the California legislature to hold back discriminatory legislation. He promised them to find means to curb Japanese immigration. In March 1907, by executive order, he terminated their entry from Hawaii and Mexico. Roosevelt also exchanged a series of six notes with the Japanese, called collectively the Gentlemen's Agreement, which committed them to restricting the immigration of laborers and farmers at the source. In turn, the American government did not by statute stigmatize the Japanese as inferiors by barring any of them from entering the country, an affront that Tokyo anxiously wished to avoid.

Regardless of this compromise, which went into effect in the summer of 1908, white racism had produced such deep anti-Americanism in Japan that it, as much as anything else, contributed to the acrimony in the formal relations between the two countries. Cultural differences and derogatory racial assumptions on both sides, particularly as combined with naval, colonial, and economic rivalry, carried the potential of conflict for years to come.

Related if not similar anti-Yankee emotions in Latin America were intensified by the ethnoracial contempt implicit in Roosevelt's "big stick" policy in the Caribbean. In 1903, when in the process of seizing the Isthmus of Panama, he made clear his contempt for the Latin Americans who had dared to oppose his plans. Roosevelt characterized the Colombians as belonging to a "corrupt pithecoid community" that was "hardly entitled to the same treatment that European nations merited."[17] He explained that the "Bogota lot of jack rabbits should not be allowed permanently to bar one of the future highways of civilization."[18] He employed force to make sure that they did not.

In the following year, in terms that he had used earlier, the president unilaterally claimed the right in the Western hemisphere "to the exercise of an international police power."[19] This Roosevelt Corollary to the Monroe Doctrine was based on the assumption that the United States as "a civilized nation" had a right to impose its will on presumedly backward, inferior, and usually "colored" peoples. A year later, in what has been described as "merely another expression of his belief in the superiority of his race," Roosevelt employed this rationale to make an informal protectorate of the Dominican Republic.[20] American troops remained stationed there for several years. Critics point out that the same ethnoracial prejudice was equally prominent in other Caribbean ventures.

An analogous racialism marked the reaction to an uprising of blacks in May 1912 in Cuba's Oriente province. They fought for privileges denied them by a government headed by José Miguel Gómez which had a close relationship with the United States. Alarmed by apparent threats to Americans and their property, and by clashes between blacks and white mobs in Havana, Washington decided on a show of force to prevent the blacks, who constituted about a third of the island's population, from gaining power. In June Washington "sent warships and marines . . . without formal intervention" to save the largely white regime.[21]

This black insurrection, known also as the "race war" or the "Negro Revolt," which was suppressed by the end of June, evidently in part for racial reasons, destroyed much of the remaining sentiment in the United States for annexation. Policymakers now became content to control Cuba indirectly through the Platt Amendment, which was embodied in the Cuban constitution and in a treaty which gave the United States the right to intervene in the island's affairs.

All the while, the dedication of the American and British elites to close friendship and even synchronization in their countries' foreign affairs remained strong. The effect of this fraternal feeling on policy was evident in an episode that had begun in December 1902 when Germany, Britain, and Italy resorted to force to collect debts from Venezuela. These interventionists sank part of Venezuela's navy and blockaded her major ports. Americans quickly assumed that Germany intended to seize Venezuelan territory and thereby violate the Monroe Doctrine. Roosevelt claimed that by threatening to use the navy under Admiral George Dewey in Venezuela, he forced a reluctant Germany to arbitrate the dispute.

Even though the British also had a hand in initiating the intervention and were at first as uncompromising as the Germans, "neither the American people nor many of its newspapers felt Britain had sinister motives." Roosevelt said later that he "knew that there was no danger from England." So, in good part because of the rapprochement and the ethnocultural bond, Britain "was on the whole exonerated from evil intent and the onus of American opinion fell on Germany."[22]

Several years later close attention to the status of the Anglo-American connection led Roosevelt and others of like persuasion to see at least something positive in the variety of the new immigration. "There is just one redeeming feature about all these new nationalities" entering the country, he explained. It "has diminished what used to be the one feeling of hostility, that against England." He also observed that "the result of this mixture of ethnic prejudice is that in a measurable degree each acts as an antiscorbutic to the others."[23]

In the desire to maintain the close relationship between the mother country and her offspring, some transatlantic leaders even became willing to step beyond the boundaries of Anglo-Saxonism. In this vein, while visiting the United States in December 1910, Britain's Admiral Lord Fisher brought up an idea that had been around for years but that was now gaining increasing acceptance in governing circles. He remarked that "nationalities of every species pour into the United States. . . . But in the second generation they are *all pure Americans*—their language English, their literature English, their traditions English! What d——d fools we shall be if we don't exploit this into a huge Federation of the English-speaking peoples."[24]

Among the American political and intellectual leaders who shared a comparable outlook, Woodrow Wilson, the scholar-politician, stood out. He cherished his English roots and loved English culture, but unlike Fisher he questioned the ability of outsiders to become a part of it even indirectly. In his academic writings Wilson held that race, more than anything else, determined a nation's destiny. He expressed a loathing for southeastern Europeans, non-whites, and minorities in general who, because of their "race," could not measure up to Anglo-Saxon standards. While still president of Princeton University, he had praised John Hay for upholding "our happy alliance of sentiment and purpose with Great Britain." Later Wilson carried this attitude, along with other "ethnocultural perceptions and assumptions," into his conduct of foreign policy.[25]

In some ways Wilson exceeded Roosevelt's ethnoracial phobias, as in his coziness with Southern racism, though Roosevelt has been characterized "as the more self-conscious white racist of the two." Wilson's words in May 1912 while he campaigned for president revealed his position. "I stand for the national policy of exclusion," he said. "The whole question is one of assimilation of diverse races. We cannot make a homogeneous population of a people who do not blend with the Caucasian race."[26] While he occupied the White House, the segregation of blacks in government agencies, a practice which he defended, and in the city of Washington increased.

Prejudices such as these quickly again affected relations with Japan. Soon after Wilson took office, he had to deal with a measure before the California legislature that would prohibit aliens "ineligible to citizenship," meaning at this point mainly Japanese immigrants, from owning or even leasing agricultural land. The Californians made it clear that "the assimilation of races and not the ownership of land is the crux of the situation." On May 9, 1913, the Japanese government strongly protested this bill as "unfair and discriminatory" and as violating its treaty rights.[27]

Although Japan, too, had laws against alien ownership of land, its people, not just the government, regarded the California legislation, because of its specific nature, as again singling them out for insult. In public demonstrations many Japanese even demanded war to avenge it. American armed forces prepared for possible hostilities. Even though Wilson tried to soften California's anti-Japanese Alien Land Law, which other western states such as Washington, Arizona, and New Mexico copied, he failed. Beyond this effort he did nothing substantive to defuse an international crisis brought on by racism rather than by the economics of land-holding.

The president and his secretary of state reacted more forcefully to crises in Latin American countries inhabited mainly by people of color. There, they launched a series of interventions more extensive than those under Roosevelt and Taft. In each instance complex attitudes of ethnoracial superiority, along with a condescending but genuine missionary zeal to uplift the assumedly benighted peoples of the Caribbean and Mexico, suffused American policy.

In July 1915 this mixture of morality, racism, and strategic concerns brought American bayonets to Haiti. Wilson justified the occupation of the country, in the wake of mob violence, as an effort to bring its people civil and financial order. Yet in the face of dogged resistance by *cacos*, or native guerrillas, the occupiers fought what critics perceived as a racial war of extermination. Before it ended, American marines slaughtered more than 2,250 Haitians while suffering less than 16 casualties.

The small number of African-Americans who at this time followed foreign-policy developments, as did other analysts, saw in the government's high-handed methods a deep "contempt for colored people." Judge Felix Frankfurter called the occupation an "exploitation of and brutality towards the 'inferior race' and degradation of the 'superior race.'"

Later, as the Haitian occupation continued, the National Association for the Advancement of Colored People, the African-American special-interest organization founded in 1910, took the lead in opposing it. The involved African-Americans wrote letters to the State Department protesting the occupation's racial injustices and "agitated for participation in the policymaking that affected Haiti." Their lobbying reflected what would become a rising sense of identity with the "kindred peoples of African descent in other parts of the world."[28]

No such lobbying softened Wilson's interventions in Mexico, the most extensive in his missionary crusade. There the anti-Yankee antagonism of the war of 1846 had never died. In the twentieth century racist discrimination and other injustices against Mexicans living in the Southwest kept the mutual antipathies alive. News of a lynching of a compatriot, as in Rocksprings, Texas, in November 1910, would inflame people in Mexico who would vent their hatred in angry demonstrations and in often-repeated slogans such as "Death to the Yankees." The Americans, one newspaper said, are "giants of the dollar, pigmies of culture, and barbarous whites of the north."[29] Such anti-Gringo sentiment permeated Mexico's revolution, which began in the same month as the Rocksprings incident, even though it was led by the pro-American idealist Francisco Madero.

That idealism gave way to the opportunism of Madero's chief of staff, General Victoriano Huerta, who in February 1913 seized power through force. A month later, after entering the White House, Wilson denounced Huerta as a usurper who had murdered Madero. The new president refused to recognize Huerta's government and instituted a policy of compelling him to abdicate his authority. Wilson aided Huerta's opponents, while stationing naval vessels off the Mexican coast to prevent him from receiving foreign arms. In resisting this pressure, Huerta whipped up the ever-present anti-Americanism. At a rally of three thousand in Nuevo Laredo, for instance, supporters announced that "Huerta would brook no insult or humiliation from the Yankees."[30]

In April 1914, when Wilson exploited a trivial incident to land troops at Tampico and then at Vera Cruz, the old and new hatreds burst into violence. At Vera Cruz over two hundred Mexicans and nineteen Americans died. More anti-Yankee demonstrations swept through Mexico. In Mexico City adults and children marched through the streets chanting "Death to the Gringos." Still, the president claimed that "We have gone down to Mexico to serve mankind if we can find a way."[31] Seeing mainly the spilled blood of their people, many Mexicans, even those who had been enemies, ignored this moral rhetoric and rallied behind Huerta. War seemed probable. It was averted when Wilson in November withdrew the American forces from Vera Cruz.

Huertistas continued, nevertheless, to exploit anti-Yankee sentiments. In January 1915 some of them, as outlined in the Plan of San Diego, Texas, attempted to foment a revolution among the Mexican-Americans and Mexican nationals in Texas that would end the "economic exploitation and racial discrimination of non-Anglos by 'white' Americans." The *revoltosos'* "Manifesto to the Oppressed Peoples of America" called for "a war to the death against all Anglo-Americans." That war never happened because immigration authorities arrested a key leader. But that summer other *revoltosos*, in bands of twenty-five to a hundred, raided "ranches, robbed stores, and burned bridges in south Texas," setting off an anti-Mexican hysteria and racial vigilantism among Anglos that added to the bloodletting.[32]

Early in the following year troops under another revolutionary leader, Francisco (Pancho) Villa, who resented the American assistance to a rival, Venustiano Carranza, raided towns in Texas and New Mexico and murdered Americans. Without the consent of any government in Mexico, Wilson sent a punitive expedition of 5,000 troops across the border in pursuit of Villa. Along the Texas border the killings and bloodier white reprisals against Mexicans "led to fears of a race war." Hawks and others who desired war denounced the Mexicans with racial epithets, saying in one instance, "They can't fight. Take a look at those stupid little peons and you will understand why."[33]

Again, when even Villa's Mexican opponents resisted this invasion, war seemed imminent. It was avoided mainly because Wilson, faced with the probability of larger conflict with Germany, in February 1917 withdrew the troops. Regardless of the president's good intentions, his effort to impose his will upon Mexico smacked of a racism that Mexicans easily recognized.

As for most Americans, they showed a greater concern over what effect ethnic affiliation might have on foreign policy because of the war in Europe, which had begun in August 1914, than over the ethnoracial aspects of the

confrontation with Mexico. At that time the foreign-born and first-generation Americans constituted about one-third of the population, or 32 out of
94 million or more people. These statistics fueled the establishment's alarm
over possible disunity because of the real or imagined affinities of minorities
for their countries of origin. "We definitely have to be neutral," Wilson was
reported as saying, "since otherwise our mixed populations would wage war
on each other."[34]

Whether or not the president believed in a true neutrality, the latter part
of his analysis was sound. The World War quickened the ethnic consciousness of minority groups. They promptly created organizations to help the
causes of their old European homelands that had become belligerents.
Through whatever means possible, the ethnic activists among them sought
to give direction to Washington on matters of policy that affected their
overseas kin, making the United States a lobbying battleground between
rival interest groups emotionally entangled in the war. The strength of the
ethnic bond among the Anglo-, Irish-, and German-Americans, whose
Americanization had long been taken for granted, and also their antagonisms, now cast doubt on assimilation theory even among habitual believers.

In the perspective of the largely assimilated German- and Irish-Americans, Wilsonian neutrality, with its acquiescence in British control of the
seas, seemed to require them to support a program that provided mountains
of American munitions and other goods to the Allied side. Resentful Ger-
man- and Irish-American organizations therefore attacked this aspect of the
administration's foreign policy. Their sometimes coordinated activity,
which many took as evidence of divided loyalty, alarmed the Anglo-American elite. It maintained that since these minorities would not conform to
national policies, "the melting pot was failing to melt."[35]

The Anglo establishment, which condemned the persistence of ethnic
diversity as incompatible with national unity, insisted anew upon a patriotic
American solidarity that it had defined. Using the hyphenate slur, which
"was never applied to Americans of English ancestry, even to those who
were noisy partisans of Great Britain," its leaders assailed the minority
groups.[36] The establishment launched an Americanization movement that
demanded the forswearing of minority ethnic identities and the immediate
acceptance of Anglo conformity, or what sociologists would later call "pres-
sure-cooking assimilation." This drive for "100 percent Americanism"
marked a peak in nativism and in the diplomacy of the rapprochement with
Britain.[37]

All the while, those nativists who deplored old-world connections other than their own practiced singularly effective ethnic politics in favor of the Allied side. They could do so with some ease because the president, almost all of his cabinet members, and most of his weighty advisers were Anglo-Americans or Anglophiles. Furthermore, the Americans of British origin still outnumbered those of any other ethnic group in the country, and their political leverage remained greater than that of their opponents. As Walter Hines Page, the Anglophile American ambassador in Britain, had explained in Southampton in August 1913, "Blood" is what "makes us all English in the last resort." Thus, despite its "fusion of races . . . the United States is yet English-led and English-ruled."[38] Even though his comments caused a minor furor when they reached the United States, seldom had the American government been as close to Britain's, and seldom had it evinced less criticism of Britain.

As with the governing elite, millions of ordinary Americans were aroused by the allegations of disloyalty in the white minority population. Therefore, to complement his pro-Allied diplomacy, Wilson began a campaign against hyphenism by attacking German- and Irish-Americans. "You cannot become thorough Americans if you think of yourselves in groups," he told newly naturalized citizens in May 1915. "America does not consist of groups." Those who regard themselves "as belonging to a particular national group in America," or trade upon the nationality of immigrants, are not worthy "to live under the Stars and Stripes."[39] In keeping with this theme, the government sanctioned the first official Americanization Day, celebrating it appropriately on July 4 with the slogan "Many Peoples But One Nation."

In October a popular journal, the *Literary Digest*, plugged this Americanization theme by declaring hyphenism the most vital issue of the day. In the following year social critic Randolph S. Bourne denounced the anti-hyphen crusaders who insisted "that the alien shall be forcibly assimilated to that Anglo-Saxon tradition which they unquestioningly label 'American.'" He added "that no more tenacious cultural allegiance to the mother country has been shown by any alien nation than by the ruling class of Anglo-Saxon descendants in these American States." Praise of Englishness has "been the cultural food that we have drunk in from our mothers' breasts."[40]

As Bourne and later critics have pointed out, the Americanizers "were very often guilty of their own kind of hyphenism. Many were, whether they recognized it or not, British-Americans."[41] Bourne explained, "It is only because it has been the ruling class that in this country bestowed the epithets that we have not heard copiously and scornfully of 'hyphenated En-glish-Americans.'"[42]

The hyphenates that the Americanizers feared most were the German-Americans, who in the decades preceding the war had formed the nation's largest and best organized white minority community. Only the Anglo-Americans had exceeded them in contributing substantively to the shaping of American society. From the start of the European conflict in 1914, knowledgeable German-American leaders realized that they could not over-come the Anglo dominance of foreign policy in any effort to obtain assis-tance for Germany. Still, they hoped to retain enough leverage to hold the government to a policy of what they perceived as impartial neutrality.

Their organizations, many of them federated in the National German-American Alliance, therefore passed resolutions opposing aid to the Allied side. In the winter of 1914–15, as American munitions flowed to Britain and France, the German-Americans launched a campaign for an embargo on the export of implements of war. Since such a prohibition would injure Britain more than Germany, the Anglo-Americans correctly construed the effort as support for the fatherland. In consequence, the status of the Ger-man-Americans, regardless of how well they may have been assimilated, quickly deteriorated.

The president fretted that the German-American resentment against him would produce a political upheaval, but as the group's power receded, so did his apprehension. The British government, however, remained anxious over any kind of German influence on American policy. Sir Cecil Spring-Rice, Britain's ambassador in Washington, summarized this worry over the potential political power of the German-Americans. "They are organised for un-American and purely German purposes," he wrote. "They propose to put pressure on all candidates for office and to carry out their policy by the intimidation of Congressmen and Presidents, either actual or would be. . . . it is not inconceivable that the formation of a strong and compact State within the State should not create a reaction."[43]

Foreign Secretary Sir Edward Grey was troubled by such views and also by reports that the German- and Irish-American pressures had given a neg-ative coloration to executive, congressional, and public opinion of the Al-lies. So, even though the American government was pro-British, he said that he might establish committees in the United States to counter anti-Allied ethnic activity with "energetic" British propaganda.

At the same time, despite being intimidated by the hostility against them, many German-Americans charged Wilson with singling them out for insult because they dared to challenge his foreign policy with demands for a strict neutrality. Of course, their kind of neutrality would benefit the Central Powers. In his campaign for reelection in 1916, Wilson expressed annoyance with the German- and Irish-Americans for just that reason. As did the Anglo nativists, they regarded Wilson's policy toward the European war as a major issue in the election. Regardless, the Anglo-Americans knew that he favored their side.

The president charged these minorities hostile to his foreign policy with "trying to levy a species of blackmail" against him and his party with the threat of punishment at the polls. At his instigation, the Democrats took a strong stand against the presumed duality of minority loyalty. Their party platform announced that hyphenism "by arousing prejudice of a racial, religious or other nature creates discord and strife among our people so as to obstruct the wholesome process of unification." It also injures the government "in its foreign relations."[44] Despite Theodore Roosevelt's equivalent views, the Republican platform remained silent on the subject of hyphenism.

Some Republicans sought to exploit the antipathy of the German-Americans toward Wilson. To offset this opposition, Democrats took to cultivating those ethnic groups whose people in the old homelands regarded the Germans as enemies. As part of this new emphasis on minority issues, Wilson in 1915 had vetoed a bill, similar to others proposed earlier, that required literacy tests for immigrants. Its proponents saw in it the means of saving the Anglo-Americans from being swamped by the Slavs, Italians, Jews, and other presumed undesirables who had been entering the country at a rate four times greater than the northern Europeans.

Soon after his renomination, Wilson again took a stand against such tests, manifesting a considerable interest in the offspring of the new immigrants he had formerly despised. He sought to balance German- and Irish-American politicking with the votes of Slavic-Americans such as the Poles, who made up by far the largest Slavic community in the United States. They endorsed his reelection "in glowing terms." Nonetheless, in February 1917, congress, in its codification of the nationality statutes, used the anti-hyphenate sentiment that Wilson had himself exploited, to pass a literacy law over his veto.

In this instance Wilson had taken a moral position in defense of immigrants in general. Otherwise he seemed unaware of his inconsistency in supporting the foreign-policy causes of some ethnic groups while attacking those of others. His belief that "England is fighting our fight" reflected his selectivity in choosing which ethnic groups to favor.[45] At this point he denounced as hyphenates mainly those, such as the German- and Irish-

Americans, who opposed his foreign policy because they were convinced that it favored the Allies.

Despite Wilson's harsh attitude toward his minority opponents in the presidential campaign, the Democrats benefited from Roosevelt's more vehement attacks on the non-Anglo ethnic groups. In addition to embarrassing Charles Evans Hughes, the Republican candidate, Teddy's fulminations made the Republican efforts to cultivate the German-Americans seem disingenuous. Even though Hughes did not himself raise the ethnic issue, many German-Americans had serious misgivings about his views on foreign policy because he seemed dominated by people such as Roosevelt. More fiercely than Wilson, Roosevelt singled out the German-Americans for affront, denouncing them for acting "purely in the sinister interest of Germany." He condemned their "adherence to the politico-racial hyphen which is the badge and sign of moral treason to the Republic."[46]

In October the Republican leaders, who were disturbed by his ranting, asked Roosevelt to soft-pedal the hyphenate issue. So strongly did he feel about it, however, that he threatened to resign from party activity rather than let up in his rhetoric. Most analysts believe that Teddy's diatribes frightened the usually Republican German-American voters to such an extent that many of them deserted Hughes. Even though they disliked Wilson, they hated Roosevelt more. Journalists noted Hughes' dilemma, commenting, for example, that to placate pro-German supporters he had to risk antagonizing his pro-British constituency which demanded war with Germany.

The Irish-Americans, too, incurred considerable hostility, because many of them acted on the assumption that an independent Ireland would emerge from the defeat of Britain. Their anti-British stance also led them to occasional cooperation with German-Americans in matters of foreign policy which could benefit their old homeland. Although less numerous than the German-Americans, they were more zealous in their ethnic politics, a quality that prompted critics to maintain that the Irish-Americans had long exercised an influence on foreign policy out of proportion to their numbers. Reflecting this point of view, Walter Hines Page suggested, for example, that "we Americans have got to hang our Irish agitators and shoot our hyphenates and bring up our children with reverence for English history and in the awe of English literature."[47]

Such sentiments, of course, enraged the Irish-Americans. Some of them who belonged to the Clan-na-Gael, which still sought to achieve independence for Ireland through anti-British violence, went along with the organization's plotting with the Germans. They also backed the plan of Roger D.

Casement, an Irish nationalist who had served in the British consular service and who had engaged in fund-raising in the United States, for an uprising in Dublin on April 24, 1916, during Easter week. When Casement returned to Ireland in a German submarine, ironically to stop the rebellion because of feared failure, British authorities captured him, crushed the rebels, and executed fifteen of their leaders. A British tribunal convicted Casement of treason and sentenced him to death.

Shocked by the killings, Irish-Americans and others asked Wilson to intervene to save Casement. The president refused, saying there was no legal case for it. Nonetheless, because many of its members desired to cultivate Irish votes, the senate on July 29 passed a resolution asking the British government to exercise clemency. Wilson unaccountably delayed his forwarding of the petition. Even if the British had been inclined to heed the plea, it arrived too late to save Casement. On August 3 British authorities hanged him without arousing significant American protest. Irish-Americans charged that the president's refusal to intervene and his foot-dragging with the congressional resolution had cost Casement his life.

This turmoil occurred during the presidential campaign while both parties were courting minority voters. The Irish-American activist organizations, which usually supported the Democrats, now vigorously opposed Wilson's reelection. He, in turn, repudiated them. In September, when Jeremiah A. O'Leary, an Irish-American leader, protested the administration's pro-British policies, Wilson responded, "I would feel deeply mortified to have you or anybody like you vote for me. Since you have access to many disloyal Americans and I have not, I will ask you to convey this message to them."[48] Such disdain infuriated many of the nation's Irish, but not enough for them to desert the Democrats in mass so as to influence the election significantly.

Even though Wilson won reelection in good measure because he ran as the peace candidate, in April 1917 the United States declared war on Germany. The reasons for the intervention are complex, and historians debate them constantly. Scholars usually agree upon Germany's resumption of unrestricted submarine warfare as the immediate cause. But for underlying causation they focus on American economic ties with the Allies, on the fear that a German victory would injure American interests or upset a world balance of power favorable to the United States and the Allies, and on other concerns. Yet even within this tangled causal web, the ethnic connection between the American and British elites stands out as a compelling reason.

In keeping with this affiliation, the United States upon becoming a belligerent sponsored "Loyalty Days" designed to inculcate a patriotic Americanism among immigrants and their kin. As had become usual, this Americanism was often equated with Englishness. A federal judge even enjoined the production of a movie, *The Spirit of '76*, because presumably it "would slacken American loyalty to Great Britain."[49] In this mood in June 1917 congress passed the Espionage Act and in May of the following year the Sedition Act. Both were designed to reinforce the patriotism of conformity by hobbling the German-Americans and others who had opposed intervention. Under the authority of the espionage law, authorities jailed Jeremiah O'Leary for continuing to attack Britain.

Even though in the course of the war the German-Americans, like the Irish-Americans, showed what seemed even to the nativist establishment a surprising loyalty to the nation, they were harassed everywhere, suffered violation of their civil rights, and were abused by local vigilantes. Superpatriots demanded the eradication of all evidence of German culture in the United States. Communities outlawed the German language in schools and burned German books. Mobs assaulted former opponents of intervention, tarred-and-feathered some, and lynched a German alien. Congress investigated the German-American Alliance because it "had been at odds with the dominant notions of Anglo-conformity." The lawmakers then canceled the alliance's charter. A German-American spokesman lamented that "we are attacked, suspected, and slandered. . . . They want us to condemn our native speech, our laboriously created societies, and even our own flesh and blood."[50]

Ethnic fidelity became an even broader international consideration following the Bolshevik Revolution in Russia in November 1917. The Bolsheviks demanded a peace "on the basis of an entire and complete recognition of the principle of self-determination for all peoples and in all states," or the right of subject peoples to decide their own status.[51] Wilson, who had already announced his support for such a concept, responded on January 8, 1918, with what would become his most famous wartime speech. Among the fourteen points that he listed as war objectives, he alluded to, but did not mention self-determination.

A month later the president declared the implementation of the self-rule idea a foremost goal of American foreign policy. "Self-determination is not a mere phrase," he said. "It is an imperative principle of action which statesmen will henceforth ignore at their peril."[52] Later he elaborated, but did not precisely define, this principle. To hasten victory, other Allied leaders more or less went along with it.

In the United States the Anglo-Americans were pleased with the address because it offered them assurance of continued solidarity with Britain. For this same reason Irish-American leaders viewed it with distrust. John Devoy, a veteran Irish revolutionary, emphasized that Wilson's points covering nationality applied "only to a portion of the world—that controlled by Germany and her allies—and utterly ignore the rest." Devoy asked bluntly, "What about English imperialism?"[53]

In general, the ethnic groups in the United States reacted to the fourteen points program according to its perceived effect on ancestral countries. Many of their spokesmen quickly hailed Wilson as a great humanitarian because his words led them to believe that self-determination applied to all their old homelands. What he had in mind was in fact much narrower. Wilson conceived the principle of national self-determination as a war measure that would be meaningful for peoples dominated by enemy nations, not for those, for example, in colonies controlled by Britain or France.

In Paris many observers, such as Ho Chi Minh, a twenty-eight-year-old Vietnamese, took Wilson's words seriously. They quickly learned that the principle did not extend to yellow, brown, and black peoples living under white rule, or even to the Europeans who inhabited territories controlled by the victorious Allied powers.

Only in the case of Poland, in his thirteenth point which called for its independence, did Wilson make an outright commitment to self-determination. This was an astonishing development, because until the close of his first term Polish-Americans had had virtually no national political influence. Furthermore, as with other minorities, he had earlier expressed contempt for Poles. Wilson's interest in Polish independence coincided with his campaign for reelection, in which he demonstrated a tolerance for hyphenates if they could bring him political benefit. After his victory, wherein Polish-Americans in several crucial states voted for him in large numbers, the president responded to their advocacy for an independent Poland.

When the United States became a belligerent, Wilson exerted considerable effort for the Polish cause. Like the Czechs and Slovaks in the United States who lobbied Washington for a state independent of Austria-Hungary, the Poles profited from the principle of self-determination. Washington contributed to the rising expectations in matters of foreign affairs among such ethnic groups by cultivating the aspirations to independence of ethnic minorities within the lands of the Central Powers and elsewhere.

The Committee on Public Information, the government's propaganda agency, headed by George Creel, was prominent in this activity. It had "intimate contact" with virtually every major immigrant group in the country.[54] In 1918, as part of this effort, Creel formed the organization of Oppressed Nationalities of Central Europe, headed by the Czech patriot

Thomas G. Masaryk and the Polish musician and patriot Ignace J. Paderewski. Creel regarded this association as the most effective of his propaganda creations.

In the case of Czechoslovakia, the ethnic politicking of "the Czech and Slovak immigrants in the United States" appeared less significant than their "moral and financial" support for kin abroad. The lobbying of prominent Czechs such as Masaryk did help in winning over Wilson, "major newspapers," and "influential congressional leaders" to the cause of their homeland's independence.[55] In the case of Poland, persuasive scholarship suggests that Wilson's backing for its regeneration came in good measure as a reward to Polish-Americans for past and anticipated political support. In the following year his endorsement contributed critically to the reestablishing of the Polish state. Thus, in this instance, another of the new minority groups, as well as its mother country, gained substantially from its ethnic politics.

All the while, the Anglo-American elite endeavored to enhance its influence over the definition of delicate issues such as self-determination which, if broadly construed, could lead to the disintegration of the British empire. In line with this objective, in July 1918 one of the elite's prominent figures provided most of the financing for the English-Speaking Union, another joint ethnocultural organization founded by leaders in Britain and America. Publicly the union sought to promote "good fellowship among the English-speaking democracies of the world."[56] Like its predecessor, the British-American Association, however, the union quickly became something more—another force for advancing British-American solidarity in world affairs.

The power of this transatlantic togetherness stood out in the peace-making in Paris in 1919, where Wilson reacted with particular awareness to British desires. Seldom did he or his diplomatists stray far from their objective of maintaining the close relationship with Britain. At times, though, they had to balance this attachment with responses to a diverse electorate more sensitized to foreign-policy issues than in the past. Minority groups were now better organized, voted their interests in larger numbers, and were more effective in politics than they had ever been. The Anglo-American elite thus could no longer dismiss their desires in foreign affairs as though they were of minor consequence within the larger pattern of American policy.

At Paris as well as at home, because of the expectations among suppressed ethnic groups everywhere for attaining liberty that Wilson's rhetoric and Creel's activity had aroused, some of Washington's propaganda backfired. Armenians, Turks, Persians, the Indians of South Asia, Southeast Asians,

African groups, and others quickly became disillusioned by the Allied policies, and particularly by Wilson's constricted commitment to self-determination. They liked the concept but resented being excluded from its application. Those subordinated groups with numerous kin in the United States, however, looked to ethnic politics to expand the American obligation to the principle of self-determination, usually as it would affect them.

Secretary of State Robert Lansing and others had anticipated that the president's perspective on the issue would cause trouble. Lansing had asked, "why, since we are so solicitous about oppressed nations, do we not take a definite stand for the independence of Ireland, Egypt, India, and South Africa . . . ?" Domestically and internationally, he regarded self-determination as "a very unwise policy," pointing out that it was incompatible with Allied colonial policies and with the close connection with England. "Great Britain," he explained, "has already an unenviable reputation for having one rule for herself and another rule for other nations."[57]

Irish-American lobbyists in particular made an issue of the British inconsistencies. Despite their disappointment with Wilson's earlier rejection of their goals, through the bargaining at Paris they also still sought to aid their overseas kin, now locked in rebellion against the British. As much as almost anything else, the Irish-Americans wanted the peacemakers to "apply to Ireland the great doctrine of national self-determination."

Three days after the armistice, the Friends of Irish Freedom, a lobby committed to influencing foreign policy, launched a nationwide campaign to pressure congress and the president to intervene with Britain for independence for the old homeland. During Self-Determination Week, December 8–15, 1918, they sponsored mass meetings across the country to generate support for their cause. They persuaded both the senate and the house of representatives to pass resolutions, by overwhelming votes, calling on the negotiators in Paris to "favorably consider the claims of Ireland to the right of self-determination."[58] Again, largely because of his English predilections and anger over being pressured, the president rebuffed the Irish-Americans.

At Paris this Anglo-Saxonist intimacy, along with an insensitivity to white racism, also brought Wilson into a confrontation with the Japanese. In Tokyo the prejudice against Japanese immigrants embedded in American laws had never ceased to rankle, especially since similar disabilities did not apply to white aliens. The Japanese foreign ministry therefore approached the peace-making determined, through international agreement, to place curbs on discrimination based on race. Newspapers such as the Tokyo *Asahi* asserted that "fairness and equality must be secured for the colored races who form 62% of the whole of mankind." Even though the Japanese said that they desired equal treatment "not only for Japan but for all the countries of Asia," as in the past their attitude on ethnoracial matters was contradictory.[59] They deplored insult to their own kind, but they continued to discriminate against others as, for example, Koreans.

Regardless of their own inconsistencies, the Japanese, on raising the racial issue at Paris, perceived Wilson as the key figure. From the start, their delegation solicited American support for the insertion of a statement on racial equality in the covenant of the League of Nations. Despite his eloquence on self-determination, however, the president had not shed his racist feelings. He also assumed that the senate would not permit the United States to join the League of Nations if its covenant stated that whites and people of color were equals. As with the Irish, therefore, he rebuffed the Japanese.

Japan's representative, Nobuaki Makino, then appealed the equality proposal to the League of Nations Commission as a whole. When Wellington Koo, representing China, backed the measure, an American delegate commented that "in this great question of world policy, it is highly significant that the Chinese, though suspicious of the Japanese in every other way, came here to their support." This was about the "only issue on which the Chinese and Japanese delegations saw eye-to-eye."[60]

In Japan, private citizens formed an Association for the Elimination of Racial Discrimination. A leading newspaper commented that although Americans were "very sensitive of race problems," they had to be reminded of their Declaration of Independence's "unmistakable guarantees of justice and equality" for "all mankind."[61] As in past agitation over issues of race, the anti-Americanism escalated. Viscount Kikujiro Ishii, Japan's ambassador to the United States, asked, "Why should this question of race prejudice, of race discrimination, of race humiliation be left unremedied?"[62] Japanese-Americans agreed with him. Those in Hawaii sent telegrams to the president's delegation urging support for the anti-racist principle.

On April 11, 1919, in the final session of the League Commission chaired by Wilson, eleven of seventeen members voted for the Japanese proposal. The American, British, and Australian representatives opposed it. Wilson then ruled that majority approval was insufficient to permit the equality measure to be included in the covenant. It required unanimous endorsement. Most of those present were shocked. They knew that on two other occasions, with Wilson himself involved, the commission had not demanded unanimity. Blaming the "Anglo-Saxons" for the defeat, the Japanese condemned the president for using one voting arrangement to carry out his ethnoracial prejudices and another for everyone else.

In failing to grasp the intensity of feeling on this issue, American policymakers appeared obtuse or racist. Friends and critics of Japan alike regarded her at Paris as the standard bearer of the colored cause and not as an inconsequential nation deserving of humiliation through parliamentary legerdemain. Furthermore, they perceived white racism as rooted in American foreign policy. This episode helped persuade the Japanese, as well as other non-whites, that what came out of Paris was a racist "Anglo-American peace."[63]

Japan and the United States also clashed over other ethnoracial issues, particularly as they touched self-determination in China. In January 1915 the Japanese had secretly pressed twenty-one demands which would have impaired China's sovereignty. Wilson's government, which learned about them, tried to block the Japanese plan, while the Chinese in the United States rushed to the support of their old homeland by organizing a boycott of Japanese goods. Even though this outside pressure persuaded the Japanese to drop some of their demands, neither the American protest nor the boycott kept them from imposing in May a coercive treaty on China. In it, among other concessions, the Chinese recognized Japan's preeminence in Shantung, which it had conquered from Germany.

When the Japanese at Paris attempted to obtain international assent for retaining Shantung, the Chinese opposed them, as did Wilson, at first. He argued, properly in this instance, that the control the Japanese desired over a Chinese population which despised their hegemony would violate the self-determination principle. Given his stand on racial equality and related issues, the Japanese viewed the American opposition as hypocritical. Of course, they again failed, or refused, to see their own hypocrisy, as in their effort to dominate the Chinese while they protested American racism. Finally, to keep the Japanese from bolting the conference, Wilson retreated from self-determination by going along with a recognition of Japan's interests in Shantung in return for her promise ultimately to return the province to China.

The president's conception of self-determination also brought him into conflict with specific Italian territorial demands. In the bargaining at Paris, Italy received, as had been promised by the Allies in a secret treaty, a rectified northern boundary that placed about 200,000 Austrians of German blood under her rule. Wilson accepted this violation of self-determination because he believed that Italy deserved a defensible frontier. When Italian nationalists demanded more, in particular part of Dalmatia including the city of Fiume, inhabited mainly by South Slavs, Wilson in a logical defense of his principle said no. Yet, like the Japanese, the Italians noted the contradictions in his diplomacy. They pointed out that he did not block the territorial claims of other Allies based on secret arrangements similar to those of Italy, arrangements which were incompatible with self-determination.

The president's selective use of the principle also antagonized Italian-American groups, which lobbied for a *Fiume Italiana*, telling the president that they "wholeheartedly supported the position of the mother country." Senator Henry Cabot Lodge, who previously had been openly contemptuous of minority hyphenates, now had a large Italian-American community in his home state. In March 1919 he assured these constituents that "Italy has no stronger friend than I—no one who will urge the satisfaction of her just claims more strongly than I."[64] In opposition to Wilson, he promised to support the Italian claim on Fiume regardless of its defiance of self-determination.

Lodge's position reflected the growing influence of assertive Italian-Americans who had persuaded the Massachusetts legislature to adopt, with only one dissenting vote, a resolution calling on the president to back Italy on the Fiume issue. At the same time, through its own ethnic politicking, America's less numerous South Slav community, composed mostly of Serbs and Croats, strove to keep the city out of Italian hands.

Former Secretary of State Elihu Root noted the president's dilemma of trying to conduct a foreign policy that wavered in its sensitivity to issues vital to ethnic constituencies. "How can we prevent dissension and hatred among our own inhabitants of foreign origin," he asked, "when the country interferes on foreign grounds between the races from which they spring?"[65] In this instance the ethnic discord did not produce any striking change in Wilson's behavior, in part because the lobbying of the South Slav and Italian-American groups virtually canceled each other's effect on foreign policy.

The advocacy of Jewish-Americans for Zionism, or a national home in Palestine, did not encounter the kind of internal opposition that confronted the Italian-Americans. The Zionist situation was striking because during the war, or at least until April 1917, American Jews had sided with the Central Powers. Initially they had rejoiced in German and Austrian victories. The editors of a Yiddish newspaper explained why. "The Jews support Germany because Russia bathes in Jewish blood . . . ," they declared. "Who will dare say that it is a crime for Jews to hate their torturers, their oppressors and murderers?"[66]

Despite this pro-German attitude among Jews, during the war British leaders desired their financial backing. The British flirted with Zionism on the premise that they could elicit goodwill among Jews and encourage them to open their purses. The British also believed that their Jewish courtship would please the United States, where Zionism had acquired support from all levels of Jewish life and with it political leverage. So, on November 2, 1917, Foreign Secretary Arthur J. Balfour tried to tap "American sympathy for the British cause" and to influence the Zionists by declaring that "His Majesty's Government view with favour the establishment in Palestine of a national home for the Jewish people and will use their best endeavours to fulfuill the achievement of this objective."[67]

Although Wilson initially was indifferent to Zionism, he endorsed the declaration because of "political considerations," because even though American Jews were divided, many stood behind it, and especially because the British desired his support.[68] Zionism also touched his "deep Christian sentiment favoring the fulfillment of biblical prophecy."[69] Scores of telegrams from proponents thanked him. Apparently, though, Wilson was unaware of, or refused to understand, the contradiction between sympathy for Arab self-determination in Palestine and support for Zionism.

At Paris, where various Zionists pressured the peacemakers to make good the Balfour pledge, the Jewish-Americans concentrated on the president. Since he was already committed to their cause and desired their political support, he responded favorably to their lobbying.

As did the Jews, Armenian-Americans looked to Wilson to help kin in their old homeland. In 1895–96, in part out of ethnic enmity, the Ottoman Turks had slaughtered thousands of Christian Armenians within their empire. Beginning in 1915, with a similar motivation enhanced by their wartime alarm over Armenian collusion or possible collusion with the Russian enemy, the Turks massacred between 600,000 and a million Armenians in what has been described as a campaign of extermination.[70] Armenian-Americans, Protestant missionaries with whom they had close ties, and other sympathizers protested and formed committees that raised over $11 million for relief for the hungry and refugees.

On other issues the Armenian-American groups, composed largely of recent immigrants who were few and not yet politically acculturated, were often divided. Yet after the Armenians in May 1918 declared themselves independent of Turkey and proclaimed a republic, Armenian-Americans and Armenophiles in organizations such as the American Committee for the Independence of Armenia and the Armenia-America Society pressured Wilson's government to aid the new state. "Armenia," they said, "must be freed from Turkish rule and receive the sympathetic support and protection of the Allied Powers." By the end of 1919, Armenian communities in the

United States had rallied to the cause, and "a host of Armenophiles were demanding intervention."[71]

Even though Turkey and the United States had severed diplomatic relations, they had never declared war on each other. For this and other reasons Wilson, who ostensibly on humanitarian grounds favored the sending of American forces to police Armenia, would not forcibly intervene, but in April 1920 his government accorded the Armenian republic de facto recognition.

Wilson also wished to accept the proposal of Allied and Armenian leaders that the United States assume a mandate over Armenia to protect it and guide its independence. Under pressure from Armenian-American and Armenophile groups, the sick president on May 24 asked congress for permission to do what he desired, to accept the mandate. On June 1 the senate denied it. In August, in the peace treaty of Sèvres, the Allies and Turkey recognized Armenia's independence, but the agreement was never implemented. In December Turkish nationalists, in cooperation with the Bolsheviks, crushed the Republic of Armenia. A small portion of partitioned Armenia around Erivan survived as a Soviet republic.

The Allies then agreed to another conference, at Lausanne, that began in November 1922 to revise the peace terms with Turkey. Even though the United States would not be a party to the peace-making, it sent observers. Since the Allied treaty of Lausanne with Turkey of the following July did not provide for Armenia's independence, the Armenian-Americans and Armenophiles viewed it as part of a sellout of their people to the Turks.

In August 1923 the United States concluded in the same city a separate agreement with Turkey for the restoration of diplomatic and commercial relations. Through the American Committee Opposed to the Lausanne Treaty, Armenian-Americans, backed by influential sympathizers and politicians, lobbied against it. They even managed to have inserted in the Democratic platform of 1924 a condemnation of the treaty because it "betrays Armenia."[72]

In January 1927 the senate refused approval for this Lausanne treaty by a minority vote. The pro-Armenian and Armenian-American lobbyists had prevailed because of the weakness of their opponents and because of the popular odium against Turkey, which had been denigrated for years "by the missionaries and relief workers" as the "Terrible Turk." Joseph C. Grew, the American negotiator, commented later that Armenian-Americans had influenced "a small but aggressive group of American senators and bishops" and hence the defeat "was purely a question of domestic politics."[73]

Numbering less than a million and divided in outlook, the Armenian-

Americans were too few, however, to exert enough sustained political influence to prevent Washington from formalizing relations with Turkey through other arrangements. Nevertheless, the Armenian-Americans and their friends did organize mass meetings and other forms of protest against this renewal of diplomatic ties.

Ethnic politics of a different kind had permeated as well the larger aspects of the nation's foreign relations. They did so with notable effect in the battle over possible United States membership in the League of Nations. The league attracted its strongest supporters from the ranks of the Anglo-Americans, though quite a few of them, as well as the members of other significant ethnic groups, opposed it. Individual die-hard enemies, such as Senator William E. Borah of Idaho, cooperated with hostile minority leaders in the effort to defeat what they regarded as Wilson's own scheme for collective security. Senator Lodge, another opponent, advised the minorities that had been disappointed with the Paris peace-making of 1919 to work against Wilson, against the Versailles treaty of which the league was a part, and against the Democratic party.

Many Irish-Americans, because they were repelled by Wilson, did just what Lodge suggested. They were also influenced by the Sinn Fein nationalist movement, whose leaders in Dublin in January 1919 had proclaimed an Irish republic and fought the British—and a civil war—in trying to make the state a reality. A month after the proclamation, at the Third Irish Race Convention in Philadelphia, the American Irish pledged $1 million to the struggle in their old homeland. The Friends of Irish Freedom used some of the money to oppose United States membership in the League of Nations. They distributed 1.3 million pamphlets and published large advertisements in newspapers across the country that carried the anti-league message.

The president's supporters such as Senator John Sharp Williams of Mississippi castigated these tactics. They also attacked Borah and Lodge for appealing to ethnic prejudice. But Williams was himself a racist who upheld Jim Crow oppression in the South and who wanted to preserve the United States as "a white man's country." His tirades were as savage as those of the anti-league extremists. For example, he characterized Wilson as representing "the American people" and his opponents as fronting for "all of the enemy hyphenates in America." Even so, by late May 1919 a number of minorities were linking forces in a kind of ethnic revolt against the league. Wilson reacted bitterly, saying repeatedly that "hyphens are the knives that are being stuck into" the treaty of Versailles.[74]

Even the German-Americans, who had become politically isolated and had no significant effect on the peace-making, joined this opposition. Their dissatisfaction with the treaty of Versailles, expressed through ethnic politics, reputedly contributed to its rejection by the senate. Wilsonians such as Senator Carter Glass of Virginia condemned the Republicans for using the dissatisfied ethnic groups to defeat the treaty. "Instead of being a real American," he said, "what Lodge has done has been to array every racial group in the United States against real Americans."[75]

Politicians such as Glass, Irish-American activists, and some historians contend that minority ethnic politics were decisive in the killing of the league. George Creel, for instance, claimed that "the forces of hyphenation were boldly called into being and no effort was spared to revive and exaggerate the divisive prejudices of American life."[76] He was convinced that ethnic rancor was responsible.

Even though persuasive in some of its particulars, this interpretation is controversial. A number of reputable analysts dismiss the ethnic thesis because they believe that it inflates the political strength of the involved groups. These scholars place the major responsibility for the rejection on Wilson's politics of confrontation, or on the willfulness of his Republican opponents.

In this instance no one really knows how potent the ethnic politics were or even to what extent they were effective. The in-group leaders were divided, while all the minorities did not join the fight. Yet those outsiders who were active believed, as did others, that for the first time on a large scale hyphenated groups had confronted the establishment over a major foreign-policy issue in a manner that contributed to the outcome they desired.

Those ethnic groups antagonistic to the Versailles settlement had a more clearly vital role in the presidential election of 1920. The German-Americans voted for Germany, the Irish-Americans voted against Britain and for Ireland, the Italian-Americans voted for Italy and against Yugoslavia, the Greek-Americans voted for the inclusion of northern Epirus in the kingdom of Greece, the Lithuanian-Americans voted against Poland, the Arab-Americans voted against Britain and France, and the Chinese-Americans voted against Japan. Along with others who disliked Wilson for other reasons, most of them rejected the Democratic candidate, James M. Cox of Ohio. Even though the ballots of these groups as individual units may not have been critical, as a total they did help make possible the return of the Republicans to power under Warren G. Harding. America's white minorities thus continued into the postwar era their intense interest in foreign policy along with their politicking on issues affecting distant kinfolk.

6
AMERICANIZATION, QUOTAS, AND WAR

The Government of the
United States does not look
with favor on any activities
designed to divide the
allegiance of any group of
American residents between
the United States and any
foreign government, in
existence or in prospect. The
first concern of the United
States must always be the
unity of the country. . . .

*Department of State, Dec. 10,
1941*

During the wartime alarm over ethnic fragmentation, the Americanization movement had spawned the American Protective League and other organizations committed to a conformist loyalty. The xenophobia on which they thrived reached its zenith in the revived nativist movement of the twenties. The superpatriots, belonging mainly to the dominant ethnocultural groups, no longer focused on the German-Americans. They now reacted angrily to the politicking of virtually all minorities. Bigots filled the ranks of the anti-Catholic, anti-foreign, anti-immigration, and anti-black Ku Klux Klan. Revived in 1915 as a small Southern organization, it mushroomed into the nation's largest nativist association and at its height in 1924 claimed over four million members.

Along with others who considered themselves patriots, these nativists insisted upon an uncompromising Americanization that they prescribed. They saw themselves as defenders of the Anglo-Saxon stock against damage by the allegedly inferior genetic endowment of the new European immigrants, Asians, blacks, and their offspring. These Americanizers were convinced that the imperfectly assimilated and sometimes radical aliens were corrupting cherished Anglo-American virtues. As Theodore Roosevelt put it just before his death, "There can be no divided allegiance here. Any man who says he is an American but something else also, isn't an American at all."[1]

Even social reformers who often felt a compassion for the recent immigrant peoples were worried about the survival of the old values. These reformers, too, argued for compliance with the nativist standard in assimilation. They maintained that Americanization would help the first-generation immigrants and their children to rise from poverty, enter mainstream culture, and gain acceptance from the establishment. The traditional American nationalists, who were perhaps equally well intentioned, urged cultural conformity because they were worried about a macro-unity which during the war years they had regarded as precarious. Regardless of their motivation and whether or not they were nativists, these people still measured Americanism with an Anglo-American yardstick, which meant to them, as to the dour Calvin Coolidge, that "America must be kept American."[2]

These convictions, along with persisting Anglo-Saxonist thinking, produced measures that went beyond the right of any nation to control immigration. They categorized peoples as superior and inferior according to ethnicity and race. Although debated in a domestic context, the proposals touched on sensitive areas in foreign relations.

Those who legislated the restructuring began with a temporary law in May 1921, passed by overwhelming majorities in both houses of congress, that imposed quotas while they worked out what they desired as a permanent policy. Their further law-making was governed by the illusion that the collective identity of the American people had been fixed in the eighteenth century and should be protected against dilution. This attitude reflected the still prevailing prejudices that the earlier ethnic groups from northwestern Europe, but especially from Britain, were superior to all others.

Among the many defenses of this bias, the words of Ellison DuRant Smith, a senator from South Carolina, offer a representative example. "Thank God we have in America," he said, "perhaps the largest percentage of any country in the world of the pure, unadulterated Anglo-Saxon stock." He wanted to preserve "that splendid stock that has characterized us."[3] Another common conviction held that the ethnic or racial origin of a newcomer indicated his or her capacity for Americanization. In this hypothesis the more a person deviated from the Anglo-American model, the less likely it was that he or she would or could become a true American.

On this basis the Euro-American exclusionists maneuvered to continue to keep out all "aliens ineligible to citizenship," including at this time the Japanese. Based on the Naturalization Act of 1790, congress had included such a sweeping "barred-zone" prohibition in the nationality and literacy law of 1917. "For reasons of diplomacy," or essentially because of the Gentlemen's Agreement, Woodrow Wilson's administration had managed to exempt the Japanese from this provision.[4] The proposed permanent legislation would for the first time also formally bar them.

Among those who supported this expanded exclusion, Senator Hiram

Johnson of California and Secretary of Commerce Herbert C. Hoover expressed biases that were popular with both the general public and the governing elite. Johnson explained to the State Department as an "inconvertible [*sic*] fact that the Japanese continue ever Japanese, that their allegiance is always to Tokyo." Thus, even if they were to become naturalized, they "would continue alien" and would not "in reality become American citizens." As for Hoover, he wanted to bar the Japanese because he perceived "biological and cultural grounds why there should be no mixture of Oriental and Caucasian blood."[5]

As in the past, the Japanese smarted from such racial slights coming out of the American government. These feelings carried over easily into diplomacy dealing mainly with geo-political issues. At the recently concluded Washington Naval Conference of 1921–22, for example, the Japanese believed that they had been harmed by "a blood-chilling conspiracy" between the English-speaking countries. "Anglo-American pressures" had forced them to give up their alliance with Britain and to accept a ratio in battleships they disliked.[6] The Japanese were convinced that at least part of the motivation behind the coalition against them had been racial. Now they felt compelled to protest once more because an immigration bill discriminated against them on the same grounds and also violated the Gentlemen's Agreement.

Other countries such as Italy, which disliked the prejudice written into the bill, also protested. So did those ethnic groups within the nation which were often treated as outsiders and which together formed a substantial percentage of the population. Slavic, Jewish, and Italian-American lobbyists, as well as others, did all that they could to defeat it. The American Jewish Committee, the Knights of Columbus, the National Liberal League, and other organizations pointed to the racial prejudice in the proposed legislation. Most of them desired a policy fair to all immigrants, but some minority groups wished, much as did the Anglo-Americans, for favorable treatment primarily for those of their own kind. In a minority report, for example, dissenting Democrats denounced the partiality for Anglo-Saxons and Nordics as based on "pseudoscientific" evidence. Regardless, the political power of those who opposed what many called the "British Origins Law" could not match that of the Anglo nativists.[7]

As for the Japanese, Secretary of State Charles Evans Hughes warned that they would view the legislation "as fixing a stigma upon them." He urged congress, "in the interest of our international relations," to eliminate the provision that would exclude them.[8] Neither his arguments nor the logic of the Japanese objections impressed congress. Indeed, it perceived one protest as a "veiled threat." So the Department of State's particular efforts in the case of Japan failed.

As for the Japanese immigrants, because they were few and lacked the right to vote they had no leverage through ethnic politics. Congress passed and the president signed the Johnson-Reed Act without change in May 1924, thereby abrogating the Gentlemen's Agreement. The barred-zone exclusion against Asians and Pacific islanders, except for Filipinos, remained intact. Regardless of the newcomers' inability to affect the legislation, Japanese-language newspapers on the West Coast denounced it as racist, saying it "planted the seeds of a racial war," or "a racial struggle" between "the yellow and white races."[9]

In this manner, almost as if the international implications did not matter, the essence of the provisional restriction of immigration through quotas based on perceived ethnicity and race became permanent. In addition to its exclusionary features, this second law tightened the quotas for most immigrants according to their national origins. "The day of unalloyed welcome to all peoples, the day of indiscriminate acceptance of all races," the law's major sponsor said, "has definitely ended."[10] As he and the other nativists desired, the exclusion and the quotas struck hard at the Chinese, Japanese, Jews, Italians, Greeks, Slavs, and others.

Again, racism expressed through legislation added to the ill will against the United States among all peoples in Asia, but in particular it poisoned relations with the Japanese. As a whole, the immigration statutes institutionalized ethnoracial prejudice on a national scale beyond anything previously enacted. Since this discrimination affected mainly foreigners, it could not avoid bringing trauma to significant aspects of relations with other peoples and countries. Ironically, the task of explaining the official bigotry fell to Foreign-Service officers who usually shared the nativist assumptions upon which the legislation was based.

Within a year, the biases that had gone into the making of the Johnson-Reed Act spilled over into debates on American membership in the Permanent Court of International Justice, known usually as the World Court. Opponents, in the words of one, attacked the judges who were sitting on the court as "aliens in tongue, and in every instance aliens in allegiance," as though an international tribunal must have on it only blood-tested Euro-Americans.[11]

Although the proponents used less fanciful reasoning, they too argued from a racist perspective. They commonly maintained that the greatest white nation on earth should align itself on the court only with its racial equals. They wanted to make sure that in any multiracial body, whether it was the court or the League of Nations, the white votes would prevail. Court supporters also objected to schemes that would cut down the voting strength of white Australia and Canada while relatively increasing that of black Haiti and Liberia. These attitudes directly affected American foreign policy because ultimately, for these and other reasons, the senate rejected adherence to the court.

The implementation of the immigration legislation, meanwhile, had not gone smoothly. For various reasons, including ethnic-group protest and matters touching on foreign relations, the government had twice postponed the application of its national-origins provisions. The nativists protested. "The bulk of opposition to National Origins was and is of hyphenated inspiration and organization . . . ," they insisted. "How long will you tolerate foreign propaganda as an agency in moulding American legislation? The time has come for the American people to end hyphenism."[12] The quota formula went into effect in July 1929.

Since the quotas favored the English above other peoples, they appeared to strengthen Anglo-American relations. Yet the legislation failed to entice the large number of British immigrants that its framers had hoped it would. By 1930 the English-born as a percentage of first-generation foreigners in the United States had dropped to 5.7 percent.[13] In these years also, diplomatic "strain and tension" and "a questioning, if not hostile" attitude arose in the two countries over a batch of issues unrelated to ethnicity.[14] For instance, Washington's decision to try to collect war debts, to achieve naval supremacy, and to pursue nationalistic economic policies that affected British goods contributed to the growth of some anti-American feelings, particularly among leftists, in Britain. Fewer people in both countries now spoke of the kinship in terms of Anglo-Saxonism.

Nonetheless, within the United States but particularly within the governing elite, the cultural and ethnic affinity for Britain remained as solid as ever. Drew Pearson, a popular Washington columnist, maintained that "The American career diplomats hold the British Foreign Office in reverence as if it were the Deity. American policy in Europe, they contend, should do nothing to offend Britain." Since the younger career men emulated their seniors, he concluded that "the adoration is self-perpetuating."[15]

At times that elite even still invoked Anglo-Saxon traits as ideals. For example, Henry L. Stimson, as governor-general of the Philippines, "believed the Malays were racially his inferiors" and that their only hope for advancement lay in the modern way of empire "along that general path the other group of English speaking peoples known as the British empire is already travelling."[16] Filipino leaders, he said, did not possess "a sufficiently

Anglo-Saxon mind" to govern their own people. A short time later, while battling the great depression, President Hoover expressed the conviction that only "the cooperation of the Anglo-Saxons" could rescue civilization from the disaster. Other peoples "could not be counted on."[17]

As for the Filipinos, such racist condescension, along with the immigration laws, had come to pose a knotty problem. Since as a subject people they traveled with United States passports, the barred-zone exclusion provisions did not apply to them. Even so, only a small number of Filipinos, employed mainly in agriculture on the Pacific Coast, came to reside on the American mainland. Largely for racial reasons, their presence, like that of other Asians, rankled labor leaders and others. In response to the demands of these nativists for exclusion, and reacting to the wishes of others who wanted no competition from Filipino sugar growers protected by the American flag, congress in May 1934 passed the Tydings-McDuffie Act.

This law promised the Philippines freedom in ten years, but it also immediately classified its people as aliens for purposes of immigration, assigning them a quota of fifty entrants a year until full independence. After that, like other Pacific islanders, the Filipinos would be totally excluded. So, once more, domestic prejudices contributed to the fashioning of racist legislation that brought into question the orientation of foreign policy toward Asian peoples.

Unlike people of color such as the Filipinos, a number of the white minorities had now acquired an economic power more substantial than in the prewar years. As usual in such circumstances, when turmoil in old homelands or elsewhere abroad injured kinfolk or co-religionists, these groups used that power in ethnic politicking geared especially to influence pertinent foreign policy. As in the past, Jewish-Americans turned to such activism in 1920, when Arabs attacked Jews and their property in Palestine, and again in August 1929, when a week of riots there between the two peoples left more than four hundred Jews dead or wounded.

Perturbed American Zionists believed that the British, who held the League of Nations mandate in Palestine, had not protected the Jews adequately because, despite the Balfour Declaration, they favored the Arabs. These Zionists therefore urged the American government to aid the Jews of Palestine by approaching the British. But President Hoover "was definitely adverse . . . to sending a warship or intervening in any way" that would "unduly embarrass the British Government." He advised the American Jews to avoid "inflammatory charges" against the British for their conduct under the mandate. So, regardless of the strength or weakness of its case, "the most powerful Jewish community in the world," with an impressive record as a pressure group, failed in this instance because it came up against the solidarity of the British and American elites.[18]

A few years later, shortly after Adolf Hitler had assumed power in Germany, public as well as governmental indifference affected the activities of American Jews against the pogroms there. Some Jewish organizaions favored official protest through the State Department. Others insisted on huge public demonstrations. So, on March 27, 1933, the American Jewish Committee, the American Jewish Congress, and the B'nai B'rith sponsored an anti-Nazi rally in New York's Madison Square Garden. Later, two other Jewish organizations launched a boycott of German products. It achieved partial success because it persuaded the Nazis to put off other planned anti-Semitic violence. Over all, the Zionists regarded the boycott as "particularly effective and militant" but others felt that it "came nowhere near accomplishing its objectives."[19]

What did seem obvious was that at this time the Jews, regardless of their ethnic politics, could not persuade other Americans to give the boycott full support. Nor could they either induce the government to intervene decisively on behalf of oppressed kin in Germany or modify immigration restrictions so as to obtain refuge for them in the United States.

Even though, as in these instances, the influence of Jewish-Americans in foreign policy fluctuated, few other groups could match their skill in ethnic politics. In the first three decades the twentieth century, for example, the nation's largest ethnoracial minority, the African-Americans, had seldom even come close. Only in rare instances since the time of their emancipation from slavery had the blacks exerted a significant influence on foreign policy. Their concerns were "considered minimally important or excluded altogether from the realm of foreign and military affairs."[20]

In addition to the obstacle of racial prejudice, a lack of broad communal cohesion contributed to the political weakness of the African-Americans. Having descended from a variety of African tribal and other entities, they were often divided on the basis of their origins. Slowly, however, as did white ethnic groups, many of them put aside their narrow differences to act more and more as part of a single interest group.

When attentive African-American organizations did become interested in international affairs, they usually concentrated on issues affecting race, Africa, and the Caribbean nations with black populations. Concerned blacks, essentially a minority of intellectuals, churchmen, and professionals, had tried for years, for example, to help Liberia survive against a possible European conquest. They also had asked Washington to intervene diplomatically in the Congo Free State by condemning oppressive Belgian rule and had expressed objection to the white racism in Southern Africa. In the case of Haiti, as we have seen, a dedicated number of African-Americans had been unusually active in lobbying against the United States occupation there. As the military presence continued, they became more effective. They persuaded "the American government to rule" that island country with "more circumspection" than it had initially.[21]

In keeping with this limited but growing black interest in foreign affairs, the most noted African-American scholar of his time, William E. B. Du Bois, contended that on the basis of a broad ethnoracial identity the desires for freedom of the African and American blacks were essentially the same. Even though he had earlier dismissed any connection with Africa, he wrote that "The problem of the twentieth century is the problem of the color line, — the relation of the darker to the lighter races of men in Asia and Africa, in America and the islands of the sea."[22] His view foreshadowed Pan Africanism, or the idea that the people of African origin, however dispersed, shared a macro-ethnicity based on race.

Beginning in 1919 in Paris, Du Bois organized a series of Pan-African congresses "which would, he hoped, eventually bring the Negroes of the world into a great international pressure group."[23] The delegates stressed black ethnoracial consciousness and passed resolutions calling for racial equality. But the meetings did not attract the mass response Du Bois desired.

Marcus Garvey, a black from Jamaica residing in the United States who also preached a form of Pan Africanism, did gain a wider though still limited African-American following through his Universal Negro Improvement Association, which he had founded five years earlier. He despaired of assimilation, taught pride of race for blacks, claimed the superiority of black over white, called for African-American separatism, inveighed against white colonialism, urged self-determination for dependent blacks, or Africa for Africans, and launched a back-to-Africa movement.

"Let Africa be our guiding star—our star of destiny," Garvey told his followers.[24] Repeatedly he urged close relations between the blacks in Africa and America, linking the fate of equality for African-Americans with the desired rise of a strong black nation in Africa. In speeches and publications, until he was jailed for fraud in 1925, Garvey spread an attractive image of the affinity between blacks at home and abroad. As in the past, though, few blacks wished to settle in Africa.

The positive feeling for the circumscribed African connection carried over into the thirties, when American blacks responded on a wider basis than ever before to a major international crisis, the coming of the Italo-Ethiopian war. Identifying racially with the Ethiopians, many African-Americans almost overnight in 1935 became international-minded. They mobilized to exert whatever pressure they could on Washington to follow a pro-Ethiopian policy. In April, before the start of hostilities, the National Association for the Advancement of Colored People telegraphed the League of Nations on behalf of "12,000,000 American Negroes," demanding action to restrain dictator Benito Mussolini's threatened invasion.

This lobbying set the African-Americans against outspoken Italian-American groups which, as a matter of ethnic pride, supported their ancestral homeland. In some eastern cities where Italian and black neighborhoods adjoined, riots erupted. African-Americans attacked Italian-American youths and smashed the windows of Italian shopkeepers. In September Lester Taylor, the chairman of the New African International League, wired Secretary of State Cordell Hull demanding that the government take a strong action against Italy. "Does State Department," Taylor asked, "intend invoke Kellogg-Briand Pact only in behalf of white European nations. . . ?"[25]

After war broke out in October, thousands of Italian-Americans participated in rallies in New York, Philadelphia, Boston, Chicago, and other cities in support of their overseas kin. When Franklin D. Roosevelt's administration imposed an arms embargo on Italy, many of them protested. Hundreds of their societies, such as the Sons of Italy and the Italian-American Union, as well as thousands of individuals, flooded the offices of influential members of congress with letters and telegrams attacking the embargo. The campaign carried some weight because most of the writers were Democrats who had sided with the administration on numerous other issues.

In opposition, the African-Americans held pro-Ethiopian demonstrations in Harlem, Chicago, Miami, Washington, D.C., and elsewhere, sent money and medical supplies to Addis Ababa, and boycotted Italian-made goods. They saw race as central to the dispute. "Ethiopia is the land of our heritage," one of them explained. "This is a war of black against white." In this context Emperor "Haile Selassie became something of a hero to Negroes all over America."[26] Langston Hughes, their foremost poet, composed a "Ballad of Ethiopia" in support of black solidarity. Paul Robeson, the outstanding African-American singer, on the other hand, questioned the depth of such unity, pointing out that three-fourths of the soldiers fighting with the Italians "are black fellows."[27]

These internal tensions over the thrust of American policy toward the war bothered administration leaders because they regarded the agitation as motivated by race rather than by concern over the national interest. Even so, for a while a few of those in Washington who were especially upset by the Fascist aggression sought to counter the well-organized Italian-American political tactics by pressing the aroused African-American groups to demand additional discriminatory embargoes against Italy. Ignoring the ideological basis for the government's anti-Fascist stance, many ethnically sensitive Italian-Americans viewed this courting of the blacks and Washington's policy in general as a continuation of the old prejudices against them.

In this competition to affect policy toward the war, the African-Americans appeared more successful than the Italian-Americans, but not basically because of black political power. Roosevelt and those around him took an anti-Italian position for a cluster of other reasons, such as an aversion to Fascism and an opposition to aggression which happened to coincide with the African-American desires. At the same time, the intensity of the black reaction to this specific international issue helped considerably in arousing a general American sympathy for Ethiopia.

Regardless of its outcome, this politicking for Ethiopia drew African-Americans closer together than in the past. As comparable activity had done among other ethnoracial groups, it also stimulated among blacks a desire for further participation in the formulation of foreign policy. Hence, in January 1937 in New York City, their leaders founded the Council on African Affairs, the first African-American organization created for the express purpose of lobbying to affect policy toward Africa.

Ethnic politics of this nature became even more intense in subsequent years. Indeed, "ethnic loyalties had much to do with the way people responded to events abroad, particularly to the outbreak of World War II in September 1939."[28] Even though ideological, strategic, and other considerations often were more important than ethnicity in shaping the conduct of the government toward the belligerent peoples, the ethnoracial ingredient was always prominent. At this time foreign-born whites constituted 8.5 percent of the population. Offspring with one or two immigrant parents made up an additional 17.5 percent. These Caucasians and their children still formed the greater part of the minorities populating many of the big cities.

Most of these people followed closely the developments in their former homelands. Understandably, all the ethnic groups that were in some way connected to the belligerents in most instances sided with their own kind. They desired a policy toward the warring powers that favored, or at least would not injure, their ancestral homelands. Whenever they could, they lobbied for that purpose. For ideological and other reasons, Americans in general were partial to the Allied side, but most of all they preferred a neutrality designed to keep the nation out of the war. Within the sweep of these broad desires, as during the First World War, this second conflict heightened ethnic awareness not only among Americans directly related to the belligerent peoples but also among those with only distant ties abroad.

Nowhere did ethnic consciousness undergo greater stimulation than in the nation's Jewish community. From the start, unlike its situation in the first world conflict, this minority committed itself wholly to the Allied side. Nazi persecutions and the murder of their brethren had made American Jews passionate advocates of any kind of aid to those who battled Germany's Hitler.

Many, but certainly not all, of the more numerous Irish-Americans were still Anglophobic, but with less acerbic emotion than in the past. Earlier, their support of the Sinn Fein nationalists in Ireland's civil war and their ethnic politics had contributed to the international pressure on the British government that had induced it in a treaty in December 1921 to grant dominion status to the Irish Free State. Ireland accepted this qualified independence in the following month. This settlement, along with considerable Irish assimilation, led a number of analysts and others to assume the "nearly total disintegration and disappearance of organized Irish-American nationalism."[29]

Yet Catholic-Irish America retained its ethnic identity. Its people, especially those located mainly in the urban centers of the northeast who maintained their ties to the old homeland, resented the partition of the largely Protestant six counties of Northern Ireland from the new and overwhelmingly Catholic state to the south. They backed the Irish nationalist contention that the Emerald Isle should be a single unified country. Anglo-Americans and their cultural allies sided with Ulster's Protestants, who insisted that they were entitled to their own self-determination, meaning union with Britain.

After Éamon de Valera, the Sinn Fein leader, became the Free State's president in 1932, he severed most official bonds with Britain. By 1936, in domestic affairs at least, he had in effect turned the south into a republic. He also appealed to President Roosevelt to intervene with Britain to help end the partition. Although much interested in an Anglo-Irish settlement, the president refused to interfere "officially or through diplomatic channels" in the controversy. After Britain went to war, because of their preoccupation with the Ulster question, the militant Irish-American organizations and newspapers opposed "any kind of assistance to the Allies." They attacked "Roosevelt's pro-British policies."[30]

At the same time, Winston Churchill, Britain's prime minister, who desired to use the Irish ports as bases against the Germans, asked Roosevelt to exert his influence with the Irish-Americans so that they would persuade Dublin to abandon its neutrality and make the ports available. De Valera countered by utilizing ethnic politics. He appealed to the Irish-Americans to support Ireland's neutrality by urging the American government to restrain Britain from seizing the ports by force. In November 1940 he also asked the American Irish to put Ireland's case against partition before the public, a political act that official Washington deplored.

Activist Irish-Americans responded favorably. In New York City they organized a special lobby, the American Friends of Irish Neutrality. In the following months, other chapters sprang up in cities throughout the country. Indirectly, this lobbying "played a vital part in convincing the British government that it had more to lose than to gain by violating Irish neutrality."[31] Britain so desperately needed American goodwill and material assistance that her leaders were reluctant to risk further antagonism from America's Irish groups, which possessed a potential for influencing Washington's overseas relations.

This possibility changed when the United States entered the war. Dublin's ability to attract support from the Irish-American nationalists almost vanished. Within days of the war declarations, the Irish-Americans disbanded their neutrality lobby. As did other minorities, they rallied behind their own government and its allies, demonstrating that they were Americans first and hyphenates second.

Nonetheless, for the balance of the war Washington's relations with Ireland remained strained. De Valera stuck to neutrality and continued to exploit his Irish-American connections. David Gray, the American minister in Dublin, who through marriage was related to Roosevelt and had direct access to him, denounced de Valera's transatlantic tampering. The incensed minister categorized all minority ethnic politics as evil.

"The time may come," Gray told the president, "when it would be advisable for you to characterise it as an insult to the American people that any foreigner should attempt to inject himself into American politics with racial pressure group methods." Gray hoped that the current national solidarity would finally kill ethnic politics through the assimilation process. "This war," he said, "should have put an end to hyphens."[32]

In this context of ethnic politics, German-American attitudes, too, differed from those during the period of American neutrality in the First World

War. This time the German-Americans as a group did not attempt openly to influence foreign policy. Nor did they parade their ethnic affinity. Only a small number of them joined the offshoots of the Nazi party, which had been organized in the United States beginning in 1924 mainly by German nationals and recent immigrants.

In the thirties, much as many Italian-Americans had admired Mussolini's strutting and imperialism, numerous German-Americans had delighted in Hitler's successes, particularly his defiance of the Treaty of Versailles. Few of them denounced Naziism. Their attitude changed with the imprisonment of Pastor Martin Niemöller, a hero to German Protestants, and with the "Night of Broken Glass" or *Kristallnacht* pogrom that began on November 10, 1938, and raged for several days against Jews throughout Germany. The impact of these deeds, along with Roosevelt's recall of the ambassador in Berlin in protest, finally moved prominent German-Americans to condemn openly the Nazi brutalities in the old fatherland.

This reaction and the overall lukewarm support from the German-American community disappointed Nazi leaders. A number of them who viewed German-Americans in irredentist terms had hoped that ethnic affinity would draw kin in America into their nationalist organizations. These Nazis mistakenly assumed that the German-Americans possessed enough political power to deflect Washington's hostility toward the Third Reich.

Hitler's own views also grew out of misperception. He held Americans in contempt as mongrels, seeing no basis for a close relationship with them even through the German-American community. Although his outlook toward the United States fluctuated, he perceived it generally in racial terms as a "decayed country, with problems of race and social inequality . . . half Judaized half negrified with everything built on the dollar."[33] Believing that blood was stronger than citizenship, Hitler wished to unify "racial comrades" at home and abroad through Naziism. Sometimes he perceived in the German-Americans the means for regenerating the United States. At other times, unlike several of his advisers, he placed small value on the ethnic connection with America unless he could manipulate it for the direct benefit of his National Socialist state.

For a while the Association of the Friends of the New Germany, which in 1936 became the American-German Peoples Society (*Amerika-deutscher Volksbund*), called usually the German-American Bund, appeared to meet the Nazi objectives. Even though the German Nazis in the United States officially were forbidden to join this anti-Semitic affiliate of their party, it became the best-known, or the most notorious, of a number of Germanic fringe organizations. Its activities so alarmed American Jews that in December 1938, under the leadership of Stephen W. Wise, they established the Council Against Intolerance in America to combat the bund. The council's anti-Nazi campaign proved so successful that a number of German-Americans complained that it "had revived the anti-German prejudices" of the First World War.[34]

Despite this opposition to the bund and its early record of sluggishness, in the months before the coming of war in Europe it experienced a revival under the leadership of Fritz J. Kuhn, a flamboyant chemical engineer born in Germany who styled himself the American *Führer*. It held spectacular mass meetings in halls decorated with American flags and swastikas and guarded by uniformed storm troopers, as in New York's Madison Square Garden in February 1939. Kuhn described the organization as nothing more than "a militant group of patriotic Americans."[35] Despite such protestation, the bund, by its noisy tactics, brawls with Jews, and racial hatred, aroused far more hostility among Americans of all persuasions than it did support for Germany.

In brief, the bund, which collapsed in November, had hardly any influence, other than a negative one, on American foreign policy. Nonetheless, the Germanic minority's overseas ethnic attachments retained a remarkable vitality. Even though most German-Americans scorned the Nazi blandishments, they also feared and resisted possible American involvement in another war against their old fatherland.

After Italy entered the war in June 1940, Italian-Americans similarly disliked the idea of perhaps having to fight their kin, no matter how distant. Many of them dreaded American belligerency because they believed it would revive the old domestic prejudices against them. In some instances they opposed the sending of arms and other forms of aid to Britain. Yet as a whole the Italian-Americans did not react as strongly against the pro-Allied policy of the American government as did organized German- or Irish-Americans.

Ethnic predilections also often swayed the willingness of Americans of other origins to risk direct participation in the war. For instance, after Soviet forces invaded Finland on November 30, 1939, even the small Finnish-American ethnic group and its friends lobbied for American intervention against the Soviets. The Finnish-Americans sought mainly money and military supplies for their mother country. Feeling an aversion to what Roosevelt called "this dreadful rape of Finland," most Americans sympathized with the Finns.[36] Yet the administration proceeded cautiously with its aid, because it did not wish to chance involvement in the conflict. As for the Finnish-Americans, like other minorities they attempted to influence foreign policy more for ethnic than for ideological reasons such as anti-Communism.

This kind of ethnic rapport is overlooked in much of the literature on the popular attitude toward the larger European war. Most histories assert or imply that Americans as a whole favored one side or the other out of ideological commitment such as a hatred of Nazism or Communism. Yet, as we have seen, for many groups, even for those of British descent, the ethnic connection was equally compelling.

Those Americans who emphasized the nation's Anglo-Saxon antecedents were the most prominent in demanding massive aid to Britain and France. As did the Irish-Americans, German-Americans, and Italian-Americans with their ethnically oriented societies, the Anglo-Americans and Anglophiles worked through their own special-interest organizations, such as the English-Speaking Union, to give guidance to policy. As in the past, the union celebrated the superiority of Anglo-Americanism over other ethnic affiliations but accentuated the common strategic, ideological, and other commitments that bound the United States and Britain together.

During the spring of 1940, these attachments and the German victories in western Europe led visionary Anglophiles to embrace the plan of Clarence Streit, a journalist who throughout the thirties had worked in Europe for the *New York Times*. In his book, *Union Now,* he advocated that the United States join with Britain to form the nucleus of a federal union of fifteen democracies. Streit maintained, as had Anglo-Saxonist predecessors, that the English-speaking nations, because of their common legal and cultural heritage, must stand together, in this instance against Fascist forces. The ethnic character of the scheme alienated some minorities but helped make it popular with the intellectual establishment and with many others of matching outlook.

Personal fidelity to England expressed itself most strongly in the northeast and southeast, where Anglo-Americans and Anglophiles were most numerous. In those sections they dominated the social, cultural, and political establishment. Critics spoke of "the Anglophile–New Deal alliance" which included men such as jurist Felix Frankfurter of Massachusetts and administration official Dean G. Acheson of Connecticut. Their support of the war had "everything to do with England," one historian wrote. "Their reverence for British customs and institutions was so pronounced that they might better be termed Anglophiliacs. When Britain was cut, they bled."[37]

Grenville Clark, another northeasterner, a prominent lawyer, and an old friend of the president, directed the Military Training Camps Association, a continuation of the preparedness movement of the previous war, which also had sought American interdependence with Britain. He and the other Anglo-Americans and Anglophiles, who now insisted that the nation's fate was entangled with Britain's, also often explained this special relationship chiefly in strategic and ideological terms. In fact, though, emotion often defined their attachment to Britain as much as it did the subjective bond of the Irish-Americans to the Emerald Isle or of the German-Americans to their fatherland.

An example of how such ethnocultural identification was used to stir opinion on foreign policy appeared on June 10, 1940, in newspaper advertisements throughout the United States. In these ads thirty private citizens who had organized the Century Group, an informal club in New York City, asked for a declaration of war on Germany. Twelve days later France fell to German forces. These men, dubbed by outsiders of different outlook as warhawks, immediately dedicated themselves to preventing the defeat of Britain, now fighting alone, by working with greater urgency for United States intervention against Nazi Germany.

All within the club belonged to or admired the eastern establishment which had long guided the course of foreign policy. This establishment's membership still remained overwhelmingly white, Anglo-American or Anglicized, and Protestant. Its people and those who shared their convictions dominated the Department of State and set the goals of organizations such as the New York–based Council on Foreign Relations, which had been founded at the end of the First World War as an Anglo-American forum modeled on a British club.

Critics often disparaged the council not just because of its ethnic orientation but because they regarded it as "the seat of boredom." Supporters, on the other hand, praised it as "the school for statesmen."[38] Regardless of how the council was viewed by outsiders, it, like the Century Group, propagated an elitist, pro-British approach to policy-making and thrust its influence into Washington's inner circle. The professional diplomats who manned the foreign service and the desks in the Department of State generally had the same background as the people of the group, of the establishment, and of the council. All held to similar Anglo-American biases.

The historian of the Century Group points out that the "Anglo-Saxonism of the Group was at least one reason why these men wanted war during the summer of 1940 and why they were so outspoken."[39] Like other Americans with ties abroad, most of them were accustomed to perceiving national interest from the vantage point of their own ethnocultural predilections. At this time they defined that interest as justifying a war policy that they regarded as proper for the welfare of the United States as well as beneficial for the hard-pressed ancestral land of most of them. These prominent individuals represented the cutting edge of the most ardent interventionists of all, the old-line believers in the "Anglo-Saxon blood and cultural tradition."

These and other concerns over policies affecting old homelands remained strong enough to stir congress and to contribute to a change in voting patterns in the presidential election of 1940. For instance, the president's hostile stance toward Germany and Italy, even though justified by the events in Europe, drove many German- and Italian-Americans away from his party and into the Republican ranks. The close friendship with Britain and France, on the other hand, attracted many new voters, such as those of British origin, to the Democratic party. The administration's criticism of the Nazi atrocities bound Jewish-Americans closer than ever to the Democratic party. Indeed, Democratic politicians called on the Jews to vote for Roosevelt as their only bulwark against Fascism.

Early in 1941, a few months after Roosevelt's victory at the polls, Louis Bean, a statistical analyst in the Department of Agriculture, completed a study of ethnic influence on the elections. He concluded that the German government was "exceedingly successful" in persuading German-Americans to use "their vote in the interest of their former homeland without regard to the interests of the United States." In his view the German-Americans voted not as Americans, but as Germans. He warned, therefore, that if their political behavior spread to other ethnic groups, the nation would shatter "into innumerable national or racial minority groups each feuding with the other and each fighting for supremacy over the other—none of them thinking of the American Nation as a unified whole and of the supreme loyalty owed to it."[40]

Even though Bean's forebodings reflected mainly old nativist prejudices rather than perceptive analysis, the war did ignite some feuding between ethnic groups over foreign policy. As had happened earlier, on occasion German-Americans and Jewish-Americans struck at each other. To a lesser extent so did some Italian-American and Jewish groups. But at this time the Italian-Americans as a whole did not attempt the futile exercise of attempting to exert heavy pressure on American policy to favor their homeland.

Overall, this persistence of ethnic loyalties among the minority groups bothered the Anglo-American majority. As in the first world conflict, but perhaps to a lesser degree, it held to an exaggerated fear that if and when the United States entered the war, those attachments "might well produce disunity and fragmentation."[41] There is an American dread "at being split," a British diplomatist commented. "There is always the fear that they will cease to be a nation."[42]

The State Department shared this attitude. Its Anglified leadership viewed ethnic pluralism as a "hydra-headed monstrosity," resented the intrusion of domestic politics in foreign affairs, lamented the continued presence of "so many 'hyphenated' Americans," and "abhorred phenomena like the 'ethnic vote.'"[43]

All the while, the bond between the elites in Britain and the United States became stronger. In August 1941 Roosevelt and Churchill met for the first time, in four days of secret conferences at Placentia Bay in Newfoundland. They discussed war aims and postwar objectives as though the United States was already a belligerent. At the close of their talks, they issued as a press release the well-known Atlantic Charter. In it, among other promises, they agreed to uphold the principle of self-determination. Six months earlier Roosevelt had committed his administration unequivocally to it, saying that "any nationality, no matter how small, has the inherent right to its own nationhood."[44]

Yet, once more, as in Wilson's time, in part because of Churchill's reservations as to its universality, self-determination had validity mainly for Europeans. Later, though, some American leaders indicated that it would apply to Asians, Africans, and others as well. From the perspectives of the transatlantic ethnocultural connection and of geo-political strategy, however, the Atlantic Charter was more important for announcing the common purpose behind what had become an unwritten alliance between the British and American peoples.

In keeping with this partnership, Roosevelt at this point promised to support Britain in the naval battle of the Atlantic even "at the risk of war, tipping from most benevolent neutrality to active belligerency." Several months later he "gave Britain a commitment of armed support in case of a Japanese attack on British or Dutch territory or on Thailand." With faith in the basic strength of the Anglo-American bond, he and his cabinet "were convinced that the American public would support intervention to aid Britain."[45]

When Americans did become belligerents in December, this implicit alliance promptly achieved formal status. Unlike the intervention in the First World War, which had been triggered by maritime issues, America's entry into war in 1941 came from a direct attack on United States soil. As in the previous intervention, the underlying causes are complicated and also controversial. Ethnic affinity for one side and antagonism toward the other had a definite place in the pattern of causation. Yet other issues, such as democratic ideology, reaction to Japanese, German, and Italian aggressions, geo-political considerations, violations of treaty commitments, and defense of the nation, were as important, if not more so, as the ethnoracial element.

Internally, belligerency quickly put to rest most of the immediate fears of disunity arising out of American minority attachments. With considerable confidence, therefore, the nation's leaders went ahead with the strategic collaboration with Britain that in the view of some scholars attained a level "never before realised or even approached" by other sovereign states. That relationship became "probably the most remarkable alliance of modern history."[46] Indeed, the partnership came to appear so close that the British historian Denis Brogan felt compelled to remind his people that even though "there are common links between the two countries. . . . the United States is not a lost dominion." It "is a foreign country and the Americans are foreigners if not aliens. . . . in short they are non-English."[47]

Again unlike the situation in 1917, this intervention and the alliance produced no widespread hyphenate hysteria. Few Americans desired, or were willing openly, to question the intimacy with Britain. In turn, as a rule, the Anglo-American leaders did not proclaim, as they had during the First World War, that ethnic pluralism menaced national survival. Yet they could not bring themselves to dismiss their anxiety over the possible effect of ethnic-group loyalty on the conduct of the war. Promptly, therefore, in January 1942, Undersecretary of State Sumner Welles, a confidant of the president, established the Interdepartmental Committee on Foreign Nationality Problems to deal with the issue. The committee's researchers estimated that there were close to forty million Americans "who have some emotional or cultural identification with other countries" and who hoped to influence foreign policy. The committee therefore monitored the activities of selected minority groups.[48]

In the spring James M. Landis, the director of the Office of Civil Defense, expressed hope that macro-patriotic sentiment would serve as a solidifying force among the disparate ethnic and racial groups. It did not do so to the extent the government desired, but neither did the ethnoracial divisions hamper the conduct of the war in any crucial way. An overriding concern with survival and then with victory repressed much of the ethnic feuding that the establishment at first had anticipated and feared. Where belligerency did stimulate a sense of national solidarity, it transcended the old Anglo-American paradigm. Various observers and historians maintain, seemingly on the basis of impression, that the war marked a turning point in establishing the patriotism of the white ethnic minorities. These writers argue that among these groups, if not among those of color, assimilation theory had worked.

Yet from the start broad ethnoracial considerations affected wartime policy. With virtual unanimity, American leaders assigned the defeat of Germany top priority. Even though grounded in sound strategic considerations, this policy also reflected the Eurocentric feelings of those in power as well as their willingness to go along with British objectives. Although sympathy for China was widespread, and the Asia-Firsters acquired a substantial following, no Asian group in the United States could exert an influence comparable to that of the Anglo-American elite that in effect made the Europe-first decision.

Asians also bore the brunt of old racial biases reflected most dramatically in the official restrictions placed on the Japanese-Americans. Throughout the twenties and thirties, journalists, academics, and even policymakers had played up the old yellow-peril idea, linking it to a possible war with Japan. Many whites had continued to believe that the Asian-Americans, even more than the European minorities, were incapable of the deep devotion to the nation that the Anglo-American elite regarded as essential.

Among the people so characterized, the Japanese-Americans had the reputation of maintaining the most intense loyalty to their ancestral land, a feeling anchored in ethnoracial pride. They, especially the *issei* or immigrant generation, had rallied behind the old homeland during three previous conflicts: the Sino-Japanese War of 1894–95, the Russo-Japanese War, and the First World War. A naval officer writing in 1937 on this trans-Pacific connection of the Japanese-Americans expressed a sentiment held by many Americans. He argued that "every Japanese born under our flag or not is always a Japanese. No matter how much he professes to be an American he is always thinking Japanese thoughts, hoping secretly for a Japanese victory."[49]

True enough, the Japanese-Americans as a whole rejoiced over the mother country's conquests in China and identified with her imperialist policies. As a specialist on the subject observes, "*Issei* leaders in every Japanese community in the western United States established emergency committees" which "disseminated pro-Japanese propaganda," collected money to send to Japan, mailed gift packages to Japanese soldiers, and sponsored patriotic meetings to enhance identification with Japan.[50] Hawaii's Japanese-language press referred to the Japanese army as "our army," and one headline read, "Our Units Advance Everywhere." From 1937 to 1939 the Japanese-Americans in the islands held rallies to support Japan's war effort and contributed millions of yen to it.[51]

Many of the *nisei*, or members of the second generation, born in the United States, regarded themselves as citizens of Japan because their parents were Japanese, a double allegiance that was often encouraged in their community. Yet this duality, and the pride of the Japanese-Americans in the military prowess of their overseas kin, was not much different from the responses of other ethnic groups which backed the regimes in their old homelands.

After the Japanese naval aviators bombed Pearl Harbor, emotions connected to race and ethnicity intruded almost everywhere in the belligerent countries of the Pacific war. Japanese propagandists even justified the attack as proper retribution for the oppression and prejudice suffered by their kin in the United States. The nature of the Japanese assault, denounced by President Roosevelt as infamous, kindled similar racial passion in the United States.

At the time 160,000 people of Japanese ancestry lived in Hawaii and 127,000 in the continental United States. More than nine out of ten of the latter resided on the Pacific Coast. There they made up only about two percent of the population, though in Hawaii they were the largest ethnic group, making up forty percent of the islands' inhabitants. Nonetheless, in the culmination of almost a century of anti-Asian prejudice, Japanese-Americans on the coast—but not those on the islands, who were too numerous to jail—quickly suffered a unique wartime discrimination.

In accord with the earlier anti-Japanese effusions of nativists such as Hiram Johnson, Secretary of War Henry L. Stimson claimed that the "racial characteristics" of the *nisei* made their loyalty suspect. His position, which he later changed, along with that of Lieutenant General John L. DeWitt, the army commander on the Pacific Coast, reflected a popular attitude that ethnoracial ties predisposed these Japanese-Americans to aid their kin as spies and saboteurs. Like millions of other white Americans, these leaders held to the old theory that immigration did not sever such affinity and "that Asians were incapable of being assimilated."[52]

In line with this racial assumption, buttressed with the evidence of *issei* and *nisei* pro-Japanese sentiment and the dubious excuse of "military necessity," the president on February 19, 1942, two months after the start of hostilities, signed Executive Order 9066. It decreed incarceration for people of Japanese ancestry on the Pacific Coast. In the view of critical analysts, Roosevelt, who reputedly had "never experienced any feeling toward Japan other than revulsion," issued the order because like most of his advisers he harbored anti-Japanese prejudices.[53] Quickly thereafter troops herded all of the Japanese-Americans in California, Oregon, and Washington, two-thirds of whom had been born in the United States, into concentration camps where most remained for the duration of the war. They were denied constitutional rights supposedly guaranteed to all residents in the nation regardless of ancestry.

In April General DeWitt publicly defended the internment. "A Jap's a Jap," he said. "You can't change him by giving him a piece of paper," meaning American citizenship.[54] This attitude reflected prejudice, but that of other officials who supported the confinement stemmed from a wartime hysteria or from a more reasoned cognizance of possible disloyalty. After all, a number of Japanese-Americans did collaborate with their homeland brethren in the planning for the attack on Hawaii. For these reasons, and most of all because the "proponents of mass evacuation sifted the nation's enemies through a racial screen," few ethnoracial groups suffered restrictions comparable to those imposed on the Japanese-Americans.[55]

Yet the government also incarcerated other resident enemy ethnic groups. Beginning in February 1942 on the Pacific Coast, approximately ten thousand Germans and Italians who were still aliens "were removed from their homes and jobs." Some were "interned in guarded army camps." In June they were permitted to return, and in October the Italians "were removed from the enemy alien category."[56] Thus, the German- and Italian-Americans, particularly the unnaturalized among them, also felt the sting of distrust, prejudice, loss of jobs, and restrictive surveillance. In comparison to their Japanese counterparts, however, their numerous offspring had achieved a level of assimilation and enough political clout to be left mostly on their own.

The harsh measures against the Japanese-Americans pleased most Euro-Americans. This attitude blended easily with the racist ideology that had long flourished in large sections of white American society. Government policy also reflected the view of many Americans, and of Britons too, that in the Pacific, though not in Europe, they were fighting a racial war. Most of the Japanese public perceived the conflict in comparable terms. Some analysts in Tokyo even regarded American racism as "the far-reaching cause of the present war."[57]

As the Japanese had done at the end of the First World War, in this conflict they announced themselves as champions of the colored peoples of Asia against white imperialists. Their publicists spoke of an Asian solidarity, of a Pan-Asian regional order of "Asia for the Asians," and of "common racial origins" with other Asians. Japanese propagandists highlighted instances of racism and enumerated the anti-"colored" laws in the United States. Their focus on race had a noticeable impact on other Asians and also on many blacks in the United States. William E. B. Du Bois wrote, for example, "I believe in Asia for the Asiatics and despite the hell of war and fascism of capital, I see in Japan the best agent for this end."[58]

Whether or not Indonesians, Malays, Burmese, and others agreed with this sentiment, they did find satisfaction in the initial Japanese victories over whites. Asians of varied ethnicity were convinced that racial antagonism lay at the heart of the war. A radio broadcast from Japan on March 12, 1943, announced that "according to observers the hatred Anglo-American nations harbor against Asiatic races is an inborn trait and it is nothing that can be overcome by any means."[59] Other programs stressed that exclusion had been, and continued to be, the ultimate insult to all Asians. This Japanese propaganda, as well as the general Asian outlook, may have been simplistic, though hardly more so than the belief of whites in such theories as Manifest Destiny and Anglo-Saxon supremacy. For most of the attentive Asians, nonetheless, the American rhetoric about freedom for all, as in the Atlantic Charter, had no meaning.

On the other hand, many in the United States were angered by the Japanese mistreatment of American prisoners of war and of civilian internees. Secretary of State Cordell Hull maintained that protests did no good, because "Japanese barbarism was too deeply rooted" for them to have effect.[60] He exaggerated, but so did the Japanese in their claimed commitment to racial brotherhood.

The Japanese made clear that their emphasis on "Asian cooperation" did not posit "an automatic racial equality." Indeed, "the assumption of Japanese superiority permeated relations with the rest of Asia."[61] In the end, the ruthless behavior of the Japanese against other Asians as well as whites, and their own xenophobia, racism, and convictions of a divinely conferred exceptionalism, earned them more hatred than support among those they had conquered, and even among those they tried to cultivate.

Still, the prodding from Pan-Asian Japanese propaganda had an effect. It, as well as highly publicized attacks in the media and elsewhere on the master-race theories coming out of Nazi Germany, persuaded America's governing elite to reassess the "yellow peril" sentiments and the impact of racist laws and policies on wartime foreign relations. In consequence, in January 1943 the government abrogated its unequal treaties with China, thereby giving up extraterritoriality—which exempted American nationals in China from the jurisdiction of local laws—and other privileges. It also acknowledged that the nation's long-standing exclusion policy was insulting to China, its major Asian ally.

A newly formed Citizens Committee to Repeal Chinese Exclusion therefore launched a campaign to eliminate the racial discrimination against the Chinese in the nation's immigration laws. To gather support, the committee capitalized on the strong pro-Chinese sentiment produced by the war. In October the president, as a backer of the movement, pointed out that repeal would "correct a historic mistake and silence the distorted Japanese propaganda."[62]

The Chinese-Americans, who in the previous decade had demonstrated a limited activism by joining those who opposed the shipment of scrap steel, petroleum, and other war supplies to Japan, of course took a keen interest in ending the discriminatory policy they had long detested. They offered the repeal advocates whatever help they could muster. It was small, however, because the Chinese-Americans were too few and not situated strategically enough, except perhaps in Hawaii, to exert meaningful political influence. Well-placed white sinophiles piloted the legislation through congress, which in November overturned the laws which had excluded the Chinese for sixty-one years.

The new statute granted Chinese immigrants the right to become naturalized citizens, assigning them an annual token quota of 105. Meager though these benefits were, only two other Asian groups allied to the United States received them: Filipinos and the previously barred peoples of India. Nonetheless, by initiating a gradual elimination of the bigotry embedded in the immigration regulations, this law cut at one root of discrimination based on race.

As the policymakers desired, the legislation also shored up foreign policy. As Roosevelt explained on signing it on December 17, 1943, "an unfortunate barrier between nations has been removed. The war effort in the Far East can now be carried on with greater vigor. . . ."[63] He thus touched on the immediate strategic objective behind the law, the need to reinforce Chinese friendship and will to fight while countering Japanese claims that Americans were waging a racist war against Asians.

Of course, racial attitudes did affect the actual conduct of the war against Japan, and vice versa. In the United States the anti-Japanese sentiment, even aside from the jailing of the Japanese-Americans, could seldom be separated from the racism rooted in popular thought. One planner, for instance, desired the almost total elimination of the Japanese as a race, saying that "Japan should be bombed so that there was little left of its civilization."[64]

There were other American leaders who believed that the conflict would determine "which race was to survive," the American or the Japanese. The media portrayed the Japanese as cruel, treacherous, "murderous little ape-men," or in other demeaning terms. Widely admired historian Alan Nevins, among others, was convinced that Americans detested the Japanese more than any other foe they had fought in all their wars.

Race hatred by both American and Japanese soldiers stimulated atrocities which in turn generated more vindictiveness. For home consumption, Japanese authorities denounced Americans as "albino apes" and "carnivorous beasts," saying there was "no way of stopping" their cruelties except by their "thorough extermination."[65] Many Asians perceived the American inhumanities as stemming from a racism that extended to all peoples of color.

From the Asian perspective, the clearest example of "indiscriminate murder" based on race was the use of atomic bombs against Japan. Asians and others cite again and again the leveling of Hiroshima rather than Berlin as *de facto* evidence of the racial orientation of United States foreign policy. Many American blacks, too, such as the poet Langston Hughes, shared this conviction. He asked, "Why wasn't the bomb used against Germany? Germans is white. So they wait until the war is over in Europe to try them out on colored folks. Japs is colored."[66]

Despite the official protestations that the bomb was "not ready" before the capitulation of Germany, and despite the lack of concrete evidence that racial hatred entered the military decision to explode it, this belief persisted long after the Asian war ended. Public-opinion polls of the time provide at least an indirect rationale for such sentiment. They indicate that most Americans, as did a number of their war leaders, wanted to destroy Japan. Almost 23 percent of the polled public wished that the air force had dropped more atomic bombs on Japan.

Earlier, a roughly comparable distrust of white motivation had permeated the thinking of numerous South Asians. They believed that the racism in the wartime British-American partnership had led the Roosevelt administration in the summer of 1942 to acquiesce in Britain's suppression of Mohandas K. Gandhi's Quit India movement and in the jailing of thousands of anti-colonial leaders. Indian nationalists were convinced also that such racism had produced famine in India.

In October 1942 a great cyclone followed by three tidal waves had struck the western district of Bengal, destroying lives and crops. India had insufficient reserves to make up for the lost food. It could not, as it had in analogous crises in the past, obtain rice from Burma, because Japanese troops occupied that country.

News of the massive starvation trickled to the United States in January 1943, but the government sent no food. Whatever provisions had initially been available in India Churchill had diverted to the Allied troops rather than to the needy civilians. Roosevelt seconded this decision. The American government therefore largely ignored the natural disaster in Bengal with its ensuing famine, which British official and non-official Indian sources estimated as taking a toll of several million lives.

Indian scholars who have gone beyond the generalized charge of Anglo prejudice in trying to pinpoint the main responsibility for the tragedy attribute it to the British prime minister and his "racist belief in the 'white man's burden.'" Churchill often spoke disparagingly about people of color and defended the idea of Anglo-Saxon superiority by claiming as a matter of fact that "We are superior." Given the closeness of America's British connection, South Asians have also insisted that Roosevelt and other Americans were "virtually silent onlookers of Churchill's actions, if not his accessories." One historian maintains that the American government would not have demonstrated "a similar indifference . . . to the plight of European people, even on a very much smaller scale."[67]

Washington's feigned ignorance of the Indians' plight reflected its policy, all during the war, of refusing to exert strong pressure against British imperial practices. That policy upset Indians, Chinese, and other Asians and undermined whatever credibility the Atlantic Charter may have had in their eyes. Obviously, despite the Roosevelt administration's professions of support for self-determination and anti-colonialism, it placed the close relationship with Britain ahead of such considerations.

Scholars, and in particular analysts from minority groups, have also criticized the American reaction to the ethnoracial horrors in Europe, but most of all to the Nazi genocide against Jews. Through organizational experience in ethnic politics, American Jewry appeared better equipped to pressure the Roosevelt administration than did any other minority group. But on the issue of aiding imperiled kin in Germany and other Nazi-controlled lands it was divided.

As for the government, it responded positively in various ways to the pleas of Jewish leaders who had access to it. Washington protested Nazi anti-Semitism and persecutions, while receiving into the country a substantial number of European Jews as refugees. A recent author has stated that "Of the some half-million Jews who managed to find refuge outside of German-dominated Europe, nearly one-half found it in the United States. . . . In percentage terms, during the late 1930s and early 1940s, Jews accounted for over half of all immigrants into the country."[68] Along with brethren already established within the nation, and the decimation of the Jews in Europe, this influx helped to make the United States the center of world Zionism.

American Jews knew that in these and other endeavors the administration had done more for their persecuted kin than had other governments. They were aware also that the ethnoracial bias in the immigration laws stood as a barrier for most refugees and that during the war so did a rise in anti-Semitism. Nonetheless, the minority critics were convinced that there had been "a gulf between the professed good intentions of the Administration and the implementation of policy."[69] The United States simply had not done enough or tried hard enough to save Europe's Jews from destruction. The Jews, and many Gentiles too, felt that anti-Semitism in Washington had offset their ethnic politics, or at least had inhibited a more extensive rescue effort.

As during the First World War, a number of other ethnic groups in the United States sought to affect at least some aspects of policy in the reshaping of Europe. Polish-Americans, for instance, lobbied to commit the government to the revival of an independent Poland as before the war. Accordingly, at a top-level conference in Teheran in November and December 1943, the president told Josef Stalin, the Soviet dictator, that he could not agree publicly, as the Russians demanded, to a truncated eastern boundary for Poland. Roosevelt said that he had to consider the views of some six million or more Polish-Americans because "as a practical man he did not wish to lose their vote."[70] Stalin was not impressed then, nor when Secretary of State Hull, who disliked "interfering minorities," nonetheless urged the Soviets not to impose a puppet government on Poland. Soviet Foreign Minister Vyacheslav M. Molotov commented, "That's domestic politics: the Polish vote."[71]

In May of the following year, when Roosevelt again sought reelection, the Poles in the United States created an umbrella organization, the Polish American Congress, to politick for a reconstituted Poland with old boundaries. Many Democrats were apprehensive about losing elections in crucial states if the government did not cultivate such key ethnic groups. The president therefore asked Stalin to agree to an independent Poland to help him retain the support of Polish-American voters.

At the Yalta Conference Roosevelt again invoked the idea of conciliating ethnic voters. Yet he also accepted the Soviet demand for a boundary that lopped off a third of Poland in the east and compensated her with German territory in the west. Polish-American leaders assailed this compromise as the "Crime of Crimea" and as a "stab in the back" for Poland.[72] Roosevelt did worry about ethnic voters such as the Polish-Americans. When, however, their immediate demands appeared unattainable, he did not permit them to intrude dangerously upon larger strategic policy considerations as he perceived them.

President Harry S Truman followed an analogous strategy. Yet the pressure of Polish-American opinion concerned him so much that in May 1945 he sent a special envoy, Harry Hopkins, to Moscow to confer with Stalin primarily about the Polish question. Two months later at the Potsdam Conference Truman informed Stalin that he would be able to handle the importunities of his millions of "Polish constituents" with less trouble if the Soviets permitted free elections in Poland.[73] Both Roosevelt and Truman had realistic policy reasons for inflating the numbers and the political power of the Polish-Americans. This tactic allowed them the flexibility of making concessions to Stalin on Polish issues that they could not control otherwise than through force while obtaining compromises of substance from the Soviets elsewhere through diplomacy.

The two presidents knew that the ethnic politics of the Polish-Americans, while sometimes crucial in their home districts, on a national scale usually had only limited influence. These leaders did not, therefore, accord their Polish constituency the same deference that they did to other more powerful interest groups, such as those headed by Anglo-Americans. Nonetheless, as politicians who were dependent on popular support, these presidents paid attention to strategically situated minority voters, and in this instance to the policy objectives of the Polish-American community. Both men appeased that group with generalities while responding to its wishes when they could, though not at the expense of major international objectives.

Up to this time, aside from Poland, the United States still had few commercial or other substantive commitments in eastern Europe. From the turn of the century its main connection with that portion of the world had been through its immigrants. As with the members of other resident ethnic groups, the eastern Europeans and their offspring at times banded together to affect policy toward their ancestral homes. Sometimes their ethnic politics succeeded; often they did not.

The efforts of Americans of Latvian, Lithuanian, and Estonian ancestry to exert influence on large policy illustrate the difficulties that small or fragmented ethnic groups can encounter in such instances. Using ideological anti-Communist arguments common in the early cold war years, these Baltic peoples urged opposition to the regimes that the Soviets imposed on their old homelands. Since Washington's policymakers agreed with this objective, the government stuck to a policy of nonrecognition of the *de facto* situation there. Like the Irish-American lobbyists of earlier years, these Baltic groups desired actions that would help their overseas kin regain independence. The Baltic ethnics could not, however, persuade Washington to do more in the face of Soviet power.

In a limited manner, also, even recently conquered Italy benefited from America's ethnic politics. Both Roosevelt and Truman were sensitive to the rising influence of the sons and daughters of Italian immigrants, particularly in key states such as New York and Massachusetts. Whenever possible, the Italian-American organizations from the northeastern states and wherever else they could muster power pressured members of congress and political strategists in the executive branch for moderation toward the former Fascist country. In the Allied occupation of Italy, and later in the peace treaty with her, American leaders therefore lightened the severe measures desired by the British. Consequently, even though the Italian-American lobby at this time could exert only a crippled effort on major policy, it did help Italy emerge from defeat with more lenient treatment than would have been accorded her if the American government had not been responsive to ethnic constituencies.

As in other instances, this sensitivity to ethnic politics as practiced by Italian, Slavic, and other minority Americans did not divert the governing elite from carrying out its major foreign-policy objectives. Yet even during the stress and anger of war, those in power could not with impunity simply ignore the wishes of such constituents. As always, though, the politics of the Anglo-Americans, for strategic as well as for ethnic reasons, took precedence over that of the others.

Anyone who has worked in the international field knows well that our failure in race relations in this country, and our open discrimination against various groups, injures our leadership in the world. It is the one point which can be attacked and to which the representatives of the United States have no answer.

Eleanor Roosevelt, Feb. 9, 1948

7
PLURALISTS AND LOBBYISTS

Following the destruction of Naziism, no nation except perhaps South Africa was as notorious in reputation "for its domestic racial policies as the United States."[1] In retrospect John Hope Franklin, the nation's foremost African-American historian, wished that the United States could have won "the war without the blatant racism that poisoned the entire effort."[2] In this vein India's *Bombay Chronicle* noted the irony that in the conflict many Americans had fought Nazi doctrines while holding racial convictions similar to them.

Despite the prevalence of these attitudes, within the United States nativists did not whip up an hysteria against foreigners comparable to that at the end of the First World War. At the conference in San Francisco in the spring of 1945 to launch the United Nations, moreover, the American government had faced the issue of racism more forthrightly than it had at Paris twenty-six years earlier.

Unlike Woodrow Wilson, President Harry S Truman put aside his own ethnoracial prejudices to accept the principle of racial equality that was backed broadly within the new international organization. At the same time, partly to counteract the widespread criticism of American racism, to win friends in Asia, and to fulfill an old pledge, Truman's government in July 1946 granted long-awaited independence to the Philippines. It also supported a commission on human rights sponsored by the United Nations that called for a commitment to end racial discrimination on a global basis.

Chaired by Eleanor Roosevelt, America's former first lady, the commission held its first meeting in January 1947. In the United States its work quickly became entangled in ethnoracial politics. As a matter of policy,

Southerners in congress blocked adherence to any general declaration by the commission to curb racial intolerance if it had legal force behind it. The State Department acquiesced in their wishes.

William E. B. Du Bois, still an activist as he approached his eightieth year, meanwhile had gained the support of the National Association for the Advancement of Colored People to petition the world organization for a redress of grievances on behalf of African-Americans. He was anxious to be heard, he said, because the United States had denied his people "elemental Justice . . . for three centuries." When he could not overcome the resistance of the American government and of commissioner Roosevelt to his proposal to "investigate discrimination against Blacks," Du Bois had it brought before the world body in October by the Soviet Union.[3] It was voted down.

In December 1948 Du Bois and other African-Americans of like persuasion experienced further disappointment when, along with a convention on the prevention of genocide, defined as the extermination of national, ethnic, racial, or religious groups, the general assembly adopted the Universal Declaration of Human Rights. The declaration had no teeth and would have none for twenty-three years, in part because the American delegates wanted it that way. Even though its adoption amounted to a small victory for the principle of racial equality, the American role in keeping the declaration weak did little to improve the nation's moral position in the world on matters of race and ethnicity. This episode illustrates what Eleanor Roosevelt observed, that as the United States became deeply involved in the cold war, racism still remained the foremost domestic issue which injured its foreign policy.

In these years, though, the environment that had long bred the ethnoracial discrimination began to change. The children and grandchildren of the new immigrants voted in massive numbers. They had, for example, helped bring Franklin D. Roosevelt and the New Dealers to power. Many of these Euro-Americans acquired substantial wealth. Most of them entered society's mainstream, often while remaining sensitive to their cultural heritages. Increasingly, some of them served in congress, captured governorships, held key positions in state legislatures, and became conspicuous in national politics. Their power, along with the emergence of even newer ethnoracial groups, made it difficult for the Anglo-American elite to deal with international issues while still discounting the nation's multiethnic makeup.

The politicians of this era who worked at the grass roots level had fewer qualms than their predecessors about dealing with minority constituents. Along with other Americans, they appeared to accept pluralism as a fact of political life. With a more explicit commitment to minority voters than in the past, leaders in both parties constructed foreign-policy planks that acknowledged the concerns of a variety of ethnic groups.

Despite this transformation in the distribution of power affecting policy, however, the institutionalized discrimination against southeastern Europeans, Asians, and others remained in the immigration regulations. Proceeding on the old assumption that immigration was essentially a matter of domestic social policy, congress refused to repeal even those portions of the legislation which rankled minorities most. Analysts often attribute the establishment's resistance to change in these early cold war years to its preoccupation with Communism and fear of the Soviet Union. A more important reason was that prejudice, like habit, dies slowly.

That the immigration legislation damaged foreign policy had long been obvious to the ethnic groups affected by it. Now even Anglo-American leaders, while trying to cope with the intricacies of global diplomacy, found themselves constantly embarrassed by the quota system and by the Jim Crow practices against blacks. In September 1946 Paul Robeson, heading a black lobby to end lynching, told Truman "that unless mob violence was soon stopped, foreign intervention would be in order." The president retorted "that the United States could handle its affairs without concern for happenings abroad."[4]

Yet four months earlier, Acting Secretary of State Dean G. Acheson had explained the need for change in matters of civil rights, saying that "the existence of discrimination against minority groups in this country has had an adverse effect on our relations with other countries." It "is a handicap in our relations with other countries."[5]

The problem had become so acute that in December Truman created a special body, the President's Committee on Civil Rights, to investigate it. The committee quickly queried State Department officials on how ethnoracial discrimination affected foreign relations. In its findings, published in the following October, the committee used that data, saying that "We cannot escape the fact that our civil rights record has been an issue in world politics. The world's press and radio are full of it."[6] The report urged a broad-gauged assault on the segregation of African-Americans. In carrying out the campaign against this old practice, the Department of Justice cited the warnings from Acheson and other State Department figures as justifying it.

As the cold war intensified, the Soviets became increasingly alert to the foreign-policy repercussions of racial inequality. Perceiving ethnoracial prejudice as the most vulnerable aspect of America's international status, they regularly attacked all aspects of it, especially to counter the criticism of their own oppressive policies in Eastern Europe and at home. They noted that the lynching of blacks persisted in the South and that those who led America's anti-Communist crusade were themselves often still tarred with the bigotry of white nativism. Indeed, racism often accompanied cold war anti-Communism. Underscoring this connection between policies abroad and at home, the Soviets more than once denounced the United States as "a hypocrite in international affairs" for demanding free elections in Europe while denying millions of its own black citizens the right to vote.[7]

The Soviets were not alone in their attacks. Other foreigners, too, criticized the lack of effective official response to minority aspirations in diverse areas of everyday life in the United States, but in particular in the regulation of immigration. Such discrimination persisted, even though in these years many more white Americans than ever had become conscious of their ethnic identities and how they affected their status in society.

This shift in popular sentiment did not translate immediately into a new public policy for many reasons, some of them being pretexts having to do with foreign relations. For example, ethnoracial groups often focused more on the objectives important to their old homelands, or to their brethren abroad, than on domestic laws. Yet the fresh social attitudes did help to modify traditional establishment practices in both domestic and foreign policy. Notable aspects of this change can be seen in the ethnic politics leading to the founding of Israel.

Since Wilson's time the Zionist lobbies, which had represented only a portion of Jewish opinion in the United States, had obtained pledges of support from presidents and congress for a Jewish state as called for by the Balfour Declaration. By 1943, even though some Jews, such as those in the recently founded American Council for Judaism, were still anti-Zionist, for the first time "practically every major Jewish organization in this country supported a demand for a homeland in Palestine."[8] Now, with a great increase in numbers representing "over 90 percent of American Jewry," the Zionists had impressive power.[9] Despite a still potent anti-Semitism, they also had sympathy from much of the general public.

In the wartime election year of 1944 American Jews used these assets to exert their heaviest pressure yet for a renewed governmental commitment to the Zionist goal. As in the past, with the support of Christian as well as Jewish organizations, they persuaded both houses of congress to take up a resolution calling for official intervention in Palestine to help create a Jewish state there. Again the major parties adopted planks favoring that policy as well as unrestricted Jewish immigration to Palestine.

On the grounds that congress' resolution would be "prejudicial to the successful prosecution of the war," the Roosevelt administration had it shelved. Prior to the election, however, the president said that he favored a "democratic Jewish commonwealth."[10] A few months later he also assured King Abdul Aziz Al Saud of Saudi Arabia "that he would do nothing to assist the Jews against the Arabs and would make no move hostile to the Arab people."[11] Whether or not the Arab communities were aware of Roosevelt's ambivalence toward them and the Jews, shortly thereafter they announced their hostility to Zionism and to American policy.

In April 1945, when Truman inherited the presidency, a larger mass of Americans than ever, many of them stirred by the suffering of the Jews in the Holocaust and others by the biblical promise of a Jewish state, favored an independent homeland for them. Although the new president, too, felt compassion for the Jews, wanting to help their displaced European survivors settle in Palestine, he indicated no noteworthy commitment to the Zionist cause. He even soon became impressed by his diplomatic and military advisers who argued that a pro-Zionist position would militate against the national interest by alienating the Arabs.

Jewish leaders in Palestine such as David Ben Gurion believed, nonetheless, that the American Jews, if united "behind the Zionist solution . . . may be the key to changing the situation."[12] Democratic political strategists such as Clark Clifford, the president's special counsel, provided good reason for such an assumption. They were concerned more with the political clout of the 5.6 million Jews in the United States, making up about half of world Jewry, than they were about the Arabs.

These advisers also perceived the national interest differently from the diplomatic and military people. Aware of Truman's dependence on private donations for his election campaigns, a large portion of which came from Jews, the politicians impressed the president with the "necessity of catering to American Jews" in an election year. To a degree, he yielded to such pressures. In opposition to the British, who still held the mandate there, Truman encouraged "illegal Jewish immigration" to Palestine.[13] After members of congress and lobbyists bombarded him with messages pressing for support of the Zionist program, Truman responded by reversing his position on this issue, too.

Accordingly, on October 4, 1946, the Jewish holy day of Yom Kippur and one month before congressional elections, the president endorsed the establishment of "a viable Jewish state" in Palestine. As he had done earlier, he also urged the British policymakers to admit 100,000 Jews immediately. Foreign Secretary Ernest Bevin had begged the president to withhold the announcement. Truman responded that if he did not release his statement, Thomas E. Dewey, the Republican governor of New York and a presidential aspirant, would come out with a similar proposal.

Two days later, while insisting that the issue "far transcended partisan politics," Dewey said that what was needed was "an immigration not of one hundred thousand but of several hundreds of thousands" of Jews to Palestine.[14] The Arabs, who opposed such immigration, stepped up a campaign of violence against the Jews and the British. Bevin, who had complained that "the Jews through their aggressive attitude were 'poisoning relations between our two [American and British] peoples,'" explained to parliament that American ethnic politics had ruined promising negotiations designed to compose Jewish-Arab differences.

Secretary of State George C. Marshall, Undersecretary Acheson, his successor, Robert Lovett, and the foreign-policy establishment, also deplored the president's support for a Jewish state to satisfy the demands of ethnic politics. Acheson wrote later that those who advocated a pro-Zionist policy "had allowed . . . their emotion to obscure the totality of American interests."[15] On the other hand, Clark Clifford "sometimes felt, almost bitterly, that they [the State Department people] preferred to follow the views of the British Foreign Office rather than those of their own President."[16]

In April 1947 the British turned over the Palestine problem to the United Nations and in October announced that they would terminate their mandate. The world organization recommended partition into Jewish and Arab states and a separate status for Jerusalem. Since the plan offered the Jews the independent homeland they desired, they accepted it. The Arabs rejected it. After some hesitation, Truman came out for the Jewish state as proposed through partition. "We had won a great victory," the Zionist lobbyists explained. "We had won because of the sheer pressure of political logistics that was applied by the Jewish leadership in the United States."[17]

Immediately Arab-Jewish hostilities spread. In November, after prolonged skirmishing, the United Nations resolution passed, and in December the British declared that in May they would withdraw from Palestine. When the Zionists proceeded with plans to erect their own state, Jewish-Americans pleaded with the Truman government to stand behind it. A few were blunt in reminding the president that "Jews who vote the Democratic ticket expect your immediate intercession in Palestine."[18]

That spring advisers warned Truman that Jewish supporters would turn against him if he delayed recognition of the state once it came into being.

Democratic leaders urged recognition "as a way to appeal to Jewish voters and perhaps head off disaster in the presidential election."[19] A torrent of pro-recognition mail flooded the White House. Truman said later that he had never been more heavily lobbied.[20]

On May 14, 1948, at 6:00 P.M. Washington time, Zionists proclaimed the independent state of Israel. Eleven minutes later, at the president's insistence, Washington announced *de facto* recognition, the first government to accord it.

Those policymakers, such as Marshall and Secretary of Defense James V. Forrestal, who regarded themselves as patriots in the Anglo-American tradition claimed that they wanted "to lift the Palestine question out of American partisan politics." Deploring what he perceived as a decision motivated by ethnic pressure, Forrestal commented bitterly, "I thought it was a most disastrous and regrettable fact that the foreign policy of this country was determined by the contributions a particular bloc of special interests might make to the party funds." Reputedly Truman responded to such criticism with, "How many American voters are Arabs?"[21]

Unlike Forrestal, Marshall, and others, historians debate the efficacy of Jewish-American ethnic politics in this decision. Those who deny that the immediate recognition of Israel sprang from Zionist pressure, or from a need "to gain Jewish votes," maintain that it evolved out of compassion for the oppressed as well as from the desire to serve "the best interests of the United States."[22] They go along with Clifford's view that the nation's interests called for keeping the Soviets out of Middle Eastern affairs by beating them to recognition. These analysts take Truman's protestations at face value. They argue that he "insisted privately and publicly that he would not be influenced by domestic politics but would act in the light of U.S. national security."[23] They conclude that he had proceeded accordingly.

Other academic students of the problem hold with the cabinet officers that ethnic politics backed "by the power of an aroused public" sympathetic to the Jews were indeed important, if not decisive, in Truman's policy.[24] They maintain that regardless of his initial ambivalence toward the Palestine issue, the president "was very considerably influenced by domestic political considerations," that "his support for Zionism was closely determined by electoral considerations," that he "sought to appease Jewish leaders," that he responded to "political and strategic realities," or that he wanted "a solid base within the Jewish community" and hence "was deliberately and calculatingly playing politics with this explosive issue."[25]

Regardless of the controversy, a minority had succeeded in molding foreign policy in a fundamental way. More impressively than had any ethnic group other than the Anglo-American, the Jewish community had achieved its objective by building public, congressional, and executive support. It also overcame the opposition of the London government and the contrary influence of the Anglo-American leadership in Washington.

Despite this accomplishment and the power attributed to the Jewish-American lobby, however, that lobby still worked within limitations. It could not, for instance, block the Displaced Persons Act of June 1948, "which, although providing for the admission of over two hundred thousand displaced persons in Europe for the next two years, discriminated against Jews." Jewish lobbyists appealed to the White House for a veto, but other minority leaders, as well as prominent Jews who believed that the legislation brought some relief, urged the president to approve it. Caught in a bind between the politics of conflicting ethnoreligious groups, he signed the bill on June 25 with "very great reluctance" because of its "callous" discrimination against Jews.[26]

"Most American Jews were outraged" by the law.[27] Many wondered how and why their lobbying had gone wrong. As for the harm Truman's signing of the legislation did to his standing with the Jewish community, it was offset by his prompt recognition of Israel in the previous month.

The Jewish community's attitude was reflected in the presidential campaign of that year, in which both parties promised support for Israel, then at war with several Arab states. Against great odds Truman won the election. It has been estimated that he received between sixty and seventy-five percent of the Jewish vote nationwide. Yet despite a strenuous effort in New York, he lost this state with the largest number of Jewish voters. The Jewish vote was not, as often claimed, a key factor in his victory that came to him as a reward for his support of Israel. As historian Zvi Ganin points out, the Jews were more important in the election "for their financial contributions to the Democratic party."[28]

Beyond such Jewish support, the causes for Truman's win are complex. People voted for him for economic as well as ethnoracial reasons. His bread-and-butter policies, which held the allegiance of blue-collar Democrats and midwestern farmers, his ability to attract votes from minorities, including eastern Europeans, Catholics, and blacks, his strong civil rights stance, and the general prosperity of the country all contributed to his upset. Truman himself attributed it to a "continuation of the policies which had been in effect for the last sixteen years."[29]

In the years that followed, the Israelis fought off Arab armies, preserved their new state and even expanded it, and with crucial help from the United States, grew in strength. In considerable measure, Jewish-American ethnic politics kept Washington's assistance from wavering. In 1951 this politicking blended with that of a newly organized Israeli lobby. As an umbrella for numerous Zionist organizations, it quickly acquired an impressive but not always decisive influence in policy affecting the Middle East. For example, its efforts to prevent arms sales to Arab states sometimes faltered.

The most notable opposition to the lobby's pressure by an American government occurred during and after the Suez War that began on October 29, 1956, when Israeli forces knifed into the Sinai Peninsula and routed Egyptian foes. Six days later, as part of a two-power collusion with the Israelis, British and French troops invaded Egypt. In a resolution pushed through the general assembly of the United Nations, the American government condemned these actions as aggression. On the following day it took measures that forced a cease-fire and compelled the Europeans to withdraw.

The Israelis proved more stubborn, making clear their intention to retain possession of the territory that their soldiers had conquered. With telegrams, letters, and other means, American Jews importuned Washington to permit the retention. President Dwight D. Eisenhower would not accede. Even though he had courted minority voters, he was much less obligated to Jewish ethnic politics than his predecessor. From the start he assumed that Israel's prime minister, David Ben Gurion, "might think he could take advantage of this country because of the approaching [presidential] election and because of the importance that so many politicians in the past have attached to our Jewish vote." To prevent that, Eisenhower added, "I gave strict orders to the State Department that they should inform Israel that we would handle our affairs exactly as though we didn't have a Jew in America."[30]

Even though political advisers told the president that his stand might cost him the election, he insisted that Israeli forces must pull back from the Sinai. In November he stopped economic aid to Israel, and in February 1957 threatened economic sanctions if its troops did not withdraw. When American Jews mobilized their resources against this caveat, the furious Secretary of State John F. Dulles complained "how almost impossible it is in this country to carry out a foreign policy not approved by the Jews. Marshall and Forrestal learned that. I am going to try and have one."[31] This assumption that America's Jews dominated the nation's policy in the Middle East, whether or not accurate, governed his own policy-making. Finally, after five months of procrastination and despite the solid support of Jewish-Americans for its stance, Israel reluctantly evacuated its troops from Egyptian territory.

Eisenhower's Democratic successors, John F. Kennedy and Lyndon B. Johnson, felt more beholden to Zionist political support than he did. While their rhetoric stressed an "even-handed" approach to Middle Eastern problems, both adopted pro-Israeli policies. In his presidential campaign, Kennedy, for instance, had criticized Arab leaders while explaining to Jewish voters that "Friendship for Israel is not a partisan matter, it is a national commitment." Whether rightly or wrongly, he became convinced "that the Jewish vote had been critical to his narrow victory over [Richard M.] Nixon."[32] An analysis of the ballots cast showed that "81.82% of the Jews voted for Kennedy."[33]

Having entered the White House, Kennedy attempted a rapprochement with Egypt to bring balance to policy-making for the Middle East without impairing the relationship with Israel. His effort failed. It could hardly have succeeded in light of his feelings for Israel as a singular friend, his concern for Jewish domestic constituents, and his view of Israel as a strategic international asset. Kennedy told Golda Meir, the Israeli foreign minister, that "the United States . . . has a special relationship with Israel in the Middle East really comparable only to that which it has with Great Britain over a wide range of world affairs."[34]

In May 1967, as the Arab states built up their armies, Egypt ordered the United Nations Emergency Force stationed on its Israeli border to withdraw and closed the Strait of Tiran to Israeli shipping. War again loomed in the Middle East. President Johnson, Kennedy's successor, made the United States' relationship with Israel even closer. He assured Israel's foreign minister, "very slowly and very positively," that "Israel will not be alone unless it decides to go alone." He also emphasized the "necessity for Israel not to make itself reponsible for the initiation of hostilities."[35] Believing their survival threatened, the Israelis disregarded the advice. On their own, on June 5, they again struck at Egypt, Syria, and Jordan, again quickly defeated them, and again seized the Sinai Peninsula along with the Gaza Strip and other territory.

As in the past, in this Six-Day War Israel benefited from widespread American sympathy and government support. Despite a publicly proclaimed embargo on arms to the Middle East, the Johnson administration secretly sent military equipment to Israel, and American planes flew reconnaissance for her during the hostilities. This time the president refused to pressure her into surrendering her gains. In opposition to the Soviets, he even stepped up his military assistance to the Israelis.

Although Israel was still beset by Arab enemies on all sides, with American support she had emerged as the most powerful state in the Middle East.

Hence, in subsequent years many Americans came to question the need for supplying her with huge sums of money as well as military assistance. The Israeli lobby, which in 1958 had become the American Israel Public Affairs Committee (AIPAC), kept the aid flowing. This phenomenon led a number of political scientists and others to recast their thinking about the nature of ethnic influence on foreign policy.

With Jewish-Americans and Israel in mind, they contended that in international affairs minority ethnic power had become lopsided. They observed that the White House usually maintained an official liaison person for the Jewish community who could, and at times did, influence foreign policy. They noted, too, that year after year politicians supported Israel without having to worry about alienating an Arab vote of any significance.

At no time since Israel's founding could its opponents rally to their cause an Arab-American community comparable in size, unity, and motivation to that of the Jewish-Americans. Before the Second World War only about 250,000 Arabs had immigrated to the United States, most of them Christians from Lebanon and Syria. After the creation of Israel and its Arab wars that followed, thousands of Palestinians and other Muslim Arabs fled to North America.

Neither these recent arrivals nor the older Arab residents formed a cohesive political force. Religious and micro-ethnic differences kept them weak and divided. Not until after the Six-Day War could they agree on specific foreign-policy objectives. That conflict brought to Arab-Americans and their supporters, such as several African-American groups, an aroused awareness of their bond to the Arab world. Still, none of these activists could compete with the Israeli lobby, which despite a lingering anti-Semitism in the United States, grew in power. As for the Arabs, public sentiment, the press, television, and the movies all remained against them. In the next few years in their efforts to effect any change in foreign policy, the Arab-Americans had to battle ethnic prejudice and a hostile socio-political environment.

Unlike the Arabs in these decades, the descendants of southeastern European immigrants other than Jews had become bolder and more effective in challenging the traditional managers of foreign policy. At the same time, much more often than in the past, the governing elite sought support from these minorities in attaining strategic international goals. In 1948, for example, it had turned to the Italian-Americans.

The policymakers reached out to this constituency because, for the first time in a quarter of a century, the people in Italy had an opportunity to choose their own deputies and senators in democratic elections. The campaign pitted pro-American Christian Democrats against a coalition of leftist parties headed by Communists. Regarding Italy at this time as a critical prize in the cold war, the American government became deeply involved in the electioneering in support of the Christian Democrats. Policymakers even weighed possible military intervention to prevent Italy from going Communist.

Truman and his advisers decided instead to beef up their effort by engaging prominent Italian-Americans to make broadcasts to Italy for the propaganda organ *Voice of America*. The administration also involved itself deeply in a campaign of "letters and telegrams to Italy," in which Italian-Americans urged relatives and friends in the old homeland to vote against the left. The Italian government, headed by Christian Democrat Alcide De Gasperi, assigned an officer in its embassy in Washington to act as liaison between it and the Italian-American community. In the spring, as the drive climaxed, the Italian-Americans responded to the prodding by flooding Italy's post offices with letters and telegrams carrying the cold war dogma that a vote for the Communists would be a vote against the United States.

The Communists denounced this American lobbying as "tortuous and Jesuitical," while some Americans, such as Vice President Henry A. Wallace, criticized the use of "bribery and threats," as in the message that Italy would lose Marshall Plan and other economic aid if the Communists gained power.[36] Weathering such criticism, the Christian Democrats won the April elections decisively. Observers believed that the Italian-American intervention had contributed significantly to the Communist defeat.

In his hard-pressed presidential campaign of that year, Truman sought to benefit from the letters campaign, in part because he and Dewey competed for the votes of the Italian-Americans, as they did for those of American Jews and other ethnic groups, with commitments on controversial foreign-policy issues. Truman claimed credit for having "saved Italy from communism."

Dewey, on the other hand, told a delegation of Italian-Americans that he favored giving Italy control of her former African colonies. He said, "after all no other ethnic group in the United States had any real interest in Africa." He soon realized how insensitive he had been to the deeper nuances of ethnic politics. The African-American press immediately attacked him. He responded with a compromise, saying that he favored Italian control "under a United Nations trusteeship."[37]

Truman's equally crude strategy proved more effective. Even though he lost New York with its large Italian population, he apparently succeeded in bringing back to the Democratic party many of the Italian-Americans who had abandoned it in the later Roosevelt years largely for reasons of foreign policy.

As this and other episodes showed, ethnic politicking retained its importance, even though under the impact of the restrictive immigration laws the first- and second-generation population had declined as a percentage of the total. Ethnic voting continued because the non-Anglo segment of society remained large, with an ethnic affiliation that stretched into the third and fourth generations and even beyond. In 1950 there were nearly 11 million foreign-born in the country and 24 million Americans with at least one parent born abroad.

To these people, to the politicians who believed that they needed ethnic votes to survive, and to the diplomats who implemented foreign policy, the national-origins formula for restricting immigration had become ever more embarrassing. As more and more former colonial peoples outside Western Europe achieved independence, the United States and the Soviet Union competed for influence among them. In this rivalry the damage abroad to American policy multiplied because of the immigration discrimination. Moreover, most of the people then coming into the country as refugees belonged to the minority groups stigmatized by law. In the matter of the refugees, after five years of consistent pressure from both Jews and Gentiles, congress in June 1952 eliminated one of the most discriminatory features of the displaced persons law so as to allow more Jews into the country.

At the same time, the executive branch had taken the lead in seeking a revision of the national-origins system. After congress had studied immigration policy for three years, had held extensive hearings on it, and had debated where changes were most needed, its unredeemed nativists prevailed. The restrictionists rejected change, and with it pluralism, by maintaining that the old-stock whites were correct in their policy of admitting primarily those "immigrants considered to be more readily assimilable because of the similarity of their cultural background to those of the principal components of our population." The nativists also warned that "we have in the United States today hard-core, indigestible blocs which have not become integrated into the American way of life but which, on the contrary, are our deadly enemies."[38] Such bias suffused the McCarran-Walter bill. The Jewish, Italian, Greek, black, and other ethnoracial groups which found it offensive condemned and tried to block it, but to no avail.

In his veto of the bill, Truman, a former believer in white-supremacy dogma, explained that "Our immigration policy [is important domestically] but is equally, if not more important, to the conduct of our foreign

relations and to our responsibilities of moral leadership in the . . . world."
Even though this bill "recognizes the great international significance of our
immigration and naturalization policy" by removing "all racial bars to naturalization," it would also "perpetuate injustices of long standing against
many nations of the world." It would continue, "practically without
change, the national origins system" which is "more than ever unrealistic
in the face of present world conditions." That system "is a constant hardship
in the conduct of our foreign relations." We need a decent immigration
program as "a fitting instrument for our foreign policy."[39]

Regardless, congress passed the Immigration and Nationality Act over
the president's veto, making it the keystone of a policy that was obnoxious
to allies as well as to most other foreigners. Yet, the legislation did eliminate
an official racial prejudice of long standing. It lifted what remained of the
ban on Asians and Pacific islanders by giving them a small quota and by no
longer excluding them from citizenship.

In January 1953 the President's Commission on Immigration repeated
the old criticisms, saying that the professions of friendship for other peoples
which usually decorated American diplomatic rhetoric were meaningless in
light of the reality under the McCarran-Walter Act. Knowledgeable foreigners could readily look beyond official verbiage to see how Americans truly
felt about them. Aware of these shortcomings, presidents Eisenhower and
Kennedy exercised executive discretion to the extent permitted by the law
to relax some of the act's most onerous restrictions. But the basic bigotry
remained.

Accordingly, in 1963 Kennedy urged congress to abolish the national-
origins formula, calling it "an anachronism" which lacked "basis in either
logic or reason" in an age of international interdependence. After Kennedy's
death, President Johnson took up his proposals. Johnson's landslide election
victory in 1964, which also brought to power new legislators sympathetic
to change, paved the way for another immigration law. "We are concerned
to see that our immigration laws reflect our real character and objectives,"
Secretary of State Dean Rusk told congress in 1964, "because what other
people think about us plays an important role in the achievement of our
foreign policies."[40]

In its hearings congress paid much more attention to statements such as
Rusk's and to numerous foreign-policy interests on which immigration had
a bearing than it had in the past. Indeed, a close student of the problem has
argued "that a key influence on immigration policy was foreign affairs."[41]
Minority lobbying was also important, particularly by Jewish, Italian, Jap-

anese-American, and other organizations. They urged the changes that would erase the old discriminatory practices.

Finally, in September 1965 congress overwhelmingly passed amendments to the Immigration and Nationality Act that would go into effect in three years. By abolishing the national-origins formula and the special restrictions on peoples in the Asia-Pacific triangle, it responded to the widespread ethnoracial sensitivity in international relations as well as in American society. By providing a stimulus for more ethnic politics, particularly as based on color, it undercut assimilationist theory. At last, on the immigration issue at least, American policymakers no longer appeared hypocritical for opposing racial discrimination abroad while sanctioning it at home.

Earlier in this period, as we have seen, ethnic sentiment and anti-Communist ideology had often become entangled in a manner that distinctively influenced foreign policy. Yet the mingling of doctrine and emotion had antecedents preceding the cold war era. From about the last decade of the nineteenth century onward, when the new immigrants began noticeably changing the electorate's ethnic mix, both the Republican and Democratic national committees had organized nationalities divisions designed to attract votes on the basis of ethnicity. These politicians usually focused on strategically situated minority groups.

In the presidential campaign of 1952, the politicians who headed the Republican nationalities division believed that the heavily anti-Communist Eastern European community, even though it amounted to only two percent of the population, could affect the election. So the ethnic strategists committed Eisenhower to a party plank that promised "liberation" for the "captive" peoples in the Soviet satellite countries. To Arthur Bliss Lane, a former ambassador to Poland, fell the task of winning over the voters of Eastern European extraction. The desire for such votes, particularly among Polish-Americans, also led Eisenhower to speak about repudiating the Yalta agreements with the Soviet Union as they applied to Poland.

Ironically, Truman, who had himself maintained close liaison with special-interest groups for political advantage, now denounced this manipulation of foreign policy for the same purpose. By stirring up "our citizens who have ties of blood" with the peoples of Eastern Europe, he said, the Republicans "are playing a cruel, gutter political game with the lives of countless good men and women behind the iron curtain."[42] The Republican leaders, who discounted this rhetoric, were convinced that the Slavic votes contributed to Eisenhower's victory. Furthermore, both the Democratic and Republican strategists of these years believed in the old theory that the descendants of immigrants voted on the basis of heredity, particularly on issues that affected ancestral lands.

The critics of these tactics contend that in this instance the exploitation of ethnic politics contributed to tragedy. In November 1956, when the Hungarians revolted against Soviet dominance, they hoped for help from the United States on the basis of the Republican oratory. They received no assistance. Eisenhower explained that "liberation" never meant encouragement for an armed uprising that could bring disaster to those the United States wished to befriend.

About three years later, Eastern European ethnic groups and cold war dogmatists pressured congress into adopting a resolution calling on the president to proclaim a "Captive Nations Week" which was to be repeated annually "until . . . freedom and independence shall have been achieved for all the captive nations of the world." Eisenhower implemented the resolution on July 17, 1959, the very day it passed. Few of the politicians who were involved considered the proclamation a major statement of foreign policy. Yet Nikita S. Khrushchev, the Soviet leader, said, "This resolution stinks."[43] He and other leaders objected to it as a blatant interference in their internal affairs. So, regardless of the administration's intent, the captive nations resolution did harm Soviet-American relations.

Despite the victory of their lobbyists in this instance, the mostly Slavic Eastern European groups in the United States failed to reach their main common goal—independence for their kindred peoples who were under Soviet domination. It eluded them at this time simply because the United States could not liberate the Eastern Europeans without the risk of another great war, something most other Americans would not tolerate. The ethnic politics of the American Slavs, like those of the other smaller minority groups, could succeed only with discrete objectives or when they were linked to larger issues. Their communities did not possess sufficient power to precipitate on their own major changes in foreign policy.

The African-Americans, too, still lacked such leverage. As always, race basically accounted for their political weakness. Only in rare instances, as in the case of the Ethiopian War, did the formulators of foreign policy seriously take into account the wishes of the nation's largest ethnoracial minority. Yet the African-Americans had regarded the United States as their own country far longer than had most minority whites. In addition, black religious and intellectual leaders such as Du Bois had long taken an interest in foreign policy as an important feature of their Americanism. They had viewed the Second World War in part from the perspective of foreign policy, but they had weighed it especially from that of race.

Whether or not President Roosevelt and his advisers were aware of these feelings, they had been worried about the apathy of blacks toward the conflict. The reports reaching them indicated that the African-Americans perceived it as a white man's affair, a "spectacle of America at war to preserve the ideal of government by free men, yet clinging to the social vestiges of the slave system." Roosevelt may even have heard the equivalent of the bitter comment of an African-American draftee: "Just carve on my tombstone, 'Here lies a black man killed fighting a yellow man for the protection of a white man.'"[44]

With its rhetoric about freedom for the oppressed, the war also had the effect of expanding the African-American interest in international affairs. As explained by Walter White, the head of the National Association for the Advancement of Colored People, that conflict restimulated in the "Negro a sense of kinship with other colored—and also oppressed—peoples of the world."[45]

Numerous American blacks, not just the dedicated Pan Africanists, now looked to "Mother Africa" as their homeland, even though few could trace their roots with certainty to specific ethnic groups there. They turned to Africa nonetheless, because they yearned for identification with her cultures and peoples and hoped with it to elevate their own status. As did the members of white ethnic groups, the African-Americans also sought more political leverage so that they could influence foreign policy in the interest of the peoples whose ancestry they shared.

In the next decade, especially after the supreme court in *Brown* v. *Board of Education of Topeka* (1954) mandated desegregation throughout the nation, the civil rights movement galvanized more African-Americans into an awareness of foreign-policy issues that carried ethnoracial implications. In limited ways the government, too, responded to this black sensitivity. Through the *Voice of America*, for instance, it immediately broadcast the news of the court's decision to foreign countries in thirty-five different languages. Thereafter African-American leaders, their organizations, and the media increasingly brought the ethnoracial aspects of international issues, especially as they pertained to Africa and Asia, to public attention. Black activists linked the civil rights struggle to the dissolution of European rule in Africa and to anticolonialism everywhere.

Finally, the foreign-policy establishment, which under Truman and Eisenhower gave highest priority to cold war European concerns, responded with concrete measures to this growing interaction between American and

African blacks. In 1956 the Department of State established a separate office of African affairs. Two years later that desk rose to bureau status with its own assistant secretary. The government also placed African-Americans in the United States' delegation to the United Nations.

Concurrently, the leaders of the newly independent African peoples followed the American civil rights movement, often identifying with it. Newspapers in their countries reported on racial tensions, violence, racist speeches in congress and elsewhere, and spoke out against segregationists. Kwame Nkrumah, the head of recently established Ghana, for example, explained that Africa's blacks felt a sense of solidarity with the "people of African descent everywhere who are striving for a richer and fuller life."[46]

Despite the heightened interest of concerned American blacks in their mother continent and their efforts to engender government support for development in the new nations there, they still could not mobilize sufficient political power to affect African issues significantly. Blacks' potential for reorienting foreign policy in that direction was diluted because they were frequently still disenfranchised and because they often voted as a bloc mainly on matters affecting their domestic welfare, which to many of them was all-absorbing. The Euro-American policymakers still prevailed. In most instances they continued to treat affairs in Africa as though Europeans still dominated that continent, and they still placed Europe first in their concerns.

What for the first time gave the international politics of black Africa the status of a major issue in American foreign policy was the violence in the Congo (Zaire) following its independence from Belgium in June 1960. After some ambivalence in its attitude, the Kennedy administration in 1962 broke with its Western European allies over policy toward the black regime there. In support of the goal of a united Congo nation, as favored by African-Americans, it cautiously helped the United Nations suppress a conservative secessionist movement in the province of Katanga. Africans and African-Americans viewed this commitment as a positive change in American foreign policy. Yet, as most of them realized, the government had acted more out of fear that "Communist influence would rise dangerously" and impair cold war objectives than out of regard for the desires of black constituents.[47]

A year earlier a group of African-Americans had organized the American Negro Leadership Conference on Africa to promote civil rights in the United States, support national independence in Africa, guide African-American opinion on Africa, and draw more blacks into positions of influence within the policy-making establishment. In the following year Kennedy backed these objectives by telling black leaders that "he felt the 20,000,000 Negroes in this country had a responsibility for the role of the United States in Africa."[48]

That advice was significant because, with most of black Africa now independent, the countries there constituted the largest regional bloc in the United Nations. In December 1963 a coalition of these nations was instrumental in persuading the Security Council to vote for a voluntary embargo on the sale of arms to racist South Africa. The African-Americans, a number of whom since late in the nineteenth century had maintained some form of contact with the blacks in South Africa, threw their weight behind it. Washington backed the embargo because the American blacks did and because apartheid, the Afrikaner program of segregating blacks that had been in force since the early forties, violated human rights.

This espousal of civil rights for foreign blacks represented another change in American policy. For African-Americans, however, it did not go far enough. They desired more government involvement, such as its sponsorship of mandatory economic measures against South Africa. They also lobbied Washington to allot to the new African nations a substantial share in the foreign-aid program.

This African-American effort to isolate the white South African regime from the rest of the world began to pick up more supporters after the passage of the Civil Rights Act of 1964 and the Voting Rights Act of the following year. By providing voter guarantees, this legislation greatly increased the black electorate, thus assuring it meaningful political power. Politicians quickly became more accountable than in the past to African-American pressures in foreign as well as domestic matters.

Nonetheless, leaders such as Martin Luther King, Jr., charged the Johnson administration with being lax in urging the Pretoria government to abandon apartheid. Militant African-Americans also adopted the language of "Black Power," a program which gained recognition for some of their views in the politics of foreign policy. As one leader explained, "Black Power recognizes—it must recognize—the ethnic basis of American politics as well as the power-oriented nature of American politics. Black power therefore calls for black people to consolidate behind their own, so that they can bargain from a position of strength."[49]

In the next several years the pride accompanying the Black Power movement in the United States influenced the rise of militant black consciousness in South Africa. African-Americans organized support for their overseas brothers by engaging in ethnic politics on their behalf, much as did the members of the white ethnic groups for kin in their motherlands. Although these tactics made little immediate headway, as evident in the collapse of the leadership lobby in 1967, blacks did attain several long-term benefits. From this time forward, for example, as was evident in the Kennedy and Johnson policies, no administration could deal with oppressive white regimes in South Africa as though oblivious to the plight of the majority black inhabitants.

Similarly, American governments could no longer follow a truly hands-off policy elsewhere in Africa, as became clear when civil war broke out in May 1967 in Nigeria. That conflict was anchored in the resentment of the Christian Ibos, the dominant ethnic group in the eastern part of the country, against the ruling regime of Muslim northerners composed mainly of rivals of Hausa, Fulani, and Kanuri stock. The Ibos proclaimed a republic of Biafra and tried to secede.

Concerned more with the Vietnam War and the cold war, President Johnson evinced little interest in the Nigerian struggle. Essentially, he went along with the views of his advisers in the State Department and elsewhere who regarded the hostilities as falling within Britain's sphere of influence. They and the British sided with the central government on the theory that if Biafra's secession succeeded, Nigeria and other parts of black Africa would become Balkanized. Influential whites within the United States who sympathized with the Ibos, however, lobbied the government to assist Biafra with food and military supplies. "Pro-Biafran groups were organized both at the national and the local levels," with several of them having chapters "in every state in almost every significant city in the U.S."[50]

At the start, attentive African-Americans, too, were divided in their views toward the Nigerian conflict, most of them desiring a peaceful resolution. Nigeria's federal government, along with the African-American press, appealed to them "for support by claiming that 'the evil manipulations' of European powers were at the root of the war" and that the white racists were exploiting it in "relentless efforts to perpetually enslave Black people."[51]

This argument, the rising pro-Biafra sentiment, and the escalation of the strife brought more and more of the African-American politicians, journalists, and others behind the Nigerian federal government. They connected its status with their own. Viewing this most populous of Africa's countries with pride as "a key to black dignity and liberation," many African-Americans assumed that if it fell apart its fate would harm their own struggle for unity and power.[52]

When Richard M. Nixon took office, he inclined toward the pro-Biafran position favored mainly by the white lobbyists. He had criticized "the central government of Nigeria" for pursuing a policy of "wholesale atrocities and genocide" against "the Ibo people."[53] This stance placed the White House at odds with most African-American leaders and with the State Department. Despite these feelings, Nigeria ranked low in Nixon's scale of priorities. In effect, he continued his predecessor's policy.

When Biafra capitulated in January 1970, after a toll of two million deaths, Nigeria's victors ventilated their resentment against the American government as well as against the band of liberal and conservative intellectuals that had attacked them. The Nigerians also expressed gratitude toward those African-Americans who, in their own limited way, through lobbying and other support, had helped to counter the Biafra lobby and to keep Washington committed to the one-Nigeria policy.

Later that year African-Americans again expressed a desire to be involved in international issues that affected their mother continent. A number of them requested observer status at a meeting of the Organization of African Unity in Addis Ababa. "It is important that our African brothers and sisters recognize that we are an African people," they explained, "and it is important for us as the major African people outside the continent to have a presence in discussions on the future of Africa."[54] At the same time, black Americans renewed their demands for a larger role in the shaping of their own country's foreign policy. They regarded their limited achievements in matters of policy as not commensurate with their numbers or with the goals they sought.

In these decades, as in the past, the white establishment's faith in its racial preeminence influenced American behavior toward much of Asia and the Pacific islands. Officials such as General Douglas MacArthur, the embodiment of American power in the occupation of Japan, maintained that the Pacific Ocean had become an "Anglo-Saxon" lake, and that it should stay that way.

However much Asian-Americans might resent such assumptions, they could do little to change them, because, like the African-Americans, these American Asians still lacked meaningful political leverage. Seldom on their own could they give direction to even limited aspects of foreign policy. Although most of them, like the Jewish- and Italian-Americans, were clustered in populous coastal cities where political activism could be especially effective, micro-ethnic fragmentation continued to weaken whatever influence they could muster on behalf of old homelands.

No Asian-American group, for example, affected the events leading to the Korean War in June 1950, or those which decided its outcome. Korean-

Americans numbered only several thousand, far too few to engage in effective ethnic politics. Indeed, students of that conflict invariably depict it as ideological from beginning to end.

Yet, as in the nation's other foreign wars, ethnoracial emotions intensified the Korean hostilities. American leaders such as Secretary of State Dean Acheson maintained that the nation fought to uphold the right of South Korea to self-determination. Nonetheless, they viewed the Koreans, and also the Chinese Communists, who intervened in Korea against the United States, with a racist condescension that "suffused the political spectrum."[55] With the enemy "seen as yellow in race and red in ideology," there were instances of Chinese-Americans' experiencing fear from nationalist hysteria and official surveillance.[56]

As in the previous American clashes with Asians, the soldiers who did the fighting disparaged their opponents in racial terms, dismissing the North Koreans and the Chinese—and even their own South Korean allies— with epithets such as "barbarians," "beasts," and "gooks."[57] Aware of this attitude, most African-Americans analyzed the conflict from their own racial perspective. Many of them and their organizations opposed it. Neither they, the few Korean-Americans, nor the more numerous Chinese-Americans exerted any meaningful pressure on the policymakers so as even to modify the war's outcome.

Sensitive to the American ethnocentrism, many Asians perceived the war as another manifestation of the white peril of imperialism, and hence as racial. Others complained that "the Americans do not recognize Koreans as human beings."[58] Focusing on the racial issue, the Chinese Communists launched a "Resist America, Aid Korea" campaign significant for "its anti-American invective."[59] In this "terribly destructive war," characterized by massive American bombing, as many as three million Koreans were killed and "many more were turned into refugees."[60] Critics took the devastation as evidence of the white Americans' callous disregard for Asian lives.

In the United States at the time, a widespread sentiment maintained that a "China lobby," which "was presumed to have tremendous influence in American politics," had had an impact on the war.[61] It consisted of Nationalist Chinese officials around whom worked other Chinese, former American military leaders, publicists, and Republican politicians. The most noted American members were publisher Henry R. Luce, Walter H. Judd, a congressman and former missionary, and California senator William F. Knowland. To achieve its main goal, the overthrow of the People's Republic of China, the lobby sought the aid of the American government, just as had the nineteenth-century Fenians who had wished to destroy British rule in Ireland.

The China lobbyists also labored "to commit the United States to a long-term program of military and economic assistance" to Chiang Kai-shek's Nationalist regime on Taiwan. The lobby expected to win such support because of the American hostility to Communism. The Nationalist Chinese employed public relations firms and others to keep this program before key policy figures and the public. Critics hence viewed the lobby as a well-financed foreign pressure group that readily manipulated aspects of foreign policy, particularly through its cooperation with Senator Joseph R. McCarthy of Wisconsin, who, beginning in February 1950, attacked government leaders for "betraying" Nationalist China. This climate of fear associated with McCarthyism reputedly transformed the China lobby from a weak "to a frighteningly powerful influence on American foreign policy."[62]

Although the lobby never did become a true ethnic pressure group, at this time individuals connected with it did attempt to exploit ethnoracial consciousness with various tactics, as by organizing block parties in the nation's Chinatowns to stimulate Chinese-American opposition to Mao Tse-tung's mainland regime. They thus gave some direction to attitudes in those communities, which could possibly have an impact on foreign policy. Whatever the extent of the lobby's influence through race, ethnicity, or ideology, ultimately it failed in its mission.

As with the involvement in Korea and in the matter of aiding Nationalist China, ethnoracial considerations in themselves initially had little to do with the American entanglement that began in the fifties in Southeast Asia. Close students of the Vietnam War maintain that the leaders who embroiled the United States saw this conflict, too, mainly in ideological terms. Yet ethnoracial attitudes still cast a shadowy influence over the nation's Asian policies.

One historian, perhaps with exaggeration, argues that "prejudice against Asians permeated the entire top levels of the administration. Exclamations of racial fear, mistrust, and disdain often intruded into the discussions of the policymakers."[63] Another analyst, who was involved in aspects of the decision-making, reveals that a number of those in high places harbored a "casual bigotry" toward nonwhites that had to have had "some effect" on policy in this conflict.[64]

More than with the Korean War, peoples in Asia and elsewhere viewed the Vietnam conflict in racial terms. In Peking Red Guards and others, in their frequent massive anti-American demonstrations, reflected this belief. So did street signs in Vietnam's old capital city of Hue. They read: DOWN

WITH THE CIA, END THE FOREIGN DOMINATION OF OUR COUNTRY, and END THE OPPRESSION OF THE YELLOW RACE.[65]

Even in the United States numerous observers regarded the intervention in Vietnam as racial. They did so for many reasons, but especially because the policymakers refused to accept the right of the Vietnamese to their own version of self-determination, a principle implicit in the Geneva agreements of July 1954. Those agreements had ended the first Indochina war, which had forced the French out of Vietnam. France and the other powers that were involved in that diplomacy then recognized the independence of Laos, Cambodia, and Vietnam, but with a proviso for the temporary division of Vietnam at the seventeenth parallel until nationwide elections could be held. The United States had blocked the elections because it would not accept Vietnam's probable unification as a Communist state.

When such unity again seemed probable through force, the United States had intervened with large military forces to prevent it. Once more the world witnessed a powerful nation controlled by whites killing people of color. Again, as in the Philippine conquest, as in the Pacific war against Japan, and as in the Korean War, American soldiers spat out hateful racial epithets. To them, all the Vietnamese, presumed friends as well as foes, were "gooks," or dehumanized creatures against whom they committed atrocities as they seldom had done against white enemies. "They came to regard the entire population as the enemy," an attitude made clear in a message printed on the T-shirts that some soldiers wore: KILL THEM ALL! LET GOD SORT THEM OUT![66]

In March 1968 this hatred of the Vietnamese exploded when American troops tortured, raped, and murdered at least 347 unarmed civilian men, women, and children in the village of My Lai. As a kind of apologia, American officials pointed out that the Vietnamese Communists, too, committed atrocities. Even though grounded in truth, such a defense of brutish behavior could not offset the Nixon administration's whitewash of the My Lai affair. Nor could it counter the anti-American racial emotions that it, similar episodes, and the war itself intensified in Asia, Africa, and elsewhere. Nor, finally, could the anti-Communist and other ideologically based arguments emanating from Washington in justification of the war overcome such feelings.

African-Americans in particular focused on race in questioning the United States' involvement in Vietnam. "It would be hard," one writer explained, "to find a serious black in the United States who does not believe that the war was profoundly racist."[67] Many of them viewed it as another of the white establishment's wars against weaker people of color.

Martin Luther King, Jr., the most prominent black to condemn the American role in Vietnam, gave this interpretation wide publicity. "We are engaged in a war that seeks to turn the clock of history back and perpetuate white colonialism," he announced.[68] Believing that his people should combat racism abroad as well as at home, especially when their own government was the oppressor, he aligned much of the civil rights movement behind the widespread protest against the war. A number of liberal whites who hitherto had supported his movement then turned against King, with the charge that his attitude betrayed the national interest. Even a few African-American leaders attacked his stand, mainly because they did not wish to jeopardize their gains in civil rights by assaulting President Johnson's foreign policy.

At the start of this anti-war agitation, the Hispanics, principally the Mexican-Americans, who were the nation's second-largest ethnoracial minority, possessed even less political clout than did the African- or Asian-Americans. Having had to cope with discrimination, poverty, fragmentation, and disregard from Mexico City, the Mexican-Americans seldom had been able to leave a mark on matters of foreign policy even when they touched their former homeland. The seeming acquiescence of the Mexican immigrants in their situation, the public attitude toward them, and their own political goals, began to shift in the sixties.

Fundamental change started late because the depressed status of Mexicans in the United States, which went back to 1848, had a long history. Through the second half of the nineteenth and into the twentieth century, as Mexicans trudged north through a porous frontier, primarily entering the American Southwest as agricultural workers, they remained an underclass. Many were itinerants recruited to work on farms, railroads, and mines. Others stayed.

As with other minority peoples, Mexicans were subject to prejudice, and at times, especially in Texas, to mob violence. The restrictionists who denounced them as undesirable wanted them out of the country, or wanted them at least to stop their border crossings. Despite this sentiment, between 1910 and 1930 a tenth of Mexico's population moved into the United States, with the surge increasing as the European immigration dropped. As in the past, the white nativists, who detested the Mexicans more than they did the southeastern Europeans, condemned these migrants as the offspring of "a mixture of Mediterranean blooded Spanish peasants with low grade Indians," and for other racial reasons.[69]

Even though these prejudices ran all through congress, it had exempted Hispanics from the quota restrictions of 1921 and 1924. It did so largely because of the State Department's sensitivity to Pan Americanism, or the concept of close relations with the Western hemisphere countries. When the Mexicans at this time came to account for 12 percent of all immigrants and about 20 percent in 1927–28, the old-stock Americans mounted a campaign to bar them along with the other peoples of color. Those who formulated foreign policy and the agriculturalists in the Southwest who desired a loose labor market objected.

Secretary of State Frank B. Kellogg told a congressional committee that quotas for the Western hemisphere "would adversely affect the present good relations of the United States with Latin America and Canada," an action "very regrettable from the point of view of international policy." Thus "considerations of foreign policy" in this instance prevailed over the widespread ethnoracial prejudices that demanded Mexican exclusion.[70]

In these years, as a defense against Anglo hostility, Mexican-Americans with a political bent began forming their first civil rights organizations. In 1929 they founded the League of United Latin American Citizens (LULAC), which urged members to fight for civil rights by turning to politics. Despite this limited activism and the Mexican government's protests against "the abusive treatment its citizens received," the discrimination against Mexicans continued without much change through the thirties.[71]

At times the ethnoracial hostility engendered by such prejudice would burst into violence. In June 1943 in the Mexican quarter of Los Angeles, for example, Mexican-American youths and white sailors and soldiers clashed in what journalists called the Zoot Suit riots, named after the distinctive clothing the Mexicans wore. This racial rioting caused a small crisis in foreign relations because the Mexican government protested to the State Department, asking for measures to curb the attacks on Mexican-Americans in the Los Angeles area.

After the Second World War, both the temporary and permanent Mexican migration increased. Indeed, as a whole it grew into a massive movement. From 1945 to 1955 some four million *braceros* (contract laborers) and *mojados* (illegal "wetbacks") poured across Mexico's northern border. Their coming and going from *México de Afuera*, as Mexicans called their community in the United States, became an international issue. The deportations and the prejudice they suffered led a small group in Phoenix in 1949 to form the short-lived radical *Asociación Nacional México-Americana* (ANMA). In addition to civil rights, it concerned itself with the peace movement and other aspects of foreign policy by encouraging "an international consciousness," especially "in respect with Mexico and the rest of Latin America."[72]

Beginning in the mid-sixties, as Mexico's birth rate soared to one of the highest on earth, and for other reasons such as the elimination of the *bracero* program for temporary Mexican workers, her people kept coming in even greater numbers, both as legal and illegal immigrants. As in the past, some returned home embittered by the racism they encountered. Most remained, however, because in the United States they had some chance at least to escape the poverty that ground them down in their birthplace.

For these reasons, and because the immigrant generation took to naturalization slowly, Mexican-Americans as a group had the reputation of being reluctant to defy the values of the white establishment. Yet at times, as we have seen, some of them had protested and even politicked. In 1959 in California a number of them organized the Mexican-American Political Association (MAPA) as a pressure group within the Democratic party to acquire political clout for their people.

For several years those Mexican-Americans who particularly despaired of ever becoming assimilated had referred to themselves as *Chicanos*, previously a derogatory term applied to lowly Mexican laborers in the American Southwest. In the sixties, along with other frustrated minorities, they took to political activism on a scale larger than in the past. Ostensibly, like the Jewish, Polish, and other ethnic groups, the Chicanos were on their way to controlling sufficient demographic, cultural, and geographic assets to challenge the Euro-American dominance of politics and of foreign policy in specific areas.

In Mexico those who observed the lowly status of their kin to the north nurtured the anti-gringo feelings that had never died. As in years past, stories of discrimination or police brutality against Chicanos could trigger demonstrations and angry speeches in Mexico City condemning the United States. Even so, only as the Mexican-Americans grew in number and mobilized resources in ethnically oriented politics did the leadership in both major parties take them seriously.

Despite this expansion of minority power, even among the Chicanos, the Americans who were descended primarily from British stock still constituted the nation's largest ethnic group, though by 1950 they had shrunk to about 50 percent of the total population. Nonetheless, they remained essentially in control of the foreign-policy establishment. It and the governing elite in Britain wished to retain the remarkably close wartime alliance and even to create a union of the two nations, an objective that Winston Churchill had been pursuing for several years. When he spoke at Fulton, Missouri, on March 5, 1946, with a text remembered mainly for its "iron curtain" metaphor, he devoted half of the address to an idea that went back to the Anglo-Saxonism of the late nineteenth century. Churchill pleaded for a strengthening of "the fraternal association of the English speaking peoples" which would, he hoped, lead to "common citizenship."[73]

That unique relationship continued well into the cold war era. Yet the rhetorical remnants of the old Anglo-Saxonism, expressed most often by the British in phrases such as "men of our race" ruling the United States and "the unity of the English-speaking peoples," struck most Americans not similarly attuned as strange. The bond between the two countries remained strong not because of an anachronistic Anglo-Saxonism but because of a shared culture, language, ethnicity, and outlook on world affairs, and because leaders of both nations were determined to keep it strong. These people at the top collaborated impressively in many areas of international relations. When differences arose between them, however, the British, being acutely aware of their diminished status in the world, did most of the striving for amicable settlements.

For example, at the start of the Suez conflict in 1956, Prime Minister Anthony Eden and others in London had assumed that because of the special relationship the United States "would support any policy choice Britain made." Their government "never dreamed that Washington . . . would actually take the lead in opposing its actions," especially with the threat of economic sanctions.[74]

After this humiliation many in Britain concluded that their alliance with the United States had been seriously, if not fatally, damaged. But the fundamental relationship was hardly dented. At the height of the crisis, Eisenhower explained privately, "Britain not only has been, but must be, our best friend in the world."[75] Such sentiment helped the British to accept their junior position with apparent grace so as to maintain the relationship's special quality. The partnership also survived the currents of anti-Americanism among vocal elements of the British public, particularly over divergent views toward the Vietnam War.

Those in Britain who desired greater power for their country in the relationship seemed not to understand the depth of America's social change in the postwar decades. In the early sixties an Englishman, in visiting the United States for the first time, was astonished to discover quickly that it "was not an Anglo-Saxon nation."[76] He had known in abstract of the society's rainbow ethnoracial character but was surprised by its depth. America's heterogeneity was more and more reflected in the intellectual, cultural, economic, and even some of the political leadership. Most likely he observed an erosion of the old Anglo-American dominance but also a widespread admiration for English values and culture.

By 1970, as numerous other visitors discerned, British-American relations on their own had lost some of their old importance in American foreign policy. Yet the old Anglo-American elite and its allies, even if occasionally forced to share power, still kept the relationship with Britain more "special" than that with any other country. As always, one of its key ingredients remained the ethnic bond.

8

ETHNORACIAL RESURGENCE

In the United States, ethnic groups exert a remarkable impact on the nation's foreign policy towards what they recognize as their homeland or country of national origin.

Maryiyawanda Nzuwah and William King
Journal of Southern African Affairs, 1977

Beginning in 1968, when the nationality law that had been enacted three years earlier went into effect, a new surge of immigrants again transformed the nation's ethnic mix. About 1 million arrived each year. Within a decade roughly 12 million legal and undocumented newcomers had crowded into the United States. These numbers approximated or exceeded those of 1900–1910, the decade with the highest previous influx. More immigrants now came from Asia and Latin America and fewer from Europe. By 1976 two persons were arriving from Asia and Hispanic America for every one from Europe.

Unlike the southeastern Europeans of a century ago, these people entered a society with such tolerance for diversity that it was "by far the world's largest receiver of refugees and immigrants for permanent settlement," accepting "twice as many as the rest of the world combined."[1] These years were also characterized as an era of ethnic revival or upsurge when America's minorities evinced a greater consciousness of their origins than they had in the past. Their interest in their roots drew nourishment from a number of sources, such as third-world nationalism, but it came especially from the civil rights movement. Millions of Americans were inspired to think afresh about pluralism and national unity.

Students of ethnicity generally viewed the upsurge as part of a worldwide phenomenon that had started earlier in industrialized Western Europe. They pointed out that in the United States the rise in ethnic pride and power punched a hole in assimilationist theory. Instead of shedding old-world connections, many second-, third-, and even fourth-generation descendants of immigrants became reinvolved in concerns over ancestral homelands.

Ethnic awareness did not diminish even though the foreign-born population as a percentage of the whole had declined.

Yet there were sociologists, historians, and others who denied that the United States had undergone a true pluralist renewal that effectively challenged assimilationist assumptions. They argued that the ethnic resurgence was "romantic," "symbolic," or a cult of "superficial enthusiasm" that "began as a gesture of protest against the Anglocentric culture" and existed mainly in the minds of journalists, intellectuals mostly "of a third generation," and "unscrupulous hucksters."[2]

Despite this dissent, most investigators accepted the idea of a new pluralism, maintaining, as did sociologist Daniel Bell, that "there has been a resurgence of ethnic identification as the basis for effective *political* action in widely divergent societies," not just in the United States.[3] More openly than had the earlier pluralists, the new ones insisted that ethnic goals in foreign policy were compatible with a macro-national loyalty along traditional lines. In other multiethnic societies, such as the Soviet Union and the People's Republic of China, pluralists advanced similar arguments, but within political contexts where coercion forced external conformity. In the United States, in contrast, the pluralists now gained wide acceptance for their postulate that expressions of ethnic consciousness were to be expected and were even to be encouraged in a diverse democratic society. This cognizance also manifested itself in discussions of foreign policy, where the phrase "ethnic politics" became much more common than in past usage.

In both the intellectual and popular literature on this pluralism, the offspring of the white minority immigrants, African-Americans, and others now became "ethnics" rather than the disparaged hyphenates of the recent past. Much as before, the politicians of both parties fished among them for votes, but with a more obvious sense of answerability than in the past. On selected issues of foreign relations, this fresh accountability, as a function of the new pluralism, produced impressive results.

Whether in foreign or domestic matters, the pluralists argued that the nation's institutions lacked meaning unless they responded to the concerns of individuals and groups regardless of their race or ethnicity. These pluralists maintained that this contemporary regard for social diversity implied an acceptance of multiple loyalties as part of being American. They suggested that because of the demographic changes, as well as of the raised consciousness of minorities, there was no basis for characterizing the American people as Anglo-Saxon, or even for tolerating this delusion.

Using what many called the "new" social history to make their point, these pluralists stressed the obvious—that the African-Americans, Asian-

Americans, Mexican-Americans, and others of color had never fitted and could not fit the Anglo model of Americanism. As had the earlier pluralists, the new ones challenged the old dogma of a melting pot of Europeans who shared a core culture, insisting that if the population had ever conformed to this assimilationist conception, it certainly did not do so now. They conceived the remodeled United States as a "world nation" with ties of kinship to peoples virtually everywhere.

Why, therefore, the diverse ethnic politicians who emerged from this demographic transformation asked, should the traditional Anglo-American control over foreign policy continue with an exclusivity approximating that of the past? The latest arrivals, along with the descendants of the white new immigrants and the intellectuals who desired a restructuring of society, pressed for meaningful participation in the institutions that managed policy. Because the managers were called to account, they acknowledged some obligation to the nation's increasingly varied populace. From the minority outlook, however, the elite's response was selective and too slow.

That lag seemed evident in the controversy over how to deal with the thousands of undocumented aliens who still swarmed across the nation's southern border, many of them smuggled into the United States as part of a booming business. In efforts to stop the influx, the Immigration and Naturalization Service from 1971 to 1980 apprehended more than 8.3 million illegal entrants, up from 1.6 million in the previous decade.[4] According to governmental and other rough estimates, 5–6 million illegals, comprising Salvadorans, Nicaraguans, Haitians, and others, but most of them Mexicans, resided in the United States. For subsequent years unofficial estimates ran higher, with the Mexicans constituting 50 to 60 percent of the nation's deportable alien population.

In September 1988 the Census Bureau reported that since 1980 the Hispanic population had increased 34.4 percent. It totaled 19.4 million, up in these years by 4.8 million, a rate of growth more than five times that of other ethnic groups. This increase included Puerto Ricans, Cubans, and others but again it was mostly made up of Mexicans, many of whom were undocumented. The Latinos were well on their way to succeeding the blacks as the nation's largest ethnoracial minority. In some areas, as in the Southwest, the influx was so great and so concentrated that Spanish supplanted English as the language of common usage.[5]

This massive movement strained the tolerance of the new pluralism for all newcomers, even for those who entered the country legally under the liberalized immigration and refugee legislation. Many Americans argued that it was in the national interest to block the undocumented stream by either enforcing the law or again revising it. Public-opinion polls indicated "that a majority of Americans opposed illegal immigration" and wanted it curbed. In one poll 91 percent of those sampled called for "an allout effort to stop the illegal entry into the United States of 1½ million foreigners" without documentation.[6] Hispanic groups regarded this attitude as reflecting crypto-racism. To combat it, they entered ethnic politics in increasing numbers.

In 1968, at the start of this political surge, Hispanics created their first umbrella lobby in Washington, the National Council of La Raza, to influence national policy, especially immigration legislation. About a decade later the few Latinos in the house of representatives, who were worried about this same problem, formed the Congressional Hispanic Caucus. Their main power base was the Mexican-American community, which was as usual the most important of the Latino groups. As the community expanded and grew more assertive, and as the foreign-policy aspect of immigration became a foremost issue in relations with the United States, Mexico's governments reversed their former aloofness. As never before, they sought cooperation with Chicano lobbies.

Mexico City and the activist Mexican-American organizations now tried to counter the popular pressure on Washington for curbs on undocumented aliens by arguing that the United States could not afford to tighten control over its southern border. To do so would create more bitter feelings in Mexico and greater strain in the relationship between the two countries. When, for instance, presidents Jimmy Carter and José Lopez Portillo met in February 1977, the Mexican leader opposed any "police solutions" to the border problem.[7] He expressed solidarity with *México de Afuera* and warned that if the United States blocked the northward passage of Mexico's surplus labor, both countries would suffer. Indicating that in Mexico it could produce revolution, he entreated Carter not to raise the level of his enforcement of the immigration laws.

In the following year, after Lopez Portillo had met with leaders of the Mexican-American community, they offered to work with him against proposed legislation in Washington affecting Latino immigration. "We've never before told Mexico that we are all ready to help Mexico in the United States," Eduardo Morga, the chairman of the League of United Latin American Citizens (LULAC), explained to reporters. "We feel that in the future Mexico can use us as Israel uses American Jews, as Italy uses Italian-Americans, and so on."[8]

As for Carter, he responded to the immigration problem by announcing a program of reform but did not carry it through. His domestic critics maintained that in granting the illegals temporary immunity from the law he had capitulated to foreign threat, as supposedly from Mexico, and had compounded a vital national problem. His administration ended in 1981 amidst a rush of undocumented aliens into the country. These newcomers included 1 million or so Mexicans, 125,000 Cuban expellees, and 10,000 Haitian boat people. Immigration and refugee policy appeared to be in shambles.[9]

In this crisis the Mexican authorities behaved much as had those in immigrant-sending European societies in the past. True enough, Mexico City feared destabilization if emigration stopped, but it also desired to retain its benefits. While providing an outlet for a surplus population, the sievelike border also brought Mexico millions of dollars each year in remittances from those nationals who slipped through it. Critics of the undocumented invasion countered that it and the *laissez-faire* acceptance of it offended notions of justice because the American government did not apply the law with an even hand to all foreign peoples. Lax enforcement, they said, discriminated against those awaiting legal entry, mocked the orderly management of the frontier, and in itself harmed relations between Mexico and the United States.

Aware of this malaise, congress in October 1978 had established a Select Commission on Immigration and Refugee Policy to study the existing legislation and to recommend changes. Three years later, when it had completed its work, Ronald Reagan had become president. Even though he had been critical of illegal immigration, he shunned the reform issue, going along in effect with the basic policies of his two predecessors, presidents Carter and Gerald Ford. In March 1982 Senator Alan W. Simpson, a Republican from Wyoming who had served on the Select Commission, and Representative Romano L. Mazzoli, a Democrat from Kentucky, sponsored a bill that "was a delicate compromise" reflecting congressional, employer, Hispanic, and foreign-policy concerns—the last meaning mainly relations with Mexico.[10] It aimed to reassert federal control over the southern border but with a temporary-worker program designed to help agriculturalists in the Southwest replace their illegal alien workers. In response to public pressure, the Reagan administration backed these reforms.

The proposed legislation galvanized Latinos into unprecedented activity. Up to this time the cooperative efforts of Hispanic pressure groups to influence national or international policy had seldom been effective. Now, because the Simpson-Mazzoli bill affected their people more than any other segment of the immigrant population, they mobilized behind the ethnic politics of a common front specifically in opposition to it.

As a rule, the Mexican-American organizations maintained that the curbing of illegals would exacerbate discrimination against all Hispanics, legal as well as undocumented residents. In some instances spokesmen contended that Mexicans had a moral right to an open border since American imperialists had wrenched the Southwest from Mexico through force. LULAC and the Mexican American Legal Defense Educational Fund (MALDEF) founded fourteen years earlier, as a self-help lobbying organization, opposed the bill for many reasons. But their main argument, as repeated often in the media and elsewhere, that there should be no restrictions on the illegals, had widespread support in the Chicano community and in Mexico.

After the United States senate approved the Simpson-Mazzoli bill, Mexico's senate passed a resolution on "this grave matter that negatively affects our good neighbor relations," declaring that the immigration legislation should be weighed "from a bilateral and even multilateral perspective." Washington's policy establishment reacted angrily to the resolution "as a flagrant attempt by a foreign power to intervene in the American legislative process."[11] Critics also pointed out that the Mexican government unilaterally tightened controls over its own southern border to block a smaller influx of refugees from the Central American and Caribbean countries, who competed for jobs with native-born Mexicans.

In October 1984 the 98th Congress adjourned without a final vote on the reform bill. A coalition of Hispanic pressure groups, white liberals, and agricultural interests in the Southwest, which traditionally desired a pool of cheap labor, defeated it. For the first time in an area touching foreign policy, the Mexican-American venture into ethnic politics could claim a noteworthy success. The euphoria did not last long. Congress and the administration persisted in their reform efforts, because the problem of illegal immigration was getting worse. As a converted Reagan explained in 1984, "the simple truth is that we've lost control of our own borders, and no nation can do that and survive."[12]

Despite the resistance from Mexico, from the Hispanic lobbies, and from others who brought up the arguments that had been directed against the earlier reform efforts, congress in October 1986 narrowly passed the comprehensive Immigration Reform and Control Act. It took into account the strong feelings of the Mexican-American community for its kin with a concession that provided an amnesty program for millions of the undocumented who could prove they had been in the United States since January 1, 1982. Otherwise, in keeping with its objective of curbing the flow of illegal aliens, the bill imposed sanctions on those who employed them. Chicano critics charged that the law represented "a major victory for North American nativists" and that "the issue was racism."[13]

In the next several years, studies of the legislation's effectiveness stimulated controversy. The government claimed success in stemming the illegals, an assertion challenged by independent researchers. Still driven by poverty and unemployment at home, Mexicans ignored the legal hurdles and continued by the thousands to slip across the border. In 1991 even government officials concluded that the law's sanctions on employers had not deterred illegal immigration as intended. As in the past, Mexico at her own southern frontier tried to keep out migrants from Central America.[14]

The Reagan administration, too, had expressed concern about emigration from south of Mexico and the Caribbean. Its policymakers justified their intervention in El Salvador, Nicaragua, and elsewhere in Central America in ethnoracial terms, as part of an effort to restrain a massive migration from Central America to the United States. It would happen, they asserted, if Central American leftists gained power or remained in power. To support their policy, the interventionists cited the example of ten percent of Cuba's population migrating to the United States since the rise of Fidel Castro. The opponents of intervention came to an opposite conclusion from the same data. They argued that violence, terror, and instability compelled the Central American Hispanics to migrate, usually to the United States.

Shortly thereafter, beginning in November 1989, aroused Euro-Americans belonging to the Alliance for Border Control demonstrated nightly on the California side of the Mexican frontier against the continued rush of illegals. Viewing the protests as a throwback to earlier nativism, counter-demonstrators chanted *No mas racismo!* The Euro-Americans denied being either racist or anti-immigrant. They were, they said, "just anti-illegal immigrant" because "we're in a crisis situation."[15]

Confrontations of this kind, with their potential for violence, coupled with the rising political influence of Mexican-Americans, led Mexican President Carlos Salinas de Gortari to do what leaders of other immigrant-sending countries had long done. He created a cultural agency, the Directorate for Mexican Communities Abroad, with the objective of stepping up the effort to establish close ties with Mexican-Americans. As did other foreign lobbies, it also sought through ethnic politics to make a difference in the American policies that affected Mexico.

In these years the United States and Mexico were not alone in their entanglement over immigration control. Other countries, some that sent as well as others that received immigrants, faced comparable problems in their foreign policies. As with Mexico, poor nations all over the world relied heavily on the monies they obtained from their emigrants. So they opposed restriction where practiced by wealthier countries, for example by those in Western Europe, where from the end of the Second World War onward foreign workers had gone and stayed.

At first, as in West Germany, invited "guest" workers came from southern Europe. Later most of the laborers, the invited and uninvited, originated in the Third World. The presence of these new aliens revived within the receiving nations ethnic animosities of perhaps greater depth than those in the United States, because anti-foreignism had been more deeply embedded in their cultures. Regardless, as in the United States, the problem of control touched on the sensitive issues of ethnicity, race, and foreign policy.

As in the United States, critics in Western Europe attacked the curtailing of immigration as racist because the restrictive laws—as for example Britain's Commonwealth Immigrants Act implemented in 1962—affected mainly people of color. In the seventies anti-immigration movements gained strength, led by right-wing politicians Enoch Powell in Britain, Jean-Marie Le Pen in France, whose xenophobic National Front party motto was "France for the French," and various conservatives in Germany.

In the eighties these countries, as well as Denmark, Switzerland, and even Italy, now a receiver rather than a dispatcher of immigrants, passed or considered additional legislation against unwanted aliens. Even so, after the demise of Communism in Eastern Europe the anti-immigrant xenophobia sometimes incited violence. In Germany, for example, a week of race riots in September 1991 forced Asian, African, and Eastern European refugee families, and guest workers also, to flee the town of Hoyerswerda, near the Polish border. The problem had become so serious that in the following month the ministers from twenty-seven European governments agreed on emergency-like, short-term measures, such as intensified frontier surveillance, to reduce illegal immigration.

Back in the United States, the Mexican-Americans, despite the setback they experienced in immigration control, had renewed their commitment to ethnic politics. Their activism had grown steadily. Between 1970 and 1988 the numbers of Hispanics elected to public office, most of them Mexican-Americans, had quadrupled, rising "from fewer than 800 to almost 3,400."[16] Their protests did help in the shaping of the Immigration Act of 1990, which modified the sanctions against the employers of illegal aliens so as to deter discrimination.

Overall, though, the Mexican-Americans remained weaker than their numbers suggested, largely because of their mixed status. About a third of them were undocumented and could not vote. Many of those who were eligible did not vote. Mexican-American leaders attentive to political reality nonetheless declared their intention to seek a more decisive role in inter-American affairs and in the formulation of foreign policy in general.

Hispanics saw in the activism of American Jews in particular a model for this goal of deeper involvement. They were aware that no minority had been able to exploit the new accountability in foreign policy more impressively than had the Jewish community. Yet from the end of the Second World War through the eighties, its people had made up no more than 2.7 percent of the nation's population.[17] Its power therefore perplexed observers. How, they asked, could so few bring effective pressure to bear on the political system so as to direct the course of policy-making in the Middle East for more than four decades?

In cooperating to support Israel, as we have seen, American Jews created nothing unique in ethnic behavior or in the American policy-making experience. As they had from a short time after they had overcome most ethno-religious discriminations, they followed the example of the Anglo-Americans in using ethnic politicking to influence foreign affairs. Some of the other minorities, when able to do so, emulated both the Anglos and the Jews.

What set apart American Jews from most other special-interest activists in these years was their handling of ethnic politics "in a particularly dedicated and intense way."[18] They made Israel the core issue of their political life, organized their resources in a manner superior to that of other groups, and derived much of their motivation from one of the foremost tragedies of the twentieth century. In part because of the Holocaust, American Jews continued to attract broad public sympathy. They also appeared to nurture a more emotional commitment to Israel than did other immigrant peoples to their ancestral homelands.

"Israel was more important to Jews," one of their historians commented, "than the concerns for racial justice and peace that they shared with other Americans. The identification with Israel was their 'religion.'"[19] In addition, as numerous writers point out, Jewish-Americans were concentrated in the nation's most politically powerful and wealthiest states, such as New York, California, Illinois, and Florida. Various analysts maintain that these bases permitted Jewish groups to exert pressure on the federal government with little effort wasted because of geographical dispersal.

Into the nineties, Jewish-Americans continued to exercise their power in foreign affairs through a number of organizations and political action committees (PACs), but most often through their disciplined AIPAC lobby. It pounced on any issue that touched the welfare of Israel, pressuring members of congress, presidents, and the whole policy-making establishment. Decision makers responded positively to it because Jews voted in higher proportion to their numbers than did other Americans, and because they provided large sums for Democratic candidates and impressive funding also for selected Republicans. In the seventies analysts estimated that the Jews, who then constituted "the most affluent group in America," normally donated "more than half the large gifts of national Democratic campaigns."[20]

Even those officeholders who did not benefit from such support feared taking on the lobby as an adversary. So it was with Richard M. Nixon, who as president "was convinced that he owed nothing to Jewish votes and that he could not increase his Jewish support regardless of what he did." Yet he respected "the strength of Israel's support in Congress and in public opinion generally."[21]

Even though many in congress backed Israel out of conviction, more did so as political realists. If they did not side with her, they knew that in the next election they would face retribution. Waverers became targets of masses of letters, telegrams, telephone calls, and visits from powerful constituents. These carrot-and-stick tactics won governmental backing for a high level of military and economic aid to Israel.

During the Yom Kippur War in October 1973, when Egypt and Syria fought Israel, "most of the Arab world viewed the United States as 'totally supporting Israel,'" an assumption borne out by events.[22] When at first Israel's position appeared grim, its supporters were "more vocal than in any previous crisis." American Jews, "business, labor, religious, and congressional leaders bombarded the White House on Israel's behalf."[23] Even though obsessed by the problems of the Watergate scandal that later forced his resignation, Nixon replaced whatever the Israelis lost on the battlefield, explaining that "We will not let Israel go down the tubes."[24]

Washington hastened arms to the Israeli forces with the largest airlift since the Second World War. It provided 566 flights carrying 72,000 tons of equipment valued at $2.2 billion. Nixon and Secretary of State Henry A. Kissinger also planned to send troops to the Middle East to counter a threatened Soviet intervention on behalf of Egypt.

This assistance, which proved crucial to Israel's victory, came in addition to the billions of dollars the United States had provided since the Jewish state's founding. Of course other factors, such as Israel's being regarded as an important asset in the nation's cold war strategy, as well as the lobbying of American Jews, produced this aid. Yet, as with other effective lobbyists, they could claim much of the credit for it, because in addition to the other reasons for supporting Israel, they formed an indigenous interest group that worked within the American political system. On many issues American Jews could be divided, but on foreign policy affecting the "single question of Israel" they were united in maintaining "political pressure and financial contributions."[25]

Jewish-American ethnic politics made headlines again in December 1974, when in response to their pressure and out of a concern for human rights, congress passed an amendment to a trade bill with the Soviet Union. Its main sponsor, Senator Henry Jackson of Washington, who was running for president, solicited Jewish financial support. This Jackson-Vanik Amendment linked trade concessions, such as most favored nation treatment and long-term credits to the Soviets, to the Jewish emigration they permitted. President Gerald Ford signed the legislation on January 3, 1975. Eleven days later the Soviet Union canceled its three-year-old trade agreement with the United States, stopped payment on lend-lease debts, and reduced Jewish emigration. Since the amendment failed in its objective, critics say it backfired. Yet the Jewish organizations once more had demonstrated their ability "to exert a great deal of influence" on a foreign-policy issue considered vital to their own kind.[26]

They did so again with Jimmy Carter, who dedicated his administration's foreign policy to the advancement of human rights. Despite this commitment, in November 1978 he boycotted a World Conference to Combat Racism because its sponsor, the United Nations, had equated Zionism with racism. He did not wish to offend Israel or alienate his Jewish constituency, as, to his regret, he had done earlier on the matter of rights for Palestinians.

Charles Percy, a popular Republican senator from Illinois, also felt the weight of ethnic politics when in January 1975 he indicated that Israel "cannot count on the United States in the future just to write a blank check," suggesting that it would have to borrow money rather than receive aid gratis.[27] Within a week he received over 4,000 letters and 2,000 telegrams from Illinois, and many others from New York and New Jersey. In all, Zionists swamped Percy with more than 20,000 pieces of mail, all critical. Later, those in Illinois organized a campaign to remove him from the senate. They succeeded.

The power of the Jews acting as "a mobilized American ethnic group" led other critics, such as George W. Ball, a former State Department official, to attack their politics. He contended that they deprived the United States "of freedom of diplomatic action on issues that deeply affect its national interest." Ball maintained further that "practically no actions touching Israel's interests can be taken, or even discussed, within the executive branch without it being quickly known to the Israeli government."[28]

Even if this was not a standard practice as Ball charged, through American Jews Israel at times did acquire privileged entry to policy-making in Washington. In itself such an advantage was not unusual; it was often a part of the business of ethnic politicking. Other governments had gained similar access. Britain had done so frequently, and in recent years so had Greece. Seemingly, though, few countries exploited the machinery of American politics as successfully as did Israel.

As had other societies with offspring in the United States, Israel's government encouraged Jewish-American organizations to work on its behalf. For instance, after negotiating a peace treaty with Egypt in March 1979, Prime Minister Menachem Begin met with two thousand American Jewish leaders in New York City. "You have great influence," he told them. "Do not hesitate to use that influence." He later reiterated this sentiment, saying of American Jews and Israel: "This is the land of their forefathers, and they have a right and a duty to support it."[29]

In March 1980 the extent of the Israeli lobby's power again impressed critics. Donald McHenry, the American representative in the United Nations, whom Jews regarded as pro-Palestinian, supported a resolution that they viewed as anti-Israel. They put such pressure on President Carter, whose administration appeared to them "philosophically inclined toward the Arab perspective," that two days later he admitted that his government had made a mistake and retracted the vote.

Critics believed that Carter had professed to error because, with the New York Democratic presidential primary only three weeks off, he wished to placate Jewish voters there. His national security adviser said that this reversal of policy in the interest of ethnic politics made the administration "look silly" and the president "look weak."[30]

These cases illustrate another reason for Jewish achievement in ethnic politics. As students of foreign policy are well aware, an interest group can exert pressure disproportionate to its size in a specific area if its demands arouse no strong opposition from the governing establishment or the public at large. For years virtually no other ethnic group effectively challenged the Israeli lobby. Hence establishment politicians and others not only benefited but also usually feared no retribution in supporting Israel.

Small-scale ethnic-group opposition to Israel had begun in 1972, when business and professional Americans of Arab stock founded the National Association of Arab-Americans (NAAA). They had organized "to protest and to register their disagreement with American policies of unquestioning support to Israel and total disregard for the security of Arab states in the Middle East."[31] For three years, or until the nation's Arab population started rising, the association was feeble. By 1981, however, there were two million Americans of Arab origin, and still more by the end of the decade. With this increase in numbers, and in wealth too, Arab influence rose, though not enough to offer meaningful political competition to the Jewish-Americans. The Arab-Americans complained that they suffered from a negative stereotyping which affected their ethnic politics and the nation's policy in the Middle East.

Jews, too, felt that the criticism directed at them was often unjust. For example, they denied charges that they practiced a dual allegiance and that their ethnic politics subordinated foreign policy to the interest of a special group at the expense of the national interest. They argued, on the contrary, that the United States supported Israel not just because of Jewish-American political clout but also because it valued that small nation as a sister democracy with strategic utility in the Middle East. In brief, in the American Jewish perspective, as well as that of others, aid to Israel benefited the national interest. It was a "cost effective" bargain because Israel's contributions to the American interest in the Middle East "more than compensate[d] for U.S. aid."[32]

Whether or not assistance to Israel or a deeper appreciation for Arab sensibilities served the nation best appeared debatable. American backing was essential to Israel, and the Jews knew that. As before, to keep that aid flowing stood out as a major objective of the American Zionists. They saw to it to the best of their ability that officials declared support for Israel when seeking office or reelection. In general, "Jewish political influence" carried more weight in determining the American commitment in the Middle East over a longer period than did ethnic politics in most other issues specifically related to foreign policy.[33]

This basis for Middle Eastern policy continued through the Ronald Reagan presidency. For a Republican, Reagan had garnered a large Jewish vote of thirty-nine percent, yet it had not notably benefited him.[34] His administration differed with the Israeli lobby over a number of issues, such as the sale of high-technology airplanes (AWACS) to Saudi Arabia in 1981 and Israel's handling of the *intifada*, an Arab uprising in Palestine. In the case of the plane dispute, in which the administration prevailed, the president even rebuked Israeli pressure, saying that "It is not the business of other nations to make American foreign policy."[35] Of course, other countries had been trying to do that for years.

Regardless, these differences were minor. From the beginning and throughout his presidency, Reagan could claim that American Jews "never had a better friend of Israel in the W[hite] H[ouse] than they have now."[36] Out of respect for Zionist political weight, as well as to counter Soviet incursions into the Middle East, he converted the "strategic partnership" with Israel of the previous decade into a closer strategic alliance.

This Israeli connection led even aggrieved Jews in the Soviet Union, in January 1985, to invoke an enigmatic ethnic bond in an effort to obtain help from the United States. They appealed to Secretary of State George P. Shultz, an Episcopalian, who they assumed was of Jewish descent seemingly because of his favorable attitude toward Israel, to intercede with Moscow on their behalf. No data reveals that he did so. The plea itself, however, indicated that like other peoples, Jews abroad were convinced that ethnicity influenced American foreign policy.

The role of ethnic politics in Middle Eastern affairs continued to provide substance for this assumption because "U.S. aid . . . flowed to Israel in record amounts." In all, despite huge budget deficits, Reagan's government granted Israel an unprecedented $40 billion in economic and military aid.[37] Critics again charged that the politics of Zionist groups intimidated politicians and corrupted the democratic process, an accusation that pluralists rebutted.

Regardless, the relationship with Israel remained close, but with tension, in the administration of George H. Bush. Noting Bush's Texas oil connections, Jewish political activists suspected him of being sympathetic to the Arabs. In several instances in 1989 and 1990, Secretary of State James A. Baker III called on the Israelis to give up their expansionist goal of a "Greater Israel." They rejected the advice. At the same time, American Jewish groups persuaded the State Department to back off from its proposals. In March 1990 Bush reassured the Israelis of his support by selling them a new, sophisticated anti-missile system. The relationship with Israel seemingly remained firm.

Strain became evident, however, after a clash on October 8, 1990, in Jerusalem between stone-throwing Arabs and Israeli police who shot to death twenty-one of the Palestinians. Anxious to retain Arab support in a confrontation with Iraq over its invasion of Kuwait, the Bush administration backed a United Nations resolution condemning Israel for the killings. This action upset American Jews, but they were assuaged when on October 22 the senate, because of the Iraq crisis, voted $700 million in additional military aid to Israel.[38] During the forty-three-day Persian Gulf War that began in January 1991, the Iraqis rained some missiles on Israel. Bush rushed to its aid with Patriot anti-missile batteries manned by Americans.

After the war minor cracks began appearing in the relationship. Yet in the spring of 1991, when Yitzhak Shamir, Israel's prime minister, was preparing a request for Washington to guarantee $10 billion worth of loans for housing for Jews fleeing the Soviet Union, he assumed success. As a backup for his policy, he "urged American Jews to lobby the U.S. government for the loan guarantees."[39]

Just before the formal request arrived, Bush and Secretary Baker spent several days imploring key members of congress to postpone action on it, but with dubious results. On September 6, therefore, the president announced, "I am going to ask every single Member of Congress to defer, just for 120 days, consideration" of the guarantee package.[40] He believed that the aid would subsidize settlements on former Arab land occupied by the Israelis and would drive Arabs away from a peace conference, scheduled for October, that he had initiated.

Despite Bush's opposition, AIPAC went ahead with its campaign for early passage of the guarantee legislation. When congress responded to the lobbying with what appeared overwhelming support, the president turned to the public. In a televised news conference on September 12, he stressed that for over forty years the United States had been "Israel's closest friend in the world" and that it would remain so as long as he was president. Citing examples of the friendship, he said that "during the current fiscal year alone and despite our own economic problems, the United States provided Israel with more than $4 billion in economic and military aid, nearly $1,000 for every Israeli man, woman, and child, as well as with $400 million in loan guarantees to facilitate emigrant absorption." Indeed, since 1976 Israel had been the largest annual recipient of foreign aid.

Saying that "too much is at stake for domestic politics to take precedence over peace," Bush threatened to veto an early approval of the loan guarantee, the first instance of a president's indicating that he would reject a congressional vote in favor of Israel. He also struck at the Israeli lobby. "I'm up against some powerful political forces," he explained. "I heard today there was something like a thousand lobbyists on the Hill working the other side of the question. We've got one lonely little guy down here doing it."[41]

This confrontation produced the White House's most serious rift with the American Jewish community and with Israel since its founding or at least since Eisenhower's presidency. A right-wing Israeli cabinet minister, Rehavam Zeevi, went so far as to call Bush an anti-Semite and a liar. Other Israelis and American Jews viewed Bush's and Secretary Baker's stance as reflecting traditional upper-class Anglo antipathy toward them as a group. This Jewish outrage and the tactics of the Israeli lobby backfired. Public-opinion polls indicated that the American people backed the president by as much as 86 percent to 12 percent. The lobby and its supporters in congress retreated.

Analysts commented that Bush demonstrated courage in forcing a showdown with the lobby just before the start of an election campaign. Others said he prevailed because he was popular, was determined to fight, could mobilize public sentiment, and faced a Democratic congress unwilling to defy him directly on this issue. Some interpreters assumed that this outcome bared the waning influence of the Israeli lobby as well as the inherent weakness of ethnic politics in foreign affairs.

One could also argue that the struggle demonstrated the power of the Israeli lobby's politics. A small country backed by a small American ethnic group had forced the president, against the advice of close political advisers, to mobilize all of his political resources, to risk the prestige of his office, and to appeal over the head of congress to the people to uphold his foreign policy. Even while losing, the Jewish-American community's ethnic politicking had shown considerable muscle.

"I'm catching hell from the party," Bush complained later. "They're afraid we could lose some Senate seats out of this—especially in California."[42] His own risk was small. He had won the presidency without much Jewish support and did not need it for reelection in 1992. Nonetheless, in some states and districts Jewish votes and donations were still important even to Republican office seekers. So the White House moved quickly to conciliate Jewish-American leaders with assurances of continued basic support for Israel.

As for the Israeli government's attitude toward ethnic politicking, Prime Minister Shamir again made it clear when he visited the United States in November 1991 to drum up support for his policies among Jewish-Americans. He dismissed a poll indicating that 80 percent of their leadership favored a freeze on Israeli settlements in occupied territories in exchange for American loan guarantees. "I don't believe it," he said. "I am sure, 100%, that the rank and file of the Jewish population, the Jewish community in the United States, support my views, my opinions."[43]

Another example of ethnic politics' challenging what critics regarded as the nation's larger strategic interests was rooted in the long-standing animosity on Cyprus between the Greeks, who made up 80 percent of the population, and the Turks. It erupted into communal violence on July 15, 1974, when a coup supported by the military regime in Athens overthrew the island republic's government, with the design of merging Cyprus with Greece.

Five days later Turkey, citing treaty rights, intervened to protect the Cypriot Turkish minority. Within weeks the invaders controlled the northern third of the island.

The repercussions quickly affected the Greek community in the United States, which formed about one percent of the population. Turkish-Americans were still fewer, numbering about 50,000, most of them recent arrivals who had yet to become politically acculturated. Like the Jews, the Greek-Americans were notably cohesive and politically active. Starting in mid-August, in a move "orchestrated by the Foreign Ministry in Athens," they campaigned for an arms embargo against Turkey, an ally of the United States since 1947.[44] Working primarily through the American Hellenic Institute, a coalition of old and new lobbies, and with the cooperation of legislators of Greek descent, they inundated congress with communications. In addition, they solicited help from other ethnic groups with anti-Turkish traditions, such as Armenians and Jews, hoping in all to generate sufficient American pressure to force the Turkish occupiers to evacuate Cyprus.

The Greek-American lobbyists argued that the mainland Turks, armed with American weapons in violation of agreements which limited the use of the arms to defensive purposes, were the aggressors. President Nixon and Secretary Kissinger, whom Greek-American militants denounced as the "killer of Cypriots" because he tilted toward Turkey, opposed the embargo. Kissinger believed that the pro-Greek legislators "were doing nothing more than simply playing ethnic politics" and thereby risking "unravelling the entire fabric of our foreign policy."[45] Congress nonetheless voted the arms embargo, which went into effect in February 1975. All parties concerned with the issue recognized the Greek lobby as the primary force in the passage of the legislation.

Greek-American groups continued politicking so as to keep the embargo in force against efforts that summer to repeal it. One congressman, who was under heavy pressure from constituents who favored the embargo, explained why he voted to retain it. "Maybe I wouldn't have lost my seat over this," he said, "but who wants the hassle?"[46]

The day after the attempted repeal had failed, Turkey closed twenty-six bases and listening posts that the United States and its allies maintained on its territory. Thus a lobby claiming the support of three million Greek-Americans had created what Kissinger and others considered a grave situation in foreign policy. The embargo remained in effect for the next three years.

All the while, relations between Turkey and the United States remained strained. On June 14, 1978, therefore, President Carter categorized the lifting of the embargo as "the most immediate and urgent foreign policy decision" before congress.[47] That summer his and his secretary of state's intensive effort for repeal finally succeeded. Despite this defeat, the Greek community in the United States had demonstrated impressive influence, but only for a limited time. In the long run it failed to achieve results commensurate with those of the Jewish community toward Arabs, because it was less powerful and could not persuade other Americans that the government served the national interest by maintaining a long-term antagonistic stance toward Turkey.

Most analysts consequently viewed the Greek ethnic politics as ineffective. Others perceived them differently. They maintained that if the Greek-Americans had not lobbied, for strategic reasons Washington might have ignored the plight of the Greek Cypriots, or the Turks might have slaughtered many of them. Furthermore, the Greek government regarded the solicited assistance of the Greek-Americans as valuable. In expressing gratitude for the help, Athens asked "that it will not remain a one-time event. We hope that in the future Greek Americans will manifest their support whenever crisis confronts the Greek people."[48]

Concurrently, the status of Northern Ireland resurfaced as a divisive issue in ethnic politics. For years the controversy that had accompanied Ireland's partition seemingly had lain dormant, but it had always smoldered with a potential for violence. Among militant Irish-Americans it helped keep alive remnants of Anglophobia. In 1948 the American League for an Undivided Ireland, which had been founded in the previous year, had "collected 200,000 signatures for a petition asking Truman to help end the partition of Ireland."[49] It was ignored because it might roil relations with Britain.

In subsequent years politicians in New York, Massachusetts, and other places where Irish-American voters were still cohesive urged an end to the communal friction between the minority Catholics and the majority Protestants in the northern counties. Like their overseas kin, these Irish-Americans desired the unification of the north, still bound to Britain, with the south, which in 1949 had become the Republic of Ireland. Moved by the example of the black civil rights movement in the United States, a group of Catholics and liberal Protestants in Northern Ireland in 1967 formed the Civil Rights Association to protest anti-Catholic discrimination.

This movement led to angry opposition from militant Protestants loyal to Britain. In August 1969, as the violence between the Catholics and the Protestants escalated, British troops entered Ulster's six counties to suppress it. London failed to find a solution to the troubles. All the while, the force-ful tactics of the British soldiers, directed mainly against the minority Cath-olic Irish, aroused the indignation of Irish-Americans. In April 1970 the militants among them formed the Irish Northern Aid Committee (NORAID) to help brethren in Ulster with money donations for clothing and other needs, but also to supply arms smuggled largely to the anti-Protestant and anti-British underground Irish Republican Army (IRA).

In August 1971 Chicago's mayor, Richard J. Daley, in conjunction with the Irish-American president of a large corporation, headed a drive for more aid, principally funds for the Catholic refugees in the Ulster strife. Daley also urged Irish-Americans to mobilize so as to pressure the British to with-draw their troops. In October Edward M. Kennedy offered a resolution in the senate also calling for withdrawal, as well as seeking backing for a united Irish Republic. Nothing came of this effort. But Republican national chair-man Robert Dole, reflecting a concern over the relationship with Britain, condemned the resolution as "a blatant attempt to interfere in the internal affairs of a friendly nation."[50]

This attitude maddened the involved Irish-Americans, but their anger rose to fever pitch when British paratroopers on "Bloody Sunday," January 30, 1972, killed fourteen Catholic demonstrators in Londonderry. The Irish Northern Aid Committee now stepped-up the supplying of weapons to the Catholic resisters in Ulster. In 1976 British authorities estimated that 85 percent of the IRA arms came from the United States.

In the United States the prominent Irish-American politicians who con-tinued to demand British withdrawal sought support from Washington. In the presidential campaign of that year, Jimmy Carter, in search of Irish-American votes, met with the Irish National Caucus, a lobby for Irish Re-publican causes that had been founded several years earlier. The Democratic party, he announced, believes that "it is a mistake for our country's govern-ment to stand quiet on the struggle of the Irish for peace, for the respect of human rights, and for unifying Ireland."[51]

Although the government persisted in its policy of passive neutrality toward the conflict, on August 30, 1977, Carter as president did intercede. He offered a "job creating investment" in Ulster "to the benefit of all the people of Ireland" if the Protestant and Catholic communities could agree on some kind of settlement. Nothing substantive came of the proposal, but as in the past, the British did recognize the "American dimension" in the Irish problem.[52]

In 1979 on Saint Patrick's Day the Speaker of the House of Representa-tives, Thomas P. "Tip" O'Neill, the governor of New York State, Hugh

Carey, and the senior senators from New York and Massachusetts, Daniel P. Moynihan and Kennedy—sometimes dubbed the Irish-American "Four Horsemen"—charged the British government with acquiescence in "gross violations of human rights" in Ulster. They also appealed for a united Ireland. Resenting their criticism, the London government did nothing about their charges. In 1981, at the behest of the Irish embassy, the four expanded their circle to include other Irish-American legislators and become the Friends of Ireland, a kind of lobby. In efforts to sway American opinion on this issue, the Irish National Caucus issued more strident accusations than did the legislators. Its activity strained, but hardly injured, the bond between the British and American establishments.

When Reagan became president, he kept that connection about as close as it had ever been. Yet he also demonstrated a sentimental interest in his roots, as for example in visits to the Irish embassy on several Saint Patrick's days. His close friend and National Security Adviser, William Clark, had an even stronger attachment to his ancestral land. Between 1981 and 1985 he visited Ireland five times to discuss a solution for the troubles in Ulster. Clark helped arrange the Anglo-Irish Agreement of November 1985 that for the first time provided Dublin with a voice in affairs in the northern counties.

The Reagan administration's economic aid to the Irish in support of the arrangement involved "an American government" more directly in a possible Irish-British settlement than any had been in the past. This involvement owed much "to the power and influence of the American connection," or to the ethnically related Irish and Irish-American lobbying by groups such as the Friends of Ireland.[53] As for the agreement, it brought a pause to Ulster's violence but did not end it.

Scholars of ethnicity often maintain that by this time the Irish-Americans had become so assimilated along lines of Anglo conformity that they manifested no real unity or even intense feeling toward Northern Ireland's fate. These analysts assert that only a minority among Americans with Irish blood concerned itself with the issues relating to Ulster. While generally sound, this assessment underrates the ability of the activist Irish-Americans to involve, if not influence, the foreign-policy establishment on Anglo-Irish problems.

More important than the extent of assimilation in accounting for the Irish lobby's questionable potency was political reality. As in the past, in a showdown those Irish-Americans who were mobilized still could not match the more powerful "British and Scotch-Irish" group and its supporters, nor could the Irish move the government to act so as to alienate "America's most powerful ally."[54] In the case of the Anglo-Irish agreement, Irish-American lobbying proved fruitful because it did not injure the relationship with Britain.

Irish-American ethnic politics were equally or more effective in obtaining preferential treatment for legal and illegal Irish immigrants in the major revision of the immigration process that President Bush signed into law on November 28, 1990. While this new act, to go into effect in the following year, expanded the total number of permitted newcomers by forty percent, it favored Europeans. Under a lottery system, it allowed the Irish "more than double the number allotted to any other nationality."[55] Instrumental in obtaining this quota was the lobbying of the Irish Reform Movement, a special-interest organization based in New York but with chapters in other cities with sizable Irish populations. Another notable feature in the legislation permitted the secretary of state, for the first time, to exclude foreigners on the basis of foreign-policy considerations.

Africans, too, benefited from the law, but in these decades African-Americans, despite impressive progress in domestic areas, still were unable to compete productively against most large white ethnic groups in the politics of foreign policy. This difficulty was evident throughout the Nixon administration. From the start in 1969, the president, and especially Henry Kissinger, then his national security adviser, viewed relations with African nations fundamentally in terms of their relevance to cold war strategy. These leaders therefore shifted tactically from the anti-colonial policies of the Kennedy and Johnson administrations.

Nixon and Kissinger cooperated more with white-supremacy regimes in South Africa and Southern Rhodesia, as well as with those in the colonies still controlled by Portugal. These leaders assumed that in those parts of Africa American policy could be effective only by dealing with the entrenched whites. A State Department critic dubbed this approach the "tar baby" option, because it stuck the government to the remnants of European colonialism. Yet in basic assumptions, Nixon followed a policy similar to that of his immediate predecessors. Over time his administration shifted its stance on the colonial issue and in April 1976 even repudiated the tar-baby approach.

African-American leaders, of course, disliked any aspect of the Nixon shift. Policymakers knew that, but they discounted black influence. They were convinced that, away from areas of heavy African-American concentration, African issues did not win votes. Yet when the president spoke on foreign policy, he often sought in some way to appease the blacks. "Is there something in it for the jigs?" he would ask speech writers and assistants such as Kissinger. From the perspective of a usual Euro-American disdain for peoples of color, administration leaders assumed also that most citizens cared little about what happened in Africa. Affairs there, consequently, remained at what one analyst called "the unchallenged bottom rung of American foreign policy priorities."[56]

Activist African-Americans who sought to disprove Nixon's presumption took advantage of the country's liberalized social climate and the global sentiment against racism to make their case. Congressman Charles C. Diggs, Jr., a black from Detroit, was one of the first to attack the Nixon policy, saying that "America has made an immoral entangling alliance with one of the most tyrannical governments in the world, the Republic of South Africa."[57]

After the 1970 congressional elections, African-Americans in the house of representatives formed the congressional Black Caucus. Although it focused mostly on domestic issues, the ethnoracial consciousness of its members compelled them to express concern about policy toward African nations. In March 1971 the caucus urged Nixon to take economic measures against South Africa's minority white regime. In May of the following year, it organized in Washington the first African-American National Conference on Africa. That body called for a "national Black Strategy on Africa" with a fresh policy toward southern Africa. In November African-American leaders announced that "some 25 million black people . . . are making clearer each day that they *are* concerned with U.S. policy toward South Africa."[58]

These tactics, supported also by white liberals, persuaded the administration, despite its friendliness with Pretoria, to move cautiously on volatile South African matters. Thus, even though the African-American use of ethnic politics in this anti-apartheid movement did not force a reversal in policy toward Africa, it did limit the government's space for maneuver.

All along, African-American leaders were convinced that racism in the governing establishment precluded it from giving their people as fair a hearing on foreign-policy issues as it did other ethnic groups. Even so, the black leadership increasingly took up international matters. In 1975 intellectuals formed the Black Forum on Foreign Policy to press the government for favorable measures toward African countries. In December the Black Caucus announced a comprehensive critique of policy toward a rebellion in Angola. Later it called for the cessation of foreign intervention there, especially for the withdrawal of South African troops.

In 1976 Diggs and Andrew Young, another congressman, brought together 130 black leaders to challenge Kissinger's policy toward white-ruled

Rhodesia. In Washington in May 1978 these men organized and launched TransAfrica, Inc., the first mass-based African-American lobby. It aspired to influence policy toward Caribbean countries as well as toward Africa, which was nevertheless its main area of concern. Within a year the lobby acquired a membership of 10,000. In subsequent years, as it became increasingly effective in mobilizing its constituency, it established itself as the foremost channel for the expression of African-American attitudes on foreign policy.

Meanwhile, Young had delivered the African-American votes which many believed provided the narrow margin in Jimmy Carter's victory. In payment, and as part of his commitment to human rights in foreign affairs, Carter appointed Young to the post of ambassador to the United Nations. Young enjoyed proximity to the top policymakers but not the power to participate in the formulating of policy. Yet his diplomacy focused attention on black Africa as had that of no previous American official.

Young frequently took the lead in emphasizing American support for majority black rule in Rhodesia and opposition to apartheid in South Africa. Yet he never succeeded in gaining as high a priority for African issues as most African-Americans believed they merited. Throughout the country, according to a survey in 1979, Euro-Americans opposed the exertion of strong pressure on the ruling white minority in South Africa. African-Americans such as Parren J. Mitchell, chairman of the Black Caucus, were convinced that "for reasons of ethnic considerations, America finds it necessary to safeguard the interests of a white minority in Southern Africa."[59]

Young's diplomacy, which reflected the desire among black leaders to act as intermediaries between the United States and Third World countries, also triggered a confrontation between African-Americans and American Jews. On July 26, 1979, on his own while president of the United Nations' Security Council, Young secretly conferred with the representative of the Palestine Liberation Organization (PLO), an Arab revolutionary group opposed to Israel. Young thereby violated America's nonrecognition policy toward the PLO, a key element for four years in the partnership with Israel. The Israelis who learned of his action promptly informed Secretary of State Cyrus R. Vance.

In mid-August, when the indiscretion became public, Jewish-Americans and others showered the White House with protests. Even though the presidential election, in which Carter needed solid black as well as Jewish support, was less than four months off, within a week he forced Young to resign. Carter explained later that "Andy had *not* violated the United States agreement with Israel concerning the PLO, but he should have informed the Secretary of State more fully about the controversial meeting."[60]

Angered African-Americans denounced the dismissal as racist. Trans-Africa flooded the White House with letters, telegrams, and telephone calls protesting the dumping. Blacks believed that Young had been forced out because he had taken a position on foreign policy outside an area directly involving his own people and because he had challenged the Israeli lobby, an allegation that American Jews denied. They argued that an angered Vance had insisted on the resignation.

This disclaimer did not assuage the African-Americans. Everywhere they upbraided Carter for allowing "one of our own" to be fired "upon the whim and caprice of a foreign power." At a meeting in August, African-American leaders insisted that Young had acted in the best interests of the nation. They rejected "the implication that anyone other than blacks themselves can determine their proper role in helping to shape and mold American foreign policies which directly affect their lives."[61] In doing so they also spoke out for the narrower interests of their own ethnoracial group.

Regardless of how one may assess this case, it did bring more venom to the antagonism between Jews and blacks that had been growing over several decades. Many African-American activists had long been anti-Semitic because while struggling for upward mobility they continually collided with Jews. They resented Jewish opposition to affirmative action in employment and education, the billions given to Israel, and Israel's friendliness with South Africa. They viewed the aid as a measure of their own limited influence in foreign policy in comparison to that of the less-numerous Jews. Israel received far more dollars than any of the African nations. African-Americans attributed this discrepancy to Jewish political power.

Blacks also frequently expressed solidarity with their "Palestinian brothers and sisters, who, like us, are struggling for self-determination and an end to racist oppression." Many Jews therefore viewed African-Americans and the civil rights movement itself as "tinctured with anti-Semitism."[62]

African-American leaders also ascribed some of their people's other disadvantages, such as unemployment and poverty, to foreign policy, as for example to cold war military expenditures. They believed that those funds could have been used instead to help them. In particular, they questioned the implementation of refugee policy, believing that the decisions which permitted the entry of thousands of Cubans as political refugees and with government subsidies amounting to $1.5 billion were racially biased.

These benefits spanned decades, because the Cubans had fled their homeland in three separate waves. The first wave followed Fidel Castro's revolution in 1959, the second came in 1965, and the third arrived in 1980, bringing in total more than a million Cubans to the United States. Most of them settled in Florida as exiles who hoped someday to go back to their island, but many gave up hope of a return, sank roots, and became politically active Cuban-Americans. Virtually all were staunch anti-Communists who opposed any official connection with Castro's Cuba, a conviction that found reward in Washington in matters affecting foreign policy.

African-Americans remained convinced that the Cuban community took their jobs and enjoyed an official favoritism that allowed it to prosper while they languished. When the third wave of immigration from the island brought some 130,000 Cuban refugees into the country, the black animosity in Miami exploded. Similar grievances produced race riots there in 1982, 1984, and January 1989. The African-Americans said they "felt cheated" by the privileges accorded Cubans, Nicaraguans, and others.

From the black perspective, the government's treatment of illegal Haitian immigrants also exuded racism. Thousands who washed ashore in flimsy vessels requested a refugee status that the Reagan administration denied on the grounds that the Haitians were fleeing economic deprivation rather than political persecution. African-Americans maintained that the Haitians would have been treated differently had they been white, as were most of the Cuban and Jewish refugees.

These frustrations did not arise necessarily out of African-American disenchantment with the nation's foreign-policy objectives as a whole. The tension derived more from their lack of power to advance toward specific goals. For instance, blacks wished to enhance the civil rights struggle at home with the prestige of having behind it the support of African nations, but that required cultivation through foreign policy.

Blacks also felt baffled by the "tilt" of Reagan and his conservative ideologues toward South Africa's minority regime. Reagan was "opposed to sanctions, opposed to the African National Congress," the militant anti-apartheid organization, because in his perspective "it was terroristic."[63] His policy of "constructive engagement" included more trade and the reestablishment of other contacts with the white regime there. African-American politicking and the anti-apartheid movement proved ineffective in reversing that policy or in inducing the government to take measures against South Africa that truly hurt.

The stymied blacks therefore turned to private organizations made up of students, leftist and civil rights activists, and others to force American corporations, and if possible the government, to sever their ties to South Africa. In the view of many, the corporate investments represented the core of

American interests there, hence the attack on the right of American companies to profit from the exploitation of black workers under apartheid was proper. Since the anti-apartheid movement still failed to mobilize mass support, however, the president virtually ignored it.

For this and other reasons, many black leaders denounced the administration as racist. In October 1984, when Reagan ordered troops into Grenada, a small island in the Caribbean belonging to the British commonwealth, he appeared, in the view of African-American leaders, to live up to the accusation. As more than eighty-five percent of Grenada's population was black, they perceived the invasion as racially motivated and criticized it as another instance of Euro-Americans' readily using guns against black people. The black congressional caucus unanimously condemned the invasion. Five of its members even desired to impeach the president.

Among the other actions in foreign affairs that struck the African-Americans as hostile to them was Reagan's veto in 1986 of a bill to ban loans, investments, and other economic activity in South Africa. In October, in response to African-American and white liberal lobbying, congress overrode the veto. In this instance black ethnic politics were effective enough to influence a major foreign-policy issue. However, that power still had severe limitations. In August 1988 the president blocked stronger legislation. He also attempted to reduce the internationally recognized nationalist movements of southern Africa to the status of terrorist groups.

Despite this opposition, African-Americans had attained at least one of their goals in the Reagan years—official acknowledgment of their international concerns. They had also frequently complained that even though they were the largest ethnoracial minority in the country, not one of their people had ever reached a position of pivotal power in the formulation of foreign policy. One did so finally in November 1987, when Reagan appointed Lieutenant General Colin L. Powell, an African-American experienced in foreign affairs, as his national security adviser.

Such quests for policy-making responsibility among minorities often fell short of aspirations because of their own confrontations, as in the case of the blacks and the Jews. When prominent African-Americans expressed sympathy for Arabs or condemned Israeli actions in Palestine as oppressive, Jewish groups often struck back in anger.

At times the encounters were bitter, as during the presidential campaign in 1988, when Jesse Jackson, the African-American clergyman and civil rights leader, sought the Democratic nomination. As in a similar campaign four years earlier, he questioned the propriety of Israeli influence in the shaping of American policy in the Middle East. His attitude infuriated many Jewish-Americans because it revived, through implication at least, the old charge that they practiced a double allegiance. In contrast, black leaders claimed pointedly that they had always "been free of this kind of dual loyalty. Like it or not," one of them explained, "Afro-Americans' single national identity is with the United States."[64]

Whether or not the generalization was sound, in these years the nature of the African-Americans' real or assumed ancestral affinity underwent greater change than in the past. More than ever, attentive blacks identified with African countries or with native groups within them, as in South Africa. They also partially inspired a black pride movement in Brazil, a country where ethnoracial considerations steered foreign policy toward a close relationship with African societies. Whenever possible the black lobby in the United States similarly sought to bend policy toward African nations.

Meanwhile, the emotions aroused by the charges of dual loyalty spilled onto Jackson's campaign when he brought it east. Edward I. Koch, New York City's blunt mayor, who took on the role of spokesman for American Jewry, announced that any Jew loyal to Israel would be "crazy" to vote for Jackson. He accused the candidate of anti-Semitism and of showing contempt for the Jewish-American attachment to Israel.

Although New Yorkers had long been accustomed to rough ethnic politics, this attack caused a furor. It highlighted how deeply felt such politics still could be when they touched sensitive areas of foreign policy. For example, when polled on how they would cast ballots if Jackson became the candidate for vice president, Jewish Democrats indicated they would vote the Republican ticket, though in the primary many backed Jackson. With an emotion equal to that of the Jews, African-Americans stood solidly by Jackson, and largely for racial reasons.

Leaders in Africa, too, applauded Jackson's candidacy in racial terms. As had Israeli politicians with American Jews, they frequently appealed to African-Americans to use their expanding political power to aid them by exerting pressure on Washington. Whenever possible, these African officials tried to influence American policy toward their countries by courting African-American opinion.

For instance, Nigerians who followed American politics praised Jackson's stand on specific foreign-policy issues, especially his call for stronger sanctions against South Africa and for America's recognition of Angola's Marxist government. These and other Africans perceived him "as a bridge between black Africa and the United States." A Nigerian journalist who recognized the effectiveness of ethnic politics commented that Jackson "believes that the same spirit of brotherhood that exists between Jews in Israel and Jewish-Americans should exist between black Africans and Afro-Americans."[65]

As for the presidential campaign, when Jackson's supporters, joined by Arab-Americans, attempted to include in the Democratic party platform a plank that endorsed self-determination for Palestinians, Jewish groups blocked it. Yet its mere consideration signified a degree of disenchantment over the Israeli tactics against an Arab uprising. Leaders of the Arab-American Institute, an ethnic lobby, regarded even the stifled debate on Middle East policy as an achievement. Most of all, this episode further corroded the Jewish relationship with African-Americans. So did Jackson's loss of the Democratic nomination to Michael S. Dukakis. Both Dukakis and George Bush, the Republican candidate, reached out for votes in crucial states with commitments of support for Israel. They courted black voters with less ardor.

Another flare-up between African-Americans and Jews occurred in June 1990, when Nelson Mandela, the South African civil rights leader recently freed after twenty-seven years in jail, toured the United States. On national television he said, "We identify with the PLO because, just like ourselves, they are fighting for the right of self-determination. . . ."[66] Jews took offense, and policymakers were troubled. If localized, such minority clashes did not affect foreign policy directly. But, as these black-Jewish confrontations demonstrated, the pronouncements of unofficial visitors, mayors, and others could impinge on sensitive international issues.

As had the attitudes of the hyphenates earlier in the century, this behavior of the "ethnics" on foreign-policy matters alarmed old-line nationalists. As in the past, they raised the old issue of dual loyalty, accusing the minority activists of placing commitment to foreign lands above allegiance to the United States. Yet these largely Anglo-American nativists themselves still practiced an equivalent loyalism. In a roughly comparable way it again became obvious during the Falkland Islands (Malvinas) War between Britain and Argentina.

Sovereignty over these islands lying 380 nautical miles off the southern tip of Argentina had been in dispute between Europeans since their discovery in 1592, and between the British and the Argentines since 1833, when the British seized control of the islands and remained. On April 2, 1982, after years of negotiation to resolve the differences, Argentine armed forces invaded and occupied the Falklands. As the British properly claimed, under the existing standards of international law the seizure was illegal.

Although the American government considered both countries friends, the relationship with Britain was much closer. From the start Washington assured the British leaders of its support. At first it aided them secretly while publicly proclaiming neutrality. Then on April 30, the day after the senate overwhelmingly passed a resolution in favor of Britain, the administration intervened openly, levying sanctions against Argentina.

Secretary of Defense Caspar W. Weinberger, "a passionate anglophile" who from the start was committed to helping the British "to the utmost of our ability," asked Nicholas Henderson, the British ambassador in Washington, "Tell me what you need."[67] Accordingly, the United States supplied Britain with sophisticated air-to-air and air-to-surface missiles, backup warplanes, and fuel and ammunition. Britain also had the use of United States naval and air bases on Ascension Island in the south Atlantic for refueling ships and planes and for bombing the Argentines, and it received other equipment, along with a wealth of intelligence on Argentina's military capability and activity.

Most analysts regard this assistance, which stopped just short of direct involvement, as decisive. They assume that without it the British could not have recaptured the Falklands and triumphed as they did in June, though others such as Weinberger argued differently.

Even though brief, the war aroused supposedly dormant ethnic passions. Latin American and Third World states supported Argentina, while Western European nations, some of them reluctantly, backed Britain. In Buenos Aires, London, and Washington too, in a rejuvenated tribalism people spoke of the old Latin—Anglo-Saxon rivalry. Both sides revived ethnic epithets. In the United States Hispanics favored Argentina, while the Anglo-American elite behaved in the usual manner of an ethnic pressure group.

Policymakers such as Secretary of State Alexander Haig openly expressed their affinity for England. "He was determined, as was the president," in the words of the British ambassador to the United States, "to do everything conceivable to help the British government."[68] Jeanne Kirkpatrick, a cabinet officer more empathic toward the Latin Americans, called Haig and his chief deputies "Brits in American clothes" who were "totally insensitive to [Latin] cultures." She asked sarcastically, "Why not disband the State Department and have the British Foreign Office make our policy?"[69]

Officially, the Reagan administration explained its intervention with a sound reason: it opposed armed aggression by a military dictatorship. In fact though, as high government officials later admitted on television and elsewhere, the perceived ethnic bond of "common Anglo-Saxon roots, a common language," or "the atavistic business of blood and language," had greater potency in their pro-British behavior. Later, for example, Queen

Elizabeth knighted Weinberger for his "fraternal role in the Falklands crisis."[70]

The administration knew beforehand that its conduct would provoke anti-Yankee bitterness throughout Latin America, a part of the world it still courted. It risked injury to its relations there, while claiming to support international law, because more than anything else, it valued the closeness of the British connection. As an American scholar observed, "it is impossible to conceive that the United States would go so far for any other nation."[71]

In keeping with the reality of the long-standing solidarity with Britain, this assumption was logical. The United States still had more in common with her than with any other country. In reverse, however, this uniqueness no longer held true for the United Kingdom. It had as strong, if not stronger, ethnic links with Australia, New Zealand, Canada, and South Africa. But the power of the United States on a global scale, and the ethnic affinity between elites, made the partnership as valuable as ever to Britain.

Despite the depth of this amity, intellectuals in both Britain and America deplored what they perceived as an ebbing of the special relationship because of the profound demographic changes in the United States. In 1979 only 22.3 percent of the population traced its ancestry to English sources. By the mid-eighties such people no longer even formed the largest single minority, and by 1990 less than 20 percent of all Americans had any British ancestors.[72] Understandably, British leaders lamented the decline of the old East Coast and essentially Anglo-American establishment that had long dominated the formulation of foreign policy. Disapprovingly, they saw the Anglophile "Atlanticists" sharing primacy with leaders who sprang from different roots or were domiciled on the West Coast and other Sunbelt areas.

Regardless of these lamentations, and of the altered basis of the Anglo-American relationship, it still retained vitality. Under Prime Minister Margaret H. Thatcher and President Reagan, it had been as close as ever. She made the special relationship the central feature of British policy. On the American side, President Bush continued the tradition. For example, in December 1989 Secretary of State Baker, while in Europe for other reasons, made an unscheduled detour to London to thwart gossip of an erosion in the friendship and to "reaffirm and reconfirm" that the bond remained intact. "The relationship with Great Britain," he announced, "is extraordinarily special."[73]

Still the talk of deterioration persisted. Four months later, Norman Tebbit, a prominent member of Britain's Conservative party, expressed a worry common in his government over the demographic shift in America because it would "inevitably" weaken the ethnic bond between the two peoples. He pointed out that "the culture of the United States has been essentially Anglo-Saxon," but now it was being diluted by the non-Caucasian immigration. "I'll be sorry to see the United States becoming a less Anglo-Saxon, a less European country," he said.[74]

In the United States disquietude of this nature, as the Falklands episode indicated, did not fundamentally affect the status of the Anglo-American elite. By adjusting selectively to the circumstances that had rearranged the ethnic mix, and by sharing some power, it retained immense influence. Even though compelled to function alongside the new pluralism, its standard of Americanism remained the foremost model for assimilationists. Furthermore, even though in numerous instances the Anglo-American elite had expanded to become a Euro-American elite, in relations with the outside world it shared less of its power than in domestic affairs. It still set the goals in most areas of foreign policy.

There has never been a
"British" vote or "English"
lobby.

Harry C. Allen, historian,
1955

9

IN PERSPECTIVE

In the seventies and eighties assimilationists still expected "the demise of ethnic influence on foreign policy."[1] Even during the ethnic resurgence, they asserted that among white Americans as a whole ancestral awareness had declined. Those who foresaw the ethnoracial bond as being replaced by class feeling, or "eroded by time or eradicated by education," were as convinced as they had ever been that in this shift the commitment to distant kin would lose its capacity to affect foreign policy.[2] They either ignored the effective politics of Anglo-Americans, Jewish-Americans, and other groups in this area or dismissed them as an exception to their hypothesis.

The pluralists of this period, on the other hand, claimed that among the pressures on foreign relations the ethnic connection remained as powerful as ever. They argued that much in the nation's past documented the toughness of the ancestral bond. They pointed out that in the present its persistence was particularly evident in the aroused ethnoracial consciousness of the African-Americans and the Hispanics. Furthermore, the demographic changes that the recent immigrant groups had brought to American society showed a rising minority involvement in specific international issues. All these groups, old and new, had an actual or potential impact on policy-making.

Others who unconsciously had long accepted assimilation theory were so puzzled by the dynamism of the ethnic connection in the politics of foreign affairs that they doubted their own assumptions.[3] Yet in domestic life the minorities, which as a rule had long been committed to pluralism, seldom totally rejected the assimilationist model. They preferred a stronger governmental commitment to pluralism mainly in foreign affairs. They desired a tolerance which, in line with their own concerns, would allow them to accept or modify the Anglo-American model of relations with the rest of the world.

In the late nineteenth century through the use of ethnic politics, as we have seen, minorities did gain choice in influencing foreign policy in limited areas. Usually, though, if they wished to avoid the stigma of dual allegiance while they were involved with large issues affecting ancestral lands, they had to accept the prevailing Anglo-American model in policymaking. In the twentieth century their options slowly expanded, until in recent years sizable minority groups have acquired sufficient power to challenge establishment standards. The minorities could, for instance, choose either assimilationism or pluralism in domestic affairs while adopting a pluralist approach to foreign policy, without necessarily being condemned as untrustworthy hyphenates.

Yet, on the basis of the perceived growth in ethnic power, scholarly pluralists concluded that assimilation theory "has clearly proven to be mistaken."[4] Even those who presumed that as the offspring of minority immigrants moved into mainstream culture their link to an ethnic homeland would weaken questioned whether it would disappear. "The mythical melting pot has failed to create a new American," a skeptic asserted; "even to the fourth and fifth generation, citizens cling to their original nationality."[5] Other analysts claimed that the sense of ethnic affinity as expressed especially in the politics of foreign policy even heightened among second- and third-generation Americans.

Whether or not such intensification occurred, affiliation on the basis of ethnicity was encouraged. More openly than in the past, Americans of diverse stock proclaimed their attachment to old homelands. In some parts of the country citizens who had long become accustomed to the "balanced ticket," meaning a slate of candidates from various ethnoracial groups, still often voted on the basis of group attachment. In these areas office seekers candidly campaigned to attract votes from their own kind. In all, by this time many Americans had seen so much of ethnic politicking that frequently touched on special foreign-policy issues that they took it for granted.

Even though historians generally regarded the stepped-up minority maneuvering in matters of foreign relations that began late in the nineteenth century as not surviving beyond the 1920s, in reality it has remained alive and healthy to the present. As in earlier times, the nativists viewed such ethnic politics as a flaw in the assimilation process. When they witnessed minorities pulling and hauling to influence foreign policy, they resented them as spoilers of the kind of stability that they believed the country should have in international affairs. These old-line Americans took for granted that ethnic striving, by sapping the traditional patriotism which in theory held the nation together against the outside world, hampered the conduct of foreign policy.

Confirmed academic assimilationists who had deplored "the curse of ethnicity in American politics," denouncing it as a "morbid experience," as "a danger to national survival," and as "a great foreign fungus," still regarded pluralism as undesirable because to them it meant a society "irreconcilably divided."[6] In turn, critics condemned these attitudes as exaggerating the danger of disunity. They pointed out that the assimilationists often failed to distinguish between cultural and political loyalties or to prove that dual allegiances constituted disloyalty to the nation. "Political disloyalty to the United States," one critic explained, "has never been predominantly a result of immigrant-ethnic old country ties" and no hard evidence supported the claim that ethnoracial "pressure politics in foreign policy have undermined or unbalanced the national interests of the United States."[7]

Yet the nation's important officeholders, who usually were assimilationists, took the possibilities of fragmentation seriously because they underestimated the strength of acculturation. Rarely, therefore, did they deviate from the traditional Anglo-American criterion of national unity. When they spoke as statesmen, for example, they gave the impression of being above capitulation to interest-group politics, whatever their source. The politicians and policymakers claimed service only to an amorphous national interest based on their own idea of a socially cohesive American nation.

Most presidents, or their advisers, have indulged in such rhetoric. Dwight D. Eisenhower did so during the Suez crisis of 1956, saying that the welfare and best interest of the whole country were the "sole criteria" of his foreign policy. In 1976 Vice President Nelson Rockefeller offered another example of the same principle, maintaining that "the United States cannot represent all its people, or its own national self-interest, if it tries, or is forced, to represent special groups ahead of the nation's interests as a whole."[8] Several years later, in his farewell to the presidency, Jimmy Carter expressed a similar view. He deplored "single-issue groups and special-interest organizations" as "a disturbing factor in American political life."[9]

Whenever lesser leaders, such as members of congress, disliked the drift in ethnic politics, they too echoed this theme. They worried openly about "the overall ethnicization of foreign policy," arguing that their performance and that of policymakers should not be measured by how well it served the desires of a particular interest group.[10] A few of them agreed that ethnic objectives should figure in the total foreign-policy process. Yet, like the others, they insisted that the welfare of America as a whole should not be chained to the politics of any single group. They also stressed logically that the sum of special interests did not make up the national interest.

This anti-ethnic viewpoint overlooked the reality that in the conduct of foreign relations the governing elite defined the national interest in its own terms, oftentimes as though it were itself a special-interest group. In a larger perspective, though, the establishment attracted popular support that cut across lines of ethnicity by portraying American foreign policy as the instrument of a "Chosen People . . . in the world community."[11] The dominant Anglo-American ethnic community also implemented the prescribed national interest so as to intimidate its possible challengers. So, when the behavior of minorities did not fit its criteria of national unity, its spokesmen condemned their politics as part of a dirty business that had no place in diplomacy.

The new pluralists, as distinguished from those prominent early in the century, viewed this approach to national loyalty as part of the assimilationist doctrine that beclouded the enduring qualities of ethnic affinity. They therefore attacked this conception of loyalty. They argued that "pluralist democratic theory assumes that the public good emerges from the conflict of private interests" and showed that in numerous societies pluralism functioned as a recognized political force without being tainted as subversive.[12] They also reiterated that pluralism had long been a part of American life, perhaps its defining feature.

Furthermore, because the United States still accepted masses of ethnically, racially, and culturally diverse immigrants, the pluralists perceived the nation as "becoming more plural every day," with "the differences . . . growing, not diminishing."[13] For this reason and because ancestral loyalties retained vitality, they were convinced that ethnoracial groups would continue to lobby for their original homelands regardless of who opposed them.

Pluralism's defenders contended also that if minority politics were as divisive as the assimilationists claimed, so were other forms of political confrontation. Ethnoracial advocacy constituted only one aspect of political behavior. Most major interest groups—agrarian, labor, and corporate—lobbied to sway foreign policy. In this perspective ethnic pressures were not much different from those in the other organized politicking in democratic government. Why, therefore, should lobbying and voting on the basis of ethnoracial considerations, as by Jewish-Americans, African-Americans, and others, be considered less legitimate than doing so for economic, regional, or ideological reasons? If government in a plural society is to be responsive to the public's desires, the argument went, it will be influenced by the ethnic affiliations of its constituent groups.

From this standpoint the alternative to a foreign policy open to the politics of all ethnoracial groups could be one dominated by a few insiders who acted primarily for the benefit of their own kind. The new pluralists maintained, therefore, that society at large benefited from sundry grass-roots efforts to influence foreign policy. They even contended that in contrast to control by one interest group, diversity, through a balance of offsetting interests, promoted peace, or that ethnoracial groups often engaged in "activities that maximize the possibilities of peace politics."[14]

The new pluralists insisted, as had the old, that regardless of the faults in minority politics, they helped to keep foreign policy open to democratic pressure. As a Greek-American activist explained, "We have a right and a duty as ethnic groups to lobby."[15] Without such politicking, the formulation of foreign policy would be a much more closed affair than it has been.

Minority leaders insisted that affinity for kin in ancestral lands represented neither a lack of patriotism nor a desire to place foreign ahead of American interests. They believed that the two commitments often coincided. In addition, they cited data demonstrating that despite the old-world attachments, in time of national crisis, as during the two world wars, loyalty to the Union generally took precedence over whatever previous ethnic affiliations groups had cherished.

Of course, many Americans of mixed stock who did not identify with any particular ethnic group saw no real meaning in specific ancestral connections. This lack of feeling for old-world roots was part of the ongoing Americanization implicit in assimilation doctrine. The result of this process was evident in the census of 1980, in which those who reported "multiple ancestry" or who gave "American" as their ethnic group (13.3 million out of a total of 226.5 million) made up the largest category under the heading of national origins.[16] Their status also reflected the flexibility in ethnic affiliation. It could and did change. Old communal attachments died and new ones were born, though in the United States no ethnic group once established had entirely disappeared.

As we have seen, the overlapping loyalties inherent in ethnic groups existed alongside considerable acculturation, or what might be termed "behavioral" as distinct from the "structural" assimilation which foundered on the rock of "Anglo-conformity."[17] In practice, therefore, neither assimilation nor pluralism functioned as separately as many of their advocates had assumed. Through intermarriage even the intractable divisions of race gave way to some extent, so that in the reality of everyday living the two conceptions were not always incompatible. Assimilation and pluralism could even be regarded as "part of the same process."[18] Indeed, out of these seemingly opposed forces could be observed the formation of the distinctively American identity that Michel-Guillaume-Jean de Crèvecoeur, Frederick Jackson Turner, and even Theodore Roosevelt, before he had become obsessed with hyphenism, had described.

Roosevelt had noted that the "English, and especially the Puritans made the mold into which the other races were run. They therefore gave the vital turn to our development." Yet, he added, the "admixture of other races made it certain that we would be what we now are, a distinct nation with its own peculiar individuality."[19] The contemporary image of the American is more mixed and less European than in his time, being based on a more expanded conception of ethnicity than Roosevelt and the others had envisaged. Today an American can trace his or her origins to one race, to one ethnic group, or to a blend of several. What we can identify as American, therefore, is less static and more fluid than is ethnic identity in most other societies.

Within the nation, however, regardless of how flexible the conception of an American ethnicity may be, there is still inconsonance. As from the beginning, it is most apparent in the cases of African-Americans, who have been in the country longer than have most of the white minorities, of American Indians, who boast of an even lengthier presence, of some Asians, and of most Hispanics. By Euro-American standards, these groups did not qualify for assimilation. Even though many did, or could, fit the similar conception called integration, most of them are still "outside the melting pot."[20]

Even so, through increasing numbers and rising affluence, Asian-Americans have overcome aspects of this unassimilability to acquire more influence in the politics of foreign policy than they had in the past. In 1989 they asserted their new strength in seeking legislation to protect the 40,000 Chinese students in American universities against being forced to return to their Communist homeland. There the returnees faced possible punishment for having agitated against the regime that in June had massacred students and other dissenters. Fearing that China would retaliate if the students did not go back and would also move away from what had been an improving relationship with the United States, President George Bush opposed the special bill. In November, after congress passed the legislation, he vetoed it.

When the mobilized Asian-Americans pressured congress to override, Senator Alan K. Simpson, the minority whip, asserted that they had created a powerful lobby. "With the fund-raising they do," he said, "they're really heavy hitters." Stewart Kwok, the executive director of the Asian Pacific American Legal Center of Southern California, responded that the senator "should understand that Asian-Americans have for a long time had no voice in Washington, D.C." Yet now that they are "making use of their democratic rights, he's reacting in a negative way."[21] Although congress sustained the veto, the president, as he had promised, protected the students against deportation with an executive order in April 1990. In all, the Asian-Americans had demonstrated that they, too, must be heard on international issues of interest to them.

Despite this instance of a racially mobilized minority overcoming cultural differences to work effectively within the political system, the racial barriers to true assimilation remained. Race, consequently, stands as a constant reminder of the nation's pluralism and remains a prominent ingredient in its relations with a large part of the world.

On the other hand, the old antagonisms between Americans of diverse European ancestry declined, because the lines that divided them often became blurred. Among them in this domestic sense, as we have seen, assimilation theory generally worked. At the same time, as the pluralists contended, the activity of the micro–Euro-American groups in the politics of foreign relations retained their vitality. These groups persisted in maintaining an often attenuated but nonetheless viable connection with kindred peoples abroad. As from the beginning of the republic, therefore, most identifiable ethnoracial groups, whether old or new, continued to concern themselves with issues of foreign policy that touched on the "consciousness of kind."

As evident in contemporary life and as throughout the past, ethnic and racial sympathies still have much to do with how Americans and their leaders respond to events abroad. Since these sentiments are often vague, they also continue to make the measuring of ethnic influence on foreign policy controversial. As in the past, the critics of special-interest lobbying ascribe the difficulty to an ineffectiveness in the politicking of most minorities. The skeptics still maintain that while ethnic groups may succeed in small ways, essentially in matters affecting "areas of the world . . . to which they have a direct connection," they are unable to define the big issues or alter fundamental foreign-policy orientation.[22] Whenever the minority aspirations clash with the national interest as prescribed by the governing elite, the ethnic politicians have to retreat. Knowing that foreign-policy issues on their own have seldom decided national elections, officeholders have at times withstood minority pressures, or have set one group against another to cancel the effectiveness of each.

When taken on its own terms, this negative appraisal of ethnic power can be persuasive. When, however, the Anglo-American group is included in any assessment, then the perspective changes. Mainly in comparison to this ethnic community do the achievements of minorities, even of the Jewish-Americans, seem less than significant in the making of foreign policy. If, as in this study, the Anglo-Americans are counted as ethnics, then we can hardly avoid considering ethnicity a significant determinant of policy.

Of course, the power of the Anglo-Americans in foreign affairs has not derived just from their favored ethnicity. The nation's leadership has usually been committed to the Anglo-American perspective out of other concerns as well, as for example the preserving of national unity. America's leaders have been practical domestic politicians as well as international policymakers. They valued survival as well as their own version of patriotic conduct. In specific instances, therefore, they strayed from, but did not abandon, the traditional commitment. When weighing policy alternatives, they could seldom forget the election that lay ahead and hence the need to listen to ethnically motivated minority as well as to majority constituents. If these officeholders disregarded the necessities of being elected, then in keeping with the theory of ultimate accountability, they would seldom be around long enough to conduct effective foreign policy.

In swing districts, even for a national ticket, minority votes sometimes could make a difference between victory or defeat. Presidents as well as members of congress, therefore, frequently had to acknowledge minority concerns over international as well as domestic matters. In seeking ethnic votes for the 1972 election, Richard Nixon, for instance, made "an absolute demand on his advisers that we do more for the Italians, Cuban Americans, Poles, and Mexicans."[23] Such practicality may even have caused elected officials at times to overestimate the power of particular interest groups and, out of fear, to accede to their wishes. In the view of nationalists, this kind of response "made cowards of our political leaders."[24]

In the case of congress, recent studies substantiate the sensitivity of its members to the opinions of constituents in matters of foreign relations. Members of congress responded in particular to pressure from those who had political clout through the control of batches of votes or through access to substantial funds for vote-getting. In turn, the accountable officeholders urged the executive branch to shape policy as the lobbyists desired. For example, for years Armenian-Americans, who were especially influential in

California, had lobbied congress for a resolution to commemorate what they termed "the Armenian genocide of 1915–23" in Turkey.

In February 1990, despite opposition from the Bush administration, from the Turkish government, and from others, the Armenian-American lobbyists appeared to have succeeded. At the last minute, however, a senate filibuster blocked their resolution. Opponents described it as "a foreign policy disaster in the making," because Turkey, an important ally, as a matter of policy denied that its people had committed genocide.[25] Turkey warned that if the memorial passed while containing the word "genocide," it would produce a grave crisis between the two countries. The resolution failed, but by the narrowest of margins.

As have comparable episodes that we have probed, this one illustrates how small ethnic groups, when well organized and capably led, can sway foreign policy. They can do so in limited ways because even if the politicians and policymakers only think, rather than know with certainty, that the ethnic politics of such a group are potent, then indeed they are. Again, as analysts point out, "intensity tends to outweigh numbers."[26] The persuasive lobbying of such interest groups also frequently has the effect of a magnifying glass. It enlarges the impact of political fund-raising and hence of ethnic votes.

The recent rise to political power of minorities has at least modified the character of the ethnic orientation in the making of foreign policy. Minorities are less awed than in the past by the establishment's invocation of the mystique of "national interest," by its purported exceptional ability to rule, or by its corollary right to shape foreign policy by its standard alone.

African-Americans, for example, regard themselves as being as much a part of the national interest as anyone else. Moreover, they do not demand that they should determine general foreign policy. They only wish to be included in the process. As do the British, Irish, Poles, Italians, Germans, Jews, and others, they want their interests recognized as a legitimate feature of policy-making. These legitimate desires meet resistance because, for one reason, the white establishment considers African-American goals deviant from its exemplar of national commitment.

In foreign relations as in domestic life, such dedication by minorities, despite their political gains, still required a considerable degree of conformity to establishment standards. In matters of war and peace, most ethnic groups were still judged by how closely they harmonized with the Anglo-American view of the world. When ethnic activists deviated markedly from this benchmark, they usually ran into trouble. Those at the top condemned them as disloyal because they appeared to be attacking the ideological foundations of the nation as well as its foreign policy.

As usual, the Anglo-Americans seldom faced such charges, because, among the other reasons we have noted, they had created the national ideology. Moreover, as have other dominant peoples in comparable circumstances, as a rule they continued to deny that they were hyphenates who engaged in ethnic politics. Even though through their mixing with outsiders they had undergone considerable dilution, the Anglo-Americans still regarded themselves as the truest of Americans. Along with Anglicized allies, they still defined their stance in foreign relations as at the center of mainstream American culture. As have others who have constituted core groups, the Anglo-Americans resisted absorption into a broader identity that would reduce their power.

These Anglo-Americans had behind them more than two hundred years of successful ethnic politics, having overcome Anglophobia and most other challenges to their authority. No other group manifested greater pride in its antecedents, distinctiveness, and accomplishments. Its people had "never ceased to be the descendants of their forefathers and the products of the culture from which they sprang." In the words of British historian Maldwyn Jones, "it could plausibly be argued that the most dominant of America's ethnic groups was also the one with the closest ties to its homeland."[27] It had prevailed in part because of its longtime majority status and because the governing elite constantly had come from its ranks. Since 1815 that elite had rarely departed in the making of policy from the Anglo-American model. It still usually sets the course for foreign policy.

This standard has survived for a bundle of reasons, including common British and American global and strategic interests. It has endured especially because the Anglo-Americans constituted the nation's ethnic core, which still retained sufficient power to impose its ideals upon, or gain their acceptance from, society. Their centuries of dominance have led the Anglo-Americans to assume, as have numerous other Americans also, that their exercise of power was part of a natural order. We should remember, though, that the Anglo behavior in channeling foreign policy so as to benefit distant kin hardly differed from that of others who have involved themselves in ethnic politics. The Anglo-Americans have, however, practiced such politics with greater success than the members of any other group.

For this reason, other groups had often insisted that the Anglo-Americans, too, must be regarded as hyphenates. In the late eighties organized minorities decided to drop the hyphen in referring to themselves because the Anglos "seldom, if ever" used it.[28] The minorities took this step also because they believed that the old implication of divided loyalty still clung to the hyphen. They did not realize that dual loyalty "is common in all complex societies with their many cross-cutting ties and different objects of attachment."[29]

The Japanese-Americans, who felt strongly the stigma of their wartime experience, led in the anti-hyphen movement. Blacks, on the other hand, embraced hyphenism. They wanted to be known as African-Americans, because the term assured them of "cultural integrity," placed them in their "proper historical context," and tied them with pride to a land of origin, as the hyphen did to members of white minority groups.[30]

In line with the nation's increasing diversity, these sensitive groups attacked the traditional leadership in foreign policy with more effect than in the past. In response, many Anglo-Americans, who had at times assumed that the main thrust of minority politics "has been to thwart Anglo-American friendship," became more openly "ethnic" in their own political tactics. They acknowledged having reacted to international situations according to their ancestral affiliation. Now, along with other Euro-Americans, they insisted that the United States must remain fundamentally an "Atlantic nation," preserving its close ties not only with Britain but with all of Western Europe. Anglo-American leaders and their counterparts in Britain also lamented the policy-making authority of individuals "concerned solely with the response of American constituencies to their actions and advocacies."[31]

This attitude stemmed from an awareness of the eroding basis of Anglo-American authority. As the census data showed, by the nineties the Anglos, too, had become a minority in a sea of diversity. Privileged entities do not relish loss of power. They seldom surrender it without a struggle. Unlike most other challenged elites, however, the Anglo-American group generally maintained its status through ethnic politics rather than through force. While other ethnic groups, as they pushed upward clashing along the way with the entrenched elite over foreign-policy issues, suffered discrimination, they did not experience institutionalized brutality.

Seldom as a matter of policy did the dominant Anglo ethnic community persecute alien groups. Even though it acted reluctantly, it did permit others to depart to a degree from its standards through peaceful means. Without this tolerance, which, regardless of its flaws, has long been a distinguishing feature of American society, there could have been no multiethnic politics within existing institutions and no ethnoracial influence in the making of foreign policy, other than that provided by the Anglo-Americans.

Despite this tolerance and the reality of national diversity, there were Anglo-American or Anglicized leaders who continued to behave as though they still represented *the* national interest. To an extent they still do exemplify it, because some group has to maintain the cultural and ethnic basis of the evolving American identity. With their cohesiveness, history, and tradition, the Anglo-Americans are still well equipped to do so. While their numbers have diminished relative to those of other groups, they are still the nation's ethnic core. That status has helped them retain dominance in the shaping of foreign policy, but with a fresh forbearance for other viewpoints. Essentially, their power has faded more in the domestic area, where there is "no longer an exercise in Anglo-Saxon domination," than it has in foreign affairs.[32]

It is in good part because of this rearrangement of power that congress and the executive branch have responded more readily than in the past to minority politics. They have further democratized the foreign-policy system through accountability to minority interests, even though they know that cleavages in ethnic groups often prevent them from delivering votes as a bloc. But policymakers also realize that on issues affecting distant kin ethnic voters usually demonstrate greater unity than on domestic matters.

Events the world over indicate that ethnic politics roughly comparable to those in the United States are inherent in plural societies. Yet, because of the nature of its heterogeneity and of its democratic institutions, the United States remains more prone to ethnoracial pressures in foreign policy than any other major nation. Analysts therefore continue to believe that "the ethnic factor in American foreign policy cannot be denied," and to insist that it should not be.[33] They do not regard ethnoracial politics as a menace to the nation's integrity, because they know that the United States has always been ethnically plural, and also, even with its civil war, unified.

Logic suggests that ultimately most of the nation's white ethnic groups will melt, as in the assimilationist model. At present they function as do the racial blocs and other interest groups. They strive for power that the strong and well-organized among them often attain. As always, the weak suffer what they must. Strong or weak, the ethnoracial groups plunge into foreign-policy issues because their members, like all peoples, feel a deep attachment to ancestral lands which may still be home to uncles, aunts, cousins, and other relatives. They seem compelled to try to help their own kind through political influence.

As pluralists believe, such politicking to influence decisions affecting international affairs appears destined to continue for years to come, because of the extent of American society's cultural, ethnic, racial, and other connections with countries the world over. These ethnic politics are distinctive because American society has been and is more multiethnic, multiracial, and multireligious than any other on a comparable scale. As its diversity increases, more than ever its decision makers must accord respect to ethno-racial differences and desires. They, and scholars too, should also realize that while ethnicity and race may not be the engine of history or be as powerful as claimed by Moynihan, Glazer, and others, ethnoracial concerns have always been, and remain a prominent determinant of American foreign policy.

NOTES

Notes to Chapter One

1. Gabriel A. Almond, *The American People and Foreign Policy* (New York, 1960), xxv.
2. *Ethnicity: Theory and Experience*, ed. Nathan Glazer and Daniel P. Moynihan (Cambridge, Mass., 1975), 23–24.
3. Quoted from George F. Kennan, *Memoirs, 1925–1950* (Boston, 1967), entry of June 23–25, 1944, 185.
4. Steven L. Spiegel, *The Other Arab–Israeli Conflict* (Chicago, 1985), 390.
5. D. Cameron Watt, "Foreword," *Anglo-American Relations in the 1920s*, ed. B. J. C. McKercher (London, 1991), xii.
6. Inis L. Claude, Jr., *The Impact of Public Opinion Upon Foreign Policy and Diplomacy* (The Hague, 1965), 17.
7. Ernest R. May, "An American Tradition in Foreign Policy: The Role of Public Opinion," in *Theory and Practice in American Politics*, ed. William H. Nelson (Chicago, 1964), 122.
8. Quoted in Martin Kriesberg, "Dark Areas of Ignorance," in Lester Markel et al., *Public Opinion and Foreign Policy* (New York, 1949), 54.
9. Quoted from Thomas G. Paterson, "Presidential Foreign Policy, Public Opinion, and Congress: The Truman Years," *Diplomatic History*, III (Winter 1979), 2–3.
10. Quoted from John Snetsinger, "Ethnicity and Foreign Policy," in *Encyclopedia of American Foreign Policy*, ed. Alexander DeConde (3 vols., New York, 1978), 1, 322.
11. Frederick Jackson Turner, *The Frontier in American History* (New York, 1920), 22–23.
12. Victor Greene, "Old Ethnic Stereotypes and the New Ethnic Studies," *Ethnicity*, V (Dec. 1978), 341.
13. Philip Gleason, "Americans All: World War II and the Shaping of American Identity," *Review of Politics*, XLIII (Oct. 1981), 485.

Notes to Chapter Two

1. Quoted from Charlotte Erickson, "English," in *Harvard Encyclopedia of American Ethnic Groups*, ed. Stephan Thernstrom (Cambridge, Mass., 1980), 319.
2. John Butler, *The Huguenots in America* (Cambridge, Mass., 1983), 104.
3. Quoted from Bernard Bailyn, *The Peopling of British North America* (New York, 1986), 96.
4. "Observations concerning the Increase of Mankind, Peopling of Countries, &c," in *The Papers of Benjamin Franklin*, ed. Leonard W. Labaree et al. (18 vols., New Haven, Conn., 1959–), IV, 234.
5. Quoted from ibid.
6. Quoted in Hermann Wellenreuther, "Image and Counterimage, Tradition and Expectation: The German Immigrants in English Colonial Society in Pennsylvania, 1700–

1765," in *America and Germans*, I, ed. Frank Trommler and Joseph McVeigh (Philadelphia, 1985), 93.

7. Quoted in Gerald Stourzh, *Benjamin Franklin and American Foreign Policy* (Chicago, 1954), 81.

8. The first quotation (Hopkinson) comes from Merle Curti, *The Roots of American Loyalty* (New York, 1946), 13, and the second from Gordon S. Wood, *Representation in the American Revolution* (Charlottesville, Va., 1969), 3.

9. Quoted in Vernon J. Jensen, "British Voices on the Eve of the American Revolution: Trapped by the Family Metaphor," *Quarterly Journal of Speech*, LXIII (Feb. 1977), 45.

10. College provost, Philadelphia, May 1776, quoted in Hans Kohn, *American Nationalism* (New York, 1957), 7.

11. The quotations come from Philip Lawson, *The Imperial Challenge* (Montreal, 1989), 150, and John P. Roche, "Immigration and Nationality: A Historical Overview of United States Policy," in *Ethnic Resurgence in Modern Democratic States*, ed. Uri Ra'anan (New York, 1980), 37.

12. The quotations come from William C. Stinchcombe, *The American Revolution and the French Alliance* (Syracuse, N.Y., 1969), 1, 61.

13. Cited in *American Nativism, 1830–1860*, ed., Ira M. Leonard and Robert D. Parmet (New York, 1971), 18.

14. Hector St. John de Crèvecoeur, *Letters from an American Farmer* (London, 1912, but published originally in 1782), 43.

15. Quoted from Winthrop D. Jordan, *The White Man's Burden* (New York, 1974), 132–33.

16. Quoted from Lawrence H. Fuchs, *The American Kaleidoscope* (Hanover, N.H., 1990), 15.

17. James H. Kettner, *The Development of American Citizenship, 1608–1870* (Chapel Hill, 1978), 226.

18. Federalist No. 2, Oct. 31, 1787, *The Federalist*, ed. Jacob E. Cooke (Middletown, Conn., 1961), 9.

19. Quoted in Reginald Horsman, *Race and Manifest Destiny* (Cambridge, Mass., 1981), 94.

20. Quoted from a report by Beckwith, Oct. 25, 1789, in Julian P. Boyd, *Number 7: Alexander Hamilton's Secret Attempts to Control American Foreign Policy* (Princeton, 1964), 24. The other quotations come from Alexander DeConde, *Entangling Alliance* (Durham, N.C., 1958), 71–72.

21. Quoted from Charles S. Ritcheson, *Aftermath of Revolution* (Dallas, 1969), 359.

22. Quoted, with italics, in Bradford Perkins, *The First Rapprochement* (Philadelphia, 1955), 1.

23. Sept. 19, 1796, in *The Writings of George Washington . . . 1745–1799*, ed. John C. Fitzpatrick (39 vols., Washington, D.C., 1931–44), XXXV, 224–36.

24. March 7, 1798, quoted in James M. Smith, *Freedom's Fetters* (Ithaca, N.Y., 1956), 21.

25. Quoted in Leonard, ed., *American Nativism*, 22.

26. Quoted in Smith, *Freedom's Fetters*, 25.

27. The statistics come from Edward C. Carter II, "A 'Wild Irishman' Under Every Federalist Bed: Naturalization in Philadelphia, 1789–1806," *Proceedings of the American Philosophical Society*, CXXXIII (No. 2, 1989), 179, 184.

28. Jefferson to James Monroe, Washington, Nov. 24, 1801, in *Works of Thomas Jefferson*, ed. Paul L. Ford (12 vols., New York 1904–5), IX, 317.

29. The quotation (Jefferson) comes from Timothy M. Matthewson, "George Washington's Policy Toward the Haitian Revolution," *Diplomatic History*, III (Summer 1979), 328.

30. Quoted in Bradford Perkins, *Prologue to War* (Berkeley, 1963), 59.

31. Clinton is quoted in Maldwyn A. Jones, *American Immigration* (Chicago, 1960), 76; Everett in Horsman, *Race*, 95–96; and anomaly comes from Ritcheson, *Aftermath of Revolution*, 359.

32. Quoted from Leon F. Litwack, *North of Slavery* (Chicago, 1961), 25.

33. Quoted from Ella Forbes, "African-American Resistance to Colonization," *Journal of Black Studies*, XXI (Dec. 1990), 219.

34. Jan. 27, 1825, quoted in Frederick M. Binder, *The Color Problem in Early National America as Viewed by John Adams, Jefferson and Jackson* (The Hague, 1968), 118.

Notes to Chapter Three

1. Quoted from Hans-Jürgen Grabb, "European Immigration to the United States in the Early National Period, 1783–1820," *Proceedings of the American Philosophical Society*, CXXXIII (June 1989), 197.

2. John J. Johnson, *A Hemisphere Apart* (Baltimore, 1990), 46.

3. Rowland T. Berthoff, *British Immigrants in Industrial America, 1790–1950* (Cambridge, Mass., 1953), 139.

4. Quoted from Yehoshua Arieli, *Individualism and Nationalism in American Ideology* (Cambridge, Mass., 1964), 254.

5. José Manuel Zozoya quoted in George W. Grayson, "Anti-Americanism in Mexico," in *Anti-Americanism in the Third World*, ed. Alvin Z. Rubinstein and Donald E. Smith (New York, 1988), 31.

6. To Mary Austin Holley, Aug. 21, 1835, Austin Papers, cited in Arnaldo DeLeón, *They Called Them Greasers* (Austin, Tex, 1983), 12.

7. Quoted in Reginald Horsman, *Race and Manifest Destiny* (Cambridge, Mass., 1981), 218.

8. Senator William Merrick of Maryland, quoted in John Hope Franklin, *Race and History* (Baton Rouge, La., 1989), 105.

9. Manuel Eduardo de Gorostiza, the Mexican minister to the United States during the Texas revolution, quoted in Gene M. Brack, "Mexican Opinion, American Racism, and the War of 1846," *Western Historical Quarterly*, I (April 1970), 170.

10. Quoted in Edward P. Crapol, "The Foreign Policy of Antislavery, 1833–1846," in *Redefining the Past*, ed. Lloyd C. Gardner (Corvallis, Ore., 1986), 90.

11. The quotations come from Stuart C. Miller, *The Unwelcome Immigrant* (Berkeley, 1969), 95, 105.

12. Quoted from Max Berger, "The Irish Emigrant and American Nativism as Seen by British Visitors, 1836–1860," *Pennsylvania Magazine of History and Biography*, LXX (April 1946), 154.

13. James Haughton, quoted in John A. Murphy, "The Influence of America on Irish Nationalism," in *America and Ireland, 1776–1976,* ed. David N. Doyle and Owen D. Edwards (Westport, Conn., 1980), 110.

14. Quoted from Marcus L. Hansen, *The Atlantic Migration, 1607–1860* (Cambridge, Mass., 1945), 169.

15. John L. O'Sullivan, Sept. 1838, quoted from Reginald L. Stuart, *United States Expansionism and British North America, 1775–1871* (Chapel Hill, 1988), 86.

16. Quoted in ibid., 104.

17. Quoted from Horsman, *Race*, 221, 224 and David M. Pletcher, *The Diplomacy of Annexation* (Columbia, Mo., 1973), 351.

18. The first quotation comes from Robert W. Johannsen, *To the Halls of Montezuma* (New York, 1985), 291, and the second from Frederick Merk, *The Oregon Question* (Cambridge, Mass., 1967), 254.

19. New York *Herald*, June 11, 1846, quoted in Pletcher, *Diplomacy of Annexation*, 414.

20. Simms is quoted in Horsman, *Race*, 166–67. The other quotations come from Thomas R. Hietala, *Manifest Design* (Ithaca, N.Y., 1985), 155, and Justin H. Smith, *The War with Mexico* (2 vols., New York, 1919), I, 104.

21. James Russell Lowell, *The Biglow Papers* [First Series], ed. Thomas Wortham (DeKalb, Ill., 1977), 62.

22. Aug. 19, 1845, quoted in Andrew L. Farrand, "Cultural Dissonance in Mexican-American Relations," Diss., University of California, Santa Barbara, 1971, 237.

23. Quoted from Paul C. Nagel, *This Sacred Trust* (New York, 1971), 64.

24. Feb. 10, 1847, quoted in Frederick Merk, *Manifest Destiny and Mission in American History* (New York, 1963), 159.

25. Jan. 4, 1848, quoted in ibid., 162.

26. Quoted from Cecil Woodham-Smith, *The Great Hunger* (New York, 1962), 206.

27. Quoted from Michael F. Holt, *The Political Crisis of the 1850s* (New York, 1978), 179.

28. William E. Gienapp, "Nativism and the Creation of a Republican Majority in the North Before the Civil War," *Journal of American History*, LXXII (Dec. 1985), 558.

29. *Albany Evening Journal*, Feb. 23, 1857, quoted in Miller, *Unwelcome Immigrant*, 123.

30. Quoted in Tyler Dennett, *Americans in Eastern Asia* (New York, 1922), 340n.

31. May 15, 1861, quoted in Martin Crawford, *The Anglo-American Crisis of the Mid-Nineteenth Century* (Athens, Ga., 1987), 106.

32. Thomas Hart Benton, quoted in Alfred N. Hunt, *Haiti's Influence on Antebellum America* (Baton Rouge, La., 1988), 185.

33. The quotations come from John Hope Franklin, *The Emancipation Proclamation* (New York, 1963), 132.

34. Quoted from James H. Kettner, *The Development of American Citizenship, 1608–1870* (Chapel Hill, 1978), 324.

35. Patrick Ford, an immigrant from Galway, is quoted in Kerby A. Miller, *Emigrants and Exiles* (New York, 1985), 337.

36. Bruce to Russell, Aug. 8, 1865, cited in William D'Arcy, *The Fenian Movement in the United States: 1858–1886* (Washington, D.C., 1947), 121.

37. Adams to Wm. West, March 7, 1866, cited in Brian A. Jenkins, *Fenians and Anglo-American Relations during Reconstruction* (Ithaca, N.Y., 1969), 90.

38. Ibid., 277.

Notes to Chapter Four

1. The quotations come from Charlotte Erickson, *American Industry and the European Immigrant, 1860–1885* (Cambridge, Mass., 1957), 3, 5.

2. By T. D. Sullivan, 1875, quoted in John B. Duff, *The Irish in the United States* (Belmont, Calif., 1971), 65.

3. *Deutsche Pioneer* (Cincinnati), 1873, quoted in G. A. Dobbert, "German-Americans Between New and Old Fatherland, 1870–1914," *American Quarterly*, XIX (Winter 1967), 670.

4. U. S. Grant, "Reasons Why Santo Domingo Should be Annexed to the United States," cited in George Sinkler, *The Racial Attitudes of American Presidents* (Garden City, N.Y., 1971), 151.

5. The quotations come from David Donald, *Charles Sumner and the Rights of Man* (New York, 1970), 442–43, and Sinkler, *Racial Attitudes of Presidents*, 153.

6. Quoted in Seán Cronin, *Washington's Irish Policy 1916–1986* (Dublin, 1987), 15.

7. Charles S. Campbell, *From Revolution to Rapprochement* (New York, 1974), 162.

8. Quoted from Paul C. Nagel, *This Sacred Trust* (New York, 1971), 262.

9. Quoted from Stuart C. Miller, *The Unwelcome Immigrant* (Berkeley, 1969), 192.

10. Quoted from Harold R. Isaacs, *Scratches on Our Minds* (New York, 1958), 198, and George Morrison, Feb. 26, 1879, in Sinkler, *Racial Attitudes of Presidents*, 193.

11. The quotations come from Thomas F. Gossett, *Race: The History of an Idea in America* (Dallas, 1963), 291, and Miller, *Unwelcome Immigrant*, 159.

12. Freda Hawkins, *Critical Years in Immigration* (Kingston and Montreal, 1989), 10.

13. First annual message, Washington, D.C., Dec. 8, 1885, in *The State of the Union Messages of the Presidents, 1790–1966*, ed. Fred L. Israel (3 vols., New York, 1966), II, 1518.

14. Quoted (1899) from Rubin F. Weston, *Racism in U.S. Imperialism* (Columbia, S.C., 1972), 27.

15. Lawrence H. Fuchs, *The Political Behavior of American Jews* (Glencoe, Ill., 1956), 24.

16. Jacob R. Marcus, *United States Jewry, 1776–1985* (2 vols., Detroit, 1989–91), I, 660.

17. Ibid., II, 327.

18. The quotations come from Richard Gambino, *Vendetta* (Garden City, N.Y., 1977), 97, 118.

19. Written in 1893 and quoted in Nagel, *Sacred Trust*, 321.

20. Finley Peter Dunne, *Mr. Dooley On Ivrything and Ivrybody*, ed. Robert Hutchinson (New York, 1963), 19.

21. Quoted in Stuart Anderson, *Race and Rapprochement* (East Brunswick, N.J., 1981), 81–82.

22. Quoted in Thomas A. Bailey, *The Man in the Street* (New York, 1948), 15.

23. The quotations come from Bradford Perkins, *The Great Rapprochement* (New York, 1968), 143; David N. Doyle, *Irish Americans, Native Rights and National Empires* (New York, 1976), 204; and Anderson, *Race and Rapprochement*, 11.

24. Quoted from Alexander E. Campbell, *Great Britain and the United States 1895–1903* (London, 1960), 195–96.

25. Quoted in William T. Stead, *The Americanisation of the World* (London, 1902), 14.

26. The quotations come from Campbell, *Revolution to Rapprochement*, 183, and Anderson, *Race and Rapprochement*, 96–102.

27. *Times* (London), May 14, 1898, quoted in R. G. Neale, *Great Britain and the United States Expansion: 1898–1900* (East Lansing, Mich., 1966), 155–56

28. Quoted from Christopher Hitchens, *Blood, Class and Nostalgia* (New York, 1990), 298.

29. Frederick Merk, *Manifest Destiny and Mission in American History* (New York, 1963), 243.

30. Quoted from Julius W. Pratt, *Expansionists of 1898* (Baltimore, 1936), 135.

31. T. Roosevelt to James Bryce, Sept. 10, 1897, quoted in Howard K. Beale, *Theodore Roosevelt and the Rise of America to World Power* (Baltimore, 1956), 29, and William A. Russ, Jr., *The Hawaiian Republic (1894–98)* (Selingsgrove, Pa., 1961), 315.

32. Quoted in Sylvester K. Stevens, *American Expansion in Hawaii 1842–1898* (Harrisburg, Pa., 1945), 288.

33. *Springfield* (Mass.) *Republican*, Aug. 25, 1898, quoted in Daniel B. Schirmer, *Republic or Empire* (Cambridge, Mass., 1972), 91–92.

34. David F. Trask, *The War with Spain in 1898* (New York, 1981), 475–76.

35. Gerald F. Linderman, *The Mirror of War* (Ann Arbor, Mich., 1974), 121, 123.

36. Quoted from Helen E. Knuth, "The Climax of American Anglo-Saxonism, 1898–1905," Diss., Northwestern University, 1958, 88, and Doyle, *Irish Americans, Native Rights*, 190.

37. Richard Olney, "International Isolation of the United States," *Atlantic Monthly*, LXXXI (May 1898), 588.

38. Quoted from Joseph H. Taylor, "The Restriction of European Immigration and the Concept of Race," *South Atlantic Quarterly*, L (Jan. 1951), 32.

39. The quotations come from Anderson, *Race and Rapprochement*, 118–19; Stuart Anderson, "Racial Anglo-Saxonism and the American Response to the Boer War," *Diplomatic History*, II (Summer 1978), 229; and Weston, *Racism in U.S. Imperialism*, 148.

40. The first quotation comes from Linderman, *Mirror of War*, 138 and the others from Louis A. Pérez, Jr., *Cuba Between Empires 1878–1902* (Pittsburgh, 1983), 206, 220, 227.

41. Quoted from Louis A. Pérez, Jr., "Cuba Between Empires, 1898–1899," *Pacific Historical Review*, XLVIII (Nov. 1979), 483.

42. Ronald T. Takaki, *Iron Cages* (New York, 1979), 269.

43. The quotations come from Weston, *Racism in U.S. Imperialism*, 92–93, and Stuart C. Miller, *"Benevolent Assimilation"* (New Haven, 1982), 15.

44. Quoted from Barbara M. Solomon, *Ancestors and Immigrants* (Cambridge, Mass., 1956), 120.

45. Quoted from Miller, *"Benevolent Assimilation,"* 52, 66.

46. The quotation comes from the *Times* (London), May 24, 1898, cited in Neale, *Britain and United States Expansion*, 90.

47. Quoted in Schirmer, *Republic or Empire*, 143.

48. From the *Milwaukee Weekly Advocate*, Aug. 17, 1899, quoted in Willard B. Gatewood, Jr., "Black Americans and the Quest for Empire, 1893–1903," *Journal of Southern History*, XXXVII (Nov. 1972), 559.

49. These figures come from Richard E. Welch, Jr., *Response to Imperialism* (Chapel

Hill, 1978), 155; John W. Dower, *War Without Mercy* (New York, 1985), 150–51 gives higher estimates.

50. Quoted in Weston, *Racism in U.S. Imperialism*, 109.

51. Quoted in Anderson, *Race and Rapprochement*, 84.

52. Willard B. Gatewood, Jr., "Black Americans and the Boer War, 1899–1902," *South Atlantic Quarterly*, LXXV (Spring 1976), 234.

53. Anderson, "Racial Anglo-Saxonism," 225–26, 230.

54. The quotations come from Perkins, *Great Rapprochement*, 93, and Lodge to Roosevelt, Feb. 2, 1900, in *Selections from the Correspondence of Theodore Roosevelt and Henry Cabot Lodge, 1884–1918*, ed. Henry Cabot Lodge (2 vols., New York, 1924), I, 446.

55. John Hope Franklin, *From Slavery to Freedom* (4th ed., New York, 1974), 313.

56. Quoted in Benjamin B. Ringer, *"We the People" and Others* (New York, 1983), 973.

Notes to Chapter Five

1. Quoted from William R. Thayer, *Democracy: Discipline: Peace* (Boston, 1919), 112.

2. July 14, 1903, quoted in Gary Bean Best, *To Free a People* (Westport, Conn., 1982), 80.

3. Quoted from Henry A. Feingold, *A Midrash on American Jewish History* (Albany, N.Y., 1982), 47.

4. The quotations come from Alan J. Ward, "Immigrant Minority 'Diplomacy': American Jews and Russia 1901–1912," *Bulletin of the British Association for American Studies*, New Series, IX (Dec. 1964), 62, and William Sulzer in Best, *To Free a People*, 196.

5. The quotations come from David A. Mayers, *George Kennan and the Dilemmas of US Foreign Policy* (New York, 1988), 56, and George F. Kennan, *Russia Leaves the War* (Princeton, 1956), 13.

6. Quoted in Delber L. McKee, *Chinese Exclusion versus the Open Door Policy 1900–1906* (Detroit, 1977), 51.

7. Quoted in Delber L. McKee, "The Chinese Boycott of 1905–1906 Reconsidered: The Role of Chinese Americans," *Pacific Historical Review*, LV (May 1986), 176.

8. Quoted in Mary R. Coolidge, *Chinese Immigration* (New York, 1909), 300.

9. To Theodore Roosevelt, March 2, 1904, quoted in Howard K. Beale, *Theodore Roosevelt and the Rise of America to World Power* (Baltimore, 1956), 214.

10. *Chicago Tribune*, May 21, 1905, quoted in ibid., 218.

11. The first quotation (Zeng Shaojing) comes from Shih-Shan Henry Tsai, *The Chinese Experience in America* (Bloomington, Ind., 1986), 78, and the second, *Nih Nih Sing* (Fukien), May 24, 1905, from Tsai, *China and the Overseas Chinese in the United States, 1868–1911* (Fayetteville, Ark., 1983), 108.

12. The quotations come from L. Eve Armentrout Ma, *Revolutionaries, Monarchists, and Chinatowns* (Honolulu, 1989), 5, 158, 165.

13. Quoted from Ronald Takaki, *Strangers from a Different Shore* (Boston, 1989), 46.

14. Quoted from Paul G. Lauren, *Power and Prejudice* (Boulder, Colo., 1988), 67.

15. Kayahara Kazan, *Shinsekai*, Nov. 16, 28, 1906, quoted in Akira Iriye, *Pacific Estrangement* (Cambridge, Mass., 1972), 140–41.

16. To Kermit Roosevelt, Washington, D.C., Oct. 27, 1906, in *The Letters of Theodore Roosevelt*, ed. Elting E. Morison (8 vols., Cambridge, Mass., 1951–54), V, 475.

17. Thomas G. Dyer, *Theodore Roosevelt and the Idea of Race* (Baton Rouge, La., 1980), 140.

18. To John Hay, Aug. 19, 1903, quoted in Richard H. Collin, *Theodore Roosevelt's Caribbean* (Baton Rouge, La., 1990), 239.

19. Annual message, Dec. 6, 1904, U.S. Department of State, *Foreign Relations of the United States, 1903–1904* (Washington, D.C., 1905), xli.

20. Quoted from David H. Burton, *Theodore Roosevelt* (Philadelphia, 1968), 120.

21. Quoted from David Healy, *Drive to Hegemony* (Madison, Wis., 1988), 215.

22. The quotations come from Beale, *Roosevelt and the Rise of America*, 145, 398.

23. To Elihu Root, Oyster Bay, July 2, 1908, in Morison, ed., *Roosevelt Letters*, VI, 1104.

24. Quoted in Bradford Perkins, *The Great Rapprochement* (New York, 1968), 80.

25. The quotations come from ibid., 291, and Paul L. Murphy, *World War I and the Origin of Civil Liberties in the United States* (New York, 1979), 254.

26. The quotations come from John M. Cooper, Jr., *The Warrior and the Priest* (Cambridge, Mass., 1983), 210, and Rubin F. Weston, *Racism in U.S. Imperialism* (Columbia, S.C., 1972), 32.

27. Quoted in Roy W. Curry, *Woodrow Wilson and Far Eastern Policy, 1913–1921* (New York, 1957), 52, 55.

28. The quotations come from Weston, *Racism*, 72, and Brenda G. Plummer, "The Afro-American Response to the Occupation of Haiti, 1915–1934," *Phylon*, XLIII (Spring 1982), 125. The casualty figures come from Hans Schmidt, *The United States Occupation of Haiti, 1915–1934* (New Brunswick, N.J., 1971), 103.

29. *El Diario del Hogar*, quoted in Frederick C. Turner, "Anti-Americanism in Mexico, 1910–1913," *Hispanic American Historical Review*, LVII (Nov. 1967), 505.

30. Aug. 1913, ibid., 512.

31. May 11, 1914, quoted in Kenneth J. Grieb, *The United States and Huerta* (Lincoln, Neb., 1969), 154. The slogan is quoted from Robert E. Quirk, *An Affair of Honor* (Lexington, Ken., 1962), 108.

32. Quoted from William Dirk Raat, *Revoltosos: Mexico's Rebels in the United States, 1903–1923* (College Station, Tex., 1981), 262–64.

33. Quoted from Linda B. Hall and Don M. Coerver, *Revolution on the Border* (Albuquerque, 1988), 15, and Mark T. Gilderhus, *Diplomacy and Revolution* (Tucson, 1977), 39.

34. Quoted in Louis L. Gerson, *The Hyphenate in Recent American Politics and Diplomacy* (Lawrence, Kan., 1964), 51.

35. Quoted from Maldwyn A. Jones, *The Old World Ties of American Ethnic Groups* (London, 1976), 4.

36. Ibid., 7.

37. See Milton M. Gordon, "Assimilation in America: Theory and Reality," in *The Ethnic Factor in American Politics*, ed. Brett W. Hawkins and Robert A. Lorinskas (Columbus, Ohio, 1970), 29–30.

38. Burton J. Hendrick, *The Life and Letters of Walter H. Page* (3 vols., Garden City, N.Y., 1922–28), I, 258.

39. Philadelphia, May 10, 1915, in *The Papers of Woodrow Wilson*, ed. Arthur S. Link (59 vols., Princeton, 1966–   ), XXXIII, 148.

40. Randolph S. Bourne, "Trans-National America," *Atlantic Monthly*, CXVIII (July 1916), 86, 88.

41. Quoting Alan J. Ward, *Ireland and Anglo-American Relations 1899–1921* (London, 1969), 100.

42. Bourne, "Trans-National America," 88.

43. To Edward Grey, Feb. 12, 1915, in *The Letters and Friendships of Sir Cecil Spring-Rice, A Record*, ed. Stephen Gwynn (2 vols., New York, 1919), II, 254.

44. The quotations come from Thomas J. Kerr IV, "German-Americans and Neutrality in the 1916 Election," *Mid-America*, XLIII (April 1961), 100, and Ward, *Ireland and Anglo-American Relations*, 133.

45. Wilson is quoted in Joseph P. Tumulty, *Woodrow Wilson as I Know Him* (Garden City, N.Y., 1921), 231.

46. Quoted from Gerson, *Hyphenate*, 66.

47. To Edwin A. Alderman, London, June 22, 1916, in Hendrick, *Life of Page*, II, 144.

48. Quoted in William M. Leary, Jr., "Woodrow Wilson, Irish Americans and the Election of 1916," *Journal of American History*, LIV (June 1967), 64.

49. Quoted from Selig Adler, *The Isolationist Impulse* (New York, 1957), 76.

50. The quotations come from Frederick C. Luebke, *Bonds of Loyalty* (DeKalb, Ill., 1974), 269, and *Nord-Amerika* (Philadelphia), Aug 12, 1918, cited in Austin J. App, "The Germans," in *The Immigrants' Influence on Wilson's Peace Policies*, ed. Joseph P. O'Grady (Lexington, Ken., 1967), 38.

51. Leon Trotsky, Dec. 29, 1917, quoted in Betty M. Unterberger, *The United States, Revolutionary Russia, and the Rise of Czechoslovakia* (Chapel Hill, 1989), 86.

52. Feb. 11, 1918, quoted in Harold S. Johnson, *Self-Determination Within the Community of Nations* (Leyden, 1967), 33.

53. New York *Gaelic-American*, Jan. 19, 1918, quoted in Joseph P. O'Grady, "The Irish," in O'Grady, ed., *Immigrants' Influence*, 58.

54. George Creel, *How We Advertised America* (New York, 1920), 173.

55. Quoted from Victor S. Mamatey, *The United States and East Central Europe, 1914–1918* (Princeton, 1957), 131, and Unterberger, *United States and Czechoslovakia*, 127.

56. Dennis J. McCarthy, "The British," in O'Grady, ed., *Immmigrants' Influence*, 91.

57. Lansing Diary, entry of Aug. 23, 1918, quoted in Ward, *Ireland and Anglo-American Relations*, 170.

58. The quotations come from O'Grady, "The Irish," in his *Immigrants' Influence*, 67, and Arthur Walworth, *Wilson and His Peacemakers* (New York, 1986), 468.

59. Quoted from Walworth, *Wilson and Peacemakers*, 38.

60. Quoted from Paul G. Lauren, "Human Rights in History: Diplomacy and Racial Equality at the Paris Peace Conference," *Diplomatic History*, II (Summer 1978), 265, and Chitoshi Yanaga, *Japan Since Perry* (New York, 1949), 373.

61. *Asahi* cited in Lauren, *Power and Prejudice*, 89.

62. Speech in New York City, March 14, 1919, quoted in Lauren, "Human Rights," 268.

63. Prince Konoye Fumimaro quoted in Akira Iriye, "Intercultural Relations" in *Encyclopedia of American Foreign Policy*, ed. Alexander DeConde (3 vols., New York, 1978), II, 439.

64. The quotations come from John B. Duff, "The Italians," in O'Grady, ed., *Immigrants' Influence*, 125, 128.

65. Root to Lodge, June 19, 1919, Henry Cabot Lodge Papers, cited in William C. Widenor, *Henry Cabot Lodge and the Search for An American Foreign Policy* (Berkeley, 1980), 325.

66. Editorial in the *Yidishes Tageblat*, Sept. 1914, quoted in Gerson, *Hyphenate*, 83.

67. Quoted from Alfred M. Lilienthal, "The Balfour Declaration: Forty Years Later," in *Issues and Conflicts*, ed. George L. Anderson (Lawrence, Kan., 1959), 103, and Ronald Sanders, *The High Walls of Jerusalem* (New York, 1983), 612–13.

68. The quotation comes from Richard N. Lebow, "Woodrow Wilson and the Balfour Declaration," *Journal of Modern History*, XL (Dec. 1968), 523.

69. The quotation comes from Frank W. Brecher, "Woodrow Wilson and the Origins of the Arab-Israeli Conflict," *American Jewish Archives*, XXXIX (April 1987), 25.

70. The numbers vary according to whether Armenian or Turkish sources are consulted. See Leo Kuper, "The Turkish Genocide of Armenians, 1915–1917," in *The Armenian Genocide in Perspective*, ed. Richard G. Hovannisian (New Brunswick, N.J., 1986), 52–53 and Michael M. Gunter, *"Pursuing the Just Cause of Their People"* (New York, 1986), 19.

71. The first quotation, Senator William H. King of Utah, Feb. 1919, comes from Richard G. Hovannisian, *The Republic of Armenia* (2 vols., Berkeley, 1971–82), I, 261, and the second from ibid., II, 402.

72. John A. DeNovo, *American Interests and Policies in the Middle East 1900–1939* (Minneapolis, 1963), 159.

73. The quotations come from Robert L. Daniel, "The Armenian Question and Turkish-American Relations, 1914–1927," *Mississippi Valley Historical Review*, XLVI (Sept. 1959), 273, and Roger R. Trask, *The United States Response to Turkish Nationalism and Reform, 1914–1939* (Minneapolis, 1971), 44.

74. The quotations come from Lloyd E. Ambrosius, *Woodrow Wilson and the American Diplomatic Tradition* (New York, 1987), 142–43, and John Higham, *Strangers in the Land* (New York, 1963), 252.

75. Quoted in Ambrosius, *Woodrow Wilson*, 209.

76. George Creel, *The War, the World, and Wilson* (New York, 1920), 330–31.

Notes to Chapter Six

1. To Richard M. Melancthon, Jan. 3, 1919, quoted in *Theodore Roosevelt and the Idea of Race* (Baton Rouge, La., 1980), 134.

2. Quoted in Geoffrey S. Smith, "Nativism," in *Encyclopedia of American Foreign Policy*, ed. Alexander DeConde (3 vols., New York, 1978), II, 664.

3. Quoted in Arthur Mann, *The One and the Many* (Chicago, 1979), 134.

4. Quoted from John Higham, *Strangers in the Land* (New York, 1963), 204.

5. Johnson to Roland Morris, Jan. 21, 1921, Johnson Mss., Bancroft Library, University of California, Berkeley, cited in Roger Daniels, *Asian America* (Seattle, 1988), 148–49. Hoover is quoted in David Burner, *Herbert Hoover* (New York, 1987), 197.

6. The quotations come from Asahi Shimbun, *The Pacific Rivals* (New York, 1972), 74.

7. Quoted from Carl Wittke, *We Who Built America* (rev. ed., Cleveland, 1964), 529.

8. Quoted in Merlo J. Pusey, *Charles Evans Hughes* (2 vols., New York, 1951), II, 512, 513.

9. *Taihoku Nippo* (Seattle), May 13, 1924, and *Shin Sekai* (San Francisco), May 21, 23, 1924, quoted in Yuji Ichioki, *The Issei* (New York, 1988), 247–48.

10. Representative Albert Johnson, quoted in Norman L. Zucker and Naomi F. Zucker, *The Guarded Gate* (San Diego, 1987), 12.

11. Senator James A. Reed of Missouri, quoted in Michael Dunne, *The United States and the World Court, 1920–1935* (London, 1988), 129.

12. Quoted in John A. Hawgood, *The Tragedy of German-America* (New York, 1940), 299.

13. The statistic comes from Christopher Thorne, *Border Crossings* (Oxford, 1988), 71.

14. Quoted from B. J. C. McKercher, "Introduction," in *Anglo-American Relations in the 1920s*, ed. B. J. C. McKercher (London, 1991), 1, and George H. Knoles, *The Jazz Age Revisited* (Stanford, 1955), 21.

15. Drew Pearson, "Washington Merry-Go-Round," Washington *Herald*, April 22, 1938, quoted in Martin Weil, *A Pretty Good Club* (New York, 1978), 95.

16. The quotations come from Richard N. Current, *Secretary Stimson* (New Brunswick, N.J., 1954), 39, and the Stimson Diaries, Jan. 17, 1929, cited in Thorne, *Border Crossings*, 263.

17. Quoted in Christopher Thorne, *The Limits of Foreign Policy* (New York, 1973), 56.

18. The quotations come from Naomi W. Cohen, *The Year After the Riots* (Detroit, 1988), 14, 48.

19. The quotations come from Aaron Berman, *Nazism, the Jews, and American Zionism, 1933–1948* (Detroit, 1990), 38, and Arnold A. Offner, *American Appeasement* (New York, 1976), 63.

20. Committee on the Status of Black Americans, *A Common Destiny*, ed. Gerald D. Jaynes and Robin Williams, Jr. (Washington, D.C., 1989), 252.

21. Quoted from Brenda G. Plummer, "The Afro-American Response to the Occupation of Haiti, 1915–1934," *Phylon*, XLIII (Spring 1982), 143.

22. William E. B. Du Bois, *The Souls of Black Folk* (New York, 1963), 23.

23. Quoted from Ben F. Rogers, "William E. B. Du Bois, Marcus Garvey, and Pan-Africa," *Journal of Negro History*, XL (April 1955), 156.

24. Quoted from E. David Cronon, *Black Moses* (Madison, Wis., 1969), 183.

25. Quoted in Alexander DeConde, *Half Bitter, Half Sweet* (New York, 1971), 216.

26. The quotations come from William R. Scott, "Black Nationalism and the Italo-Ethiopian Conflict, 1934–1936," *Journal of Negro History*, LXIII (April 1978), 123, and Cedric J. Robinson, "Fascism and the Intersections of Capitalism, Racialism, and Historical Consciousness," *Humanities in Society*, VI (Fall 1983), 344.

27. Cited in Sterling Stuckey, *Slave Culture* (New York, 1987), 347.

28. Richard Polenberg, *One Nation Indivisible* (New York, 1980), 39.

29. Kerby A. Miller, "Class, Culture, and Immigrant Group Identity in the United States: The Case of Irish-American Ethnicity," in *Immigration Reconsidered*, ed. Virginia Yans-McLaughlin (New York, 1990), 118.

30. The quotations come from T. Ryle Dwyer, *Irish Neutrality and the USA, 1939–47* (Dublin, 1977), 12, 24, 27, 49.

31. Ibid., x.

32. To Roosevelt, April 14, 1944, quoted in T. Ryle Dwyer, *Strained Relations* (Dublin, 1988), 149.

33. Quoted in James V. Compton, *The Swastika and the Eagle* (Boston, 1967), 17.

34. Quoted from Richard W. Steele, "The War on Intolerance: The Reformulation of American Nationalism, 1939–1941," *Journal of American Ethnic History*, IX (Fall 1989), 25.

35. Quoted in Geoffrey S. Smith, *To Save a Nation* (New York, 1973), 94.

36. Quoted in Robert Dallek, *Franklin D. Roosevelt and American Foreign Policy, 1932–1945* (New York, 1979), 209.

37. Quoted from Weil, *Pretty Good Club,* 109.

38. Quoted in Robert D. Schulzinger, *The Wise Men of Foreign Affairs* (New York, 1984), ix–x.

39. Mark L. Chadwin, *The Hawks of World War II* (Chapel Hill, 1968), 70.

40. Quoted from Louis L. Gerson, *The Hyphenate in Recent American Politics and Diplomacy* (Lawrence, Kan., 1964), 120–122.

41. Quoted from Polenberg, *One Nation Indivisible*, 45.

42. Diary entry, Aug. 13, 1941, Harold Nicolson, *Diaries and Letters,* ed. Nigel Nicolson (3 vols., New York, 1966–68), II, 184.

43. Philip J. Baram, *The Department of State in the Middle East, 1919–1945* (Philadelphia, 1978), 327.

44. Quoted in Gary R. Hess, "Franklin D. Roosevelt and Anti-Colonialism," *Indian Journal of American Studies,* XIII (Jan. 1983), 23.

45. The quotations come from Waldo H. Heinrichs, *Threshold of War* (New York, 1988), 159, and Raymond A. Esthus, "President Roosevelt's Commitment to Britain to Intervene in a Pacific War," *Mississippi Valley Historical Review,* L (June 1963), 35, 36.

46. Quoted from John Baylis, *Anglo-American Defence Relations 1939–1984* (2nd ed., London, 1984), xvi, and David Reynolds, "Roosevelt, Churchill, and the Wartime Anglo-American Alliance, 1939–1945: Towards a New Synthesis," in *The "Special Relationship,"* ed. William R. Louis and Hedley Bull (Oxford, 1986), 38.

47. Denis W. Brogan, "Transatlantic Strains," *The Spectator,* CLXI (July 3, 1942), 8.

48. Peter H. Irons, "'The Test is Poland': Polish Americans and the Origins of the Cold War," *Polish American Studies,* XXX (Autumn 1973), 14–15.

49. Quoted in Rubin F. Weston, *Racism in U.S. Imperialism* (Columbia, S.C., 1972), 79.

50. Yuji Ichioka, "Japanese Immigrant Nationalism: The Issei and the Sino-Japanese War, 1937–1941," *California History,* LXIX (Fall 1990), 260.

51. John J. Stephan, *Hawaii Under the Rising Sun* (Honolulu, 1984). The quotations come from pp. 27, 28, and the statistics from p. 33.

52. The quotations come from Henry L. Stimson and McGeorge Bundy, *On Active Service in Peace and War* (New York, 1948), 406, and Eric J. Sundquist, "The Japanese-American Internment: A Reappraisal," *American Scholar,* LVII (Autumn 1988), 531.

53. Quoted from Frederick W. Marks, III *Wind Over Sand* (Athens, Ga., 1988), 52.

54. Quoted from John W. Dower, *War Without Pity* (New York, 1986), 81, and Roger Daniels, *Concentration Camps: North America* (Malabar, Fla., 1981), 72.

55. Quoted from Morton Grodzins, *Americans Betrayed* (Chicago, 1949), 175.

56. Stephen Fox, *The Unknown Internment* (Boston, 1990), xii–xiii. Richard Gambino, *Blood of My Blood* (Garden City, N.Y., 1974), 288, states that initially 4,000 Italian-Americans were arrested.

57. July 2, 1943, quoted from Fred W. Riggs, *Pressures on Congress* (New York, 1950), 163.

58. Quoted in Gerald Horne, *Black and Red* (Albany, N.Y., 1986), 10.

59. Quoted in Riggs, *Pressures*, 162.

60. *The Memoirs of Cordell Hull* (2 vols., New York, 1948), II, 1589.

61. Quoted from Saburo Ienaga, *The Pacific War* (New York, 1978), 154.

62. Quoted in Riggs, *Pressures*, 211.

63. Ibid.

64. Harry L. Pence, quoted in Akira Iriye, "Intercultural Relations," in DeConde, ed., *Encyclopedia*, II, 440.

65. The quotations come from Christopher Thorne, *The Issue of War* (London, 1985), 127–28, 130–31, and Dower, *War Without Pity*, 11, 34, 146, 262–90.

66. "Simple and the Atom Bomb," *Chicago Defender*, Aug. 18, 1945, is quoted from Paul Boyer, *By the Bomb's Early Light* (New York, 1986), 199.

67. The quotations come from M. S. Venkataramani, *Bengal Famine of 1943* (Delhi, 1973), viii, ix, 80.

68. Frank W. Brecher, *Reluctant Ally* (New York, 1991), 88.

69. Henry L. Feingold, *The Politics of Rescue* (New Brunswick, N.J., 1970), 296.

70. Meeting of Dec. 1, 1943, U.S. Department of State, *Foreign Relations of the United States: The Conferences at Cairo and Tehran* (Washington, D.C., 1961), 594.

71. The quotations come from Piotr S. Wandycz, *The United States and Poland* (Cambridge, Mass., 1980), 279, 283.

72. Thomas A. Bailey, *The Man in the Street* (New York, 1948), 29.

73. Meeting of Dec. 1, 1945, U.S. Department of State, *Foreign Relations of the United States: The Conference of Berlin 1945* (2 vols., Washington, D.C., 1960), II, 216.

Notes to Chapter Seven

1. Paul G. Lauren, *Power and Prejudice* (Boulder, Colo., 1988), 187.

2. "Round Table: The Living and Reliving of World War II," ed. Richard W. Fox, *Journal of American History*, LXXXVII (Sept. 1990), 579.

3. The quotations come from Lauren, *Power and Prejudice*, 173, and Gerald Horne, *Black and Red* (Albany, N.Y., 1986), 80.

4. Quoted from Donald R. McCoy and Richard T. Ruetten, *Quest and Response* (Lawrence, Kan. 1973), 48.

5. May 8, 1946, quoted in *To Secure These Rights: The Report of the President's Committee on Civil Rights* (Washington, D.C., 1947), 146–47.

6. Ibid., 147.

7. Richard Polenberg, *One Nation Indivisible* (New York, 1980), 115.

8. Leonard Dinnerstein, *America and the Survivors of the Holocaust* (New York, 1982), 6.

9. Quoted from Aaron Berman, *Nazism, the Jews, and American Zionism, 1933–1948* (Detroit, 1990), 124.

10. Quoted from George Kent, "Congress and American Middle East Policy," in *Middle East*, ed. Willard A. Beling (Albany, N.Y., 1973), 288.

11. Memorandum of conversation, Feb. 14, 1945, U.S. Department of State, *Foreign Relations of the United States, 1945: The Near East and Africa* (9 vols., Washington, D.C., 1969), VIII, 2–3.

12. Quoted from Zvi Ganin, *Truman, American Jewry, and Israel, 1945–1948* (New York, 1979), 35.

13. Arieh J. Kochavi, "Anglo-American Discord: Jewish Refugees and United Nations Relief and Rehabilitation Administration Policy, 1945–47," *Diplomatic History*, XVI (Fall 1990), 550.

14. *New York Times*, Oct. 7, 1946, 1.

15. Bevin is quoted from William R. Louis, *The British Empire in the Middle East 1945–1951* (Oxford, 1984), 426, and Dean Acheson from his *Present at the Creation* (New York, 1969), 169.

16. Clark M. Clifford, *Counsel to the President* (New York, 1991), 4–5.

17. Report of Leo Sack to the American Zionist Emergency Council, Oct. 13, 1974, quoted in Michael J. Cohen, *Truman and Israel* (Berkeley, 1990), 159–60.

18. Leon Blank to Truman, Feb. 1, 1948, quoted in John Snetsinger, *Truman, the Jewish Vote, and the Creation of Israel* (Stanford, 1974), 78.

19. Quoted from Robert J. Donovan, *Conflict and Crisis* (New York, 1977), 380.

20. "In 1947, 1948, and 1949 the White House received 86,500 letters, 841,903 postcards, and 51,400 telegrams on the subject of Palestine." Margaret Truman, *Harry S. Truman* (New York, 1943), 384.

21. The quotations come from James V. Forrestal, *The Forrestal Diaries*, ed. Walter Millis (New York, 1951), entries of Nov. 7 and Dec. 3, 1947, 344, 347, and Kennan Lee Teslik, *Congress, the Executive Branch, and Special Interests* (Westport, Conn., 1982), 33.

22. Ian J. Bickerton, "President Truman's Recognition of Israel," *American Jewish Historical Quarterly*, LVIII (Dec. 1968), 226, 221.

23. Steven L. Spiegel, *The Other Arab-Israeli Conflict* (Chicago, 1985), 39.

24. Quoted from Bruce J. Evensen, "A Story of 'Ineptness': The Truman Administration's Struggle to Shape Conventional Wisdom on Palestine at the Beginning of the Cold War," *Diplomatic History*, XV (Summer 1991), 359.

25. The quotations come from Evan M. Wilson, *Decision on Palestine* (Stanford, 1979), 58; Cohen, *Truman and Israel*, 259; Kenneth R. Bain, *The March to Zion* (College Station, Tex., 1979), 200, 201 and Snetsinger, *Truman*, 114, 132.

26. The quotations come from McCoy and Ruetten, *Quest and Response*, 117.

27. Dinnerstein, *Survivors of the Holocaust*, 176.

28. Ganin, *American Jewry and Israel*, 180.

29. Truman to Winston Churchill, Nov. 23, 1948, cited in Donovan, *Conflict and Crisis*, 438.

30. Eisenhower to Edward E. Hazlett, Nov. 2, 1956, in Dwight D. Eisenhower, *Ike's Letters to a Friend, 1941–1958*, ed. Robert Griffith (Lawrence, Kan., 1984), 175.

31. Eisenhower diaries, Feb. 12, 1957, quoted in Isaac Alteras, "Eisenhower, American Jewry, and Israel," *American Jewish Archives*, XXXVII (Nov. 1985), 269.

32. The quotations come from Robert Silverberg, *If I Forget Thee O Jerusalem* (New York, 1970), 551, and Douglas Little, "From Even-Handed to Empty-Handed: Seeking

Order in the Middle East," in *Kennedy's Quest for Victory*, ed. Thomas G. Paterson (New York, 1989), 159.

33. Mordechai Gazit, *President Kennedy's Policy Toward the Arab States and Israel* (Tel Aviv, 1983), 35.

34. Department of State memorandum, Dec. 27, 1962, quoted in Stephen Green, *Taking Sides* (New York, 1984), 181.

35. Quoted from Lyndon B. Johnson, *The Vantage Point* (New York, 1971), 293, and William B. Quandt, *Decade of Decisions* (Berkeley, 1977), 54.

36. Quoted from Alexander DeConde, "Foreign Intervention in Domestic Politics," in *Atti del I Congresso Internazionale de Storia Americana*, ed. Raimondo Luraghi (Genoa, 1978), 120–21.

37. Arnaldo Cortesi and "Observer" in Lester Markel et al., *Public Opinion and Foreign Policy* (New York, 1949), 199, and Louis L. Gerson, *The Hyphenate in Recent American Politics and Diplomacy* (Lawrence, Kan., 1964), 31.

38. The quotations come from *Clamor at the Gates*, ed. Nathan Glazer (San Francisco, 1985), 6, and Leonard Dinnerstein and David M. Reimers, *Ethnic Americans* (New York, 1975), 83.

39. Message of June 25, 1952, in *Public Papers of the Presidents of the United States, Harry S. Truman* (8 vols., Washington, D.C., 1961–66), VIII, 441, 442, 444.

40. Quoted in Milton D. Morris, *Immigration—The Beleaguered Bureaucracy* (Washington, D.C., 1985), 40.

41. David M. Reimers, *Still the Golden Door* (New York, 1985), 244.

42. Quoted in Gerson, *Hyphenate*, 195.

43. The quotations come from Bennett Kovrig, *The Myth of Liberation* (Baltimore, 1973), 230.

44. The quotations come from Gunnar Myrdal, *An American Dilemma* (New York, 1944), 1006, 1008.

45. Walter White, *A Rising Wind* (New York, 1945), 144.

46. Quoted (1958) in Morrell Heald and Lawrence S. Kaplan, *Culture and Diplomacy* (Westport, Conn., 1977), 318.

47. Quoted from Stephen R. Weissman, *American Foreign Policy in the Congo, 1960–1964* (Ithaca, N.Y., 1974), 184.

48. Dec. 1962, quoted in Gerson, *Hyphenate*, 274n25.

49. Stokely Carmichael and Charles V. Hamilton, "Black Power," in *Ethnic Group Politics*, ed. Henry A. Bailey, Jr., and Ellis Katz (Columbus, Ohio, 1969), 299.

50. F. Chodozie Ogene, *Interest Groups and the Shaping of Foreign Policy* (New York, 1983), 94.

51. Martin Staniland, *American Intellectuals and African Nationalists, 1955–1970* (New Haven, 1991), 207.

52. Quoted from Ogene, *Interest Groups*, 72.

53. Campaign speech, Sept. 8, 1968, quoted in Suzanne Cronje, *The World and Nigeria* (London, 1972), 226.

54. Quoted in Herschelle S. Challenor, "The Influence of Black Americans on U.S. Foreign Policy Toward Africa," in *Ethnicity and U.S. Foreign Policy*, ed. Abdul Aziz Said (New York, 1977), 159.

55. Bruce Cumings, *The Origins of the Korean War* (2 vols., Princeton, 1981–90), II, 695.

56. Ronald Takaki, *Strangers from a Different Shore* (Boston, 1989), 415.

57. See, for example, Max Hastings, *The Korean War* (New York, 1987), 29, 306–8.

58. Quoted in Cumings, *Origins of Korean War*, II, 697.

59. David L. Shambaugh, "Anti-Americanism in China," in *Anti-Americanism: Origins and Context*, ed. Thomas P. Thornton, a special issue of the *Annals* of the American Academy of Political and Social Science, CDXCII (May 1988), 147.

60. Rosemary Foot, *A Substitute for Victory* (Ithaca, N.Y., 1990), 207–8.

61. Warren I. Cohen, "The China Lobby," in *Encyclopedia of American Foreign Policy*, ed. Alexander DeConde (3 vols., New York, 1978), I, 104.

62. The quotations come from Nancy B. Tucker, *Patterns in the Dust* (New York, 1983), 81, 167.

63. Gordon H. Chang, *Friends and Enemies* (Stanford, 1990), 170.

64. Roger Morris, *Uncertain Greatness* (New York, 1977), 132.

65. Frances FitzGerald, *Fire in the Lake* (Boston, 1972), 282–83.

66. Quoted from George C. Herring, "'Peoples Quite Apart': Americans, South Vietnamese, and the War in Vietnam," *Diplomatic History*, XIV (Winter 1990), 18, and Loren Baritz, *Backfire* (New York, 1985), 291.

67. Quoted from Roger Wilkins, "What Africa Means to Blacks," *Foreign Policy*, XIV (Summer 1974), 137.

68. Feb. 25, 1967, quoted in Peter B. Levy, "Blacks and the Vietnam War," in *The Legacy*, ed. D. Michael Shafer (Boston, 1990), 216.

69. Congressman John Cox of Texas, Feb. 9, 1928, quoted in Robert A. Divine, *American Immigration Policy, 1924–1952* (New Haven, 1957), 57.

70. The quotations come from ibid., 60, 67.

71. Quoted from Leobardo F. Estrada et al., "Chicanos in the United States: A History of Exploitation and Resistance," *Daedalus*, CX (Spring 1981), 113.

72. Quoted from Mario F. Garcia, *Mexican-Americans* (New Haven, 1989), 207–9.

73. Quoted in Henry B. Ryan, *The Vision of Anglo-America* (Cambridge, Eng., 1987), 170.

74. Quoted from Diane B. Kunz, *The Economic Diplomacy of the Suez Crisis* (Chapel Hill, 1991), 3, 5.

75. Quoted in Geoffrey Warner, "The Anglo-American Special Relationship," *Diplomatic History*, XIII (Fall 1989), 487.

76. E. Digby Baltzell, *The Protestant Establishment* (New York, 1964), 46.

Notes to Chapter Eight

1. Michael S. Teitelbaum, "Right Versus Right: Immigration and Refugee Policy in the United States," *Foreign Affairs*, LIX (Fall 1980), 23.

2. Quoted from Gunnar Myrdal, "The Case Against Romantic Ethnicity," Dialogue Discussion Paper, Center for the Study of Democratic Institutions, May 13, 1974, 9, deposited in Special Collections, University of California, Santa Barbara Library; Herbert J. Gans, "Symbolic Ethnicity: The Future of Ethnic Groups and Cultures in America," *Ethnic and Racial Studies*, II (Jan. 1979), 1, 5; and Arthur M. Schlesinger, Jr., *The Disuniting of America* (Knoxville, Tenn., 1991), 17, 78.

3. Daniel Bell, "Ethnicity and Social Change," in *Ethnicity*, ed. Nathan Glazer and Daniel P. Moynihan (Cambridge, Mass., 1975), 141.

4. See Arthur F. Corwin, "The Numbers Game: Estimates of Illegal Aliens in the United States, 1970–81," in *U.S. Immigration Policy*, ed. Richard R. Hofstetter (Durham, N.C., 1984), 247. For an analysis of statistical estimates, see Guillermina Jasso and Mark R. Rosenzweig, *The New Chosen People* (New York, 1990), 8–10.

5. The statistics come from the Santa Barbara *News-Press*, Sept. 5, 1988, A3, and the *New York Times*, Oct. 26, 1988, 1.

6. The quotations come from David Simcox, "Introduction," *U.S. Immigration in the 1980s*, ed. David Simcox (Boulder, Colo., 1988), 4, and Teitelbaum, "Right Versus Right," 21.

7. Carlos H. Zazueta, "Mexican Political Actors in the United States and Mexico: Historical and Political Contexts of a Renewed Dialogue," in *Mexican–U.S. Relations*, ed. Carlos Vásquez and Manuel García y Griego (Los Angeles, 1983), 469.

8. Quoted in Michael S. Teitelbaum, *Latin Migration North* (New York, 1985), 34.

9. *Clamor at the Gates*, ed. Nathan Glazer (San Francisco, 1985), 11 and Patricia W. Fagen, "Latin American Refugees: Problems of Mass Migration and Mass Asylum," in *From Gunboats to Diplomacy*, ed. Richard Newfarmer (Baltimore, 1984), 238–39.

10. Quoted from David M. Reimers, *Still the Golden Door* (New York, 1985), 237.

11. The quotations come from Teitelbaum, *Latin Migration North*, 32.

12. Reagan, press conference, June 14, 1984, quoted in Robert A. Pastor and Jorge G. Castañeda, *Limits to Friendship* (New York, 1988), 345.

13. Quoted from Rodolfo Acuña, *Occupied America* (3rd. ed., New York, 1988), 440.

14. In 1990 Mexican authorities arrested and deported to Guatemala 110,000 Central Americans. This number was 30 percent higher than in 1989, which had a 500 percent increase of deportees over 1988. From Bill Frelick, refugee policy analyst, Los Angeles *Times*, June 25, 1991, B7.

15. See the Los Angeles *Times*, March 16, 1990, A27; March 17, A27; May 26, A1, A38.

16. Lawrence H. Fuchs, *The American Kaleidoscope* (Hanover, N.H,, 1990), 263.

17. Nimrod Novik, *The United States and Israel* (Boulder, Colo., 1985), 56, which also points out that "American Jewry is the largest Jewish community in history."

18. Quoted from Robert Silverberg, *If I Forget Thee O Jerusalem* (New York, 1970), 6.

19. Arthur Hertzberg, *The Jews in America* (New York, 1989), 375.

20. The quotations come from Steven D. Isaacs, *Jews and American Politics* (Garden City, N.Y., 1974), 6, 124.

21. Quoted from Henry Kissinger, *Years of Upheaval* (Boston, 1982), 202, and William B. Quandt, *Decade of Decisions* (Berkeley, 1977), 93.

22. Quoted from John F. Roehm, Jr., "Congressional Participation in U.S. Middle Eastern Policy, October 1973–1976: Congressional Activism vs. Policy Coherence," in *Congress, the Presidency and American Foreign Policy*, ed. John Spanier and Joseph Nogee (New York, 1981), 23.

23. Steven L. Spiegel, *The Other Arab-Israeli Conflict* (Chicago, 1985), 253.

24. *R N: The Memoirs of Richard Nixon* (New York, 1978), 611.

25. Melvin I. Urofsky, *We Are One!* (Garden City, N.Y., 1978), x, 445.

26. Quoted from Dan Caldwell, "The Jackson-Vanik Amendment," in Spanier, ed., *Congress*, 18.

27. Quoted in Russell W. Howe and Sarah H. Trott, *The Power Peddlers* (Garden City, N.Y., 1977), 275.

28. George W. Ball, "The Coming Crisis in Israeli-American Relations," *Foreign Affairs*, LVIII (Winter 1979–80), 231, 233.

29. Quoted in Yossi Lapid, "Ethnic Mobilization and U.S. Foreign Policy: Current Trends and Conflicting Assessments," *Studies in Contemporary Jewry*, III (1987), 9.

30. The quotations come from David H. Goldberg, *Foreign Policy and Ethnic Interest Groups* (New York, 1990), 62, and Zbigniew Brzezinski, *Power and Principle* (New York, 1983), 441–42.

31. Quoted in Charles McC. Mathias, Jr., "Ethnic Groups and Foreign Policy," *Foreign Affairs*, LIX (Summer 1981), 994.

32. Quoted from A. F. K. Organski, *The $36 Billion Bargain* (New York, 1990), 203, and Steven L. Spiegel, "Israel as a Strategic Asset," *Commentary*, LXXV (June 1983), 55.

33. Quoted from Steven S. Rosenfeld, "Pluralism and Policy," *Foreign Affairs*, LII (Jan. 1974), 270.

34. Spiegel, *Other Arab-Israeli Conflict*, 397.

35. Quoted in Steven S. Rosenfeld, "Dateline Washington: Anti-Semitism and U.S. Foreign Policy," *Foreign Policy*, XLVII (Summer 1982), 175.

36. Diary entry, April 1, 1981, Ronald Reagan, *An American Life* (New York, 1990), 412.

37. The quotation and the statistics come from Edward Tivnan, *The Lobby* (New York, 1987), 216–17, and the Los Angeles *Times*, Sept. 15, 1991, M5.

38. Los Angeles *Times*, Oct. 23, 1990, A4.

39. Ibid., June 30, 1991, A12.

40. U.S. President, *Weekly Compilation of Presidential Documents*, XXVII, no. 36 (Washington, D.C., Sept. 9, 1991), 1229.

41. Ibid., no. 37 (Sept. 16, 1991), 1252–54. For the statistics on aid to Israel, see the *Wall Street Journal*, Sept. 19, 1991, A16.

42. Los Angeles *Times*, Sept. 30, 1991, A16.

43. Ibid., Nov. 25, 1991, A7.

44. Quoted from Keith R. Legg, "Congress as Trojan Horse? The Turkish Embargo Problem, 1974–1978," in Spanier, ed., *Congress*, 107.

45. Quoted in Paul Y. Watanabe, *Ethnic Groups, Congress, and Foreign Policy* (Westport, Conn., 1984), 129, 156.

46. Quoted in Howe and Trott, *Power Peddlers*, 444.

47. Quoted in Mathias, "Ethnic Groups," 989.

48. Quoted in Lapid, "Ethnic Mobilization," 9.

49. Seán Cronin, *Washington's Irish Policy 1916–1986* (Dublin, 1987), 194.

50. Quoted in Perry L. Weed, *The White Ethnic Movement and Ethnic Politics* (New York, 1973), 146.

51. Quoted in Cronin, *Washington's Irish Policy*, 312.

52. Quoted from Jack Holland, *The American Connection* (New York, 1987), 128, and Thomas E. Hachey, "Irish Republicanism Yesterday and Today: The Dilemma of Irish Americans," in *Ethnicity and War*, ed. Winston A. Van Horne and Thomas V. Tonnesen (Madison, Wis., 1984), 167.

52. Quoted from Holland, *American Connection*, 151.

54. Terrance G. Carroll, "Northern Ireland," in *Ethnic Conflict in International Relations*, ed. Astri Suhrke and Lela G. Noble (New York, 1977), 38.

55. Los Angeles *Times*, Nov. 18, 1990, A32.

56. The first quotation comes from Roger Morris, *Uncertain Greatness* (New York, 1977), 131, and the second from Donald F. McHenry, "Captive of No Group," *Foreign Policy*, XIV (Summer 1974), 143.

57. Quoted in Steven Metz, "Congress, the Antiapartheid Movement, and Nixon," *Diplomatic History*, XII (Spring 1988), 168.

58. The quotations come from J. K. Obatala, "Black Consciousness and American Policy in Africa," in *Ethnicity in an International Context*, ed. Abdul Said and Luiz R. Simmons (New Brunswick, N.J., 1976), 71, and Goler T. Butcher, "Congress and American Relations with South Africa," *Issue*, III (Winter 1973), 54.

59. Quoted in Mariyawanda Nzuwah and William King, "Afro-Americans and U.S. Policy Toward Africa: An Overview," *Journal of Southern African Affairs*, II (April 1977), 235–36.

60. Jimmy Carter, *Keeping Faith* (New York, 1982), 491.

61. Quoted in Henry F. Jackson, *From the Congo to Soweto* (New York, 1982), 161.

62. The quotations come from Carl H. Voss and David A. Rausch, "American Christians and Israel, 1948–1988," *American Jewish Archives*, XL (April 1988), 72–73.

63. Robert I. Rotberg, "The Reagan Era in Africa," in *Reagan and the World*, ed. David E. Kyvig (New York, 1990), 122.

64. Nathan I. Huggins, "Afro-Americans," in *Ethnic Leadership in America*, ed. John Higham (Baltimore, 1978), 116.

65. Quoted in the International *Herald Tribune* (Rome), April 20, 1988, 1.

66. Los Angeles *Times*, June 23, 1990, A23.

67. Quoted from Caspar W. Weinberger, *Fighting for Peace* (New York, 1990), 205; Lawrence Freedman and Virginia Gamba-Stonehouse, *Signals of War* (London, 1990), 189; and Michael Charlton, *The Little Platoon* (Oxford, 1989), 179.

68. Nicholas Henderson, "America and the Falklands: Case Study in the Behaviour of an Ally," *The Economist*, CXXXI (Nov. 12, 1983), 33.

69. Quoted in "War Over Foreign Policy: Reagan Aides at War," *Newsweek*, XCIX (June 7, 1982), 29.

70. Reagan, General Vernon Walters, and Elizabeth are quoted from Reagan, *An American Life*, 357, and Christopher Hitchens, *Blood, Class and Nostalgia* (New York, 1990), 357.

71. William D. Rogers, "The 'Unspecial Relationship' in Latin America," in *The "Special Relationship,"* ed. William R. Louis and Hedley Bull (Oxford, 1986), 343.

72. For the demographic data, see William Issel, *Social Change in the United States, 1945–1983* (London, 1985), 9, 154, and David H. Fischer, *Albion's Seed* (New York, 1989), 6, 872.

73. Los Angeles *Times*, Dec. 12, 1989, A6.

74. Ibid., April 19, 1990, A10.

Notes to Chapter Nine

1. Richard J. Barnet, *Roots of War* (Baltimore, 1973), 321.

2. Quoted from Thomas Sowell, *The Economics and Politics of Race* (New York, 1983), 17.

3. See, for example, Edgar Litt, *Beyond Pluralism* (Glenview, Ill., 1970), 9, 42.

4. Yossi Lapid, "Ethnic Political Mobilization and U.S. Foreign Policy: Current Trends and Conflicting Assessments," *Studies in Contemporary Jewry*, III (1987), 5.

5. Quoted from Melvin Small, "Public Opinion," in *Encyclopedia of American Foreign Policy*, ed. Alexander DeConde (3 vols., New York, 1978), III, 854.

6. Quoted from John Higham, *Send These to Me* (rev. ed., Baltimore, 1984), xi, xiii; Louis L. Gerson, *The Hyphenate in Recent American Politics and Diplomacy* (Lawrence, Kan., 1964), xxvi, 201, 235; and Thomas A. Bailey, *The Man in the Street* (New York, 1948), 31.

7. Lawrence H. Fuchs, "Ethnicity and Foreign Policy: The Question of Multiple Loyalties," in *Ethnicity and War*, ed. Winston A. Van Horne and Thomas V. Tonnesen (Madison, Wis., 1984), 55, 62.

8. Quoted in Russell W. Howe and Sarah H. Trott, *The Power Peddlers* (Garden City, N.Y., 1977), 4.

9. Quoted in Elliott P. Skinner, "Ethnicity and Race as Factors in the Formation of United States Foreign Policy," in *American Character and Foreign Policy*, ed. Michael P. Hamilton (Grand Rapids, Mich., 1986), 91.

10. Quoted from Thomas M. Franck and Edward Weisband, *Foreign Policy by Congress* (New York, 1979), 190.

11. Quoted from Johan Galtung, "U.S. Foreign Policy as Manifest Theology," in *Culture and International Relations*, ed. Jongsuk Chay (New York, 1990), 139.

12. Quoted from Seymour M. Lipset, "The 'Jewish Lobby' and the National Interest," *New Leader*, LXIV (Nov. 16, 1981), 9.

13. Henry Cisneros and Rysard Kapuscinski, "American Dynamism and the World Culture," *New Perspectives Quarterly*, V (Summer 1988), 40, 45–46.

14. Winston A. Van Horne and W. Werner Prange, "Introduction," in Van Horne, ed., *Ethnicity and War*, 20.

15. Marilyn Prasinos quoted in Paul Y. Watanabe, *Ethnic Groups, Congress, and American Foreign Policy* (Westport, Conn., 1984), 157.

16. Stanley Lieberson and Mary C. Waters, *From Many Strands* (New York, 1988), 264–65.

17. Milton M. Gordon, "Assimilation in America: Theory and Reality," *Daedalus*, XC (Spring 1961), 280, 283.

18. Thomas F. Pettigrew, "Ethnicity in American Life: A Social Psychological Perspective" in *Ethnic Identity in Society*, ed. Arnold Dashefsky (Chicago, 1976), 17.

19. To Thomas St. John Gaffney, Oyster Bay, April 30, 1900, in *The Letters of Theodore Roosevelt*, ed. Elting E. Morison (8 vols., Cambridge, Mass., 1951–54), II, 1274.

20. Donald F. McHenry, "Captive of No Group," *Foreign Policy*, XIV (Summer 1974), 143.

21. *Los Angeles Times*, Jan. 24, 1990, A6, and April 11, A5.

22. Quoted from Bernard C. Cohen, *The Influence of Non-Governmental Groups on Foreign Policy-Making* (Boston, 1959), 12.

23. Quoted in Hugh D. Graham, *The Civil Rights Era* (New York, 1990), 317.

24. Bailey, *Man in the Street*, 32.

25. *Los Angeles Times*, Feb. 23, 1990, A14, B7, and Feb. 28, A11.

26. Quoted from Robert A. Dahl, *Congress and Foreign Policy* (New York, 1950), 42.

27. The quotations come from James H. Powell, "The Concept of Cultural Pluralism in American Social Thought, 1915–1965," Diss., University of Notre Dame, 1971, 46, and Maldwyn A. Jones, *The Old World Ties of American Ethnic Groups* (London, 1976), 26.

28. M. Mark Stolarik, "To Hyphenate or Not to Hyphenate," in *New Dimensions*, The Balch Institute for Ethnic Studies, Philadelphia (Fall 1988), 4.

29. Anthony D. Smith, *The Ethnic Origins of Nations* (Oxford, 1987), 152.

30. Quoted from the *New York Times*, Dec. 21, 1988, A12.

31. The quotations come from Lawrence H. Fuchs, "Minority Groups and Foreign Policy," in *American Ethnic Politics*, ed. Lawrence H. Fuchs (New York, 1968), 160–61, and D. C. Watt, "Demythologizing the Eisenhower Era," in *The "Special Relationship,"* ed. William R. Louis and Hedley Bull (Oxford, 1986), 84–85.

32. Arthur M. Schlesinger, Jr., *The Disuniting of America* (Knoxville, Tenn., 1991), 67.

33. Quoted from the editors of *Foreign Policy*, XIV (Summer 1974), 108.

BIBLIOGRAPHY

The footnotes indicate the sources of the quotations or at times of statistical data. Despite its length, this is a select bibliography that lists the books, articles, dissertations, documents, and other materials that were directly or indirectly useful in my research. Its purpose is to aid readers who may wish to explore topics beyond the treatment they receive in this study or who may wish to trace the source of specific data or ideas presented in it.

Abraham, Sameer Y., and Nabeel Abraham (eds.). *Arabs in the New World: Studies on Arab-American Communities.* Detroit, 1983.

Abramson, Harold J. *Ethnic Diversity in Catholic America.* New York, 1973.

Abu-Laban, Baha, and Faith T. Zeady (eds.). *Arabs in America: Myths and Realities.* Wilmette, Ill., 1975.

Acevedo, Domingo E. "The U.S. Measures against Argentina Resulting from the Malvinas Conflict," *American Journal of International Law,* LXXVIII (April 1984), 323–44.

Acheson, Dean. *Present at the Creation: My Years in the State Department.* New York, 1969.

Acuña, Rodolfo. *Occupied America: A History of Chicanos.* 3rd ed. New York, 1988.

Adams, Ephraim D. *Great Britain and the American Civil War.* 2 vols. New York, 1925.

Adler, Selig. "Franklin D. Roosevelt and Zionism—The Wartime Record," *Judaism,* XXI (Summer 1973), 265–76.

———. *The Isolationist Impulse: Its Twentieth Century Reaction.* New York, 1957.

Agoncillo, Teodoro A. *Malolos: The Crisis of the Republic.* Quezon City, Philippines, 1960.

Alba, Richard D. *Ethnic Identity: The Transformation of White America.* New Haven, 1990.

——— (ed.). *Ethnicity and Race in the U.S.A.: Toward the Twenty-First Century.* London, 1985.

———. "The Twilight of Ethnicity Among Americans of European Ancestry: The Case of Italians," in *Ethnicity and Race in the U.S.A.,* ed. Richard D. Alba. London, 1985, 134–58.

Allen, Harry C. *Great Britain and the United States: A History of Anglo-American Relations (1783–1952).* New York, 1955.

Almond, Gabriel A. *The American People and Foreign Policy.* 2nd. ed. New York, 1960.

Alteras, Isaac. "Eisenhower, American Jewry, and Israel," *American Jewish Archives,* XXXVII (Nov. 1985), 257–74.

Ambrosius, Lloyd E. "The President, the Congress and American Foreign Policy: The Ethnic Factor," in *Congress and American Foreign Policy,* ed. Göran Rystad. Lund, Sweden, 1981, 63–77.

———. *Woodrow Wilson and the American Diplomatic Tradition: The Treaty Fight in Perspective.* New York, 1987.

Anderson, George L. (ed.). *Issues and Conflicts: Studies in Twentieth Century American Diplomacy.* Lawrence, Kan., 1959.

Anderson, Stuart. *Race and Rapprochement: Anglo-Saxonism and Anglo-American Relations, 1895–1904.* East Brunswick, N.J., 1981.

————. "Racial Anglo-Saxonism and the American Response to the Boer War," *Diplomatic History*, II (Summer 1978), 219–36.

App, Austin J. "The Germans," in *The Immigrants' Influence on Wilson's Peace Policies*, ed. Joseph P. O'Grady. Lexington, Ken., 1967, 30–55.

Archdeacon, Thomas J. *Becoming American: An Ethnic History*. New York, 1983.

Arieli, Yehoshua. *Individualism and Nationalism in American Ideology*. Cambridge, Mass., 1964.

Aruri, Naseer, et al. *Reagan and the Middle East*. Belmont, Mass., 1983.

Asahi Shimbun. *The Pacific Rivals: A Japanese View of Japanese-American Relations*. New York, 1972.

Atherton, Alfred L., Jr. "Arabs, Israelis—and Americans: A Reconsideration," *Foreign Affairs*, LXII (Summer 1984), 1194–1209.

Bach, Robert L. "Mexican Immigration and the American State," *International Migration Review*, XII (Winter 1978), 536–58.

Bachrack, Stanley D. *The Committee of One Million: "China Lobby" Politics, 1953–1971*. New York, 1971.

Bailey, Henry A., Jr., and Ellis Katz (eds.). *Ethnic Group Politics*. Columbus, Ohio, 1969.

Bailey, Thomas A. *America Faces Russia: Russian-American Relations from Early Times to Our Day*. Ithaca, N.Y., 1950.

————. *The Man in the Street: The Impact of American Public Opinion on Foreign Policy*. New York, 1940.

————. *Woodrow Wilson and the Great Betrayal*. New York, 1947.

————. *Woodrow Wilson and the Lost Peace*. New York, 1947.

Bailyn, Bernard. *The Ideological Origins of the American Revolution*. Cambridge, Mass., 1967.

————. *The Peopling of British North America: An Introduction*. New York, 1981.

————. *Voyagers to the West: A Passage in the Peopling of America on the Eve of the Revolution*. New York, 1986.

Bain, Kenneth R. *The March to Zion: United States Policy and the Founding of Israel*. College Station, Tex., 1979.

Baker, Donald G. *Race, Ethnicity, and Power: A Comparative Study*. London, 1983.

Ball, George W. "The Coming Crisis in Israeli-American Relations," *Foreign Affairs*, LVIII (Winter 1979), 231–56.

————. "How to Save Israel in Spite of Herself," *Foreign Affairs*, LV (April 1976), 453–71.

Baltzell, E. Digby. *The Protestant Establishment: Aristocracy and Caste in America*. New York, 1964.

Banks, James A., and Geneva Gay. "Ethnicity in Contemporary American Society: Toward the Development of a Typology," *Ethnicity*, V (Sept. 1978), 238–51.

Banton, Michael P. *The Idea of Race*. London, 1977.

————. *Race Relations*. New York, 1967.

————. *Racial and Ethnic Competition*. Cambridge, Eng., 1983.

————. *Racial Theories*. Cambridge, Eng., 1987.

Banton, Michael P., and Jonathan Harwood. *The Race Concept*. Newton Abbot, Eng., 1975.

Baram, Philip J. *The Department of State in the Middle East, 1919–1945*. Philadelphia, 1978.

Baritz, Loren. *Backfire: A History of How American Culture Led Us into Vietnam and Made Us Fight the Way We Did*. New York, 1985.

Barnet, Richard J. *The Rockets' Red Glare: When America Goes to War: The Presidents and the People*. New York, 1990.

————. *Roots of War: The Men and Institutions Behind U.S. Foreign Policy*. Baltimore, 1973.

Barnett, Lawrence I. *Gambling with History: Reagan in the White House*. Harmondsworth, Eng., 1984.

Barrera, Mario. *Beyond Aztlan: Ethnic Autonomy in Comparative Perspective*. New York, 1988.

Barzun, Jacques. *Race: A Study in Superstition*. Rev. ed. New York, 1965.

Baskin, Darryl. "American Pluralism: Theory, Practice, and Ideology," *Journal of Politics*, XXXII (Feb. 1970), 71–95.

Baylis, John. *Anglo-American Defense Relations 1939–1984: The Special Relationship*. 2nd ed. London, 1984.

Bayor, Ronald H. "Italians, Jews and Ethnic Conflict," *International Migration Review*, VI (Winter 1972), 377–91.

Beale, Howard K. *Theodore Roosevelt and the Rise of America to World Power*. Baltimore, 1956.

Beck, Peter. *The Falklands Islands as an International Problem*. London, 1988.

Beisner, Robert L. *Twelve Against Empire: Anti-Imperialists, 1898–1900*. New York, 1968.

Beling, Willard A. (ed.). *The Middle East: Quest for an American Policy*. Albany, N.Y., 1973.

Bell, Daniel. "Ethnicity and Social Change," in *Ethnicity*, ed. Nathan Glazer and Daniel P. Moynihan. Cambridge, Mass., 1975, 141–74.

Bemis, Samuel F. *John Quincy Adams and the Foundations of American Foreign Policy*. New York, 1949.

Benedict, Ruth. *Race: Science and Politics*. New York, 1940.

Bennett, Marion T. *American Immigration Policies: A History*. Washington, D.C., 1963.

Benson, Lee. *The Concept of Jacksonian Democracy: New York as a Test Case*. Princeton, 1961.

Berens, John F. "The Sanctification of American Nationalism, 1789–1912: Prelude to Civil Religion in America," *Canadian Review of Studies in Nationalism*, III (1976), 172–91.

Berger, Max. "The Irish Emigrant and American Nativism as Seen by British Visitors, 1836–1860," *Pennsylvania Magazine of History and Biography*, LXX (April 1946), 146–60.

Bergquist, James M. "The Forty-Eighters and the Politics of the 1850s," in *Germany and America*, ed. Hans L. Trefousse. New York, 1980, 111–21.

Berman, Aaron. *Nazism, the Jews, and American Zionism, 1933–1948*. Detroit, 1990.

Berthoff, Rowland T. *British Immigrants in Industrial America, 1790–1950*. Cambridge, Mass., 1953.

Best, Gary Dean. *To Free a People: American Jewish Leaders and the Jewish Problem in Eastern Europe, 1890–1914*. Westport, Conn., 1982.

Bickerton, Ian J. "President Truman's Recognition of Israel," *American Jewish Historical Quarterly*, LVIII (Dec. 1968), 173–239.

Billigmeier, Robert H. *Americans from Germany: A Study in Cultural Diversity*. Belmont, Calif., 1974.

Billington, Ray Allen. *The Protestant Crusade, 1800–1860: A Study of the Origins of American Nativism*. New York, 1938.

Binder, Frederick M. *The Color Problem in Early National America as Viewed by John Adams, Jefferson and Jackson*. The Hague, 1968.

Biskupski, M. B. "Re-creating Central Europe: The United States 'Inquiry' into the Future of Poland in 1918," *International History Review*, XII (May 1990), 249–79.

Blaisdell, Donald C. "Pressure Groups, Foreign Policies, and International Politics," *Annals of the American Academy of Political and Social Science*, CCCXIX (Sept. 1959), 149–57.

Blakeslee, George H. "Hawaii: Racial Problem and Naval Base," *Foreign Affairs*, XVII (Oct. 1938), 90–99.

Bloom, Jack M. *Class, Race, and the Civil Rights Movement*. Bloomington, Ind., 1987.

Blumenthal, Henry. "Woodrow Wilson and the Race Question," *Journal of Negro History*, XLVIII (Jan. 1963), 1–21.

Bonadio, Felice A. "The Failure of German Propaganda in the United States, 1914–1917," *Mid-America*, XLI (Jan. 1950), 40–57.

Borden, Philip. "Found Cumbering the Soil: Manifest Destiny and the Indian in the Nineteenth Century," in *The Great Fear*, ed. Gary B. Nash and Richard Weiss. New York, 1970, 71–97.

Botsas, Eleftherios N. "The American Hellenes," in *America's Ethnic Politics*, ed. Joseph S. Roucek and Bernard Eisenberg. Westport, Conn., 1982, 29–45.

Bourne, Randolph S. "Trans-National America," *Atlantic Monthly*, CXVIII (July 1916), 86–97.

Bowers, David F. (ed.). *Foreign Influences in American Life*. New York, 1952.

Boyd, Julian P. *Number 7: Alexander Hamilton's Secret Attempt to Control American Foreign Policy*. Princeton, 1964.

Boyer, Paul. *By the Bomb's Early Light: American Thought and Culture at the Dawn of the Atomic Age*. New York, 1986.

Brack, Gene M. "Mexican Opinion, American Racism, and the War of 1846," *Western Historical Quarterly*, I (April 1970), 161–74.

———. *Mexico Views Manifest Destiny, 1821–1846: An Essay on the Origins of the Mexican War*. Albuquerque, 1975.

Braddick, Henderson B. "A New Look at American Policy During the Italo-Ethiopian Crisis, 1935–36," *Journal of Modern History*, XXXIV (March 1962), 64–73.

Braithwaite, E. R. "The Colored Immigrant in Britain," *Daedalus*, XCVI (Spring 1967), 496–511.

Brantz, Rennie W. "German-American Friendship: The Carl Shurz *Vereinigung*, 1926–1942," *International History Review*, XI (May 1989), 229–51.

Brauer, Kinley J. "The Slavery Problem in the Diplomacy of the American Civil War," *Pacific Historical Review*, XLVI (Aug. 1977), 439–69.

Brecher, Frank W. *Reluctant Ally: United States Foreign Policy Toward the Jews from Wilson to Roosevelt*. New York, 1991.

———. "Woodrow Wilson and the Origins of the Arab-Israeli Conflict," *American Jewish Archives*, XXXIX (April 1987), 23–47.

Breitman, Richard, and Alan M. Kraut. *American Refugee Policy and European Jewry, 1933–1945*. Bloomington, Ind., 1987.

Brogan, Denis W. "Transatlantic Strains," *The Spectator*, CLXIX (July 3, 1942), 8–9.

Brown, Peter G., and Henry Shure (eds.). *The Border That Joins: Mexican Migrants and U.S. Responsibility*. Totowa, N.J., 1983.

Brown, Thomas N. *Irish-American Nationalism, 1870–1890*. Philadelphia, 1966.

Browne, Robert S. *Race Relations in International Affairs*. Washington, D.C., 1961.

Bryson, Thomas A. "An American Mandate for Armenia: A Link in British Near Eastern Policy," *Armenian Review*, XXI (No. 2, 1968), 23–41.

———. "The Armenia-America Society: A Factor in American-Turkish Relations, 1919–1924," *Records of the American Catholic Historical Society*, LXXXII (June 1971), 83–105.

————. "Woodrow Wilson and the Armenian Mandate: A Reassessment," *Armenian Review*, XXI (No. 3, 1968), 10–29.

Brzezinski, Zbigniew. *Power and Principle: Memoirs of the National Security Adviser, 1977–1981.* New York, 1983.

Burgess, M. Elaine. "The Resurgence of Ethnicity: Myth or Reality?" *Ethnic and Racial Studies*, I (July 1978), 265–85.

Burns, Edward McNall. *The American Idea of Mission: Concepts of National Purpose and Destiny.* New Brunswick, N.J., 1957.

Burns, Robert A. *Diplomacy, War, and Parliamentary Democracy: Further Lessons from the Falklands or Advice from Academe.* Lanham, Md., 1985.

Burton, David H. *Theodore Roosevelt: Confident Imperialist.* Philadelphia, 1968.

Bustamente, Jorge A., and Geronimo G. Martinez. "Undocumented Immigration from Mexico: Beyond Borders but Within Systems," *Journal of International Affairs*, XXXIII (Fall-Winter 1979), 265–84.

Butcher, Goler T. "Congress and American Relations with South Africa," *Issue*, III (Winter 1973), 54–64.

Butler, John. *The Huguenots in America: A Refugee People in New World Society.* Cambridge, Mass., 1983.

Butterfield, Herbert. *Christianity, Diplomacy and War.* New York, 1953.

Butterfield, Herbert, and Martin Wright (ed.). *Diplomatic Investigations: Essays in the Theory of International Relations.* Cambridge, Mass., 1966.

Caldwell, Dan. "The Jackson-Vanik Agreement," in *Congress, the Presidency and American Foreign Policy*, ed. John Spanier and Joseph Nogee. New York, 1981, 1–21.

Calvert, Peter. "Latin America and the United States During and After the Falklands Crisis," *Millennium*, XII (Spring 1983), 69–78.

————. *The Mexican Revolution, 1910–1914: The Diplomacy of Anglo-American Conflict.* Cambridge, Eng., 1968.

Campbell, Alexander E. *Great Britain and the United States 1895–1903.* London, 1960.

Campbell, Charles S., Jr. *From Revolution to Rapprochement: The United States and Great Britain, 1783–1900.* New York, 1974.

————. *The Transformation of American Foreign Relations, 1865–1900.* New York, 1976.

Cardoso, Lawrence A. *Mexican Emigration to the United States, 1897–1931.* Tucson, 1980.

Carmichael, Stokely, and Charles V. Hamilton, "Black Power," in *Ethnic Group Politics*, ed. Henry A. Bailey, Jr. and Ellis Katz. Columbus, Ohio, 1969, 297–306.

Carroll, Terrance G. "Northern Ireland," in *Ethnic Conflict in International Relations*, ed. Astri Suhrke and Lela G. Noble. New York, 1977, 21–42.

Carter, Edward C. II."Naturalization in Philadelphia: A 'Wild Irishman' under Every Federalist's Bed—Revisited Twenty Years Later," *Proceedings of the American Philosophical Society*, CXXX III (No. 2, 1989) 175–77.

————. "A 'Wild Irishman' under Every Federalist's Bed: Naturalization in Philadelphia, 1789–1806," *Proceedings of the American Philosophical Society*, CXXXIII (No. 2, 1989), 178–89.

Carter, Jimmy. *Keeping Faith: Memoirs of a President.* New York, 1982.

Cazemajour, Jean, and Jean-Pierre Martin. *La Crise de melting pot: ethnicité et identité aux Etats-Unis de Kennedy à Reagan.* Paris, 1983.

Chadwin, Mark L. *The Hawks of World War II.* Chapel Hill, 1968.

Challener, Richard D. *Admirals, Generals, and American Foreign Policy, 1898–1914.* Princeton, 1973.

Challenor, Herschelle S. "The Influence of Black Americans on U.S. Foreign Policy Toward Africa," in *Ethnicity and U.S. Foreign Policy,* ed. Abdul Aziz Said. New York, 1977, 139–74.

Chalmers, David M. *Hooded Americanism: The First Century of the Ku Klux Klan, 1865–1965.* Garden City, N.Y., 1965.

Chang, Gordon H. *Friends and Enemies: The United States, China, and the Soviet Union, 1948–1972.* Stanford, 1990.

Charlton, Michael. *The Little Platoon: Diplomacy and the Falklands Dispute.* Oxford, 1989.

Cheng, Charles W. "The Cold War: Its Impact on the Black Liberation Struggle Within the United States," *Freedomways,* XIII (No. 3, 1973) and (No. 4, 1973), 184–99, 281–93.

Chester, Edward W. *Clash of Titans: Africa and U.S. Foreign Policy.* Maryknoll, N.Y., 1979.

Child, Clifton J. *The German Americans in Politics 1914–1917.* Madison, Wis., 1939.

Chomsky, Noam. *The Fateful Triangle: The United States, Israel and the Palestinians.* Boston, 1983.

Chorbajian, Leon S. "Armenians and Middle Eastern Americans," in *America's Ethnic Politics,* ed. Joseph S. Roucek and Bernard Eisenberg. Westport, Conn., 1982, 65–88.

Christol, Hélène, and Serge Ricard (eds.). *Hyphenated Diplomacy: European Immigration and U.S. Foreign Policy, 1914–1984.* Aix-en-Provence, 1985.

Christopher, Robert C. *Crashing the Gates: The De-WASPing of America's Power Elite.* New York, 1989.

Cisneros, Henry, and Rysard Kapuscinski. "American Dynamism & The World Culture," *New Perspectives Quarterly,* V (Summer 1988), 36–46.

Claude, Inis L., Jr. *The Impact of Public Opinion Upon Foreign Policy and Diplomacy.* The Hague, 1965.

———. "UN Efforts at Settlement of the Falkland Islands Crisis," in *The Falklands War,* ed. Alberto R. Coll and Anthony C. Arend. Boston, 1985, 118–31.

Clendenen, Clarence, Robert Collins, and Peter Duignan. *Americans in Africa, 1865–1900.* Stanford, 1966.

Clifford, Clark M. *Counsel to the President: A Memoir.* New York, 1991.

Clymer, Kenton J. "The Education of William Phillips: Self-Determination and American Policy Toward India, 1942–1945," *Diplomatic History,* VIII (Winter 1984), 13–35.

———. "Franklin D. Roosevelt, Louis Johnson, and Anticolonialism: Another Look," *Pacific Historical Review,* LVII (Aug. 1988), 261–84.

Coben, Stanley. "The Failure of the Melting Pot," in *The Great Fear,* ed. Gary B. Nash and Richard Weiss. New York, 1970, 144–85.

———. "A Study in Nativism: The American Red Scare of 1919–1920," *Political Science Quarterly,* LXXIX (March 1964), 52–75.

Cohen, Bernard C. *The Influence of Non-Governmental Groups on Foreign Policy-Making.* Boston, 1959.

Cohen, Michael J. *Palestine and the Great Powers, 1945–1948.* Princeton, 1982.

———. *Truman and Israel.* Berkeley, 1990.

Cohen, Naomi W. "The Abrogation of the Russo-American Treaty of 1832," *Jewish Social Studies,* XXV (Jan. 1963), 3–41.

————. *The Year After the Riots: American Responses to the Palestine Crisis of 1929–30.* Detroit, 1988.

Cohen, Warren I. "The China Lobby," in *Encyclopedia of American Foreign Policy*, ed. Alexander DeConde. 3 vols. New York, 1978, I, 104–10.

Coker, Christopher. *The United States and South Africa: Constructive Engagement and Its Critics.* Durham, N.C., 1986.

Cole, Wayne S. *America First: The Battle Against Intervention, 1940–1941.* Madison, Wis., 1953.

Coll, Alberto R., and Anthony C. Arend (eds.). *The Falklands War: Lessons for Strategy, Diplomacy, and International Law.* Boston, 1985.

————. "Philosophical and Legal Dimensions of the Use of Force in the Falklands War," in *The Falklands War*, ed., Alberto R. Coll and Anthony C. Arends. Boston, 1985, 34–51.

Collin, Richard H. *Theodore Roosevelt's Caribbean: The Panama Canal, the Monroe Doctrine, and the Latin American Context.* Baton Rouge, La., 1990.

Comerford, R. V. *The Fenians in Context: Irish Politics and Society 1848–82.* Dublin, 1985.

Compton, James V. *The Swastika and the Eagle: Hitler, the United States, and the Origins of World War II.* Boston, 1967.

Connor, Walker. "The Politics of Ethnonationalism," *Journal of International Affairs*, XXVII (No. 1, 1973), 1–21.

Conner, Walker (ed.). *Mexican-Americans in Comparative Perspective.* Washington, D.C., 1985.

Conzen, Kathleen N. "German-Americans and the Invention of Ethnicity," in *America and the Germans*, ed. Frank Trommler and Joseph McVeigh. Philadelphia, 1985, 131–47.

Cook, J. G. *Anglophobia: An Analysis of Anti-British Prejudice in the United States.* Boston, 1919.

Coolidge, Mary R. *Chinese Immigration.* New York, 1909.

Cooper, John M., Jr. *The Warrior and the Priest: Woodrow Wilson and Theodore Roosevelt.* Cambridge, Mass., 1983.

Cornelius, Wayne A. *Mexican Migration to the United States: Causes, Consequences, and U.S. Responses.* Cambridge, Mass., 1978.

Cornelius, Wayne A., and Jorge A. Bustamente (eds.). *Mexican Migration to the United States: Origins, Consequences, and Policy Options.* San Diego, 1989.

Cornelius, Wayne A., and Ricardo Anzaldua Montaya (eds.). *America's New Immigration Law: Origins, Rationales, and Potential Consequences.* San Diego, 1983.

Cortada, James W. *Two Nations Over Time: Spain and the United States, 1776–1977.* Westport, Conn., 1987.

Corwin, Arthur F. "The Numbers Game: Estimates of Illegal Aliens in the United States, 1970–81," in *U.S. Immigration Policy*, ed. Richard R. Hofstetter. Durham, N.C., 1984, 223–97.

Costigliola, Frank. *Awkward Dominion: American Political, Economic, and Cultural Relations with Europe, 1919–1933.* Ithaca, N.Y., 1984.

Couloumbis, Theodore A. *The United States, Greece, and Turkey: The Troubled Triangle.* New York, 1983.

Crabb, Cecil V., Jr., and Kevin V. Mulcahy. *Presidents and Foreign Policy Making: From FDR to Reagan.* Baton Rouge, La., 1986.

Craig, Richard B. *The Bracero Program: Interest Groups and Foreign Policy.* Austin, Tex., 1971.

Crapol, Edward P. *America for Americans: Economic Nationalism and Anglophobia in the Late Nineteenth Century.* Westport, Conn., 1973.

———. "The Foreign Policy of Antislavery, 1833–1846," in *Redefining the Past,* ed. Lloyd C. Gardner. Corvallis, Ore., 1986, 85–103.

Crawford, Martin. *The Anglo-American Crisis of the Mid-Nineteenth Century: The Times and America, 1850–1862.* Athens, Ga., 1987.

Creel, George. *How We Advertised America.* New York, 1920.

———. *The War, the World, and Wilson.* New York, 1920.

Cressy, David. *Coming Over: Migration and Communication between England and New England in the Seventeenth Century.* New York, 1987.

Crèvecoeur, Hector S. John de. *Letters from an American Farmer.* London, 1912.

Crewdson, John. *The Tarnished Door: The New Immigrants and the Transformation of America.* New York, 1983.

Cronin, Seán. *Washington's Irish Policy 1916–1986: Independence, Partition, Neutrality.* Dublin, 1987.

Cronje, Suzanne. *The World and Nigeria: The Diplomatic History of the Biafran War 1967–1970.* London, 1972.

Cronon, E. David. *Black Moses: The Story of Marcus Garvey and the Universal Negro Improvement Association.* Madison, Wis., 1955.

Cuddy, Joseph E. *Irish-America and National Isolationism, 1914–1920.* New York, 1976.

Cumings, Bruce. *The Origins of the Korean War:* Vol. II: *The Roaring Cataract, 1947–1950.* Princeton, 1990.

Current, Richard N. *Secretary Stimson: A Study in Statecraft.* New Brunswick, N.J., 1954.

Curry, Roy W. *Woodrow Wilson and Far Eastern Policy, 1913–1921.* New York, 1957.

Curti, Merle. *The Roots of American Loyalty.* New York, 1946.

Curtiss, Richard H. *Stealth PACs: How Israel's American Lobby Seeks to Control U.S. Middle East Policy.* Washington, D.C., 1990.

Dabat, Alejandro, and Luis Lorenzano. *Argentina: The Malvinas and the End of Military Rule.* Trans. from the Spanish by Ralph Johnstone. London, 1984.

Dahl, Robert A. *Congress and Foreign Policy.* New York, 1950.

———. *Pluralist Democracy in the United States.* Chicago, 1967.

Dallek, Robert. *The American Style of Foreign Policy: Cultural Politics and Foreign Affairs.* New York, 1983.

———. *Franklin D. Roosevelt and American Foreign Policy, 1932–1945.* New York, 1979.

Daly, John C. *What Should Be the Role of Ethnic Groups in U.S. Foreign Policy?* Washington, D.C., 1980.

Danaher, Kevin. *In Whose Interest? A Guide to U.S.–South African Relations.* Washington, D.C., 1984.

Dangerfield, George. *The Era of Good Feelings.* New York, 1952.

Daniel, Robert L. "The Armenian Question and Turkish-American Relations, 1914–1927," *Mississippi Valley Historical Review,* XLVI (Sept. 1959), 252–75.

Daniels, Roger. *Asian America: Chinese and Japanese in the United States since 1850.* Seattle, 1988.

———. *Concentration Camps: North America: Japanese in the United States and Canada During World War II.* Rev. ed. Malabar, Fla., 1981.

———. *The Politics of Prejudice: The Anti-Japanese Movement in California and the Struggle for Japanese Exclusion.* 2nd ed. Berkeley, 1977.

Daniels, Roger, and Harry H. L. Kitano. *American Racism: Exploration of the Nature of Prejudice*. Englewood Cliffs, N.J., 1970.

D'Arcy, William. *The Fenian Movement in the United States: 1858–1886*. Washington, D.C., 1947.

Davis, John A. "Black Americans and United States Policy Toward Black Africa," *Journal of International Affairs*, XXIII (Summer 1969), 236–49.

Dawidowicz, Lucy S. *On Equal Terms: Jews in America, 1881–1981*. New York, 1982.

DeBenedetti, Charles. *An American Ordeal: The Antiwar Movement of the Vietnam Era*. Syracuse, N.Y., 1990.

DeConde, Alexander. "Dwight D. Eisenhower: Reluctant Use of Power," in Edgar E. Robinson et al., *Powers of the President in Foreign Affairs, 1945–1965*. San Francisco, 1966, 79–132.

————. *Entangling Alliance: Politics and Diplomacy under George Washington*. Durham, N.C., 1958.

————. "Ethno-Racial Influences in American Foreign Policy," *American Studies* (Warsaw), X (1991), 7–33.

————. "Foreign Intervention in Domestic Politics," in *Atti del I Congresso Internazionale de Storia Americana*, ed. Raimondo Luraghi (Genoa, 1978), 120–21.

————. *Half Bitter, Half Sweet: An Excursion into Italian-American History*. New York, 1971.

————. *The Quasi-War: The Politics and Diplomacy of the Undeclared War with France, 1797–1801*. New York, 1966.

————. "The South and Isolationism," *Journal of Southern History*, XXIV (Aug. 1958), 332–46.

————. *This Affair of Louisiana*. New York, 1976.

DeConde, Alexander (ed.). *Encyclopedia of American Foreign Policy*. 3 vols. New York, 1978.

De La Garza, Rodolfo O. "Chicanos and U.S. Foreign Policy: The Future of Chicano-Mexican Relations," *Western Political Quarterly*, XXXIII (Dec. 1980), 571–82.

————. "Mexican Americans, Mexican Immigrants, and Immigration Reform," in *Clamor at the Gates*, ed. Nathan Glazer. San Francisco, 1985, 93–105.

De León, Arnaldo. *They Called Them Greasers: Anglo Attitudes Toward Mexicans in Texas, 1822–1900*. Austin, Tex., 1983.

Demolins, Edmond. *A quoi tient la supériorité des anglo saxons*. Paris, 1897.

Dennett, Tyler. *Americans in Eastern Asia*. New York, 1922.

De Novo, John A. *American Interests and Policies in the Middle East, 1900–1939*. Minneapolis, 1963.

De Santis, Hugh. *The Diplomacy of Silence: The American Foreign Service, the Soviet Union, and the Cold War, 1933–1947*. Chicago, 1980.

Destler, I. M., Leslie H. Gelb, and Anthony Lake. *Our Own Worst Enemy: The Unmasking of American Foreign Policy*. New York, 1984.

Diamond, Sander A. *The Nazi Movement in the United States, 1924–1941*. Ithaca, N.Y., 1974.

Diesing, Paul. "National Self-Determination and U.S. Foreign Policy," *Ethics*, LXXVII (Jan. 1967), 85–94.

Diggins, John P. *Mussolini and Fascism: The View From America*. Princeton, 1972.

Dillon, G. M. *The Falklands: Politics and War*. London, 1989.

Dimbleby, David, and David Reynolds. *An Ocean Apart: The Relationship Between Britain and America in the Twentieth Century*. London, 1988.

Dinnerstein, Leonard. *America and the Survivors of the Holocaust*. New York, 1982.

————. "The Origins of Black Anti-Semitism in America," *American Jewish Archives*, XXXVIII (Nov. 1986), 113–22.

Dinnerstein, Leonard, and David M. Reimers. *Ethnic Americans: A History of Immigration and Assimilation*. New York, 1975.

Divine, Robert A. *American Immigration Policy, 1924–1952*. New Haven, 1957.

————. "The Cold War and the Election of 1948," *Journal of American History*, LIX (June 1972), 90–110.

————. *The Illusion of Neutrality*. Chicago, 1962.

————. *Second Chance: The Triumph of Internationalism in America During World War II*. New York, 1967.

Dobbert, G. A. "German-Americans Between New and Old Fatherland, 1870–1914," *American Quarterly*, XIX (Winter 1967), 663–80.

Dobkowski, Michael N. "The Policies of Restrictionism: Anti-German Refugees Face a Cold World," in *Germany and America*, ed. Hans L. Trefousse. New York, 1980, 199–214.

Donald, David. *Charles Sumner and the Rights of Man*. New York, 1970.

Donovan, Robert J. *Conflict and Crisis: The Presidency of Harry S. Truman, 1945–1948*. New York, 1977.

Dorpalen, Andreas. "The German Element and the Issues of the Civil War," *Mississippi Valley Historical Review*, XXIX (June 1942), 55–76.

————. "The Political Influence of the German Element in Colonial America," *Pennsylvania History*, VI (1939), 147–58.

Dower, John W. *War Without Mercy: Race and Power in the Pacific War*. New York, 1986.

Doyle, David N. *Ireland, Irishmen and Revolutionary America, 1760–1820*. Dublin, 1981.

————. *Irish Americans, Native Rights and National Empires*. New York, 1976.

Doyle, David N., and Owen D. Edwards (eds.). *America and Ireland, 1776–1976: The American Identity and the Irish Connection*. Westport, Conn., 1980.

Du Bois, William E. B. "Inter-Racial Implications of the Ethiopian Crisis: A Negro View," *Foreign Affairs*, XIV (Oct. 1935), 82–92.

————. *The Souls of Black Folk*. New York, 1963.

Duff, John B. "The Italians," in *The Immigrants' Influence on Wilson's Peace Policies*, ed. Joseph P. O'Grady. Lexington, Ken., 1967, 111–39.

————. "The Versailles Treaty and the Irish Americans," *Journal of American History*, LV (Dec. 1968), 582–98.

Duignan, Peter, and L. H. Gann. *The United States and Africa*. New York, 1984.

Dunne, Finley P. *Mr. Dooley On Ivrything and Ivrybody*, ed. Robert Hutchinson. New York, 1977.

Dunne, Michael. *The United States and the World Court, 1920–1935*. London, 1988.

Dwyer, T. Ryle. *Irish Neutrality and the USA, 1939–47*. Dublin, 1977.

————. *Strained Relations: Ireland at Peace and the USA at War, 1941–45*. Dublin, 1988.

Dyer, Thomas G. *Theodore Roosevelt and the Idea of Race*. Baton Rouge, La., 1980.

Ealy, Lawrence O. *Yanqui Politics and the Isthmian Canal*. University Park, Pa., 1971.

Eddy, William A. *F.D.R. Meets Ibn Saud*. New York, 1954.

Egnal, Marc. *A Mighty Empire: The Origins of the American Revolution*. Ithaca, N.Y., 1988.

Eisenhower, Dwight D. *Ike's Letters to a Friend, 1941–1958*, ed. Robert Griffith. Lawrence, Kan., 1984.

El-Khawas, Mohamed, and Samir Abed-Rabbo. *American Aid to Israel: Nature and Impact*. Brattleboro, Vt., 1984.

El-Khawas, Mohamed, and Barry Cohen (eds.). *The Kissinger Study of Southern Africa: National Security Memorandum 39*. Westport, Conn., 1976.

Elsbree, Willard H. *Japan's Role in Southeast Asian Nationalist Movements 1940 to 1945*. Cambridge, Mass., 1953.

Emerson, Rupert, and Martin Kilson. "The American Dilemma in a Changing World: The Rise of Africa and the Negro American," *Daedalus*, XCIV (Fall 1965), 1055–84.

Enloe, Cynthia H. "The Growth of the State and Ethnic Mobilization: The American Experience," *Ethnic and Racial Studies*, IV (April 1981), 123–36.

Erickson, Charlotte. *American Industry and the European Immigrant, 1860–1885*. Cambridge, Mass., 1957.

———. "English," in *Harvard Encyclopedia of American Ethnic Groups*, ed. Stephan Thernstrom. Cambridge, Mass., 1980, 319–36.

———. *Invisible Immigrants: The Adaptation of English and Scottish Immigrants in Nineteenth-Century America*. Coral Gables, Fla., 1972.

Esthus, Raymond A. "President Roosevelt's Commitment to Britain to Intervene in a Pacific War," *Mississippi Valley Historical Review*, L (June 1963), 28–38.

———. *Theodore Roosevelt and Japan*. Seattle, 1966.

Estrada, Leobardo F., et al. "Chicanos in the United States: A History of Exploitation and Resistance," *Daedalus*, CX (Spring 1981), 103–31.

Evans, Laurence. *United States Policy and the Partition of Turkey, 1914–1924*. Baltimore, 1965.

Evensen, Bruce J. "A Story of 'Ineptness': The Truman Administration's Struggle to Shape Conventional Wisdom on Palestine at the Beginning of the Cold War," *Diplomatic History*, XV (Summer 1991), 339–59.

Fagen, Patricia W. "Latin American Refugees: Problems of Mass Migration and Mass Asylum," in *From Gunboats to Diplomacy*, ed. Richard Newfarmer. Baltimore, 1984, 228–43.

Fairbank, John K. (ed.). *The Missionary Enterprise in China and America*. Cambridge, Mass., 1974.

———. *The United States and China*. 3rd ed. Cambridge, Mass., 1971.

Farrand, Andrew L. "Cultural Dissonance in Mexican-American Relations: Ethnic, Racial and Cultural Images and the Coming of War, 1846." Unpublished Ph.D. dissertation, University of California, Santa Barbara, 1979.

Feingold, Henry L. *A Midrash on American Jewish History*. Albany, N.Y., 1982.

———. *The Politics of Rescue: The Roosevelt Administration and the Holocaust*. New Brunswick, N.J., 1970.

Ferguson, John H. *American Diplomacy and the Boer War*. Philadelphia, 1939.

Ferrell, Robert H. *Woodrow Wilson and World War I, 1917–1921*. New York, 1985.

Field, James A., Jr. *America and the Mediterranean World, 1776–1882*. Princeton, 1969.

Findley, Paul. *They Dare to Speak Out: People and Institutions Confront Israel's Lobby*. Westport, Conn., 1985.

Finer, Herman. *Dulles Over Suez: The Theory and Practice of His Diplomacy*. Chicago, 1964.

Fischer, David H. *Albion's Seed: Four British Folkways in America*. New York, 1989.

Fitzgerald, Frances. *Fire in the Lake: The Vietnamese and the Americans in Vietnam*. Boston, 1972.

Fitzgibbon, Russell H. *Cuba and the United States, 1900–1935*. New York, 1964.

Fitzhugh, David. "The Silent Invasion," *Foreign Service Journal*, LIII (Jan. 1976), 8–26.

Foot, Rosemary. *A Substitute for Victory: The Politics of Peacemaking at the Korean Armistice Talks.* Ithaca, N.Y., 1990.

Forbes, Ella. "African-American Resistance to Colonization," *Journal of Black Studies,* XXI (Dec. 1990), 210–23.

Forrestal, James V. *The Forrestal Diaries,* ed. Walter Millis. New York, 1951.

Forsyth, Frederick. *The Biafra Story.* Baltimore, 1969.

Fox, Moshe. "Backing the 'Good Guys': American Governmental Policy, 'Jewish Influence,' and the Sinai Campaign of 1956," *American Jewish Archives,* XL (April 1988), 83–109.

Fox, Stephen C. "General John DeWitt and the Proposed Internment of German and Italian Aliens during World War II," *Pacific Historical Review,* LVII (Nov. 1988), 407–38.

———. *The Unknown Internment: An Oral History of the Relocation of Italian Americans during World War II.* Boston, 1990.

Franck, Thomas M., and Edward Weisband. *Foreign Policy by Congress.* New York, 1979.

Franklin, Benjamin. *The Papers of Benjamin Franklin,* ed. Leonard W. Labaree et al. 18 vols. New Haven, 1959– .

Franklin, Frank G. *The Legislative History of Naturalization in the United States: Revolutionary War to 1861.* Chicago, 1906.

Franklin, John Hope (ed.). *Color and Race.* Boston, 1968.

———. *The Emancipation Proclamation.* New York, 1963.

———. *From Slavery to Freedom: A History of Negro Americans.* 4th ed. New York, 1974.

———. *Race and History.* Baton Rouge, La., 1989.

Fraser, T. G. *The USA and the Middle East Since World War 2.* New York, 1989.

Freedman, Lawrence, and Virginia Gamba-Stonehouse. *Signals of War: The Falklands Conflict of 1982.* London, 1990.

Frey, Sylvia R. *Water from the Rock: Black Resistance in a Revolutionary Age.* Princeton, 1991.

Friedländer, Saul. *Hitler et les États-Unis (1939–1941).* Geneva, 1963.

Friend, Theodore. *Between Two Empires: The Ordeal of the Philippines, 1929–1946.* New Haven, 1965.

Fritz, Harry. "Racism and Democracy in Tocqueville's America," *Social Science Journal,* XIII (Oct. 1976), 65–75.

Fuchs, Lawrence H. (ed.). "American Jews and the Presidential Vote," in *Ethnic Group Politics,* ed. Henry A. Bailey, Jr., and Ellis Katz. Columbus, Ohio, 132–53.

———. *The American Kaleidoscope: Race, Ethnicity, and the Civic Culture.* Hanover, N.H., 1990.

———. "Ethnicity and Foreign Policy: The Question of Multiple Loyalties," in *Ethnicity and War,* ed. Winston A. Van Horne and Thomas V. Tonnesen. Madison, Wis., 1984, 46–69.

———. "From Select Commission to Simpson-Mazzoli: The Making of America's New Immigration Law," in *America's New Immigration Law,* ed. Wayne A. Cornelius and Ricardo Anzaldua Montaya. San Diego, 1983, 43–50.

———. "Immigration, Pluralism, and Public Policy: The Challenge of the *Pluribus* to the *Unum,*" in *U.S. Immigration and Refugee Policy: Global and Domestic Issues,* ed. Mary M. Kritz. Lexington, Mass., 1983, 289–315.

———. "Immigration Reform in 1911 and 1981: The Role of the Select Commissions," *Journal of American Ethnic History,* III (Fall 1983), 58–89.

————. "Minority Groups and Foreign Policy," *Political Science Quarterly*, LXXIV (June 1959), 161–75.

————. *The Political Behavior of American Jews*. Glencoe, Ill., 1956.

Fuchs, Lawrence H. (ed.). *American Ethnic Politics*. New York, 1968.

Galtung, Johan, "U.S. Foreign Policy as Manifest Theology," in *Culture and International Relations*, ed. Jongsuk Chay. New York, 1990, 119–40.

Gambino, Richard. *Blood of My Blood: The Dilemma of the Italian-Americans*. Garden City, N.Y., 1974.

————. *Vendetta: A True Story of the Worst Lynching in America*. . . . Garden City, N.Y., 1977.

Ganin, Zvi. *Truman, American Jewry, and Israel, 1945–1948*. New York, 1979.

Gann, L. H., and Peter Duignan. *The Hispanics in the United States*. Boulder, Colo., 1986.

Gans, Herbert J. "Symbolic Ethnicity: The Future of Ethnic Groups and Culture in America," *Ethnic and Racial Studies*, II (Jan. 1979), 1–18.

Garcia, Mario T. *Mexican Americans: Leadership, Ideology, and Identity, 1930–1960*. New Haven, 1989.

Gardner, Lloyd C. (ed.) *Redefining the Past*. Corvallis, Ore., 1986.

————. *Safe for Democracy: The Anglo-American Response to Revolution, 1913–1923*. New York, 1987.

Gardner, Robert K. A. "Race and Color in International Relations," *Daedalus*, XCVI (Spring 1967), 296–311.

Garrett, Stephen A. "Eastern European Ethnic Groups and American Foreign Policy," *Political Science Quarterly*, XCIII (Summer 1978), 301–23.

————. "The Ties That Bind: Immigrant Influence on U.S. Policy Toward Eastern Europe," in *Ethnicity and U.S. Foreign Policy*, ed. Abdul Aziz Said. New York, 1977, 59–82.

Gatewood, Willard B., Jr. "Black Americans and the Boer War, 1899–1902," *South Atlantic Quarterly* (Spring 1976), 226–44.

————. "Black Americans and the Quest for Empire, 1893–1903," *Journal of Southern History*, XXXVIII (Nov. 1972), 545–66.

————. *Black Americans and the White Man's Burden, 1898–1903*. Urbana, Ill., 1975.

Gazit, Mordechai. *President Kennedy's Policy toward the Arab States and Israel*. Tel Aviv, 1983.

Gazley, John G. *American Opinion of German Unification, 1848–1871*. New York, 1926.

Gelber, Lionel M. *The Rise of Anglo-American Friendship: A Study in World Politics, 1898–1906*. London, 1938.

George, Alexander L. *Presidential Decisionmaking in Foreign Policy: The Effective Use of Information and Advice*. Boulder, Colo., 1980.

Gerson, Louis L. *The Hyphenate in Recent American Politics and Diplomacy*. Lawrence, Kan., 1964.

————. "Immigrant Groups and American Foreign Policy," in *Issues and Conflicts*, ed. George L. Anderson. Lawrence, Kan., 1959, 171–92.

————. "The Influence of Hyphenated Americans on U.S. Diplomacy," in *Ethnicity and U.S. Foreign Policy*, ed. Abdul Aziz Said. New York, 1977, 46–58.

————. *Woodrow Wilson and the Rebirth of Poland, 1914–1920*. New Haven, 1953.

Ghareeb, Edmund A. (ed.). *Split Vision: The Portrayal of Arabs in the American Media*. Rev. ed. Washington, D.C., 1983.

Gibson, Florence E. *The Attitudes of the New York Irish toward State and National Affairs, 1848–1892*. New York, 1951.

Gidney, James B. *A Mandate for Armenia*. Kent, Ohio, 1967.

Gienapp, William E. "Nativism and the Creation of a Republican Majority in the North Before the Civil War," *Journal of American History*, LXXII (Dec. 1985), 529–59.

Gilderhus, Mark T. *Diplomacy and Revolution: U.S.–Mexican Relations under Wilson and Carranza.* Tucson, 1977.

———. *Pan American Visions: Woodrow Wilson in the Western Hemisphere, 1913–1921.* Tucson, 1981.

Glass, Andrew. "Nixon Gives Israel Massive Aid but Reaps No Jewish Political Harvest," *National Journal*, V (Jan. 8, 1972), 57–72.

Glazer, Nathan (ed.). *Clamor at the Gates: The New American Immigration.* San Francisco, 1985.

Glazer, Nathan, and Daniel P. Moynihan. *Beyond the Melting Pot: The Negroes, Puerto Ricans, Jews, Italians, and Irish of New York City.* Cambridge, Mass., 1963.

Glazer, Nathan, and Daniel P. Moynihan (eds.). *Ethnicity: Theory and Experience.* Cambridge, Mass., 1975.

Gleason, Philip. "American Identity and Americanization," in *Harvard Encyclopedia of American Ethnic Groups*, ed. Stephan Thernstrom. Cambridge, Mass., 1980, 31–58.

———. "Americans All: World War II and the Shaping of American Identity," *Review of Politics*, XLIII (Oct. 1981), 483–518.

———. "The Melting Pot: Symbol of Fusion or Confusion?" *American Quarterly*, XVI (Spring 1964), 20–46.

———. "Pluralism and the New Pluralism," *America*, CX (March 7, 1964), 308–12.

Glick, Edward B. *The Triangular Connection: America, Israel, and American Jews.* London, 1982.

Goering, John M. "The Emergence of Ethnic Interests: A Case of Serendipity," *Social Forces*, XLIX (March 1971), 379–84.

Goldberg, David H. *Foreign Policy and Ethnic Interest Groups: American and Canadian Jews Lobby for Israel.* New York, 1990.

Gomez-Quiñones, Juan. "Notes on an Interpretation of the Relations Between the Mexican Community in the United States and Mexico," in *Mexican-U.S. Relations*, ed. Carlos Vásquez and Manuel García y Griego. Los Angeles, 1983, 417–39.

Gordon, Milton M. "Assimilation in America: Theory and Reality," *Daedalus*, XC (Spring 1961), 263–85.

———. *Assimilation in American Life: The Role of Race, Religion, and National Origins.* New York, 1964.

———. *Human Nature, Class and Ethnicity.* New York, 1978.

Gossett, Thomas F. *Race: The History of an Idea in America.* Dallas, 1963.

Grabbe, Hans-Jürgen. "European Immigration to the United States in the Early National Period, 1783–1820," *Proceedings of the American Philosophical Society*, CXXXIII (June 1989), 190–214.

Graber, Doris A. *Public Opinion, the President and Foreign Policy.* New York, 1968.

Graebner, Norman A. *Empire on the Pacific: A Study in American Continental Expansion.* New York, 1955.

Graham, Hugh D. *The Civil Rights Era: Origins and Development of National Policy, 1960–1972.* New York, 1990.

Graham, Otis L., Jr. "Illegal Immigration and the New Restrictionism," *Center Magazine*, XII (May–June 1979), 54–63.

―――. "Immigration and the National Interest," in *U.S. Immigration in the 1980s*, ed. David E. Simcox. Boulder, Colo., 1988, 124–36.

―――. "The Problem That Will Not Go Away: Illegal Immigration," *Center Magazine*, X (July–Aug. 1977), 56–66.

―――. "Uses and Misuses of History in the Debate Over Immigration Reform," *Public Historian*, VIII (Spring 1986), 41–64.

Grayson, George W. "Anti-Americanism in Mexico," in *Anti-Americanism in the Third World*, ed. Alvin Z. Rubinstein and Donald E. Smith. New York, 1985, 31–48.

Greeley, Andrew M. *The Irish Americans: The Rise to Money and Power*. New York, 1981.

―――. *Why Can't They Be Like Us? America's White Ethnic Groups*. New York, 1971.

Green, Stephen. *Living by the Sword: America and Israel in the Middle East, 1968–87*. Brattleboro, Vt., 1988.

―――. *Taking Sides: America's Secret Relations with a Militant Israel*. New York, 1984.

Greene, Victor. *For God and Country: The Rise of Polish and Lithuanian Ethnic Consciousness in America*. Madison, Wis., 1975.

―――. "Old Ethnic Stereotypes and the New Ethnic Studies," *Ethnicity*, V (Dec. 1978), 328–50.

Grenville, John A. S., and George B. Young. *Politics, Strategy and American Diplomacy: Studies in Foreign Policy, 1873–1917*. New Haven, 1966.

Grieb, Kenneth J. *The United States and Huerta*. Lincoln, Neb., 1969.

Griswold del Castillo, Richard. *The Treaty of Guadalupe Hidalgo: A Legacy of Conflict*. Norman, Okla., 1990.

Grodzins, Morton. *Americans Betrayed: Politics and the Japanese Evacuation*. Chicago, 1949.

―――. *The Loyal and the Disloyal: Social Boundaries of Patriotism and Treason*. Chicago, 1956.

Grubb, Farley. "German Immigration to Pennsylvania, 1709–1820," *Journal of Interdisciplinary History*, XX (Winter 1990), 417–36.

Gunter, Michael M. *"Pursuing the Just Cause of Their People": A Study of Contemporary Armenian Terrorism*. New York, 1986.

Gürün, Kamuran. *The Armenian File: The Myth of Innocence Exposed*. London, 1985.

Gustafson, Lowell S. *The Sovereignty Dispute over the Falkland (Malvinas) Islands*. New York, 1988.

Gwynn, Stephen (ed.). *The Letters and Friendships of Sir Cecil Spring Rice, a Record*. 2 vols. New York, 1929.

Hagopian, Elaine C., and Ann Paden (eds.). *The Arab Americans: Studies in Assimilation*. Wilmette, Ill., 1969.

Haig, Alexander M., Jr. *Caveat: Realism, Reagan, and Foreign Policy*. New York, 1984.

Haley, Edward P. *Revolution and Intervention: The Diplomacy of Taft and Wilson with Mexico, 1910–1917*. Cambridge, Mass., 1970.

Hall, Linda B., and Don M. Coerver. *Revolution on the Border: The United States and Mexico, 1910–1920*. Albuquerque, 1988.

Halliday, Jon, and Bruce Cumings. *Korea: The Unknown War*. London, 1988.

Halperin, Samuel. *The Political World of American Zionism*. Detroit, 1961.

Hamby, Alonzo L. "The Accidental Presidency: Truman vs. Dewey: The 1948 Election," *Wilson Quarterly*, XII (Spring 1988), 48–85.

Hamilton, Alexander, James Madison, and John Jay. *The Federalist*, ed. Jacob E. Cooke. Middletown, Conn., 1961.

Hamilton, Michael P. (ed.). *American Character and Foreign Policy.* Grand Rapids, Mich., 1986.

Handlin, Oscar. "The Immigrant and American Politics," in *Foreign Influences in American Life,* ed. David F. Bowers. New York, 1952, 84–98.

———. *Race and Nationality in American Life.* Garden City, N.Y., 1957.

———. *The Uprooted.* Boston, 1971.

Handlin, Oscar, and Mary E. Handlin. "The New History and the Ethnic Factor in American Life," *Perspectives in American History,* IV (1970), 524.

Hansen, Marcus L. *The Atlantic Migration, 1607–1860.* Cambridge, Mass., 1945.

———. *The Immigrant in American History.* New York, 1940.

Hargrove, Erwin C. *Jimmy Carter as President: Leadership and the Politics of the Public Good.* Baton Rouge, La., 1988.

Harrington, Fred H. " 'Europe First' and Its Consequences for the Far Eastern Policy of the United States," in *Redefining the Past,* ed. Lloyd C. Gardner. Corvallis, Ore., 1986, 103–20.

———. "Politics and Foreign Policy," in *Encyclopedia of American Foreign Policy,* ed. Alexander DeConde. 3 vols, New York, 1978, III, 773–89.

Harrington, Mona. "Loyalties: Dual and Divided," in *Harvard Encyclopedia of American Ethnic Groups,* ed. Stephan Thernstrom. Cambridge, Mass., 1980, 676–86.

Harris, Brice, Jr. *The United States and the Italo-Ethiopian Crisis.* Stanford, 1964.

Hartley, Stephen. *The Irish Question as a Problem in British Foreign Policy, 1914–18.* London, 1987.

Hartmann, Edward G. *The Movement to Americanize the Immigrant.* New York, 1948.

Harvard Encyclopedia of American Ethnic Groups, ed. Stephan Thernstrom. Cambridge, Mass., 1980.

Hathaway, Robert M. *Great Britain and the United States: Special Relations since World War II.* Boston, 1990.

Hawgood, John A. *The Tragedy of German-America.* New York, 1940.

Hawkins, Brett W., and Robert A. Lorinskas (eds.). *The Ethnic Factor in American Politics.* Columbus, Ohio, 1970.

Hawkins, Freda. *Critical Years in Immigration: Canada and Australia Compared.* Kingston and Montreal, 1989.

Heald, Morrell, and Lawrence S. Kaplan. *Culture and Diplomacy: The American Experience.* Westport, Conn., 1977.

Healy, David. *Drive to Hegemony: The United States in the Caribbean, 1898–1917.* Madison, Wis., 1988.

———. *Gunboat Diplomacy in the Wilson Era: The U.S. Navy in Haiti, 1915–1916.* Madison, Wis., 1976.

———. *The United States in Cuba, 1898–1902.* Madison, Wis., 1963.

Heindel, Richard H. *The American Impact on Great Britain, 1898–1914: A Study of the United States in World History.* Philadelphia, 1940.

Heinrichs, Waldo H. *Threshold of War: Franklin D. Roosevelt and American Entry into World War II.* New York, 1988.

Henderson, Nicholas. "America and the Falklands: Case Study in the Behaviour of an Ally," *The Economist,* CXXXI (Nov. 12, 1983), 31–42.

Hendrick, Burton J. *The Life and Letters of Walter H. Page.* 3 vols. Garden City, N.Y., 1922–28.

Henry, Charles P. *Culture and African American Politics*. Bloomington, Ind., 1990.

Hermann, Margaret G., and Charles F. Hermann. "Who Makes Foreign Policy Decisions and How: An Empirical Inquiry," *International Studies Quarterly*, III (Dec. 1989), 361–87.

Hero, Alfred O., Jr. "American Negroes and U.S. Foreign Policy: 1937–1967," *Journal of Conflict Resolution*, XIII (June 1969), 220–51.

Herring, George C. *America's Longest War: The United States and Vietnam, 1950–1975*. New York, 1979.

———. "'Peoples Quite Apart': Americans, South Vietnamese, and the War in Vietnam," *Diplomatic History*, XIV (Winter 1990), 1–23.

Herring, Pendleton. *Group Representation Before Congress*. Baltimore, 1929.

Hersh, Seymour M. *The Sampson Option: Israel's Nuclear Option and American Foreign Policy*. New York, 1991.

Hertzberg, Arthur. *The Jews in America: Four Centuries of an Uneasy Encounter*. New York, 1989.

Hess, Gary R. *America Encounters India, 1941–1947*. Baltimore, 1971.

———. "Franklin D. Roosevelt and Anti-Colonialism," *Indian Journal of American Studies*, XIII (Jan. 1983), 23–37.

Hicks, Sally M., and Theodore A. Couloumbis. "The 'Greek Lobby': Illusion or Reality?" in *Ethnicity and U.S. Foreign Policy*, ed. Abdul Aziz Said. New York, 1977, 83–116.

Hietala, Thomas R. *Manifest Design: Anxious Aggrandizement in Late Jacksonian America*. Ithaca, N.Y., 1985.

Higham, John. "Current Trends in the Study of Ethnicity in the United States," *Journal of American Ethnic Studies*, II (Fall 1982), 5–15.

———. "Integrating America: The Problem of Assimilation in the Nineteenth Century," *Journal of American Ethnic History*, I (Fall 1981), 7–25.

———. "Integration vs. Pluralism: Another American Dilemma," *The Center Magazine*, VII (July–Aug. 1974), 67–73.

———. *Send These to Me: Immigrants in Urban America*. Rev. ed. Baltimore, 1984.

———. *Strangers in the Land: Patterns of American Nativism, 1860–1925*. New York, 1963.

Higham, John (ed.). *Ethnic Leadership in America*. Baltimore, 1978.

Hildebrand, Robert C. *Power and the People: Executive Management of Public Opinion in Foreign Affairs, 1897–1921*. Chapel Hill, 1981.

Hill, Robert A. *Marcus Garvey: Life and Lessons*. Berkeley, 1987.

Hilsman, Roger. *The Politics of Policy Making in Defense and Foreign Affairs*. New York, 1971.

Hirschman, Charles. "America's Melting Pot Reconsidered," *Annual Review of Sociology*, IX (1983), 397–423.

Hitchens, Christopher. *Blood, Class and Nostalgia: Anglo-American Ironies*. New York, 1990.

Hoadley, J. Stephen. "Black Americans and U.S. Policy Toward Africa," *Journal of Black Studies*, II (June 1972), 489–502.

Hoffman, Stanley. "A New Policy for Israel," *Foreign Affairs*, LIII (April 1975), 405–31.

Hofstadter, Richard. *Social Darwinism in American Thought*. Rev. ed. Boston, 1955.

Hofstetter, Richard R. (ed.). *U.S. Immigration Policy*. Durham, N.C., 1984.

Hogan, J. Michael. *The Panama Canal in American Politics: Domestic Advocacy and the Evolution of Policy*. Carbondale, Ill., 1986.

Hogan, Michael J. *The Marshall Plan: America, Britain, and the Reconstruction of Western Europe, 1947–1952*. New York, 1987.

Hohenberg, John. *Between Two Worlds: Policy, Press, and Public Opinion in Asian-American Relations.* New York, 1967.

Holland, Jack. *The American Connection: U.S. Guns, Money, and Influence in Northern Ireland.* New York, 1987.

Holt, Michael. *The Political Crisis of the 1850s.* New York, 1978.

————. "The Politics of Impatience: The Origins of Know Nothingism," *Journal of American History,* LX (Sept. 1973), 309–31.

Holtzman, Abraham. *Interest Groups and Lobbying.* New York, 1966.

Horne, Gerald. *Black and Red: W. E. B. Du Bois and the Afro-American Response to the Cold War, 1944–1963.* Albany, N.Y., 1985.

Horowitz, Donald L. *Ethnic Groups in Conflict.* Berkeley, 1985.

Horowitz, Irving L. "Ethnic Politics and U.S. Foreign Policy," in *Ethnicity and U.S. Foreign Policy,* ed. Abdul Aziz Said. New York, 1977, 175–80.

Horsman, Reginald. "Origins of Racial Anglo-Saxonism in Great Britain before 1850," *Journal of the History of Ideas,* XXXVII (July-Sept. 1976), 387–410.

————. *Race and Manifest Destiny: The Origins of American Racial Anglo-Saxonism.* Cambridge, Mass., 1981.

Hovannisian, Richard G. *Armenia on the Road to Independence, 1918.* Berkeley, 1967.

————. *The Republic of Armenia.* 2 vols. Berkeley, 1971–82.

Hovannisian, Richard G. (ed.). *The Armenian Genocide in Perspective.* New Brunswick, N.J., 1986.

Howe, Russell W. *Along the Afric Shore: An Historical Review of Two Centuries of U.S.-African Relations.* New York, 1975.

Howe, Russell W., and Sarah H. Trott. *The Power Peddlers: How Lobbyists Mold America's Foreign Policy.* Garden City, N.Y., 1977.

Huckfeldt, Robert, and Carol W. Kohfeld. *Race and the Decline of Class in American Politics.* Urbana, Ill., 1989.

Hughes, Barry B. *The Domestic Context of American Foreign Policy.* San Francisco, 1978.

Hughes, H. Stuart. *The United States and Italy.* Cambridge, Mass., 1953.

Hull, Cordell. *The Memoirs of Cordell Hull.* 2 vols. New York, 1948.

Hunt, Michael. "The Forgotten Occupation: Peking, 1900–1901," *Pacific Historical Review,* XLVIII (Nov. 1979), 501–30.

————. *Ideology and U.S. Foreign Policy.* New Haven, 1987.

————. *The Making of a Special Relationship: The United States and China to 1914.* New York, 1983.

Ichioka, Yuji. *The Issei: The World of the First Generation Japanese Immigrants, 1885–1924.* New York, 1988.

————. "Japanese Immigrant Nationalism: The Issei and the Sino-Japanese War, 1937–1941," *California History,* LXIX (Fall 1990), 260–75.

Ienaga, Saburo. *The Pacific War: World War II and the Japanese, 1931–1945.* New York, 1978.

International Herald-Tribune. Selected issues, 1988.

Iriye, Akira. *Across the Pacific: An Inner History of American–East Asian Relations.* New York, 1967.

————. *After Imperialism: The Search for a New Order in the Far East, 1921–1931.* Cambridge, Mass., 1965.

————. "Intercultural Relations," in *Encyclopedia of American Foreign Policy,* ed. Alexander DeConde. 3 vols. New York, 1978, II, 428–42.

————. *Pacific Estrangement: Japanese and American Expansion, 1897–1911*. Cambridge, Mass., 1972.

————. *Power and Culture: The Japanese-American War, 1941–1945*. Cambridge, Mass., 1981.

Iriye, Akira (ed.). *Mutual Images: Essays in American-Japanese Relations*. Cambridge, Mass., 1975.

Irons, Peter H. "America's Cold War Crusade: Domestic Politics and Foreign Policy, 1942–1948." Unpublished Ph.D. dissertation, Boston University, 1972.

————. "Race and the Constitution: The Case of the Japanese-American Internment," *This Constitution*, III (Winter 1986), 18–26.

————. " 'The Test is Poland': Polish Americans and the Origins of the Cold War," *Polish American Studies*, XXX (Autumn 1973), 5–63.

Isaacs, Harold I. "American Race Relations and the United States Image in World Affairs," *Journal of Human Relations*, X (1962), 266–80.

————. *Idols of the Tribe: Group Identity and Political Change*. New York, 1975.

————. "The One and the Many: What Are the Implications of the New Ethnic Revival?" *American Educator*, II (1978), 4–14.

————. "Race and Color in World Affairs," *Foreign Affairs*, XLVII (Jan. 1969), 235–50.

————. *Scratches on Our Minds: American Images of China and India*. New York, 1958.

Isaacs, Steven D. *Jews and American Politics*. Garden City, N.Y., 1974.

Israel, Fred L. (ed). *The State of the Union Messages of the Presidents, 1790–1966*, 3 vols. New York, 1966.

Issel, William. *Social Change in the United States, 1945–1953*. London, 1985.

Jackson, Henry F. *From the Congo to Soweto: U.S. Foreign Policy Toward Africa Since 1960*. New York, 1982.

Jasso, Guillermina, and Mark R. Rosenzweig. *The New Chosen People: Immigrants in the United States*. New York, 1990.

Jaynes, Gerald D., and Robin Williams, Jr. (eds.). *A Common Destiny: Blacks and American Society*. Washington, D.C., 1980.

Jefferson, Thomas. *The Works of Thomas Jefferson*, ed. Paul L. Ford. 12 vols. New York, 1904–5.

Jenkins, Brian A. *Fenians and Anglo-American Relations during Reconstruction*. Ithaca, N.Y., 1969.

Jennings, Francis. *Empire of Fortune: Crowns, Colonies, and Tribes in the Seven Years' War in America*. New York, 1988.

————. *The Invasion of America: Indians, Colonialism, and the Cant of Conquest*. Chapel Hill, 1975.

Jiobu, Robert M. *Ethnicity and Inequality*. Albany, N.Y., 1990.

Johannsen, Robert W. *To the Halls of the Montezumas: The Mexican War in the American Imagination*. New York, 1985.

Johnson, John J. *A Hemisphere Apart: The Foundations of United States Policy toward Latin America*. Baltimore, 1990.

Johnson, Sheila. *The Japanese Through American Eyes*. Stanford, 1988.

Johnson, Walter. *The Battle Against Isolation*. Chicago, 1944.

Jones, Howard. *To the Webster-Ashburton Treaty: A Study in Anglo-American Relations, 1783–1843*. Chapel Hill, 1977.

Jones, Maldwyn A. *American Immigration*. Chicago, 1960.

———. *The Old World Ties of American Ethnic Groups*. London, 1976.

Jordan, Winthrop D. *The White Man's Burden: Historical Origins of Racism in the United States*. New York, 1974.

———. *White Over Black: American Attitudes Toward the Negro, 1550–1812*. Chapel Hill, 1968.

Kallen, Horace M. *Cultural Pluralism and the American Idea: An Essay in Social Philosophy*. Philadelphia, 1956.

Kammen, Michael. *People of Paradox: An Inquiry Concerning the Origins of American Civilization*. New York, 1972.

Kamphoefner, Walter D. "Dreissiger and Forty-Eighter: The Political Influence of Two Generations of German Political Exiles," in *Germany and America*, ed. Hans L. Trefousse. New York, 1980, 89–102.

Kaplan, Lawrence S. "Nationalism," in *Encyclopedia of American Foreign Policy*, ed. Alexander DeConde. 3 vols. New York, 1978, II, 610–22.

Kariel, Henry S. *The Decline of American Pluralism*. Stanford, 1961.

Karst, Kenneth L. *Belonging to America: Equal Citizenship and the Constitution*. New Haven, 1989.

Katz, Friedrich. *The Secret War in Mexico: Europe, the United States and the Mexican Revolution*. Chicago, 1981.

Kaufman, Jonathan. *Broken Alliance: The Turbulent Times Between Blacks and Jews in America*. New York, 1988.

Kegley, Charles W., Jr. and Eugen Wittkopf, "Beyond Consensus: The Domestic Context of American Foreign Policy," *International Journal*, XXXVIII (Winter 1982–83), 77–106.

Kelley, Robert. *The Cultural Pattern in American Politics: The First Century*. New York, 1979.

———. *The Transatlantic Persuasion: The Liberal-Democratic Mind in the Age of Gladstone*. New York, 1969.

Kenen, Isaiah L. *Israel's Defense Line: Her Friends and Foes in Washington*. New York, 1981.

Kennan, George F. *Memoirs, 1925–1950*. Boston, 1967.

———. *Russia Leaves the War*. Princeton, 1956.

Kennedy, Philip W. "Race and American Expansion in Cuba and Puerto Rico, 1895–1905," *Journal of Black Studies*, I (March 1971), 306–16.

———. "The Racial Overtones of Imperialism as a Campaign Issue, 1900," *Mid-America*, XLVIII (July 1966), 196–205.

Kent, George. "Congress and American Middle East Policy," in *Middle East*, ed. Willard A. Beling. Albany, N.Y., 1973, 286–305.

Kern, Montague, Patricia W. Levering, and Ralph B. Levering. *The Kennedy Crises: The Press, the Presidency, and Foreign Policy*. Chapel Hill, 1983.

Kerr, Thomas J. IV. "German-Americans and Neutrality in the 1916 Election," *Mid-America*, XLIII (April 1961), 95–105.

Keto, Clement T. "Black American Involvement in South Africa's Race Issue," *Issue*, III (Spring 1973), 6–11.

Kettner, James. H. *The Development of American Citizenship, 1608–1870*. Chapel Hill, 1978.

Key, V. O., Jr. *Politics, Parties, and Pressure Groups*. 5th ed. New York, 1964.

———. *Public Opinion and American Democracy*. New York, 1961.

Kinney, Douglas. *National Interest/National Honor: The Diplomacy of the Falklands Crisis*. New York, 1989.

Kirkendall, Richard S. "Elitism and Foreign Policy," in *Encyclopedia of American Foreign Policy,* ed. Alexander DeConde. 3 vols. New York, 1978, I, 302–9.

Kissinger, Henry. *White House Years.* Boston, 1979.

———. *Years of Upheaval.* Boston, 1982.

Kivisto, Peter. "Finnish Americans and the Homeland, 1918–1958," *Journal of American Ethnic History,* VII (Fall 1987), 7–28.

Kivisto, Peter, and Dag Blanck (eds.). *American Immigrants and Their Generations: Studies and Commentaries on the Hansen Thesis After Fifty Years.* Urbana, Ill., 1990.

Knee, Stuart E. "The Diplomacy of Neutrality: Theodore Roosevelt and the Russian Pogroms of 1903–06," *Presidential Studies Quarterly,* XIX (Winter 1989), 71–78.

Knobel, Dale T. *Paddy and the Republic: Ethnicity and Nationality in Antebellum America.* Middletown, Conn., 1986.

Knoles, George H. *The Jazz Age Revisited: British Criticism of American Civilization During the 1920s.* Stanford, 1955.

Knuth, Helen E. "The Climax of American Anglo-Saxonism, 1898–1905." Unpublished Ph.D. dissertation, Northwestern University, 1958.

Kochavi, Arieh J. "Anglo-American Discord: Jewish Refugees and United Nations Relief and Rehabilitation Administration Policy, 1945–1947," *Diplomatic History,* XIV (Fall 1990), 529–51.

Koen, Ross Y. *The China Lobby in American Politics.* New York, 1974.

Koenig, Louis W. *Congress and the President: Official Makers of Public Policy.* Glenview, Ill., 1965.

Kohn, Hans. *American Nationalism.* New York, 1957.

Kolko, Gabriel. *Confronting the Third World: United States Foreign Policy, 1945–1980.* New York, 1989.

———. *The Roots of American Foreign Policy: An Analysis of Power and Purpose.* Boston, 1969.

Kolsky, Thomas A. *Jews Against Zionism: The American Council for Judaism, 1942–1948.* Philadelphia, 1990.

Kornegay, Francis A., Jr. *Washington and Africa: Reagan, Congress, and an African Affairs Constituency.* Washington, D.C., 1982.

Kovrig, Bennett. *The Myth of Liberation: East-Central Europe in U.S. Diplomacy and Politics since 1941.* Baltimore, 1973.

Krieger, Joel. *Reagan, Thatcher, and the Politics of Decline.* Cambridge, Eng., 1986.

Kritz, Mary M. (ed.). *U.S. Immigration and Refugee Policy: Global and Domestic Issues.* Lexington, Mass., 1983.

Kunz, Diane B. *The Economic Diplomacy of the Suez Crisis.* Chapel Hill, 1991.

Kuper, Leo. "The Turkish Genocide of Armenians, 1915–1917," in *Armenian Genocide,* ed. Hovannissian. New Brunswick, N.J., 43–59.

Kusnitz, Leonard A. *Public Opinion and Foreign Policy: America's China Policy, 1949–1979.* Westport, Conn., 1984.

Kyvig, David E. (ed.). *Reagan and the World.* Westport, Conn., 1990.

La Feber, Walter. *The New Empire: An Interpretation of American Expansion, 1860–1898.* Ithaca, N.Y., 1963.

———. *The Panama Canal: A Crisis in Historical Perspective.* New York, 1989.

Lake, Anthony. *The "Tar Baby" Option: American Policy Toward Southern Rhodesia.* New York, 1976.

Lamm, Richard D., and Gary Imhoff. *The Immigration Time Bomb: The Fragmenting of America*. New York, 1985.

Landsman, Ned C. "Ethnicity and National Origin Among British Settlers in the Philadelphia Region: Pennsylvania Immigration in the Wake of *Voyagers to the West*," *Proceedings of the American Philosophical Society*, CXXXIII (No. 2, 1989), 170–74.

Langer, William L., and S. Everett Gleason. *The Challenge to Isolation, 1937–1940*. New York, 1952.

———. *The Undeclared War, 1940–1941*. New York, 1953.

Langley, Lester D. *The Banana Wars: An Inner History of American Empire*. Lexington, Ken., 1983.

Lapid, Yossi. "Ethnic Political Mobilization and U.S. Foreign Policy: Current Trends and Conflicting Assessments," *Studies in Contemporary Jewry*, III (1987), 3–25.

Lasch, Christopher. "The Anti-Imperialists, the Philippines, and the Inequality of Man," *Journal of Southern History*, XXIV (Aug. 1958), 319–31.

Lauren, Paul G. "Human Rights in History: Diplomacy and Racial Equality at the Paris Peace Conference," *Diplomatic History*, II (Summer 1978), 257–78.

———. *Power and Prejudice: The Politics and Diplomacy of Racial Discrimination*. Boulder, Colo., 1988.

Lavender, Abraham D. "United States Ethnic Groups in 1790: Given Names as Suggestions of Ethnic Identity," *Journal of American Ethnic History*, IX (Fall 1989), 36–66.

Lawson Philip. *The Imperial Challenge: Quebec and Britain in the Age of the American Revolution*. Montreal, 1989.

Leary, William M., Jr. "Woodrow Wilson, Irish Americans and the Election of 1916," *Journal of American History* (June 1967), 57–72.

Lebow, Richard N. "Woodrow Wilson and the Balfour Declaration," *Journal of Modern History*, XL (Dec. 1968), 501–23.

Legg, Keith R. "Congress as Trojan Horse? The Turkish Embargo Problem, 1974–1978," in *Congress, the Presidency and American Foreign Policy*, ed. John Spanier and Joseph Nogee. New York, 1981, 107–31.

Leigh, Michael. *Mobilizing Consent: Public Opinion and American Foreign Policy, 1937–1947*. Westport, Conn., 1976.

LeMay, Michael C. *From Open Door to Dutch Door: An Analysis of U.S. Immigration Policy since 1820*. New York, 1987.

———. *The Struggle for Influence: The Impact of Minority Groups on Politics and Public Policy in the United States*. Lanham, Md., 1985.

LeMelle, Tilden J. "Race, International Relations, U.S. Foreign Policy, and the African Liberation Struggle," *Journal of Black Studies*, III (Sept. 1972), 95–102.

Leonard, Ira M., and Robert D. Parmet. *American Nativism, 1830–1860*. New York, 1971.

Leonard, Kevin A. "'Is That What We Fought For?': Japanese Americans and Racism in California, The Impact of World War II," *Western Historical Quarterly*, XXI (Nov. 1990), 463–82.

Lerda, Valeria Gennaro (ed.). *From "Melting Pot" to Multi-Culturalism: The Evolution of Ethnic Relations in the United States and Canada*. Rome, 1990.

Levering, Ralph B. *The Public and American Foreign Policy, 1918–1978*. New York, 1978.

———. "Public Opinion, Foreign Policy and American Politics since the 1960s," *Diplomatic History*, XIII (Summer 1989), 383–93.

Levy, Jack S. "Domestic Politics and War," *Journal of Interdisciplinary History*, XVIII (Spring 1988), 653–73.

Levy, Mark R., and Michael S. Kramer. *The Ethnic Factor: How America's Minorities Decide Elections*. New York, 1972.

Levy, Peter B. "Blacks and the Vietnam War," in *The Legacy*, ed. D. Michael Shafer. Boston, 1990, 209–32.

Lewis, Allen I. "WASP—From Sociological Concept to Epithet," *Ethnicity*, II (June 1975), 153–62.

Lewis, Michael. "Why Political Interference is Good for the State Department," *Orbis*, XXXII (Spring 1988), 167–85.

Leyburn, James G. *The Scotch-Irish: A Social History*. Chapel Hill, 1962.

Lieberson, Stanley. *A Piece of the Pie: Blacks and White Immigrants Since 1880*. Berkeley, 1980.

———. "Unhyphenated Whites in the United States," *Ethnic and Racial Studies*, VIII (Jan. 1985), 159–80.

Lilienthal, Alfred M. "The Balfour Declaration: Forty Years Later," in *Issues and Conflicts*, ed. George L. Anderson. Lawrence, Kan, 1959, 99–126.

Linderman, Gerald F. *The Mirror of War: American Society and the Spanish-American War*. Ann Arbor, Mich., 1974.

Link, Arthur S. *Wilson the Diplomatist: A Look at His Major Foreign Policies*. New York, 1974.

———. *Wilson: The Struggle for Neutrality, 1914–1915*. Princeton, 1960.

Lippmann, Walter. *Isolation and Alliances: An American Speaks to the British*. Boston, 1952.

Lipset, Seymour M. "The 'Jewish Lobby' and the National Interest," *New Leader*, LXIV (Nov. 16, 1981), 8–10.

Litt, Edgar. *Beyond Pluralism: Ethnic Politics in America*. Glenview, Ill., 1970.

Little, Douglas. "From Even-Handed to Empty-Handed: Seeking Order in the Middle East," in *Kennedy's Quest for Victory*, ed. Thomas G. Paterson. New York, 1989, 156–77.

———. "The New Frontier on the Nile: JFK, Nasser, and Arab Nationalism," *Journal of American History*, LXXV (Sept. 1988), 501–27.

Little, Kenneth. "Some Aspects of Color, Class, and Culture in Britain," *Daedalus*, XCVI (Spring 1967), 512–26.

Litwack, Leon F. *North of Slavery: The Negro in the Free States, 1790–1860*. Chicago, 1961.

Llanes, José. *Cuban Americans: Masters of Survival*. Cambridge, Mass., 1982.

Lodge, Henry Cabot (ed.). *Selections from the Correspondence of Theodore Roosevelt and Henry Cabot Lodge, 1884–1918*. 2 vols. New York, 1925.

Loewenberg, Peter. "The Psychology of Racism," in *The Great Fear*, ed. Gary B. Nash and Richard Weiss. New York, 1970, 186–201.

Logan, Rayford W. *The Diplomatic Relations of the United States with Haiti, 1776–1891*. Chapel Hill, 1941.

Lomax, Louis E. *The Negro Revolt*. New York, 1963.

Lorinskas, Robert A. "The Political Impact of Anglo-Saxon Ethnicity," *Ethnicity*, I (Dec. 1974), 417–21.

Los Angeles *Times*. Selected issues, 1985–91.

Louis, William R. *The British Empire in the Middle East 1945–1951: Arab Nationalism, the United States, and Postwar Imperialism*. Oxford, 1984.

———. *Imperialism at Bay: The United States and the Decolonization of the British Empire, 1941–1945*. New York, 1978.

Louis, William R., and Hedley Bull (eds.). *The "Special Relationship": Anglo-American Relations Since 1945*. Oxford, 1986.

Love, Janice. *The U.S. Anti-Apartheid Movement: Local Activism in Global Politics*. New York, 1985.

Lovell, S. D. *The Presidential Election of 1916*. Carbondale, Ill., 1980.

Lowell, James Russell. *The Biglow Papers* [First Series], ed. Thomas Wortham. DeKalb, Ill., 1977.

Lubell, Samuel. *The Future of American Politics*. New York, 1952.

Luebke, Frederick C. *Bonds of Loyalty: German-Americans and World War I*. DeKalb, Ill., 1974.

————. *Ethnic Voters and the Election of Lincoln*. Lincoln, Neb., 1971.

Ma, L. Eve Armentrout. *Revolutionaries, Monarchists, and Chinatowns: Chinese Politics in the Americas and the 1911 Revolution*. Honolulu, 1989.

McCaffrey, Lawrence J. *The Irish Diaspora in America*. Bloomington, Ind., 1976.

McCarthy, Dennis J. "The British," in *The Immigrants' Influence on Wilson's Peace Policies*, ed. Joseph P. O'Grady. Lexington, Ken., 1967, 85–110.

McConnell, Scott. "The New Battle Over Immigration," *Fortune*, CXVII (May 9, 1988), 89–102.

McCoy, Donald R., and Richard T. Ruetten. *Quest and Response: Minority Rights and the Truman Administration*. Lawrence, Kan., 1973.

McHenry, Donald F. "Captive of No Group," *Foreign Policy*, XIV (Summer 1974), 142–49.

McKee, Delber L. "The Chinese Boycott of 1905–1906 Reconsidered: The Role of Chinese Americans," *Pacific Historical Review*, LV (May 1986), 165–91.

————. *Chinese Exclusion versus the Open Door Policy, 1900–1906: Clashes over China Policy in the Roosevelt Era*. Detroit, 1977.

McKercher, B. J. C. (ed.). *Anglo-American Relations in the 1920s: The Struggle for Supremacy*. London, 1991.

————. "Wealth, Power, and the New International Order: Britain and the American Challenge in the 1920s," *Diplomatic History*, XII (Fall 1988), 411–41.

McWilliams, Wilson C. *The Idea of Fraternity in America*. Berkeley, 1973.

Mahoney, Richard D. *J F K: Ordeal in Africa*. New York, 1983.

Maingot, Anthony P. "Ideology, Politics, and Citizenship in the American Debate on Immigration Policy: Beyond Consensus," in *U.S. Immigration and Refugee Policy*, ed. Mary M. Kritz. Lexington, Mass., 1983, 361–79.

Mamatey, Victor S. *The United States and East Central Europe, 1914–1918: A Study in Wilsonian Diplomacy and Propaganda*. Princeton, 1957.

Mann, Arthur. *The One and the Many: Reflections on the American Identity*. Chicago, 1979.

Marcus, Jacob R. *United States Jewry 1776–1985*. 2 vols. Detroit, 1989–91.

Markel, Lester, et al. *Public Opinion and Foreign Policy*. New York, 1949.

Marks, Frederick W. III. *Velvet on Iron: The Diplomacy of Theodore Roosevelt*. Lincoln, Neb., 1979.

————. *Wind Over Sand: The Diplomacy of Franklin Roosevelt*. Athens, Ga., 1988.

Martin, Philip M., and Marion F. Houston. "European and American Immigration Policies," in *U.S. Immigration Policy*, ed. Richard R. Hofstetter. Durham, N.C., 1984, 29–54.

Masland, John W. "Pressure Groups and American Foreign Policy," *Public Opinion Quarterly*, VI (Spring 1942), 115–22.

Mathias, Charles McC., Jr. "Ethnic Groups and Foreign Policy," *Foreign Affairs*, LIX (Summer 1981), 975–98.

Matray, James I. *The Reluctant Crusade: American Foreign Policy in Korea, 1941–1950.* Honolulu, 1985.

Mathews, Fred. "Cultural Pluralism in Context," *Journal of Ethnic Studies*," XII (Summer 1984), 63–78.

Matthewson, Timothy M. "Slavery and Diplomacy: The United States and Saint Domingue, 1791–1793." Unpublished Ph.D. dissertation, University of California, Santa Barbara, 1976.

May, Ernest R. *American Imperialism: A Speculative Essay.* New York, 1968.

————. "An American Tradition in Foreign Policy: The Role of Public Opinion," in *Theory and Practice in American Politics,* ed. William H. Nelson. Chicago, 1964, 101–22.

————. *Imperial Democracy: The Emergence of America as a Great Power.* New York, 1961.

————. *The World War and American Isolation, 1914–1917.* Cambridge, Mass., 1959.

May, Glenn A. "Filipino Resistance to American Occupation: Batangas, 1899–1902," *Pacific Historical Review,* XLVIII (Nov. 1979), 531–56.

Mayers, David, A. *George Kennan and the Dilemmas of US Foreign Policy.* New York, 1988.

Meier, Matt S., and Feliciano Rivera. *The Chicanos: A History of Mexican Americans.* New York, 1972.

Melbourne, Roy M. "The American Response to the Nigerian Conflict, 1968," *Issue,* III (Summer 1973), 33–42.

Menzel, Paul T. (ed.). *Moral Argument and the War in Vietnam.* Nashville, Tenn., 1971.

Merk, Frederick. *Manifest Destiny and Mission in American History: A Reinterpretation.* New York, 1963.

————. *The Oregon Question: Essays in Anglo-American Diplomacy and Politics.* Cambridge, Mass., 1967.

Metz, Steven. "The Anti-Apartheid Movement and the Populist Instinct in American Politics," *Political Science Quarterly,* CI (Fall 1986), 379–85.

————. "Congress, the Antiapartheid Movement, and Nixon," *Diplomatic History,* XII (Spring 1988), 165–85.

Miles, Robert, and Annie Phizacklea (eds.). *Racism and Political Action in Britain.* London, 1979.

————. *White Man's Country: Racism in British Politics.* London, 1984.

Miller, Abraham. "Ethnicity and Political Behavior: A Review of Theories and an Attempt at Reformulation," *Western Political Quarterly,* XXIV (Sept. 1971), 483–500.

Miller, Jake C. *The Black Presence in American Foreign Affairs.* Washington, D.C., 1978.

Miller, James E. "Taking Off the Gloves: The United States and the Italian Elections of 1948," *Diplomatic History,* VII (Winter 1983), 35–55.

Miller, John C. *The Wolf by the Ears: Thomas Jefferson and Slavery.* New York, 1977.

Miller, Kerby A. "Class, Culture, and Immigrant Group Identity in the United States: The Case of Irish-American Ethnicity," in *Immigration Reconsidered,* ed. Virginia Yans-McLaughlin. New York, 1990, 96–129.

————. *Emigrants and Exiles: Ireland and the Irish Exodus to North America.* New York, 1985.

Miller, Stuart C. *"Benevolent Assimilation": The American Conquest of the Philippines, 1899–1903.* New Haven, 1982.

————. *The Unwelcome Immigrant: The American Image of the Chinese, 1785–1882.* Berkeley, 1969.

Miller, Warren E., and Donald E. Stokes. "Constituency Influence in Congress," *American Political Science Review*, LVII (March 1963), 45–56.

Millis, Walter. *The Martial Spirit: A Study of Our War with Spain*. New York, 1965.

Mills, C. Wright. *The Power Elite*. New York, 1956.

Mirak, Robert. "Armenian Emigration to the United States to 1915: Leaving the Old Country," *Journal of Armenian Studies*, I (No. 1, 1975), 5–42.

Montague, Ashley. *Man's Most Dangerous Myth: The Fallacy of Race*. 4th ed. New York, 1964.

Morris, Milton D. "Black Americans and the Foreign Policy Process: The Case of Africa," *Western Political Quarterly*, XXV (Sept. 1972), 451–63.

———. *Immigration—The Beleaguered Bureaucracy*. Washington, D.C., 1985.

Morris, Roger. *Uncertain Greatness: Henry Kissinger and American Foreign Policy*. New York, 1977.

Mower, A. Glenn, Jr. *Human Rights and American Foreign Policy: The Carter and Reagan Experiences*. Westport, Conn., 1985.

Mueller, John E. *War, Presidents and Public Opinion*. New York, 1973.

Muñoz, Carlos, Jr. *Youth, Identity, Power: The Chicano Movement*. London, 1989.

Munro, Dana G. *Intervention and Dollar Diplomacy in the Caribbean, 1900–1921*. Princeton, 1964.

Murphy, John A. "The Influence of America on Irish Nationalism," in *America and Ireland*, ed. David N. Doyle and Owen D. Edwards. Westport, Conn., 1980, 105–15.

Murphy, Paul L. "Sources and Nature of Intolerance in the 1920's," *Journal of American History*, LI (June 1964), 60–76.

———. *World War I and the Origin of Civil Liberties in the United States*. New York, 1979.

Murphy, Thomas P. *Pressures Upon Congress: Legislation by Lobby*. Woodbury, N.Y., 1973.

Murray, Robert K. *Red Scare: A Study of National Hysteria, 1919–1920*. New York, 1964.

Myers, Gustavus. *History of Bigotry in the United States*. New York, 1943.

Myrdal, Gunnar. *An American Dilemma: The Negro Problem and Modern Democracy*. New York, 1944.

———. "The Case Against Romantic Ethnicity," Dialogue Discussion Paper, Center for the Study of Democratic Institutions, May 13, 1974. Special Collections, University of California Library, Santa Barbara.

Naff, Alixa. "Arabs in America: A Historical Overview," in *Arabs in the New World*, ed. Sameer Y. Abraham and Nabeel Abraham. Detroit, 1983, 8–29.

Nagel, Joane. "The Ethnic Revolution: The Emergence of Ethnic Nationalism in Modern States," *Sociology and Social Research*, LXVIII (July 1984), 417–34.

Nagel, Paul C. *This Sacred Trust: American Nationality, 1798–1898*. New York, 1971.

Narayan, T. G. *Famine Over Bengal*. Calcutta, 1944.

Nash, Gary B. *Red, White, and Black: The Peoples of Early America*. Englewood Cliffs, N.J., 1974.

———. *Race, Class, and Politics*. Urbana, Ill., 1986.

Nash, Gary B., and Richard Weiss (eds.). *The Great Fear: Race in the Mind of America*. New York, 1970.

Nathan, James A., and James K. Oliver. *Foreign Policy Making and the American Political System*. 2nd ed. Boston, 1987.

Neale, R. G. *Great Britain and United States Expansion, 1898–1900*. East Lansing, Mich., 1966.

Nelson, Keith L. "The Black Horror on the Rhine: Race as a Factor in Post World War I Diplomacy," *Journal of Modern History*, XXXII (Dec. 1970), 606–27.

———. "The 'Warfare State': History of a Concept," *Pacific Historical Review*, XL (May 1971), 127–43.

Nelson, William H. (ed.). *Theory and Practice in American Politics*. Chicago, 1964.

Neu, Charles E. *An Uncertain Friendship: Theodore Roosevelt and Japan, 1906–1909*. Cambridge, Mass., 1967.

Nevins, Allan. *Hamilton Fish: The Inner History of the Grant Administration*. 2 vols. New York, 1936.

Newfarmer, Richard (ed.). *From Gunboats to Diplomacy: New U.S. Policies for Latin America*. Baltimore, 1984.

New York Times. Selected issues, 1940–91.

Nicolson, Harold. *Diaries and Letters*, ed. Nigel Nicolson. 3 vols. New York, 1966–68.

———. *Peacemaking, 1919*. London, 1933.

Ninkovich, Frank A. *The Diplomacy of Ideas: U.S. Foreign Policy and Cultural Relations, 1938–1950*. New York, 1981.

Noer, Thomas J. *Briton, Boer, and Yankee: The United States and South Africa, 1870–1914*. Kent, Ohio, 1978.

———. *Cold War and Black Liberation: The United States and White Rule in Africa, 1948–1968*. Columbia, Mo., 1985.

Norman, John. "Italo-American Opinion in the Ethiopian Crisis: A Study of Fascist Propaganda." Unpublished Ph.D. dissertation, Clark University, 1942.

Novak, Michael. *The Rise of the Unmeltable Ethnics: Politics and Culture in the Seventies*. New York, 1972.

Novik, Nimrod. *The United States and Israel: Domestic Determinants of a Changing U.S. Commitment*. Boulder, Colo., 1985.

Nzuwah, Mariyawanda, and William King. "Afro-Americans and U.S. Policy Toward Africa: An Overview," *Journal of Southern African Affairs*, II (April 1977), 235–44.

Obatala, J. K. "Black Consciousness and American Policy in Africa," in *Ethnicity in an International Context*, ed. Abdul Aziz Said and Luiz R. Simmons. New Brunswick, N.J., 1976, 64–75.

O'Brien, Lee. *American Jewish Organizations and Israel*. Washington, D.C., 1986.

O'Brien, Peter. "Continuity and Change in Germany's Treatment of Non-Germans," *International Migration Review*, XXII (Fall 1988), 109–34.

O'Connor, Richard. *The German-Americans: An Informal History*. Boston, 1968.

Odlozilik, Otakar, "The Czechs," in *Immigrants' Influence on Wilson's Peace Policies*, ed. Joseph O'Grady. Lexington, Ken., 1967, 204–23.

Offner, Arnold A. *American Appeasement: United States Foreign Policy and Germany, 1933–1938*. Cambridge, Mass., 1969.

Ogene, F. Chidozie. *Interest Groups and the Shaping of Foreign Policy: Four Case Studies of United States African Policy*. New York, 1983.

O'Grady, Joseph P. *How the Irish Became Americans*. New York, 1973.

———. *Irish Americans and Anglo-American Relations, 1880–1888*. New York, 1976.

O'Grady, Joseph P. (ed.). *The Immigrants' Influence on Wilson's Peace Policies*. Lexington, Ken., 1967.

Olney, Richard. "International Isolation of the United States," *Atlantic Monthly*, LXXXI (May 1898), 577–88.

Olorunsola, Victor A. "Interaction Between Africans and Black Americans," *Pan-African Journal*, II (Winter 1969), 64–68.

Olson, James S. *The Ethnic Dimension in American History.* New York, 1979.

Orbach, William W. *The American Movement to Aid Soviet Jews.* Amherst, Mass., 1979.

Orfalea, Gregory. *Before the Flames: A Quest for the History of Arab Americans.* Austin, Tex., 1988.

Organski, A. F. K. *The $36 Billion Bargain: Strategy and Politics in U.S. Assistance to Israel.* New York, 1990.

Ornstein, Norman J., and Shirley Elder. *Interest Groups, Lobbying and Policymaking.* Washington, 1978.

Orman, John. "The President and Interest Group Access," *Presidential Studies Quarterly,* XVIII (Fall 1988), 787–91.

Osborne, Thomas J. *"'Empire Can Wait': American Opposition to Hawaiian Annexation, 1893–1898.* Kent, Ohio, 1981.

Osgood, Robert E. *Ideals and Self-Interest in America's Foreign Relations: The Great Transformation of the Twentieth Century.* Chicago, 1953.

Ott, Thomas O. *The Haitian Revolution, 1789–1804.* Nashville, Tenn., 1973.

Parenti, Michael. "Ethnic Politics and the Persistence of Ethnic Identification," *American Political Science Review,* LXI (Sept. 1967), 717–26.

Park, Robert E. *Race and Culture.* Glencoe, Ill., 1950.

Paterson, Thomas G. "Presidential Foreign Policy, Public Opinion, and Congress: The Truman Years," *Diplomatic History,* III (Winter 1979), 1–18.

Paterson, Thomas G. (ed.). *Kennedy's Quest for Victory: American Foreign Policy, 1961–1963.* New York, 1989.

Pastor, Robert A., and Jorge G. Castañeda. *Limits to Friendship: The United States and Mexico.* New York, 1988.

Patterson, Orlando. *Ethnic Chauvinism: The Reactionary Impulse.* New York, 1977.

Payne, Richard J., and Eddie Ganaway. "The Influence of Black Americans on US Policy Toward Southern Africa," *African Affairs,* LXXIX (Oct. 1980), 585–98.

Pearce, George F. "Assessing Public Opinion: Editorial Comment and the Annexation of Hawaii—A Case Study," *Pacific Historical Review,* XLIII (Aug. 1974), 324–41.

Pelenski, Jaroslaw (ed.). *The American and European Revolutions, 1776–1848: Socio-Political and Ideological Aspects.* Iowa City, 1980.

Pérez, Louis A., Jr. *Cuba and the United States: Ties of Singular Intimacy.* Athens, Ga., 1990.

———. *Cuba Between Empires, 1878–1902.* Pittsburgh, 1983.

———. "Cuba Between Empires, 1898–1899," *Pacific Historical Review,* XLVIII (Nov. 1979), 473–500.

———. *Cuba under the Platt Amendment, 1902–1934.* Pittsburgh, 1986.

Perkins, Bradford. *Castlereagh and Adams: England and the United States, 1812–1823.* Berkeley, 1964.

———. *The First Rapprochement: England and the United States, 1795–1805.* Philadelphia, 1955.

———. *The Great Rapprochement: England and the United States, 1895–1914.* New York, 1968.

Perkins, Whitney T. *Constraint of Empire: The United States and Caribbean Interventions.* Westport, Conn., 1981.

Persons, Stow. "American Ethnicity in the Revolutionary Era," in *The American and European Revolutions, 1776–1848*, ed. Jaroslaw Pelenski. Iowa City, 1980, 38–53.

Peterson, Horace C., and Gilbert C. Fite. *Opponents of War, 1917–1918*. Madison, Wis., 1957.

Pierre, A. J. (ed.). *A Widening Atlantic? Domestic Change and Foreign Policy*. New York, 1986.

Pika, Joseph A. "Interest Groups and the White House under Roosevelt and Truman," *Political Science Quarterly*, CII (Winter 1987–88), 647–88.

Pitt, Leonard. "The Beginnings of Nativism in California," *Pacific Historical Review*, XXX (Feb. 1961), 23–38.

Plax, Martin. "On Group Behavior and the Ethnic Factor in Politics," *Ethnicity*, I (Oct. 1974), 295–316.

———. "On Studying Ethnicity," *Public Opinion Quarterly*, XXXVI (Spring 1972), 99–104.

———. "Towards a Redefinition of Ethnic Politics," *Ethnicity*, III (March 1976), 19–33.

Plesur, Milton. *America's Outward Thrust: Approaches to Foreign Affairs, 1865–1890*. DeKalb, Ill., 1971.

Pletcher, David M. *The Diplomacy of Annexation: Texas, Oregon, and the Mexican War*. Columbia, Mo., 1973.

———. "Manifest Destiny," in *Encyclopedia of American Foreign Policy*, ed. Alexander DeConde. 3 vols. New York, 1978, II, 526–34.

Plummer, Brenda G. "The Afro-American Response to the Occupation of Haiti, 1915–1934," *Phylon*, XLIII (Spring 1982), 125–43.

———. *Haiti and the Great Powers, 1902–1915*. Baton Rouge, La., 1988.

Pogue, Forrest C. *George C. Marshall: Statesman, 1945–1959*. New York, 1987.

Polenberg, Richard. *One Nation Indivisible: Class, Race and Ethnicity in the United States Since 1938*. New York, 1980.

Polk, William R. *The United States and the Arab World*. 3rd ed. Cambridge, Mass., 1975.

Pollock, David. *The Politics of Pressure: American Arms and Israeli Policy Since the Six Day War*. Westport, Conn., 1982.

Pomerance, Michla. "The United States and Self-Determination: Perspectives on the Wilsonian Conception," *American Journal of International Law*, LXX (Jan. 1976), 1–27.

Postal, Bernard, and Henry W. Levy. *And the Hills Shouted for Joy: The Day Israel Was Born*. New York, 1973.

Postiglione, Gerard A. *Ethnicity and American Social Theory: Toward a Critical Pluralism*. Lanham, Md., 1983.

Potter, David M. "The Historian's Use of Nationalism and Vice Versa," *American Historical Review*, LXVII (July 1962), 924–50.

Potter, George W. *To the Golden Door: The Story of the Irish in Ireland and America*. Boston, 1960.

Powell, James H. "The Concept of Cultural Pluralism in American Social Thought, 1915–1965." Unpublished Ph.D. dissertation, Notre Dame University, 1971.

Power, Jonathan. "The Great Debate on Illegal Immigration—Europe and USA Compared," *Journal of International Affairs*, XXXIII (Fall–Winter 1979), 239–48.

Poyo, Gerald E. *"With All and for the Good of All": The Emergence of Popular Nationalism in the Cuban Communities of the United States, 1848–1898*. Durham, N.C., 1989.

Pratt, Julius W. *Expansionists of 1898: The Acquistion of Hawaii and the Spanish Islands*. Baltimore, 1936.

Pressly, Thomas J. *Americans Interpret Their Civil War*. New York, 1962.

Price, Glenn W. *Origins of the War with Mexico: The Polk-Stockton Intrigue*. Austin, Tex., 1967.

Proudfoot, Malcolm J. *European Refugees, 1939–1952: A Study in Forced Population Movement*. Evanston, Ill., 1956.

Puddington, Arch. "Jesse Jackson, the Blacks and American Foreign Policy," *Commentary*, LXXVII (April 1984), 19–27.

Pusey, Merlo J. *Charles Evans Hughes*. 2 vols. New York, 1951.

Quandt, William B. *Decade of Decisions: American Policy Toward the Arab-Israeli Conflict, 1967–1976*. Berkeley, 1977.

———. "Domestic Influences on U.S. Foreign Policy: The View from Washington," in *Middle East*, ed. Willard A. Beling. Albany, N.Y., 1973, 263–85.

Quester, George H. *The Falklands and the Malvinas: Strategy and Arms Control*. Los Angeles, 1984.

Quinones, Juan Gómez. *Chicano Politics: Reality and Promise 1940–1990*. Albuquerque, 1990.

Quirk, Robert E. *An Affair of Honor: Woodrow Wilson and the Occupation of Veracruz*. Lexington, Ken., 1962.

Ra'anan, Uri (ed.). *Ethnic Resurgence in Modern Democratic States: A Multidisciplinary Approach to Human Resources and Conflict*. New York, 1980.

Raat, William Dirk. *Revoltosos: Mexico's Rebels in the United States, 1903–1923*. College Station, Tex., 1981.

Radkau, Joachim. *Die deutsche Emigration in den USA: Ihr Einfluss auf die Amerikanische Europapolitik, 1933–1945*. Düsseldorf, 1971.

Reagan, Ronald. *An American Life: The Autobiography*. New York, 1990.

Rees, David. *Korea: The Limited War*. New York, 1964.

Reich, Bernard. *Quest for Peace: United States–Israel Relations and the Arab-Israeli Conflict*. New Brunswick, N.J., 1977.

———. *The United States and Israel: Influence in the Special Relationship*. New York, 1984.

Reid, John T. *Spanish American Images of the United States, 1790–1960*. Gainesville, Fla., 1977.

Reimann, Elisabeth. *Las Malvinas: Traición Made in USA*. Mexico City, 1983.

Reimers, David M. *Still the Golden Door: The Third World Comes to America*. New York, 1985.

———. "An Unintended Reform: The 1965 Immigration Act and Third World Immigration to the United States," *Journal of American Ethnic History*, III (Fall 1983), 9–28.

Remak, Joachim. " 'Friends of the New Germany': The Bund and German-American Relations," *Journal of Modern History*, XXIX (March 1957), 38–41.

Reuter, William C. "Anglophobia in American Politics, 1865–1900." Unpublished Ph.D. dissertation, University of California, Berkeley, 1966.

Rex, John, and David Mason (eds.). *Theories of Race and Ethnic Relations*. Cambridge, Eng., 1986.

Reynolds, David. "Roosevelt, Churchill, and the Wartime Anglo-American Alliance, 1939–1945: Towards a New Synthesis," in *The "Special Relationship,"* ed. William R. Louis and Hedley Bull, Oxford, 1986, 17–41.

Ricard, Serge. "World War One and the Rooseveltian Gospel of Undiluted Americanism," in *Hyphenated Diplomacy*, ed. Hélène Christol and Serge Ricard. Aix-en-Provence, 1985, 19–30.

Richardson, E. Allen. *Strangers in This Land: Pluralism and the Response to Diversity in the United States.* New York, 1988.

Richmond, A. "Ethnic Nationalism and Postindustrialism," *Ethnic and Racial Studies,* VII (Jan. 1984), 4–18.

Ridder, Herman. *Hyphenations.* New York, 1915.

Rigby, Barry. "The Origins of American Expansion in Hawaii and Samoa, 1865–1900," *International History Review,* X (May 1988), 221–37.

Riggs, Fred W. *Pressures on Congress: A Study of the Repeal of Chinese Exclusion.* New York, 1950.

Ringer, Benjamin B. *"We the People" and Others: Duality and America's Treatment of Its Racial Minorities.* New York, 1983.

Ringer, Benjamin B., and Elinor R. Lawless. *Race, Ethnicity and Society.* New York, 1989.

Rischin, Moses. *"Our Own Kind": Voting by Race, Creed, or National Origin.* Santa Barbara, 1960.

Ritcheson, Charles S. *Aftermath of Revolution: British Policy Toward the United States, 1783–1795.* Dallas, 1969.

Robinson, Cedric J. "Fascism and the Intersections of Capitalism, Racialism, and Historical Consciousness," *Humanities in Society,* VI (Fall 1983), 325–49.

Roche, John P. "Immigration and Nationality: A Historical Overview of United States Policy," in *Ethnic Resurgence,* ed. Uri Ra'anan. New York, 1980, 30–76.

———. *The Quest for the Dream: The Development of Civil Rights and Human Relations in Modern America.* New York, 1963.

Roehm, John F., Jr. "Congressional Participation in U.S. Middle East Policy, October 1973–1976: Congressional Activism vs. Policy Coherence," in *Congress, the Presidency and American Foreign Policy,* ed. John Spanier and Joseph Nogee. New York, 1981, 22–43.

Roett, Riordan. "La Guerra del Atlántico Sur: Una Perspectiva de Estados Unidos," *América Latina y la Guerra del Atlántico Sur,* comp. Roberto Russell. Buenos Aires, 1984, 137–48.

Rogers, Ben F. "William E. B. Du Bois, Marcus Garvey, and Pan-Africa," *Journal of Negro History,* XL (April 1955), 154–65.

Rogers, William D. "The 'Unspecial Relationship' in Latin America," in *The "Special Relationship,"* ed. William R. Louis and Hedley Bull. Oxford, 1986, 341–53.

Rogin, Michael P. *Fathers and Children: Andrew Jackson and the Subjugation of the American Indian.* New York, 1975.

Roosevelt, Theodore. *The Letters of Theodore Roosevelt,* ed. Elting E. Morison. 8 vols. Cambridge, Mass., 1951–54.

Rose, Peter I. *The Subject Is Race.* New York, 1968.

———. *They and We: Racial and Ethnic Relations in the United States.* 3rd ed. New York, 1981.

Rosenau, James N. (ed.). *Domestic Sources of Foreign Policy.* New York, 1967.

———. *Public Opinion and Foreign Policy: An Operational Formula.* New York, 1961.

———. *Race in International Relations.* Denver, 1969–70.

Rosenbaum, Robert J. *Mexicano Resistance in the Southwest: "The Sacred Right of Self-Preservation."* Austin, Tex., 1981.

Rosenberg, Emily S. *Spreading the American Dream: Economic and Cultural Expansion 1890–1945.* New York, 1982.

Rosenfeld, Steven S. "Dateline Washington: Anti-Semitism and U.S. Foreign Policy," *Foreign Policy*, XLVII (Summer 1982), 172–83.

———. "Pluralism and Policy," *Foreign Affairs*, LII (Jan. 1974), 263–72.

Rotberg, Robert I. "The Reagan Era in Africa," in *Reagan and the World*, ed. David E. Kyvig. Westport, Conn., 119–37.

Rothermund, Dietmar. "The German Problem of Colonial Pennsylvania," *Pennsylvania Magazine of History and Biography*, LXXXIV (Jan. 1960), 3–21.

Rothschild, Joseph. *Ethnopolitics: A Conceptual Framework*. New York, 1981.

Roucek, Joseph S., and Bernard Eisenberg (eds.). *America's Ethnic Politics*. Westport, Conn., 1982.

———. "Foreign Politics and Our Minority Groups," *Phylon*, II (No. 1, 1941), 44–56.

Royster, Charles. *A Revolutionary People at War: The Continental Army and the American Character, 1775–1783*. Chapel Hill, 1979.

Rubenberg, Cheryl A. *Israel and the American National Interest: A Critical Examination*. Champaign, Ill., 1986.

———. "U.S. Policy Toward the Palestinians: A Twenty Year Assessment," *Arab Studies Quarterly*, X (Winter 1988), 1–43.

Rubinstein, Alvin Z., and Donald E. Smith. *Anti-Americanism in the Third World: Implications for U.S. Foreign Policy*. New York, 1985.

Russ, William A., Jr. *The Hawaiian Republic (1894–98) and Its Struggle to Win Annexation*. Selingsgrove, Pa., 1961.

———. *The Hawaiian Revolution (1893–1894)*. Selingsgrove, Pa., 1959.

Russell, Roberto (comp.). *América Latina y la Guerra del Atlántico Sur*. Buenos Aires, 1984.

Russet, Bruce M. *Community and Contention: Britain and America in the Twentieth Century*. Cambridge, Mass., 1963.

Ryan, Henry B. *The Vision of Anglo-America: The US-UK Alliance and the Emerging Cold War, 1943–1946*. Cambridge, Eng., 1987.

Rystand, Göran. *Ambiguous Imperialism: American Foreign Policy and Domestic Politics at the Turn of the Century*. Stockholm, 1975.

Rystad, Göran (ed.). *Congress and American Foreign Policy*. Lund, Sweden, 1981.

———. "Congress and the Ethnic Lobbies: The Case of the 1974 Arms Embargo on Turkey," in *Hyphenated Diplomacy*, ed. Hélène Christol and Serge Ricard. Aix-en-Provence, 1985, 89–111.

Safran, Nadav. *Israel: The Embattled Ally*. Cambridge, Mass., 1978.

Said, Abdul Aziz (ed.). *Ethnicity and U.S. Foreign Policy*. New York, 1977.

———. "A Redefinition of National Interest, Ethnic Consciousness, and U.S. Foreign Policy," in *Ethnicity and U.S. Foreign Policy*, ed. Abdul Aziz Said. New York, 1977, 1–15.

Said, Abdul Aziz, and Luiz R. Simmons (eds.). *Ethnicity in an International Context*. New Brunswick, N.J., 1976.

Said, Edward. "Spurious Scholarship and the Palestinian Question," *Race & Class*, XXIX (Winter 1988), 23–39.

Sanders, Ronald. *The High Walls of Jerusalem: A History of the Balfour Declaration and the Birth of the British Mandate for Palestine*. New York, 1983.

Santa Barbara *News-Press*. Selected issues, 1983–91.

Sarna, Jonathan D. "From Immigrants to Ethnics: Toward a New Theory of Ethnicization," *Ethnicity*, V (Dec. 1978), 370–78.

Satz, Ronald N. *American Indian Policy in the Jacksonian Era*. Lincoln, Neb., 1975.

Savelle, Max. "Nationalism and Other Loyalties in the American Revolution," *American Historical Review*, LXVII (July 1962), 901–23.

Saveth, Edward N. *American Historians and European Immigrants, 1875–1925*. New York, 1948.

Sawada, Mitziko. "Culprits and Gentlemen: Meiji Japan's Restrictions of Emigrants to the United States, 1891–1909," *Pacific Historical Review*, LX (Aug. 1991), 339–59.

Schatzberg, Michael G. "Military Intervention and the Myth of Collective Security: The Case of Zaire," *Journal of Modern African Studies*, XXVII (June 1989), 315–40.

Schirmer, Daniel B. *Republic or Empire: American Resistance to the Philippine War*. Cambridge, Mass., 1972.

Schlesinger, Arthur M., Jr. *The Disuniting of America: Reflections on a Multicultural Society*. Knoxville, Tenn., 1991.

———. "Foreign Policy and the American Character," *Foreign Affairs*, LXII (Fall 1983), 1–16.

Schmidt, Hans. *The United States Occupation of Haiti, 1915–1934*. New Brunswick, N.J., 1971.

Schmitt, Karl M. *Mexico and the United States, 1821–1973: Conflict and Coexistence*. New York, 1974.

Schneider, William, Michael Berman, and Mark Schultz. "Bloc Voting Reconsidered: Is There a Jewish Vote?" *Ethnicity*, I (Dec. 1974), 345–92.

Schonberger, Howard. "The Japan Lobby in American Diplomacy, 1947–1952," *Pacific Historical Review*, XLVI (Aug. 1977), 327–59.

Schrag, Peter. *The Decline of the WASP*. New York, 1971.

Schroeder, John H. *Mr. Polk's War: American Opposition and Dissent, 1846–1848*. Madison, Wis., 1973.

Schulzinger, Robert D. *The Making of the Diplomatic Mind: The Training, Outlook, and Style of United States Foreign Service Officers, 1908–1931*. Middletown, Conn., 1975.

———. *The Wise Men of Foreign Affairs: The History of the Council on Foreign Relations*. New York, 1984.

Scott, William R. "Black Nationalism and the Italo-Ethiopian Conflict, 1934–1936," *Journal of Negro History*, LXIII (April 1978), 118–34.

Seabury, Paul. "Ideology and Foreign Policy," in *Encyclopedia of American Foreign Policy*, ed. Alexander DeConde. 3 vols. New York, 1978, II, 398–408.

———. "Racial Problems and American Foreign Policy," in *Racial Influences on American Foreign Policy*, ed. George W. Shepherd, Jr. New York, 1970, 60–78.

Seller, Maxine. *To Seek America: A History of Ethnic Life in the United States*. New York, 1977.

Shadid, Mohammed K. *The United States and the Palestinians*. London, 1981.

Shafer, D. Michael (ed.). *The Legacy: The Vietnam War in the American Imagination*. Boston, 1990.

Shambaugh, David L. "Anti-Americanism in China," in *Anti-Americanism: Origins and Context*, ed. Thomas P. Thornton. *Annals* of the American Academy of Political and Social Science, CDXCVII (May 1988), 141–56.

Sheehan, Neil. *A Bright Shining Lie: John Paul Vann and America in Vietnam*. New York, 1988.

Shepherd, George W., Jr. *Anti-Apartheid: Transnational Conflict and Western Policy in the Liberation of South Africa*. Westport, Conn., 1977.

————. "The Study of Race in American Foreign Policy and International Relations," *Studies in Race and Nations*, I (No. 4, 1969–70), 1–28.

Shepherd, George W., Jr. (ed.). *Racial Influences on American Foreign Policy.* New York, 1970.

Shepperson, George. "Notes on Negro American Influences on the Emergence of African Nationalism," *Journal of African History,* I (No. 2, 1960), 299–312.

Silbey, Joel H., Allan G. Bogue, and William H. Flanigan. *The History of American Electoral Behavior.* Princeton, 1978.

Silverberg, Robert. *If I Forget Thee O Jerusalem: American Jews and the State of Israel.* New York, 1970.

Simcox, David (ed.). *U.S. Immigration in the 1980s: Reappraisal and Reform.* Boulder, Colo., 1988.

Sinkler, George. *The Racial Attitudes of American Presidents: From Abraham Lincoln to Theodore Roosevelt.* Garden City, N.Y., 1971.

Skinner, Elliott P. "Ethnicity and Race as Factors in the Formation of United States Foreign Policy," in *American Character and Foreign Policy*, ed. Michael P. Hamilton. Grand Rapids, Mich., 1986, 87–136.

Slotkin, Richard. *Regeneration Through Violence: The Mythology of the American Frontier, 1600–1860.* Middletown, Conn., 1973.

Small, Melvin. *Johnson, Nixon and the Doves.* New Brunswick, N.J., 1988.

————. "Public Opinion," in *Encyclopedia of American Foreign Policy,* ed. Alexander DeConde. 3 vols. New York, 1978, III, 844–55.

———— (ed.). *Public Opinion and Historians: Interdisciplinary Perspectives.* Detroit, 1970.

Smertenko, Johan J. "The Emerging Hyphen," *Harper's Magazine,* CCIII (Aug. 1951), 63–71.

Smith, Anthony D. *The Ethnic Origins of Nations.* Oxford, 1987.

————. *The Ethnic Revival.* London, 1981.

Smith, Arthur L., Jr. *The Deutschtum of Nazi Germany and the United States.* The Hague, 1965.

Smith Geoffrey S. "Nativism," in *Encyclopedia of American Foreign Policy,* ed. Alexander DeConde. 3 vols. New York, 1978, II, 651–67.

————. *To Save a Nation: American Countersubversives, the New Deal, and the Coming of World War II.* New York, 1973.

Smith, James M. *Freedom's Fetters: The Alien and Sedition Laws and American Civil Liberties.* Ithaca, N.Y., 1956.

Smith, Justin H. *The War with Mexico.* 2 vols. New York, 1919.

Smith, Robert F. *The United States and Revolutionary Nationalism in Mexico, 1916–1932.* Chicago, 1972.

Snetsinger, John. "Ethnicity and Foreign Policy," in *Encyclopedia of American Foreign Policy,* ed. Alexander DeConde. 3 vols. New York, 1978, I, 322–29.

————. *Truman, the Jewish Vote, and the Creation of Israel.* Stanford, 1974.

Snowman, Daniel. *Kissing Cousins: An Interpretation of British and American Culture, 1945–1975.* London, 1977.

Solomon, Barbara M. *Ancestors and Immigrants: A Changing New England Tradition.* Cambridge, Mass., 1956.

Sowell, Thomas. *The Economics and Politics of Race: An International Perspective.* New York, 1983.

————. *Ethnic America: A History.* New York, 1981.

Sowell, Thomas (ed.). *Essays and Data on American Ethnic Groups.* New York, 1978.

Spanier, John, and Joseph Nogee (eds.). *Congress, the Presidency and American Foreign Policy.* New York, 1981.

Spiegel, Steven L. "Carter and Israel," *Commentary,* LXIV (July 1977), 35–40.

———. "Israel as a Strategic Asset," *Commentary,* LXXV (June 1983), 51–55.

———. *The Other Arab-Israeli Conflict: Making America's Middle East Policy, from Truman to Reagan.* Chicago, 1985.

Sprout, Harold H. "Pressure Groups and Foreign Policies," *Annals* of the American Academy of Political and Social Science, CLXXIX (May 1935), 114–23.

Staniland, Martin. *American Intellectuals and African Nationalists, 1955–1970.* New Haven, 1991.

Stead, William T. *The Americanization of the World; or, the Trend of the Twentieth Century.* London, 1902.

Steele, Richard W. "The War on Intolerance: The Reformulation of American Nationalism, 1939–1941," *Journal of American Ethnic History,* IX (Fall 1989), 9–35.

Stein, Howard F., and Robert F. Hill. *The Ethnic Imperative: Examining the New White Ethnic Movement.* University Park, Pa., 1977.

Stein, Judith. *The World of Marcus Garvey: Race and Class in Modern Society.* Baton Rouge, La., 1986.

Steinberg, Stephen. *The Ethnic Myth: Race, Ethnicity, and Class in America.* New York, 1981.

Stephan, John J. *Hawaii Under the Rising Sun: Japan's Plans for Conquest After Pearl Harbor.* Honolulu, 1984.

Stern, Paula. *Water's Edge: Domestic Politics and the Making of American Foreign Policy.* Westport, Conn., 1979.

Stevens, Sylvester K. *American Expansion in Hawaii 1842–1898.* Harrisburg, Pa., 1945.

Stimson, Henry L., and McGeorge Bundy. *On Active Service in Peace and War.* New York, 1948.

Stinchcombe, William C. *The American Revolution and the French Alliance.* Syracuse, N.Y., 1969.

Stivers, William. *America's Confrontation with Revolutionary Change in the Middle East, 1948–83.* Hampshire, Eng., 1986.

Stolarik, M. Mark. "To Hyphenate or Not to Hyphenate," *New Dimensions,* Balch Institute for Ethnic Studies, Philadelphia (Fall 1988), 4.

Stookey, Robert W. *America and the Arab States: An Uneasy Encounter.* New York, 1975.

Stourzh, Gerald. *Benjamin Franklin and American Foreign Policy.* Chicago, 1954.

Streit, Clarence K. *Union Now with Britain.* New York, 1941.

Strout, Cushing. *The American Image of the Old World.* New York, 1963.

Stuart, Reginald C. *United States Expansionism and British North America, 1775–1871.* Chapel Hill, 1988.

Stuckey, Sterling. *Slave Culture: Nationalist Theory and the Foundations of Black America.* New York, 1987.

Stueck, William W., Jr. "The Korean War as International History," *Diplomatic History,* X (Fall 1986), 191–309.

———. *The Road to Confrontation: American Policy toward China and Korea, 1947–1950.* Chapel Hill, 1981.

Suleiman, Michael W. "The Effect of American Perceptions of Arabs on Middle East Issues," in *Split Vision,* ed. Edmund Ghareeb. Washington, D.C., 1983, 337–44.

Suhrke, Astri, and Lela G. Noble (eds.). *Ethnic Conflict in International Relations.* New York, 1977.

Sundquist, Eric J. "The Japanese-American Internment: A Reappraisal," *American Scholar,* LVII (Autumn 1988), 529–47.

Takaki, Ronald T. *Iron Cages: Race and Culture in Nineteenth Century America.* New York, 1979.

———. *Strangers from a Different Shore: A History of Asian Americans.* Boston, 1989.

Tansill, Charles C. *America and the Fight for Irish Freedom, 1866–1922.* New York, 1957.

Tate, Merze. *Hawaii: Reciprocity or Annexation.* East Lansing, Mich., 1968.

———. *The United States and the Hawaiian Kingdom.* New Haven, 1965.

Taylor, Joseph H. "The Restriction of European Immigration and the Concept of Race," *South Atlantic Quarterly,* L (Jan. 1951), 25–37.

Taylor, Philip A. M. *The Distant Magnet: European Immigration to the U.S.A.* London, 1971.

Teitelbaum, Michael S. *Latin Migration North: The Problem for U.S. Foreign Policy.* New York, 1985.

———. "Right Versus Right: Immigration and Refugee Policy in the United States," *Foreign Affairs,* LIX (Fall 1980), 29–59.

tenBroek, Jacobus, Edward N. Barnhart, and Floyd W. Matson. *Prejudice, War and the Constitution.* Berkeley, 1954.

Teslik, Kennan L. *Congress, the Executive Branch, and Special Interests: The American Response to the Arab Boycott.* Westport, Conn., 1982.

Thayer, William R. *Democracy: Discipline: Peace.* Boston, 1919.

Thistlethwaite, Frank. *The Anglo-American Connection in the Early Nineteenth Century.* Philadelphia, 1959.

Thorne, Christopher. *Allies of a Kind: The United States, Britain, and the War against Japan, 1941–1945.* London, 1978.

———. *Border Crossings: Studies in International History.* Oxford, 1988.

———. *The Issue of War: States, Societies, and the Far Eastern Conflict of 1941–1945.* London, 1985.

———. *The Limits of Foreign Policy: The West, the League and the Far Eastern Crisis of 1931–1933.* New York, 1973.

———. "Racial Aspects of the Far Eastern War of 1941–1945," *Proceedings of the British Academy,* LXVI (1980), 329–77.

Tillman, Seth. *Anglo-American Relations at the Paris Peace Conference, 1919.* Princeton, 1961.

Tingley, Donald F. "The Rise of Racialistic Thinking in the United States in the Nineteenth Century." Unpublished Ph.D. dissertation, University of Illinois, 1952.

Tivnan, Edward. *The Lobby: Jewish Political Power and American Foreign Policy.* New York, 1987.

To Secure These Rights: The Report of the President's Committee on Civil Rights. Washington, D.C., 1947.

Tocqueville, Alexis de. *Democracy in America.* Trans. George Lawrence. New York, 1966.

Tompkins, E. Berkeley. *Anti-Imperialism in the United States: The Great Debate, 1890–1920.* Philadelphia, 1970.

Trani, Eugene P. *The Treaty of Portsmouth: An Adventure in American Diplomacy.* Lexington, Ken., 1969.

Trask, David F. *The War with Spain in 1898.* New York, 1981.

Trask, Roger R. *The United States Response to Turkish Nationalism and Reform, 1914–1939.* Minneapolis, 1971.

Trefousse, Hans L. (ed.). *Germany and America: Essays on Problems of International Relations and Immigration.* New York, 1980.

Trice, Robert H. "Congress and the Arab-Israeli Conflict: Support for Israel in the U.S. Senate, 1970–1973," *Political Science Quarterly,* XCII (Fall 1977), 443–63.

———. *Interest Groups and the Foreign Policy Process: U.S. Policy in the Middle East.* Beverly Hills, Calif., 1977.

Trommler, Frank, and Joseph McVeigh (eds.). *America and the Germans: An Assessment of a Three-Hundred-Year History.* Vol. I. *Immigration, Language, Ethnicity.* Philadelphia, 1985.

Truman, Harry S. *Public Papers of the Presidents of the United States, Harry S Truman.* 8 vols. Washington, D.C., 1961–66.

Truman, Margaret. *Harry S. Truman.* New York, 1973.

Tsai, Shih-shan Henry. *China and the Overseas Chinese in the United States, 1868–1911.* Fayetteville, Ark., 1983.

———. *The Chinese Experience in America.* Bloomington, Ind., 1986.

———. "Chinese Immigration through Communist Eyes: An Introduction to the Historiography," *Pacific Historical Review,* XLIII (Aug. 1974), 395–408.

———. "Reaction to Exclusion: The Boycott of 1905 and Chinese National Awakening," *Historian,* XXXIX (Nov. 1976), 95–110.

Tucker, Nancy B. *Patterns in the Dust: Chinese-American Relations and the Recognition Controversy, 1949–50.* New York, 1983.

Tucker, Robert W. "Reagan's Foreign Policy," *Foreign Affairs,* LXVIII (No. 1, 1989), 1–27.

Tulchin, Joseph S. *Argentina and the United States: A Conflicted Relationship.* Boston, 1990.

Tumulty, Joseph P. *Woodrow Wilson as I Know Him.* Garden City, N.Y., 1921.

Turner, Arthur C. *The Unique Partnership: Britain and the United States.* New York, 1971.

Turner, Frederick C. "Anti-Americanism in Mexico, 1910–1913," *Hispanic American Historical Review,* LVII (Nov. 1967), 502–18.

Turner, Frederick Jackson. *The Frontier in American History.* New York, 1920.

Tyrell, Ian. "American Exceptionalism in an Age of International History," *American Historical Review,* XCI (Oct. 1991), 1031–55.

U.S. Department of State. *Foreign Relations of the United States, 1903–1904.* Washington, D.C., 1905.

———. *Foreign Relations of the United States: The Conference of Berlin 1945.* 2 vols. Washington, D.C., 1960.

———. *Foreign Relations of the United States: The Conferences at Cairo and Tehran.* Washington, D.C., 1961.

———. *Foreign Relations of the United States: Diplomatic Papers 1945: The Near East and Africa.* 9 vols. Washington, D.C., 1969.

U.S. President. *Weekly Compilation of Presidential Documents.* Washington, D.C., XXVII, nos. 36–37, Sept. 1991.

U.S. Select Commission on Immigration and Refugee Policy. *U.S. Immigration Policy and the National Interest: Final Report.* Washington, D.C., March 1, 1981.

Unterberger, Betty M. "National Self-Determination," in *Encyclopedia of American Foreign Policy,* ed. Alexander DeConde. 3 vols. New York, 1978, II, 635–50.

———. *The United States, Revolutionary Russia, and the Rise of Czechoslovakia.* Chapel Hill, 1989.

Urofsky, Melvin I. *American Zionism From Herzl to the Holocaust.* Garden City, N.Y., 1975.

————. *We Are One! American Jewry and Israel.* Garden City, N.Y., 1978.

Van Horne, Winston A. (ed.). *Ethnicity and Public Policy.* Madison, Wis., 1982.

Van Horne, Winston A., and Thomas V. Tonnesen (eds.). *Ethnicity and War.* Madison, Wis., 1984.

Varg, Paul A. *Missionaries, Chinese, and Diplomats: The American Protestant Missionary Movement in China, 1890–1952.* Princeton, 1958.

Vásquez, Carlos, and Manuel García y Griego (eds.). *Mexican–U.S. Relations: Conflict and Consequence.* Los Angeles, 1983.

Vecoli, Rudolph J. "European Americans: From Immigrants to Ethnics," *International Migration Review,* VI (Winter 1972), 403–34.

————. "Return to the Melting Pot: Ethnicity in the United States in the Eighties," *Journal of American Ethnic History,* V (Fall 1985), 7–20.

Venkataramani, M. S. *Bengal Famine of 1943: The American Response.* Delhi, 1973.

Venkataramani, M. S., and B. K. Shrivastava. *Quit India: The American Response to the 1942 Struggle.* New Delhi, 1979.

Vieyra, Ferrer. *Las islas Malvinas y el derecho internacional.* Buenos Aires, 1984.

Villareal, Robert E., and Philip Kelly. "Mexican-Americans as Participants in U.S.–Mexican Relations," *International Studies Notes,* IX (Winter 1982), 1–6.

Vinson, John C. *The Parchment Peace: The United States Senate and the Washington Conference, 1921–1922.* Athens, Ga., 1955.

Voss, Carl H., and David A. Rausch. "American Christians and Israel, 1948–1988," *American Jewish Archives,* XL (April 1988), 41–81.

Waltz, Kenneth N. *Foreign Policy and Democratic Politics: The American and British Experience.* Boston, 1967.

Walworth, Arthur. *America's Moment: 1918. American Diplomacy and the End of World War I.* New York, 1977.

————. *Wilson and His Peacemakers: American Diplomacy at the Paris Peace Conference, 1919.* New York, 1986.

Walzer, Michael, et al. *The Politics of Ethnicity.* Cambridge, Mass., 1982.

Wandycz, Piotr S. *Soviet-Polish Relations, 1917–1921.* Cambridge, Mass., 1969.

————. *The United States and Poland.* Cambridge, Mass., 1980.

"War Over Foreign Policy: Reagan's Aides at War," *Newsweek,* XCIX (June 7, 1982), 29–30.

Ward, Alan J. "Immigrant Minority 'Diplomacy': American Jews and Russia 1901–1912," *Bulletin of the British Association for American Studies,* New Series, IX (Dec. 1964), 7–23.

————. *Ireland and Anglo-American Relations 1899–1921.* London, 1969.

Warner, Donald F. *The Idea of Continental Union: Agitation for the Annexation of Canada to the United States, 1849–1893.* Lexington, Ken., 1960.

Warner, Geoffrey. "The Anglo-American Special Relationship," *Diplomatic History,* XIII (Fall 1989), 479–99.

Washington, George. *The Writings of George Washington . . . 1745–1799,* ed. John C. Fitzpatrick. 39 vols. Washington, D.C., 1931–44.

Watanabe, Paul Y. *Ethnic Groups, Congress, and Foreign Policy: The Politics of the Turkish Arms Embargo.* Westport, Conn., 1984.

Waters, Mary C. *Ethnic Options: Choosing Identities in America.* Berkeley, 1990.

Watt, D. Cameron. "Demythologizing the Eisenhower Era," in *The "Special Relationship,"* ed. William R. Louis and Hedley Bull. Oxford, 1986, 65–85.

———. *Succeeding John Bull: America in Britain's Place.* Cambridge, Eng., 1984.

Watts, Stephen. *The Republic Reborn: War and the Making of Liberal America, 1790–1820.* Baltimore, 1989.

Weaver, Glenn. "Benjamin Franklin and the Pennsylvania Germans," *William and Mary Quarterly,* 3rd Series, XIV (Oct. 1957), 536–59.

Weber, David J. (ed.). *Foreigners in Their Native Land: Historical Roots of the Mexican Americans.* Albuquerque, 1973.

Weed, Perry L. *The White Ethnic Movement and Ethnic Politics.* New York, 1973.

Weil, Martin. "Can the Blacks Do for Africans What the Jews Did for Israel?" *Foreign Policy,* XIV (Summer 1974), 109–30.

———. *A Pretty Good Club: The Founding Fathers of the U.S. Foreign Service.* New York, 1978.

Weinberg, Albert K. *Manifest Destiny: A Study of Nationalist Expansionism in American History.* Baltimore, 1935.

Weinberg, Gerhard L. "Hitler's Image of the United States," *American Historical Review,* LXIX (July 1964), 1006–21.

Weinberger, Caspar W. *Fighting for Peace: Seven Critical Years in the Pentagon.* New York, 1990.

Weintraub, Sidney, and Stanley R. Ross. *The Illegal Alien from Mexico: Policy Choices for an Intractable Issue.* Austin, Tex., 1980.

Weisbord, Robert G. "Black America and the Italian-Ethiopian Crisis: An Episode in Pan Negroism," *The Historian,* XXXIV (Feb. 1972), 230–41.

———. *Ebony Kinship: Africa, Africans, and the Afro-American.* Westport, Conn., 1973.

Weissman, Stephen R. *American Foreign Policy in the Congo, 1960–1964.* New York, 1974.

Welch, Richard E., Jr. "American Atrocities in the Philippines: The Indictment and the Response," *Pacific Historical Review,* XL (May 1974), 233–53.

———. *Response to Imperialism: The United States and the Philippine-American War, 1899–1902.* Chapel Hill, 1978.

Wesley, Charles H. "The Struggle for the Recognition of Haiti and Liberia as Independent Republics," *Journal of Negro History,* II (Oct. 1917), 369–83.

Westerfield, H. Bradford. *Foreign Policy and Party Politics: Pearl Harbor to Korea.* New Haven, 1955.

Westin, Rubin F. *Racism in U.S. Imperialism: The Influence of Racial Assumptions on American Foreign Policy, 1893–1946.* Columbia, S.C., 1972.

White, Naomi R. "Ethnicity, Culture and Cultural Pluralism," *Ethnic and Racial Studies,* I (April 1978), 139–53.

White, Walter. *A Rising Wind.* New York, 1945.

Wilkins, Roger. "What Africa Means to Blacks," *Foreign Policy,* XIV (Summer 1974), 130–42.

Wilkinson, Rupert. *The Pursuit of American Character.* New York, 1988.

Williams, William A. *The Tragedy of American Diplomacy.* Rev. ed. New York, 1988.

Wilson, Evan M. *Decision on Palestine: How the U.S. Came to Recognize Israel.* Stanford, 1979.

Wilson, William J. *The Declining Significance of Race: Blacks and Changing American Institutions.* 2nd ed. Chicago, 1980.

Wilson, Woodrow. *The Papers of Woodrow Wilson,* ed. Arthur S. Link. 59 vols. Princeton, 1966– .

Wittke, Carl. F. *Refugees of Revolution: The German Forty-Eighters in America*. Philadelphia, 1952.

———. *We Who Built America: The Saga of the Immigrant*. Rev. ed. Cleveland, 1964.

Wolfinger, Raymond E. "The Development and Persistence of Ethnic Voting," *American Political Science Review*, LIX (Dec. 1965), 896–908.

Wolgemuth, Kathleen L. "Woodrow Wilson and Federal Segregation," *Journal of Negro History*, XLIV (April 1959), 158–73.

Wood, Gordon S. *Representation in the American Revolution*. Charlottesville, Va., 1969.

Woodham-Smith, Cecil B. *The Great Hunger: Ireland 1845–1849*. New York, 1962.

Woods, Randall B. *A Changing of the Guard: Anglo-American Relations, 1941–1946*. Chapel Hill, 1990.

Woodward, C. Vann. *The Strange Career of Jim Crow*. 2nd ed. New York, 1966.

Wyman, David S. *The Abandonment of the Jews: America and the Holocaust, 1941–1945*. New York, 1984.

———. *Paper Walls: America and the Refugee Crisis 1938–1941*. Amherst, Mass., 1968.

Wynn, Neil A. "The Impact of the Second World War on the American Negro," *Journal of Contemporary History*, VI (No. 2, 1971), 42–53.

Yanaga, Chitoshi. *Japan Since Perry*. New York, 1949.

Yans-McLaughlin, Virginia (ed.). *Immigration Reconsidered: History, Sociology, and Politics*. New York, 1990.

Yinger, J. Milton. "Toward a Theory of Assimilation and Dissimilation," Ethnic and Racial Studies, IV (July 1981), 249–64.

Young, Lewis. "American Blacks and the Arab-Israeli Conflict," *Journal of Palestine Studies*, II (Autumn 1972), 70–85.

Young, Marilyn B. *The Rhetoric of Empire: American China Policy, 1895–1901*. Cambridge, Mass., 1968.

Young, Steven B. "Ethnicity and the Indochina War: Reasons for Conflict," in *Ethnicity and War*, ed. Winston A. Van Horne and Thomas V. Tonnesen. Madison, Wis., 1984, 21–45.

Zazueta, Carlos H. "Mexican Political Actors in the United States and Mexico: Historical and Political Contexts of a Renewed Dialogue," in *Mexican–U.S. Relations*, ed. Carlos Vásquez and Manuel García y Griego. Los Angeles, 1983, 441–82.

Zeigler, Harmon. *Interest Groups in American Society*. Englewood Cliffs, N.J., 1964.

Zivojinović, Dragon R. "Yugoslavs before the United States Senate (1919)," in *Hyphenated Diplomacy*, ed. Hélène Christol and Serge Ricard. Aix-en-Provence, 1985, 41–57.

Zolberg, Aristide R. "Reforming the Back Door: The Immigration Reform and Control Act of 1986 in Historical Perspective," in *Immigration Reconsidered*, ed. Virginia Yans-McLaughlin. New York, 1990, 315–39.

Zucker, A. E. (ed.). *The Forty-Eighters: Political Refugees of the German Revolution of 1848*. New York, 1950.

Zucker, Norman L., and Naomi F. Zucker. *The Guarded Gate: The Reality of American Refugee Policy*. San Diego, 1987.

Zunz, Olivier, et al. "American History and the Changing Meaning of Assimilation," *Journal of American Ethnic History*, V (Spring 1985), 53–84.